VIJAYANAGARA VOICES

The Vijayanagara Empire flourished in South India between 1336 and 1565. Conveying the depth and creativity of Hindu religious and literary expression during that time, *Vijayanagara Voices* explores some of the contributions made by poets, singer-saints, and philosophers. Through translations and discussions of their lives and times, Jackson presents the voices of these cultural figures and reflects on the concerns of their era, looking especially into the vivid images in their works and their legends. He examines how these images convey both spiritual insights and physical experiences with memorable candour. The studies also raise intriguing questions about the empire's origins and its response to Muslim invaders, its 'Hinduness', and reasons for its ultimate decline.

Vijayanagara Voices is a book about patterns in history, literature and life in South India. By examining the culture's archetypal displays, by understanding the culture in its own terms, and by comparing associated images and ideas from other cultures, this book offers unique insights into a rich and influential period in Indian history.

To Marcia, to Rose, and to Roselle.

Vijayanagara Voices

Exploring South Indian History and Hindu Literature

WILLIAM J. JACKSON
Indiana University-Purdue University at Indianapolis, USA

ASHGATE

Published by
Ashgate Publishing Limited
Gower House
Croft Road
Aldershot
Hampshire GU11 3HR
England

Ashgate Publishing Company
Suite 420
101 Cherry Street
Burlington, VT 05401-4405
USA

Ashgate website: http://www.ashgate.com

British Library Cataloguing in Publication Data
Jackson, William J.
    Vijayanagara voices : exploring South Indian history and Hindu literature
    1. Hindu literature – History and criticism 2. Indic literature – To
    1500 – History and criticism 3. Vijayanagar (Empire) – History 4. Vijayanagar (Empire) –
    Intellectual life I. Title.
    954.8′024

Library of Congress Cataloging-in-Publication Data
Jackson, William J. (William Joseph)
    Vijayanagara voices : exploring South Indian history and Hindu
literature / William J. Jackson.
        p. cm.
    Includes bibliographical references and index.
    ISBN 0-7546-3950-9
    1. Vijayanagar (Empire)—History. 2. Vijayanagar
(Empire)—Intellectual life. 3. Hindu literature—History and
criticism. 4. Indic literature—To 1500—History and criticism. I.
Title.

    DS485. V6J33 2004
    954′.8024—dc22

                                                           2003024007

ISBN 0 7546 3950 9

Typeset by D.C. Graphic Design Ltd, Swanley, Kent.
Printed and bound in Great Britain by TJ International Ltd, Padstow, Cornwall.

Contents

List of Figures

Introduction

'New earths, new themes expect us.'   H.D. Thoreau[3]

'We are not in dependent entities, alien to Earth.
The earth in turn is not adrift in a vacuum
unrelated to the cosmos. The cosmos itself is
no longer cold and hostile – because it is
our universe. It brought us forth and it maintains
our being. We are, in the very literal sense of the
word, children of the universe.'   Eric J. Chaisson[4]

Vijayanagara: Where Cultural Fates Met Like Tectonic Plates

The lower half of the Indian subcontinent, the Deccan plains, south of the Vindhya mountains, was the location of the Vijayanagara empire, which flourished between 1336 and 1565. These Deccan plains were formed by a tremendous outpouring of basalt (lava) 65–63 million years ago. From a geological perspective, India can be viewed as two distinctly different regions – the very ancient southern crater and the comparatively recent northern section formed as a response to the Himalayan orogeny. The Deccan plains did not sink, and so we study the life that grew up there, the societies that organized themselves there. The Deccan plateau of the Marathi-speaking people is made of rich soil from long-weathered lava. The southern Deccan is more hilly, and inland from the southern coast the soil is not as rich as in the upper Deccan. Vijayanagara was the name of the capital and, by extension, has often been used in later times to name the empire that grew from that centre near the life-giving south-easterly flowing Tungabhadra river.

The special central quality and potential knot of meaning of Vijayanagara involves the way in which this empire both reaches back and flows forward, as a nucleus of Hinduism rooted in the ancient past and blossoming onward into the modern era. Vijayanagara came into existence, figuratively speaking, because of the crash of two great 'tectonic plates'[5] of religious civilization: Muslim civilization, with its origins in the Islamic Crescent, collided with the civilization of South Asia – the Hindu lifeway on the Indian subcontinent. These 'plates' gnashed and ground against each other in historic earthquakes of war, population movement and social reorganization, as Hindu India, invaded and dominated by Muslim forces, relinquished and then reasserted indigenous Hindu power. The Vijayanagara empire ended as the reverberations of the next great crash of 'tectonic plates' of civilizations began to occur: European traders, colonizers and rulers arriving to make their impacts on traditional patterns of Hindu life, in the sixteenth century and later, and India's response, the synthesis of cultures in (post)colonial South India. I do not use the image of cultural collision in a condemnatory way, but as a fact of life, just as continents' collisions are a fact of life. The greater the distance from the sorrows of the invaded and the exploits of the invaders, the more it looks like an inevitable move in the forces of human history, like a step in a cosmic dance of Shiva in Hindu mythology. The participants were agents of change in a vast play or *lila* in which civilizations rhythmically rise and fall.

On yet another level, that of visual likeness, the fracture patterns of interfacing rift lines along the lithosphere plates are similar to the sutures, the seam-lines which unite the bones of an individual's skull in immovable articulation. Of course, in this case the zigzagging edges of the interface did not slide and crash together, but grew that way, allowing the skull flexibility to grow to maturity and solidify. According to some Hindu traditions, these interlacing sutures in the skull are lines of fate written at birth by the Creator (or by Chitragupta, Yama's accountant, the archetypal keeper of karmic records).[6] To hold such a view is a way of observing that life is dynamic with choices and change but is also anchored and shaped by tendencies, inherent forces, possibilities remembered from the past. Thus, life is complex and chaotic but also time-rhythmed, consciousness-shaped, code-organized. There are patterns, physical and psychic habits, and beyond what can be known there is also life's elusive mystery. Figuratively speaking, it is through the 'cracks' (life-changing events, unexpected challenges) in the smooth surfaces of life that tensions are released and we become vulnerable to the sacred, open to more than the usual. Some would say that providence breaks hearts and lives, so that depths may be known and healing may be sought and found.[7] The cracks in the surface allow inspiration in, the 'breaks' allow serendipity to work beyond manipulation and control, giving life a dynamic wildness, a power of energy. The 'writing' made by inward/outward interfaces and ancestral continuities and current pressures is profound, with curious signs.

One link which we humans share, whether we are from Vijayanagara or postmodernity, is found in archetypes of our psyches: deep images such as the Mother figure, Child, Warrior and Dragon, Trickster and Chaos Flood. These archetypes involve us in the aches and pains of development, the dynamics of complete cycles of fulfilment, showing that the psyche or soul is partial to the whole. Archetypes appear in dreams, in art and in religion, in lyrics and narratives, in fantasies and inspiring historic exemplars, and they have been called 'the voice of the earth'.[8]

This book presents a selection of 'Vijayanagara voices' and it explores some of the archetypes of South Indian culture, the lives of poets and kings, saints and sages, and the images and arts of spiritual creativity. It explores how such voices provided a traditional order and renewed a pathway in a world of contingencies, chaos and uncertainty.

Walk through a Ghost Town: Vijayanagara as Visceral-level India

When I was in Hampi, another name for the old capital of Vijayanagara, walking in a 100° heat through a wild landscape of boulders shaped like huge potatoes strewn over rocky ridges and hills, the Tungabhadra river was high, almost flooding its banks. The huge boulders everywhere looked like leftover debris from a much earlier, almost imponderable series of geological events and processes; they were inescapable signs of a remoteness. What happened here long ago? The memories in the rough and tumble ruins, the remnants of life in the carved and rugged litter, call out with hints of experiences undergone here long ago.

In India bodies are more often cremated than buried, so there are not as many tombs as there are in Western countries. A few *samadhis* of sages and saints are venerated (for example, the resting place of Vidyaranya), but the bodies of kings and queens were normally burnt, and there are few memorable tombs. Signs of the vandalism of the looting spree of 1565 remain, such as defaced stone images. And though one may not see blood staining the stones, one senses a disruption of life lived here once, and traumatic experiences undergone here. No one lives in large areas of the old capital today. Parts of old buildings still stand on the bare land, sometimes balanced precariously, green grass growing in the roof-cracks. Nobel Prize-winning Indian poet, storyteller and philosopher Rabindranath Tagore wrote a tale about haunting echoes in old Indian ruins, places where hearts touched and skins caressed with loving spirals, where songs burst and signs fell:

> A strange delight, slightly tinged with fear, passed through my body, and although there was no figure before my eyes, I thought I saw a bevy of maidens coming down the steps to bathe ... . I distinctly heard the maidens' gay and mirthful laugh, like the gurgle of a spring gushing forth in a hundred cascades ... . The river was perfectly calm, but I felt that its clear and shallow waters were suddenly stirred by the splashes of arms jingling with bracelets, and that the girls laughed and splattered water at one another ... .[9]

Similarly here, seeing the bathing places and reading visitors' accounts ('All the inhabitants ... [e]ven down to the artificers of the bazaar, wear jewels and gilt ornaments in their ears and around their necks, arms, wrists and fingers'[10]), the imagination conjures up charming and poignant sights amid the scattered boulders.

Locals explain the boulders as remnants of an earlier 'monkey civilization' which flourished in ancient times – the period described in the Ramayana epic. (Monkey chieftains Sugriva and Vali in the Rama story were said to have lived here, for example.) All agree that this place changed from wilderness to a great capital of civilization and then reverted back to wilderness again.[11] Near Hampi, Hospet is a town built over the remains of a Vijayanagara royal home laid out by Krishnadevaraya. Old descriptions of the city picture its charms, saying that the high points of the city had palaces white like autumn clouds and that there was a celestial atmosphere of music, with groups promenading and women playing on the roofs of mansions. Visitors there 500 years ago recorded that it was indeed a highly cultured cosmopolitan city.[12] Vijayanagara, the capital, at the height of the empire in the early sixteenth century covered 25 square miles on the southern side of the Tungabhadra river with about 100 000 households. The Tungabhadra heartland supported 2 million people; altogether 25 million lived south of the Krishna river.[13]

Picturing Methods and Goals

> '*All that we call sacred history attests that the birth of a poet is the principle event in chronology.*'

Ralph Waldo Emerson[14]

The great twentieth-century Indologist Heinrich Zimmer called the empire whose capital was Vijayanagara a creative oasis which was 'the last nucleus of Hindu civilization to survive the sandstorm of the Muslim invasion'. It was one final grand summation of the *sanatana* (ancient) Hindu lifeway before the flood came from the West.[15] (Of course other summations of the Hindu lifeway do continue to be formed, but they come after that influx, or 'sandstorm', as Zimmer puts it.) We will be exploring facets of that nucleus through biography and literature. What are the 'attractors' around which our exploration meanders[16] and iterates its way? Basically, I wish to convey some of the depth and creativity of Hindu religious and literary expression during the Vijayanagara empire. This is not to say that all the people whose 'voices' we hear were living in the capital city of Vijayanagara, but that they lived in the Karnataka empire during the period when South India's chief ruler was centred there. Taken too literally 'Vijayanagara' becomes a source of confusion. It has very often been used to mean simply 'the realm of provinces which had Vijayanagara as their capital'.

India's creative culture reveals interesting views on basic human predicaments, such as the unity (and rivalries) of mind, body and spirit. Exploring the spiritual and psychological depths of significant images, examining issues of 'mind/body'[17] relationships and recurrent patterns in legends, song lyrics, stories, poetry and philosophy, *Vijayanagara Voices* is a book of essays on history, literature and life in South India. By cultivating an openness to a culture's archetypal displays and by comparing associated images and ideas from other cultures, this book offers a series of views of a rich and intriguing era of South Indian history. As Margaret Trawick wisely says, 'Learning a culture, like learning a language, is largely an unconscious process, which means precisely that one cannot control it',[18] as aspects of it gradually dawn upon one. In South India one often sees sets of vessels which nestle one inside another very snugly and conveniently. That image is a reminder of how, in everyday life in India, culture is inside religion and religion is inside culture. In premodern India politics was nestled in religious ritual and outlook, and social life was often nestled in bhakti (devotion-oriented) values and practices.

The Vijayanagara empire can reveal ideas for our own world to reflect on. Vijayanagara is far enough away in time to consider with some perspective, yet not so far away as to be entirely obscure. Cultural artefacts and texts of the Vijayanagara empire represent an accessible world, which, through reflection, can reveal things to our own world. This book explores some of the traits of the religious thinkers, poets and heroic figures of Vijayanagara (such as Vidyaranya, Krishnadevaraya, Ganga Devi, Kanakadasa and others) for visions of human existential potentials explored, played out, lost and rediscovered. It takes note of a pool of Hindu resources, texts and life stories, and living customs. The court poets celebrated love between humans. The singer-saints gave voice to bhakti – devotion, or spiritual love. Culturally creative lives like these refresh and correct the societies which give birth to them. In this literature – in Vidyaranya's writings, the lower-caste woman poet Molla's poetry and Kanakadasa's lyrics, for example – we can find full-bodied Hindu poetry reflecting a full palette of passions and experiences, not yet shamed by Victorian colonizers into hypocritical prudishness or rigid narrowness. Motifs in this book include meaning as meeting of mind and body; the significance of mind embodied, of the unity of body and soul; and the poetic means used to portray the human situation of heart and mind embodied together. I explore the weave of these strands by examining powerful images of subtle unity which creative arts, such as music and poetry, can express.

The study of religion is a creative discipline involving the efforts of both arts and sciences in its explorations and representations. It requires being creatively open to the exploration of a wide spectrum of what N. Katherine Hayles calls 'chaotics,'[19] anomalous points through which it is sometimes possible to focus on hidden cultural dynamics. 'To see and know a place is a contemplative act. It means emptying our minds and letting what is there, in all its multiplicity and endless variety, come in',[20] as Gretel Ehrlich writes. This is Taoism's traditional artistic procedure, too – to be filled with the subject so that its spirit in the artist does the painting.[21] This study is an experiment in trying to understand cultural depths; new ideas often develop in response to crises.[22] Humans are at home in a world of trouble; Vijayanagara itself arose from a crisis of survival and renewal. I believe this is a theme of interest for many living today – an enduring concern we share.

The Essays

When traditional Hindu polity reconstitutes itself, self-organizing a new incarnation of its historical identity amidst political change and social turbulence, it leaves memories and records which reveal something of its complex character. Chapters 1, 2, 3, explore the origins of the empire and the influential sage Vidyaranya. I present the colourful legends and memories of those early days based on Telugu literature of the time and from later generations. Chapter 1 presents the legendary version of the beginning of the empire and notes a concept from chaos science – the way in which conditions at the outset of a system which is coming into existence play an important trend-setting part in the trajectory and duration of the whole. 'For want of a nail' on the hoof of a horse, as the famous saying goes, an empire can falter and be lost; under the right conditions a mere butterfly's flutter of impact can generate far-reaching effects.

I also present the story about a mysterious woman appearing and giving a sword to a king, written in Sanskrit by poet-queen Ganga Devi. (Chapter 4) This essay explores a scenario of the heroic reclaiming of lands to the South of the early Vijayanagara kingdom. In it I discuss symbolic meanings, psychological and spiritual associations of the 'magical sword' image, and explore the way in which the image of conquest with an indomitable weapon goes back to earliest Vedic imagery and functions as a deep background for dynamic historical scenarios and spiritual ideals. The powerful woman with a sword is important in other cultures as well.

Chapter 5 discusses how Shripadaraya wrote influential colloquial songs, and the woman poet Molla wrote a celebrated version of the Ramayana epic in Telugu. I explore her work as a fractal-like part of a larger whole body of Ramayana works in Hindu culture.

Chapter 6 explores frank observations and worldly wisdom in the oral traditions of two popular Telugu poets: Vemana's and Baddena's verses are still part of everyday speech. These concise and vivid verses have spiced up South India conversations for centuries. In my study I consider how such a multiplication and constant currency of values and attitudes in these verses create a recursive network of usages and outlooks in many lives of a society.

Historians usually regard Krishnadevaraya's rule as embodying the height of the Vijayanagara empire's power and accomplishments. In Chapter 7 I explore this great king's life and consider the story of a crisis which led to his resolve to strengthen his realm. Krishnadevaraya was creative in recognizing weaknesses in the messy conditions and unbalanced powers around him, and he subtly found a systematic way to change things. His imagination and resolve did not fail him as he improvised necessary steps toward the realm's prosperity and security. Chapter 8 includes stories about Krishnadevaraya's famous court jester and poet-philosopher Tenali Rama, a humorous trickster-hero whose tales are told all over South India. This chapter also explores the prosperity symbolism of water imagery and eros involved in the traditional role of the devadasis (the king's temple dancers and courtesans) in the thriving Vijayanagara empire.

Whilst Shripadaraya and Molla used everyday colloquial Telugu language, the lower-caste poet Kanakadasa wrote Kannada works, as well as some works in Sanskrit, the language of Brahmanic Hinduism and classical literature. In Chapter 9 I examine Kanakadasa's life and his protests against the caste biases which existed in his age.

Chapter 10 is about the coronation of Krishnadevaraya's successor, Achyutadevaraya, and the symbolisms of coronation rituals and the king's body.

Chapter 11 consists of concluding musings on patterns of self-organization and decline, drawing on traditional thinkers and indigenous voices, such as Kanakadasa's, as well as contemporary thinkers, relating complexity theory in life sciences and culture studies. It consists of a series of reflections prompted by touring the ruins of the old capital, considering the ways in which civilizations come and go. In this chapter, and throughout the book, some concepts which are referred to in passing are further elaborated in the endnotes. Although empires and centuries of cultural life humble our attempts to encompass them, both origins and capitulations can be pondered in terms of patterns and multiple perspectives – voices.

Thus, in this book of essays I present reflections on artefacts from South India: legends and biographies, poetry, rituals and symbolisms. In consultation with Indian scholars I translate from Telugu and Kannada and Sanskrit items selected from the most vividly interesting and readily available texts. In the essays I convey basic information about significant events and representative figures in history – writers, sages, kings and queens – exploring the meanings of key symbols, philosophical concepts, cultural and spiritual focal points of order. The interrelatedness of beauty and psyche, cosmos and power, body and mind, the sacred and society are among the themes I delve into in these essays.

A field (such as history of religion) is inseparable from the language it uses to define itself and transact its work. History of Religion already has a large vocabulary. To deal with the examples of human spirituality which it encounters, a discipline naturally incorporates new terms which prove their usefulness. History of Religion explores human resources and memories in innumerable cultures. The historian reimagines situations, finding ways that best characterize what he or she sees. I believe the terms 'fractals' and 'attractors', for example, are proving their usefulness in helping us conceptualize certain situations. I agree with other scholars, such as John Lewis Gaddis, who argues convincingly in his new book *The Landscape of History*[23] that historians (and social scientists) can learn much from recent natural science, from complex adaptive systems theory and chaos science, and the concept of fractals.[24] Visual models help us conceptualize life situations and relationships, processes and patterns (see Figures I.1 to I.4).

Religions studied are storehouses of sacred images and lives, world-views and practices. Religions often concern 're-linking', connecting to a greater wholeness. The structures of the sacred, though mysterious, can sometimes be depicted in terms of chaotic systems, such as fractal images suggestive of infinite networks of consciousness. Various chapters of this study of Vijayanagara's spiritually creative figures explore such concepts when they seem useful. We live in a time of new paradigms and I tend to draw on available ideas as needed. In answer to the question, 'Are these concepts just more arbitrary constructs imposed on a living tradition?' I would suggest, first, that in our time an emerging way of asserting the world's coherence is being put forward in the study of systems and networks, wholeness and complexity. Principles such as fractals and attractors seem to stand for universal processes – basics of nature – including processes found in human life. From these, specialists can learn ways to consider larger wholes. Second, because these pattern recognitions are universal, people often noticed them in their own way and in their own terms long ago, and incorporated them into their depiction of how things happen. For both of these reasons it seems natural to employ these concepts as a useful vocabulary for furthering our understanding of the processes we discuss.

Figure I.1 **Fractal patterns, with the whole reflected in self-similar parts, are found in ferns and other structures in nature**

**Figure I.2   Fractal qualities are evident in snowflakes, with the same shape
found on several scales**

Figure I.3 These spiral shapes, generated by computers, show fractal reiterations of shapes on a series of scales

Figure I.4 **Examples of strange attractions, recursive variations of a path in phase space**

About the Translations and Texts

> ' ... it is the issue of translation, that 'this' is never quite 'that,' and, therefore
> that acts of interpretation are required, which marks the Human Sciences. It is
> thought about translation ... that energizes the Human Sciences or disciplines
> and suggests the intellectual contributions they make'.

Jonathon Z. Smith[25]

A culture often takes for granted its most basic metaphors; we need to seek these in
our search to understand Vijayanagara, as well as look for them in our own backyard,
by reflecting on our own lives. In order to let voices of the past speak for themselves,
translations form part of this work. I worked with Indian scholars and members of
the traditions and, in some cases, consulted existing translations in order to
understand the original texts better, and over several years put the Telugu and
Kannada into English. Unless otherwise noted, I am responsible for the translations
in this study; in all cases, whether translating from the original with the help of
dictionaries and secondary sources or adapting from a number of translations after
discussions with members of the tradition, I have tried to carry the original ideas into
understandable enjoyable English. The translations of A.K. Ramanujan (*Hymns for
the Drowning*), David Rosenberg's *A Poet's Bible* and Coleman Barks' *Unseen Rain*
are examples of the kind of work I admire.

To non-specialists, jargon-laden writings seem a closed book or, worse, a cryptic
tomb of moribund bodies of knowledge which even sincere interest on the reader's
part cannot bring to life. I have prepared this work in the hope that both specialists
and non-specialists will find plentiful treasures of vital interest. Knowledge of
cultures such as the Hinduism of Vijayanagara can help ground moderns in a sense
of deep natural structures, a sense of the dynamic enterprise of human life. Such
knowledge reveals classical responses in the human condition and helps us cultivate
the wisdom that negates self-absorbed narcissism.

It is my purpose here to convey and promote understanding of the folk traditions
of South India. Thus, pursuing such questions as proof of authorship of each of
Kanakadasa's songs, or the exact date a text was composed has not usually been my
first concern. Those who are sleuths in such matters should be consulted for that
information; they specialize in arguing pros and cons of details in those issues. In
this book I wanted to look into the character of the folk mind, to discover the kinds
of creativity it prizes. As the songs commonly believed to be by Kanakadasa and the
works attributed to Vidyaranya reveal aspects of the folk memory process, they are
fair game in my explorations. Because I am more concerned with exploring the
religious meanings of the images and ideas of the traditionally accepted literature of
the Vijayanagara empire era than with the historical-critical method, I have often
worked with the popularly available texts – paperback and hardcover song texts,
poetry and biographies used by the ordinary members of the living tradition. I have
usually paraphrased stories and versified passages from song and poetry texts.
Throughout, the endnotes at the conclusion of each chapter indicate specific texts I

used or further options for locating texts. Many of them are abundantly available in India but not often found elsewhere, except in a few large research libraries.

Regarding translations: as with all else in this study, I have tried to be true to the need for a mixture of the right proportions of both rigorous reason and artistic imagination. My translations are guided by these goals: first, to present with clarity the reasonableness and system which informs each song and its ideas; second, to use a familiar and agreeable tone to communicate *bhakti* expressions to moderns; third, to convey faithfully the original meaning, the literal sense, without loss of poetic resonance. The first test of a translation is that it can be humanly experienced and is not repellent to the very reading and digesting of its basic content. In order to best provide this experience, the translator does well to go through all the tryable variations, seeking the most dynamic and satisfying formulation, willing to take the necessary time. Then the results must survive readings by members of the tradition who know both the original and English. In all the places where I present texts of vernacular poetry, folk tales, song lyrics and passages from Sanskrit books I have versified, paraphrased or rewritten the text to convey the original meanings in language familiar to the modern ear. My thanks to the various other translators and thinkers who have worked on these and related texts. As one who is not primarily a linguist I am deeply indebted to their work. I am also indebted to the many historians and writers in this field. Their technical knowledge in various aspects of the empire is a rich resource for someone like myself, whose primary interest is in the stories, biographies and impressions conveyed in poetic images.

Notes

1   *The Upanishads*, tr. Swami Nikhilananda, New York: Harper and Row, 1963. The full text of this invocation at the beginning of *Isha Upanishad* is: 'Om. That is full; this is full. This fullness has been projected from that fullness. When this fullness merges in that fullness, all that remains is fullness. Om. Peace! Peace! Peace!' (p. 89).

2   Walt Whitman, Leaves of Grass, Philadelphia: David McKay, 1900, number 151, 'Voices'. Also Bartleby.com, 1999 at www.bartleby.com/142/accessed 25 June, 2003.

3   Henry David Thoreau, *Journal*, 22 October 1857. Thoreau's journals are available in a number of editions. For example, *The Heart of Thoreau's Journals*, ed. Odell Shepard, New York: Dover, 1961. See p. 185.

4   Eric J. Chaisson, 'The Scenario of Cosmic Evolution', *Harvard Magazine*, November–December 1977, pp. 21–33.

5   In the early twentieth century German theorist Alfred Wegener speculated about continental drift. In 1965 Canadian scientist John Tuzo Wilson confirmed the existence of a network of belts of mantle and crust able to move around the Earth, dividing the Earth's surface into huge rigid tectonic plates.

6   One reference to this belief is in a work by the Sanskrit author Kalidasa (not the famous poet of the same name). In his *Dvatrimsatputtalika* (*Thirty-two Sacred Images*), there is a line which asserts that even Brahma, Vishnu and Shiva are not able to change the writing on a person's forehead. In Tamil Nadu I have often heard this belief about fate or luck. In Tamil the forehead writing is *talai vidi* or *talai azhuttu*. Among Tamil villagers the headwriting representing the fate inscribed at birth is rather arbitrary, not necessarily related to previous actions. In one of Tyagaraja's songs, *Kaligiyunte gada*

in Telugu, he says 'I can have my wishes fulfilled only if the writing on my head is favourable'. (Thanks to T.S. Parthasarathy for information on this.) In the North, (in Nepal, for example) Hindus say that Chitragupta, the accountant who assists Yama, god of death, writes a child's destiny on its forehead on the sixth day afer birth. At that time the family ritually lights oil lamps and give a bracelet to the baby. In Bengal a pot of ink and a pen are set out in the birth room, and on the night of the sixth day Chitragupta invisibly arrives, dips pen in ink and writes the baby's fate on his or her forehead. See Adwaita Mallabarman's novel, *A River Called Titash*, tr. Kalpana Barhan, Berkeley: University of California Press, 1993, p. 102. Telugu poet Vemana also wrote about this fate-writing. 'Brahma distributes gifts depending on what's written on your forehead; the writing on your forehead spells out exactly your past actions. Brahma is the author of the writing on your forehead; you are the author of your acts.' (Paraphrased from text in Vemana, *Selected Verses of Vemana*, ed. and tr. J.S.R.L. Narayana Moorty and Elliot Roberts, New Delhi: Sahitya Akademi, 1995, p. 106. See also pp. 91, 105, 119.

7   For example, Andrew Solomon, a writer on his own and others' depression, despite his suffering, said that the experience revealed to him his soul, in his book *The Noonday Demon: The Atlas of Depression*. New York: Scribner, 2001.

8   Theodore Roszak, *The Voice of the Earth*, New York: Touchstone, 1992, pp. 301–302 ff. James Hillman's writings about archetypes in *A Blue Fire*, New York: HarperCollins, 1991 and elsewhere are very useful. C.G. Jung's non-dogmatic view was that the 'concept of the archetype … is only an auxilliary idea which can be exchanged at any time for a better formula'. See C.G. Jung, *Collected Works, Volume II, Psychology and Religion: West and East*, New York: Pantheon Books, 1958, in an essay entitled 'Forward to White's "God and the Unconscious"', p. 306. In this study I have used occasionally, for example, the term 'attractor'. I have written of such archetypal images as the irresistible divine sword, the ruler of earth and the women of waters, the images used in popular wisdom verses, symbols of royal enthronement, conundrums of origin and dissolution, thinking of them all as archetypal 'attractors'. Why? The psychological process goes on inside us – dreams, fantasies, slips of the tongue, ideals, story images, symbols systems. And the facts do not change whatever names we give them, as Jung remarked. See C.G. Jung, *Psychological Reflections*, ed. Jolande Jacobi, New York: Harper and Row, 1961, p. 347. 'Archetypes', 'daimonia', 'deep images', 'powerful symbols' or 'attractors' all indicate images of numinosity which compel behaviour, inspire impulses, attracting attention and energies, hence determining somewhat the scenarios which our lives play out. Adapting the term 'attractor' from 'strange attractor' – a term used in non-linear dynamical systems thinking – for use in our discussion of culture is an experiment. The attempt to employ a new and vivid parallel model from a science studying external reality, conceptualizing anew physical processes for our times, is to try out a new way of picturing reality in our human world of culture and psyche. We are still, as always, moved by these images – moved as if by a hidden whirlwind energy we name 'sacred attractor' rather than archetype, or god, or compelling image. ('Strange attractor' is a positive name which gives a positive attitude to 'strange', implying that we accept a mystery, that we are more aware of the limits of conventional logic and better appreciate the depth dynamics of complexity of the situation. As scientists say, 'The world is not only stranger than you imagine, it's stranger than you can imagine'.) A strange attractor is a pattern; it pictures the lines made by an evolving dance of circumambulations, the energies of a psyche relating to traditions of the holy, playing out archetypal scenarios, hopefully bringing the sacred closer to awareness, to actual experience in life. The attractive within the attractor is like the spirit in the pattern, in a manner of speaking.)

9   Rabindranath Tagore, 'The Hungry Stones', in *A Tagore Reader*, ed. Amiya Chakravarty, Boston, MA: Beacon Press, 1966, p. 55.

10   Abdu'r-Razzak cited by A.K. Coomaraswamy, *History of Indian and Indonesian Art*, New York: Dover Publications, 1965, p. 123.

11   There are some ruins in America, cellar holes, and Indian mounds, but it's hard to find an atmosphere such as this, with ancient ruins like bleached bones in the scorching light of the sun.

12   Burton Stein, *Peasant, State and Society in Medieval South India,* Delhi: Oxford University Press, 1985, pp. 380–81. Domingo Paes wrote: 'In this city you will find men belonging to every nation and people.' Robert Sewell, *A Forgotten Empire (Vijayanagar),* New Delhi: Asian Educational Services, 1983 (reprint of 1900 edn.). The jewellery, lifelike paintings of animals, the carvings of ivory, wood and stone, and a summary of architectural features are described by Coomaraswamy in *History of Indian and Indonesian Art,* pp. 123–24.

13   Burton Stein, 'Vijayanagara', in *The New Cambridge History of India, I.2,* Cambridge: Cambridge University Press, 1989, pp. 50, 75, 44. Some historians estimate that the world population in 1350 was 345 million.

14   Emerson wrote this in his essay 'The Poet.' See *The Selected Writings of Ralph Waldo Emerson,* ed. Brooks Atkinson, New York: Modern Library, 1968, p. 325.

15   Heinrich Zimmer, *Philosophies of India,* New York: Meridian, 1956, p. 68. Evidently, Zimmer does not place the later kingdoms ruled by Maratha kings in the same category as Vijayanagara.

16   For some people the word 'meander' has negative connotations. For me it is rich with associations such as the necessary flow of rivers, markings in primal peoples' caves, explorations along the line of least resistance. 'Attractor' in physics is a region of 'phase space' which generates a pull that draws a system towards it again and again. In this book it connotes patterns of repeated return – reiterations with variations.

17   William H. Poteat argues that formalized rationality which 'estranges thought about our minds from thought about our bodies' silently pervades 'the atmosphere of our life like a chronic depression'. See *A Philosophical Daybook, Post-Critical Investigations,* Columbia: University of Missouri Press, 1990, p. 5. I attempt to avoid this dilemma of one-sidedness prevalent in our age by exploring issues 'mind/body' interrelationships.

18   Margaret Trawick, *Notes on Love in a Tamil Family,* Berkeley: University of California Press, 1990.

19   Katherine Hayles uses the term 'chaotics' suggestively in *Chaos and Order: Complex Dynamics in Literature and Science,* Chicago: Chicago University Press. See also N. Katherine Hayles, *Chaos Bound: Orderly Disorder in Contemporary Literature and Science,* Ithaca: Cornell University Press, 1990. Friedrich Schiller in a 1788 letter to Theodor Korner wrote ' ... where there is a creative mind, Reason ... relaxes its watch upon the gates, and the ideas rush in pellmell, and only then does it look them through and through and examine them in a mass ... critics ... are ashamed or frightened of the extravagances which are to be found in all truly creative minds.' Cited by Sigmund Freud, *Interpretation of Dreams,* New York: Avon, 1965, p. 135. Control-obsessed reason can censor, amputating creative possibilities, willl 'reject too soon and discriminate too severely' and result in unfruitfulness. I am arguing that the study of religion is ideally not only a science but also an art. Thus allowing more leeway in modes of investigation and presentation would expand the optics and options of possible understanding. It requires the self-awareness to question the forms of reasonableness in the lives and lyrics then, and in our approaches now, and the use of the unconscious.

20   Gretel Ehrlich in her essay, 'Landscape', in *Legacy of Light,* ed. Constance Sullivan, New York: Knopf, 1987, p. 20. Bernard DeVoto wrote 'history is a social expression of geography ... ' in his foreword to *A Treasury of Western Folklore,* ed. B.A. Botkin, New York: Crown Publishers, Inc., 1951, p. viii.

21   This Zenlike openness and reflectivity was also part of Freud's 'Recommendations to Physicians Practicing Psychoanalysis'. To do a deeper analysis one must bend one's 'own unconscious like a receptive organ toward the transmitting unconscious' of the subject, which in this work is the court poets, philosophers and bhakti poets of the Karnataka empire's cultural life. Cited in Janet Malcolm, *Psychoanalysis: The Impossible Profession,* New York: Vintage-Random, 1981, p. 26.

22   David L. Hall writes about this in 'On Seeking a Change of Environment', in J.B. Callicott and R.T. Ames (eds), *Nature in Asian Traditions of Thought,* Albany, NY: SUNY, 1989. See also Hall's 'Reason and Its Rhyme' in *Journal of Indian Council of Philosophical Research,* IX(2), January – April, 1992, pp. 42–43.

23 John Lewis Gaddis, *The Landscape of History: How Historians Map the Past*, New York: Oxford University Press, 2002, pp. 71–89.

24 See Benoit Mandelbrot, *The Fractal Geometry of Nature*, New York: W.H. Freeman and Company, 1982. See also my book *Heaven's Fractal Net: Retrieving Lost Visions in the Humanities*, Bloomington: Indiana University Press, 2003.

25 Jonathon Z. Smith, *Differential Equations: On Constructing the Other*, University Lectures in Religion, Tempe: Department of Religious Studies, Arizona State University, 1992, p. 14.

CHAPTER 1

The Legend of Vijayanagara's Historical Origins

'[The concept] of sensitive dependence on initial conditions was not an altogether new notion. It had a place in folklore.'   James Gleick[1]

The Reversals of Fortune

Today Vijayanagara, 'the City of Victory', on the southern banks of the Tungabhadra river in Karnataka, lies in ruin, its fallen roofs and empty courtyards overgrown with weeds and unruly shrubs. The atmosphere is lonely. Vast vacant spaces predominate. The bright green parrots still play there as they did long ago, on the stones of the massive walls, on the peaks of the steep-rising temples. The parrots look out now on empty land where busy roads used to run. They chatter and survey the ruins, flying over crumbling stone structures, scattered as far as the eye can see – old-style buildings still slowly being dismantled by the workings of the sun and rain, wind and gravity. The parrots glide in the sunny air, calling out while looking for something to eat in the desolation. What invading Muslims did not topple in 1565, neglect has been pulling down gradually ever since.

If one pieces together the story from the guides, the guidebooks and the literature in libraries in India and elsewhere, the following story of the empire emerges.

Islamic forces had begun to make an impact in India as early as the beginning of the eleventh century, when Mahmud of Ghazni (Afghanistan) led raids into the North. By the thirteenth century Muslim rule had attained political dominance in much of the North and some of the South. At the time of the beginnings of the city of Vijayanagara, in the second quarter of the fourteenth century, Muslim domination was expanding from North India. A eunuch general named Malik Kafur, a Hindu converted to Islam, led a number of raids in the South on behalf of the Sultan of Delhi, Ala'ud-din Khalji, who ruled until 1315. The Deccan kingdoms could not defend themselves against him, and Muslim rule established itself in southern centres. Muslim traders and mercenary soldiers became a common sight in the South Indian landscape. Islamicate culture became a factor that shaped styles of prestige and matters of substance and power – in clothing, in vocabulary and in methods of armouring horses for warfare, for example.[2]

The origin story presented here is a composite of legends and memories, Hindu inscriptions and accounts written by Muslim historians. It includes the standard and popular tellings of the founding of the Vijayanagara empire.

Before Vijayanagara (literally the 'City of Victory') was built, south of the Tungabhadra river (in what is now Karnataka State) to revive and reassert Hindu rule in South India, Muslim ruler Muhammad bin Tughlak succeeded Ghiyasu-din Tughlak in Delhi and became sultan of the South as well as the north of the subpeninsula we call India. From what we can make of his biography, Tughlak, who ruled from 1325 until 1351, like other sultans, could be now suspicious and vindictive, now magnanimous, now harsh and now caring.[3]

He placed his nephew, Baha-ud-Din Gushtasp, in charge of a southern province of the realm. When Muhammad-bin-Tughlak died, Baha-ud-Din Gushtasp would not give his oath of fealty to the late sultan's son and successor. In a certain sense, this stubborn stance of independence was the beginning of the drama that led to the founding of Vijayanagara. In response to the refusal to vow loyalty, the sultan sent an army to pursue the rebel nephew and, when the two forces met, a battle ensued. The sultan's army won. Baha-ud-Din Gushtasp fled, seeking refuge with a Hindu king, Rai of Kampili, in an inaccessible mountain region of what is now Karnataka State. He was pursued by soldiers, who surrounded the king's palace there at Warangal. When the Hindu king saw how the siege was strangling his forces, and that the grain was running out, he knew that the enemy soldiers would surely attack him in this weakened state. Knowing that he could not win, he decided to fight to the death. He informed his wives and followers that he would enter the battle and never return, and his wives and daughters are said to have washed, and rubbed fragrant sandalwood oil and paste on their smooth bodies. Then they kissed the earth as they knelt before their king and then walked into a great and fatal fire to take control of their fates from the invaders. Nobles, ministers and chief men and their wives did likewise, choosing death in the flames over life without honour.[4]

Rai of Kampili washed, put on sandalwood oil, and picked up his sword. He did not put on his protective breastplate. His men followed him into battle. Confronting their enemy, according to traditional accounts, they all fought until they died, following the ideals of the warrior caste to the end.[5] Muhammad-bin-Tughlak ordered that his nephew, Baha-ud-Din-Gushtasp, be flayed alive; his skin was stuffed and exhibited in the region. According to reports, his flesh was cooked and sent to his wife.[6]

But five brothers on the Hindu king's side, the sons of a powerful chief named Sangama,[7] as the moment of death approached, wondered: 'Should a Muslim victory mean the death of all of us? Rather than die, if we join the Muslims, we will at least stay alive.' Following this realistic line of thought, they surrendered and were taken prisoner and locked up. They submitted to circumcision, a ritual sign of conversion, and made the profession of faith, 'There is no God but God, and Muhammad is His prophet', and thus they became Muslims. The three eldest brothers, Harihara, Bukka and Kampana had been chieftains defending the northern frontier. Mudappa and Marappa were the two youngest brothers.

In some stories it is said that one night while Harihara and Bukka were being held captive by the sultan a terrible thunderstorm came and caused confusion, and in the chaos another prisoner ran away. The two brothers did not try to flee, even though they were near an open door, and thus impressed the sultan as trustworthy. The sultan felt grateful for their apparent loyalty and took a liking to the brothers, gradually giving them more and more responsibilities. He made them his officials and gave them the task of controlling the newly won territories – work which they performed well.

There were roving warriors in the South in those days, rivalling each other for rule, seeking land to dominate and people to govern and tax.[8] The incessant warfare among the many Hindu kingdoms of the South had in fact made the whole region unstable and vulnerable to Muslim invasion. Parties of plundering warriors riding down into rich valleys, to take wealth, capture elephants and run off with gold and women, were feared by those who lost possessions and autonomy to them. These plunderers continually disrupted and embittered the lives of the many peasants who worked the land and the landlords who owned it, by causing them repeated losses. The five brothers who worked for the sultan were not only sons of Sangama, they were also grandsons of Bukkaraya Vodayalu, who had governed part of what is now Nellore District for king Prataparudra II around 1314.[9]

But in the wilderness by the Tungabhadra river lived another group of brothers, Madhava, Sayana and Bhoganatha.[10] These three were *smarta*[11] brahmans, the sons of a pious couple, Mayana and Shrimati. All three, though very different in their temperaments, were disciples of the same guru at the Shringeri *matha* (monastery), Jnanendra Saraswati.

The first brother, Madhava, who had studied the Vedas, lived a full life as a householder, and then become a sannyasin, was a hermit,[12] and his name at this stage of life was Vidyaranya ('Woods of Wisdom'). This silent sage sat in meditation for days at a time. He prayed and studied, and was inspired with wisdom which would help restore Hindu dharma. In some stories it was the news of the destruction of the entire ruling family of Anegondi by Muslims that gave him the determination to take action against the invaders.[13]

The second brother, Sayana, was a pandit who constantly studied the Vedas. He was immersed in the mantras and their meanings, and was more deeply conversant with that ancient timeless system of visions than anyone else alive. Earlier in their lives these two sages had been householders, pious family men who were priests, conductors of Vedic sacrifices. Sayana had two sons, and Vidyaranya had one son.

The third brother's name, Bhoganatha, means 'Lord of Enjoyment', but also suggests a clown's name: 'Master of Amusement'. History tells us little about him.[14] The three brothers also had a sister, who gave birth to a son who later became a famous minister in the court named Lakshmidhara.[15]

Vidyaranya the sage, endowed with many talents and merits, was a *smarta* (carrier of traditional brahman knowledge of orthodox ways, texts and laws) able to draw on practical resources and a farsighted vision. He waited for the right moment to play his role. He sought and found a way to re-establish the Hindu dharma, social order and religion, which had been the mainstay of society in the region for so long.

In 1334 the sultan's respected and trusted military leader, the Muslim convert Harihara, one of the five brothers mentioned above, turned his back on the sultan and on Islam, stirring a revolt among the people of his region. He ruled an independent kingdom, Kampili, from 1334 onwards. The people there grew their own food, defended their own small territory and lived free from the dictates of Muslim authorities. They had broken away to decide their own lives.[16] Like the Pandava brothers in exile in the Mahabharata epic, Harihara sought wise advice.

It was not until Harihara and his brothers came under the guidance of the sage Vidyaranya that they fully returned to the ideals of Hindu dharma and dedicated their rule to preserving and expanding that ancient way of life.[17] Members of the Sangama family, they established a new Hindu empire around 1336.

The following story, based on the traditional accounts,[18] describes the empire's earliest stirrings of formation.

King Harihara was ruling his small realm from Kunjarakona, north of the Tungabhadra river.[19] One day he crossed the river to hunt in the forest with some warriors on the southern bank, not too far from the old Virupaksha shrine, a holy place from ancient days, which still drew pilgrims from all over the region.

Figure 1.1   Royal hunter depicted in a sculpture in Vijayanagara

Harihara saw something very curious near the spot where sage Vidyaranya often sat in meditation. On that day, Vidyaranya meditated while Harihara hunted nearby. As the king passed, he was astonished to see a hare stop and turn against the dogs who were pursuing him, fearlessly biting them and chasing them away.[20]

The king could not get the image out of his mind, and when he came upon the hermit sage he described it to him. 'The brave hare was like a lion the way it took off after those dogs', he marvelled.

The hermit Vidyaranya opened his eyes and said, 'O king, this country deserves to be the residence of a worthy family of great dharmic kings; by its very nature it is the source of great power! You can found a city based on wisdom here'.

'Where will the soldiers and gold come from, the might and the glory of prosperity? Who will construct a kingdom from these rough stones?'

'There is a power which will provide all those things. It is dharma, the law of righteousness, fulfilling the obligations of your inborn nature. The hare who turned has shown you a sign. Follow the sign, find victory and enduring power.'

'How do you know this?' Harihara asked.

'The hare bit the dog. The meaning of this is clear. What do men fear most? Death. What do good men fear most? Death of dharma. You should not fear death of dharma, but instead fight for dharma and you are sure to win a life of blessings for yourself and the people's dharma. We can work together. Found your capital city on the very spot where the hare overpowered the dog. There you can base an indomitable empire, where, against all odds, force cannot overpower weakness.'[21]

'Can a freak event serve as foundation for the building of a civilization?' Harihara wondered. He was used to the tempered sword's sharp edge and the strength of arm and horse determining events, not curious omens.

'This place is holy from ancient times, sanctified by the divine heroes Rama and Laksmana and their great helper Hanuman', the sage explained.

'How do you know all this with such certainty?' Harihara asked.

Vidyaranya replied, 'When gazing upon the valley and hills thinking about a future capital for dharma, I myself saw the fearless hare on Matanga hill. The hare came from a cave and boldly approached a dog watching a herd of cows, and without fear he chased the dog away. The meaning is, no foe will be able to harm even the weak here. The sign is not a freak of nature but comes from the divine nourisher of dharma.'

Vidyaranya's brother Sayana, the pandit known for his Vedic studies, stood nearby, overhearing the conversation. He approached and explained: 'My brother Vidyaranya has intended for some time to found the empire of Victory here. It is his fate. We knew it from the way his guru Jnanendra Saraswati led him in that direction. Vidyaranya used to return with royal pudding from his begging rounds, when the other disciples had received just plain rice. There were many other signs. And he has secret knowledge.'[22]

The king was impressed by the brothers and the signs they eloquently interpreted: 'Shiva as Virupaksha revealed to me that long ago a kingdom of Vijayanagara thrived here, and that it should now be refounded. The ruler must first surrender the territory to Lord Virupaksha, whose shrine is near, then receive the kingdom back as trustee.'[23]

'How do you know this?'

'I made a pilgrimage to Banaras. Amazing things happened on that journey. On the way there I met the forest ascetic, Singiri Bhatlu.[24] This ancient one had served Rama and knew the past, as well as the future. He told me that through the grace of the devas, 'the Shining Ones' whom I would meet in Kashi, I would cause a city to be built on the Tungabhadra river, and would install the king, and would serve as preceptor to the occupants of the Lotus Throne. Favoured with the grace of the gods, if all begins well, and the work is undertaken as a sacred trust, the city will enjoy great prosperity, thanks to Lakshmi.'[25]

'What else happened on your pilgrimage?' Harihara asked the brahman.

'The ascetic gave me directions to meet the ancient legendary seer Vyasa, compiler of the Vedas, in Kasi. No one else could recognize Vyasa because of his disguise – he was dressed as a pariah wearing a leather hat, carrying water and accompanied by four dogs. Seeing through the vile externals to the real light of the sage within, I won his friendship and he told me secrets, regarding the lifespan and political functions of the city – the goddess Lakshmi, queen of prosperity would grace the capital for many years, and many kings would rule one after the other. As preceptor of the dynasty, I was to instruct the kings to feed a thousand brahmans a day, and the city would be invincible. This will increase the sacred power here.'[26]

'A thousand brahmans a day,' Harihara pondered. 'What else?'

'Vyasa told me that the sage Matanga in ancient times had placed a curse on Vali (brother of Sugriva, who was friend of Lord Rama), and from that time, the place by the Tungabhadra river at Matangi hill would be protected from harm by animals or men. Hence the curious relationship between the hare and the dog.'[27]

'So that's it,' the king said. 'While I have been involved in the world of the Muslims you received a revelation about the future.'

'I returned and met Sayana and his son Mayana who were to be my helpers in this venture of building the great city. As I told you, Shiva as Virupaksha revealed to me that there was once long ago a kingdom, and that it should now be refounded. The founding ruler must first surrender the territory to Lord Virupaksha, then receive it back and govern it as trustee.'[28]

'What about the Muslims I work for?' Harihara asked.

'You can outsmart them at their own game. "I am the trickster's hoax," Krishna said in the *Bhagavad Gita*. Instead of being their fool, you can fool them.'

Harihara was impressed. He sensed that this sannyasin would be an extraordinary guide to protectors of the realm. He asked Vidyaranya to tell him Manu's description of a king's duties.

'I'll tell you the obligations of kings and explain the best behaviour for a king and outline the way he can win supreme success. A *kshatriya* who's received, according to law, the sacrament which the Veda prescribes has to protect the whole realm from harm, for when beings have no ruler they run off helter-skelter in terror. God made the king to keep all from harm. Even a baby king should not be belittled, or thought of as just a mere mortal – he's a great deity in the shape of a man. The whole world is saved from chaos via penalties. The innocent are few and far between. Punishments bring order so the whole world yields due pleasures. If a king is slack in punishing the guilty, the strong will roast the weak like fish on a stick over an open flame,' the sage said.[29]

Harihara respected this sannyasin hermit, and felt inspired to work with him to found the new city and empire.

Orienting and Founding the City of Victory

In order to found securely the capital city, to centre it stably in abiding strength and spiritual being, Vidyaranya consulted his brother Sayana, collected various *shastra* authorities, mantra experts and soothsayers to set up in the sunshine the gnomon, *shanku-sthapana* – a symbolic pole which casts a shadow, a marking peg to locate a ritually specific place on earth and the north–south axis around which the city would be laid out and organized. The axis was determined by finding the star Trishanku in the south and the pole star Dhruva. On the night of the full moon they took water three times and planted the gnomon, marking, once and for all, east and west.[30]

Two weeks later, at the auspicious time of the full moon in the month of Chaitra (the first day of the first month of the year in the traditional Hindu calendar), they formed the *vastupurusha* (literally 'person of the dwelling place'), the symbolic microcosm of the genius of the place, the embodiment of the cosmic spirit of the site. They made the *vastupurusha* using 16 *manuvu*s of gold,[32] and fixed it in an upright position in a very strong pillar. They prepared an area around the pillar that could be filled with water, so that the *vastupurusha* would be immersed in water up to the head. The proper placement of the *vastupurusha* at precisely the right time would constitute the official founding of the important place.[33]

Now that the preliminary work had been done with ritual care and precision, it was almost time to install the foundation in its place. At the exact moment of perfect auspiciousness Vidyaranya was prepared to blow the conch shell from a nearby spot to mark the official beginning of the new capital. But things don't always go according to plan. It so happened that a *jangam* (Shaivite mendicant monk) came wandering along gathering alms, and he blew the conch shell he always carried to announce his presence. And the assistants of Vidyaranya, thinking that their master had blown the conch, took this as their cue to begin placing the *vastupurusha* at the wrong time. It was as if Shiva as trickster, the divine wild joker beyond all the conventions of time and human life, had whimsically spoiled the plans. A little later Vidyaranya blew his conch, and the confused helpers went to see what was happening. Vidyaranya knew that a mistake had been made, and that the city had not been started in a manner conducive to long-term order. Now, instead of 3600 years of glory, the kingdom's duration had been reduced to a mere 360 years, and even that period would not all be smooth going.

This traditional story is a legend which dramatizes the intuition that the time of an important enterprise's beginning is a fateful period when trajectories are set into motion. In the age of Chaos Theory we often hear that the very essence of chaos is that small initial errors grow exponentially until they dominate any regular motion.[34] In the Hindu view, auspicious beginnings ensure regular unfolding; ritual impurity, badly timed false starts and signs of confusion all portend difficulties. A chance wanderer happened to pass through a momentous event – he had a conch shell and he blew it. The brahman helpers, thinking it was Vidyaranya's signal, began the ritual prematurely.

Vidyaranya went on and finished establishing the *vastupurusha* in its place. Knowing that the ritual act had been performed a little off-centre, and that those initial conditions would make the kingdom's career somewhat wobbly, he felt sad. Metaphorically speaking, it was as if Merlin of King Arthur's Kingdom knew that Camelot could not endure very long and that nothing could be done about it, except to make the best of things and get on with the efforts at dedicated activity. (It is thought that Vidyaranya, being a sage, performed his social duties in the spirit of karma yoga – without concern for personal reward.) For generations many South Indians have believed that the goddess Bhuvaneshwari showered gold on Vidyaranya for over an hour as a boon. Because he was a sannyasin and was not supposed to handle money he had householders gather it to establish a Vijayanagara treasury.[35]

Harihara Devaraya, the king, immediately got busy, ordering masons to construct buildings of stone, adding to the fortifications and protective walls already in place. He built a palace and a temple, pavilions and a treasury, as well as a bastion with nine gates,[36] like the *vastupurusha*, the cosmic person first envisioned in *Rig Veda* chants – a body like that of humans, with nine openings.[37] Harihara soon moved his own family and his people there, and named the place after the hermit, calling it 'Vidyanagara', 'City of Wisdom'. He also built a temple of stone there in honour of the sage Vidyaranya. Harihara ruled for many years in the goodly city of Vijayanagara; with this capital the Karnataka empire flourished.

In 1356 Bukkaraja I, brother of Harihara Devaraya, was granted the leadership of the Vijayanagara capital and the wealth of the empire. After conquering the surrounding regions, he built up the great City of Victory beyond what it had been in his brother Harihara's days. One old inscription describes those illustrious days in poetic terms, saying that when valorous Vira Bukka ascended to the throne in the new city of Vijayanagara (central jewel in the pearl necklace of Tungabhadra river encircling Hemakuta mountain as if it were the throat of Mother Earth), the surrounding feudatories were all compelled to fall at his feet in obeisance, giving him tribute.[38]

A poet, alive when the capital city was flourishing, celebrated it by inviting listeners to:

> Walk around the great City of Victory. Go where you will on city streets. Everywhere you walk bright assembly halls decked out with golden vessels will dazzle your eyes. On many streets homes with mirrored doors will shine, and sugarcane and plaintain all around will invite you with Welcomes. You'll find able-bodied fighters, and horses, elephants and riders; you'll smell aromas of camphor and musk from breasts of exquisite doe-eyed women. You will face gardens lush with enjoyments, precious stones and glowing gold – a city of wealth and glory gleaming. You'll agree that this magnificent city is the most enchanting place you've ever seen.

Vidyaranya and his brother pandit, Sayana, worked to help the kings pattern the Vijayanagara kingdom after the old ways, gathering together the sources of learning, copying and commenting on texts, teaching a new generation, arranging the kingdom according to *sanatana dharma*. After Harihara, and then his brother Bukka, Harihara II took the throne: 'By the grace of Vidyaranya muni [Harihara II] acquired the empire of knowledge unattainable by other kings.'[40] The folk memory of Vidyaranya considers him a culture hero – '[a] poet, saint and hero' – who brought courage and self-respect to a people who had forgotten their own greatness, and even a military tactician involved in retaking the fort of Goa from the Muslims, as well as a prime minister who organized the empire, extended it and conducted affairs of state in a selfless manner, causing Vijayanagara to prosper.[41]

The kings did not take the audacious hare as emblem, but took the already familiar *varaha* – (Vishnu as a powerful boar, able to dive under flood waters and rescue earth and Vedas, retrieving them to safety on dry land) and the upright sword of might. Vijayanagara thrived for generations.

But after 300 years it was as if the dog began to come to his senses – blurting, 'What's this all about?', then turning round and chasing the hare right back into the dark cool cave, back in the hill of boulders. The brave hare's time had passed; time had removed the curse and the blessing. The sage's beautifully envisioned kingdom fell to ruin, as it stands today, scattered and abandoned in forlorn disarray, the remnants of old glory days tumbled down, broken to pieces, dusty with time.

Empire and Regional Provinces: The Whole and the Fractal Parts

For over two centuries (1336–1536) the fragmentary empire was a great embodiment of Hindu polity, following in some ways the patterns of the earlier South Indian Chola dynasty:

> Vijayanagara kings seemed to have had the sense that the kingdom established in the fourteenth century revived an earlier universal sovereignty in Karnataka, that of the Chalukyas of Badami [and] adopted the emblem of the Chalukyas, the boar ... .[42]

The Vijayanagara kingship of the Tungabhadra river core region was like the Chola kingship around the Kaveri river: in both cases 'locality units of the political system were not merely self-governing – linked to imperial centres neither by resource flows nor command – but were reduced images of the ... centres', as Burton Stein observed.[43] (The smaller units or segments were smaller-scale replicas, microcosms, a fractal-like pattern to which we shall return.) Another historian, K.A. Nilakanta Sastri, has written that, in its day-to-day workings, the whole Vijayanagara empire could best be understood 'as a military confederacy of many chieftains cooperating under the leadership of the biggest among them'.[44] And yet in cosmic religious symbolism and the context of moral order over which the Vijayanagara kings presided, the capital City of Victory was 'never less than the whole world, and its parts [were] the parts of the world'.[45] Wholeness is the religious concept which Hindu social organization, religious practice, and spiritual vision cannot do without. Scales of parts and conceptions of wholeness patterns orient with a sense of cosmic order, how things should be done, how things cohere, how things thrive. The wholeness–partness symbolisms are potent in the *vastupurusha* ritual of laying out the grid on the ground to begin the capital construction. From the early days, when Vidyaranya worshipped Goddess Durga in the form of Bhuvaneshvari to gain her blessings, to the glorious reign of Krishnadevaraya who ruled in the early sixteenth century and onwards, the imagery of cosmic wholeness and sacred patterns of consciousness and power are constant. The fractal-like[46] organization of the political system composed of cooperative smaller centres modelled on the larger centre, which itself was modelled on cosmic rule, was integrated with the religious institutions which were at the heart of South Indian life. 'Not only did these institutions directly fulfill the narrowly construed religious needs of the most respectable (*sattvik*) groups in South Indian society, but served as models *for* and models *of* an appropriate order for even ordinary folk by the Vijayanagara period.'[47] What was done at *mathas* and temples by brahmans was replicated and adapted by ordinary folk on a smaller scale and in humbler situations. Similarly, the representative 'voices' in translations which are the core feature of this book were echoed by local singers, lesser teachers and villagers, serving as poets, and living in the memories of South Indians. There are continuities, intertextual relationships and echoing reiterations.

Madeleine Biardeau writes of the fractal-like social structure of classical Hinduism: ' ... in each territorial "unit" – which can be as small as a village with its chief – one finds, theoretically at least, the totality of the Hindu socio-religious structure and its values.'[48] The attempt to continue the totality is a deep Hindu concern at all levels. What was done in the capital by the greatest chieftain was a pattern to be followed; he was an 'attractor' whose ways were emulated on a smaller scale by the smaller chieftains in outlying segmentary regions. Thus, in fourteenth-century Hindu tradition, autonomy continually reasserted and reiterated itself on several levels of scale, all affiliated under the Vijayanagara banner emblemed with the sword and boar. The popular story, with archetypal images, meanings and uses, which people have found satisfaction in telling, is experientally timeless rather than historically-oriented in the modern sense. I have presented a composite of the traditional tellings, with the idea, asserted by S. Krishnaswami Aiyangar and followed by Nilakanta Sastri, that Hindu–Muslim conflict was the motive force shaping Vijayanagara – its reason for being. However, the story has been challenged by modern scholarship. Burton Stein rejects it. Kulke and Wagoner present alternative views, saying that evidence of various Islamicate[49] influences, such as titles for those in authority, weaponry and the fashions of clothing, show an attempt to Islamicize and gain validity from ascendant Muslim power rather than an attempt to preserve Hinduism.[50] I will discuss this briefly here, and again when exploring Vidyaranya's role, as well as later, in the book's conclusion.

Adapting to new times necessitates a viable creative process – not so turbulent as to prohibit building structure, not so stable as to be stagnant. The adaptation of Hindu tradition is a complex process[51] involving energies, life, form and enduring systems that are dynamic. Heartbeats and brain activity are chaotic systems[52] in the human organism; on the level of social life cultural activities such as festivals, education and the organization of resources are also chaotic systems. When Stein, Wagoner, Kulke and others notice that the new regime is outwardly shaped by Muslim styles, they are noticing that the order and forms in the existing (Muslim) rule and potentials taking shape in the Hindu rule involve chaotic energies, self-organizing changes, at the interface – 'the edge of chaos' – which is the optimal condition. Neither too much one or the other (neither too rigid nor too mutable) but dynamically, viably, both – vitality is an edged, interfaced balancing act of life's reality. As Tagore wrote: 'It is the constant harmony of chance and determination which makes [the drama of existence] eternally new and living.' The spontaneous and the given, the new energies and old laws and conditions in dynamic interaction, form one long ancient story of tradition and improvisation.

Systems of nature and systems of human culture both rigorously follow patterns and adapt to new conditions – a tree grows in a predetermined shape but may grow around an obstacle and a prayer recited in a service of worship may need to be adapted to changing circumstances. Systems of nature and culture are necessarily interdependent. The person reciting a prayer needs energy from food and water produced by the natural world. The tree needs carbon dioxide which the person reciting the prayer produces, and so on in an intricate dance of mutuality.

The Muslims did not succeed in causing the majority of South Indians to live in harmony with their tune. How are we to imagine the transition from Muslim rule back to a Hindu kingdom as Vijayanagara became strong? First of all, the Muslim sultans who took over South India for a time had no stable base there. Geographically, the vast plateau was too extensive to control, and the blistering tropical heat and recurrent monsoons added to the difficulties. The adjacent mountainous regions prevented easy access to the Malabar coast where foreign trade flourished. Many areas of the wilderness were populated by a variety of tribal peoples and in diverse provinces a number of regional languages were spoken.

Peasant communities in the *nadus,* regional districts, had their own identities, longstanding customs and forms of self-organization. These communities were independent enough to need constant local attention in governing. The many small kingdoms of the South, 'ruled by groups of peasant-warriors who derived political legitimacy from Hindu brahmanic consent',[53] had their own defences and traditional systems of authority and cooperation which multitudes of people accepted as the social norm. The South Indian segmented Vijayanagara empire gravitated to the Hindu patterns because the habits and traditions of the people, like water 'remembering' the channels it had flowed in previously, were the preferred configurations. The people resisted Muslim regimes because of their intrusive violence. Turkic armies with their plundering and anti-Hindu policies did not win grassroots support. Their 'tune' was too foreign to gain deep acceptance in most of South India.

As Frank Kermode wrote in *The Sense of an Ending,* 'It is not that we are connoisseurs of chaos, but that we are surrounded by it, and equipped for co-existence with it only by our fictive powers'.[54] When surrounded by chaos, the imagination deals with it by turning impressions into meaningful stories, selecting and ordering. Using 'fictive' powers means narrative-making, creating a world-view that makes the most of life in familiar terms. We are not connoisseurs (*rasikas*) exactly, but also not haters of the chaotic processes which run through all existence. As humans we collaborate with chaos, working with it as a given, bringing out its inherent potentials – we conspire with the energies in chaos, make music out of noise, kingdoms out of the epoch's conditions.

One last comment on the image of the hare chasing the dog away: it is an archetypal symbol, and its relation to empire-founding is not unique to Vijayanagara. The Hoysala capital – Shashakapura, the 'City of the Hare', was said to have been built where *a hare chased a tiger.* The capital of the Bahmanis at Bidar, the fort of the Nayakas of Tarikere and other places have similar stories of origin.[55] Imagined visually, an archetype like this, with its variations on small and grand scales, distributed over time and space in human culture, forms a fractal-like network of culture. Founding stories seem to be aimed at giving clues to identity. The images of the hare and the dog seem intended to assure: 'We are a people whose lives are not entirely precarious, because we are founded on a power and destiny from beyond us.' It seems to be an archetype reminding South Indian listeners that 'It was against all odds that we exist at all, but we do, as ourselves, a favoured and fortunate people.'[56] Modern scholarship acknowledges that building an empire involves composing or selecting a narrative, calling to mind a past that gives identity and hopeful direction. The identity and life of the sage Vidyaranya, who was the source of much of this memory formation, has been the subject of much discussion and debate. As we shall see, clues about Vidyaranya's life are still being investigated, continuing to stir controversies even to this day.

Notes

1   James Gleick, *Chaos: Making a New Science*, New York: Penguin Books, 1988, p. 23. Gleick is referring to the observation that small-scale shifts accumulate and cause large-scale shifts – that, 'for the want of a nail' in a horse's shoe, a battle was lost and history was changed. The reason why it endures in folklore is worth noting. It involves the survival of a useful observation of pattern put into symbolic narrative form for safekeeping. Forewarned is forearmed. Another famous saying on this theme causes us to ask how much was contingent on the fact that Cleopatra's attractiveness hinged on her proportions – if her nose was differently shaped, would the lives of Caesar and Marc Anthony, and the course of history, have turned out differently? Chaos theory uses the term 'butterfly effect' to picture small initial causes generating large effects.

2   Phillip B. Wagoner, 'Harihara, Bukka, and the Sultan … ' in David Gilmartin and Bruce B. Lawrence (eds), *Beyond Turk and Hindu: Shaping Religious Identities in Islamicate India*, Gainesville: University of Florida Press, 2000.

3   Robert Sewell, *The Historical Inscriptions of Southern India*, New Delhi: Asian Educational Services, 1983 (reprint), pp. 345, 182–85. The Arab conquest of Sind occurred in 712. From 997 to 1030, Mahmud of Ghazni and his men plundered north-western India but did not try to govern it. At the end of the twelfth century invading Muslim armies began to conquer and occupy North India. Afghan and Turkic soldiers with cavalry overcame the local Hindu kings' forces and set up headquarters in Delhi. Turkic forces took the south Indian regional centres, Devagiri (1294), Warangal (1308), Dvarasamudram (1310) and Madurai (1311). This was part of a vast Muslim expansionist movement; a wide swathe of conquest stretched from North Africa to China. What gave the Muslim leaders the drive to venture so far from home and take others' land? Was it rootlessness or the feeling that their own homes were secure? What practical necessity, what ideological push, what restlessness caused the massive invasion, violence and looting? Did they assume that pillaging an infidel land of inferior idolators was divinely sanctioned? Was greed masked by a sense of divine mission? See Joan-Pau Rubies, *Travel and Ethnology in the Renaissance: South India through European Eyes, 1250–1625*, Cambridge: Cambridge University Press, 2000, p. 13.

4   Sewell, *Historical Inscriptions of Southern India*, p. 184. Ibn Battuta's account is summarized in N. Venkata Ramanayya, *Vijayanagara: Origin of the City and the Empire*, Madras: University of Madras, 1933, pp. 91–92. See also Robert Sewell, *A Forgotten Empire (Vijayanagar)*, New Delhi: Asian Educational Services, 1982 (reprint), pp. 17–18.

5   Venkata Ramanayya, *Vijayanagara: Origin of the City and the Empire*, p. 92.

6   Sewell, *Historical Inscriptions of Southern India*, p. 184.

7   Venkata Ramanayya, Vijayanagara: Origin of the City and the Empire, p. 98.

8   For example, before the founding of the Vijayanagara empire, Mummaddi Singa (d. 1324) a warrior who sought land to rule, founded Kampili, and later built a fortress at Anegondi, near the rocky land along the Tungabhadra river where the Vijayanagara founders were to settle. A little later, Kampiladevaraya consolidated Singa's conquest with the assistance of Bukka and his brothers. See Burton Stein, 'Vijayanagara', *The New Cambridge History of India*, 1.2, Cambridge: Cambridge University Press, 1989. p. 18

9   Venkata Ramanayya, *Vijayanagara: Origin of the City and the Empire*, p. 100.

10   In the preface to *Parasarasmriti*, Madhava Vidyaranya says that Shrimati and Mayana were his parents, and Sayana, Bhoja and Somanatha are his brothers. It is said Madhava was born in Pampanagaram. See A.K. Balasundaram, *Relics of the Vijayanagar Glory*, Anantapur: Rayalaseema Krishnaraya Publishing Works, 1948, p. 7. In *Tidings of the King*, written at a later time, they were not brothers, but Vidyaranya and his helpers.

11   Smarta brahmans, custodians of the 'remembered' traditions of Hinduism, the lawbooks and Puranas, are perhaps comparable to the Kohens in Judaism, in that both are priestly lineages, with learning and lore passed down many generations from fathers to sons. Mahatma Gandhi, who was not a brahman learned in traditional Sanskrit texts, took a different approach. He said that, without knowing the old texts, one could go to a village and observe a simple woman and learn Hinduism's basics.

12   According to legend, Vidyaranya desired to have a vision of Gayatri Devi (the Goddess of the
     Gayatri mantra). He tried ritual means, gathering learned brahmans from various regions and, at the
     auspicious time, commencing *Gayatripurascharana*, but failed to bring her presence there. His
     absorption in unfulfilled striving was so intense that it made him numb to the joys of the world, and
     he became a recluse. It was only in this turned-off, interiorized mode that he was able to attain the
     experience of Gayatri Devi, who appeared to him and offered him a favour. He asked for an
     auspicious shower of gold to fall from the sky in the Karnataka region, so that the kingdom would
     prosper, and, according to legend, his wish was fulfilled. See *Panchadasi of Sreemut Vidyaranya
     Swami*, Calcutta: Society for the Resuscitation of Indian Literature, 1899, pp. 3–4.

13   Balasundaram, *Relics of the Vijayanagar Glory*, p. 7.

14   Bhoganatha is said to have been the companion and 'minister of amusement' of King Sangama II,
     and was a Sanskrit poet. See Hermann Kulke, 'Maharajas, Mahanbts and Historians: Reflections on
     the Historiography of Early Vijayanagara and Sringeri', in Anna Libera Dallapiccola with S.Z.
     Lallemant (eds), *Vijayanagara – City and Empire*, Stuttgart: Steiner Verlag, 1985, p. 128.

15   Variations on this name include Lakkanna and Lakshmanamantri. According to an inscription he
     saved Devaraya from conspirators planning to kill him, according to Vasundhara Filliozat,
     Vijayanagar, Delhi: National Book Trust, 1999, p. 37.

16   Known facts about Harihara are well summarized by Venkata Ramanayya, *Vijayanagara: Origin of
     the City and the Empire*, p. 101.

17   The narrative I have presented thus far is synthesized from a variety of sources. These are primarily
     Venkata Ramanayya, *Vijayanagara: Origin of the City and the Empire*, pp. 1–56 as well as Burton
     Stein, 'Vijayanagara', and *Peasant, State and Society in Medieval South India*, Delhi: Oxford
     University Press 1985; T.V. Mahalingham, *Administration and Social Life under Vijayanagar*,
     Madras: University of Madras, 1940; John M. Fritz, 'Vijayanagara: Authority and Meaning of a
     South Indian Imperial Capital', *American Anthropologist*, 88(1) 1986, pp. 44–55; George Michell
     (ed.), *Splendours of the Vijayanagara Empire – Hampi*, Bombay: Marg Publications, 1981;
     Vijayanagara Sexcentenary Commemoration Volume, Dharwar: Vijayanagara Empire Sexcentenary
     Association, 1936; Phillip B. Wagoner, *Tidings of the King: A Translation and Ethnohistorical
     Analysis of the Rayavacakamu*, Honolulu: University of Hawaii Press, 1993.
     The reader will notice that this rendering of the Vijayanagara empire's origins is a narrative of
     chronological events and tale-like dialogues and descriptions. My purpose in synthesizing the salient
     modern historians' accounts, and the accounts told by tradition (for example *Tidings of the King*) is
     to present a holistic overview from which certain observations can be made. The study of the
     separate accounts' differences would require a book in itself, and in my view would be of interest to
     a far smaller audience. Hence, following Heinrich Zimmer and others, I am piecing together a
     coherent story of Hindu traditions and exploring the meanings connected to them.

18   Much of the following narrative is based on Wagoner's *Tidings of the King*. I am presenting the basic
     traditional story suggested by this and other texts to give the context for the exploration of archetypal
     images and events. I am not so concerned in this book with arguing literal veracity or historical
     accuracy, but with considering themes in the commonly accepted popular stories. I rely on typical
     tellings of the old stories to discuss Hindu patterns and traditional religious imagination.

19   In some stories, Harihara and Bukka, after a battle with the Hoysala king, Ballala, who had rebelled
     against the sultan, were resting under a tree in the forest. While Harihara slept a yogi called Revana
     came to him in a dream and gave him a *linga*, an aniconic image of the sacred associated with Shiva,
     saying, 'This *linga* will bring you certain victory and prosperity. Soon you'll meet the sage
     Vidyaranya and then become a ruler with your own throne.' See *Vidyaranya-kalajnana* in *Further
     Sources of Vijayanagara History*, cited by Wagoner in 'Harihara, Bukka, and the Sultan … ' pp.
     300–26, see esp. pp. 305–306.

20   In Wagoner's *Tidings of the King* it is Vidyaranya who saw the hare and dogs. See p. 84.

21   The lesser animal turning against the more ferocious one is a kind of archetypal sign of an
     unexpected turn of events, the non-linear nature of life: 'Instead of the hunting dog barking at the

musk deer, it's the musk deer barking at the hunting dog.' See *Tibetan Proverbs*, compiled by Lhamo Pemba, Bharamsala: Library of Tibetan Works and Archives, 1996, p. 28.

22   This anecdote is related in the text of Wagoner's translation of *Tidings of the King*, p. 80. As noted in note 18, the narrative presented here is a composite from traditional sources. I am especially interested in the rather timeless legend with its archetypal images, which people find satisfying to repeat, regardless of historical certainty.

23   This tradition, rule on behalf of Shiva Virupaksha, is noted by historians, including Romila Thapar, *A History of India*, vol. I, London: Penguin, 1990, p. 333.

24   In some tellings when Vidyaranya rested under a tree on his way to Banaras, a voice in the tree asked him a puzzle, and he answered it, and this released 'Sringagiri Bhatta' who had been cursed to remain in the tree. The released man told Vidyaranya how to find Vyasa, who would be in disguise as a toddy-carrier with four dogs (the Vedas in disguise). Vidyaranya found him and Vyasa and the four dogs and the toddy blessed the writings Vidyaranya was carrying with him. The image shows how in Hinduism divine power is sometimes disguised as what is normally polluting. See Balasundaram, *Relics of the Vijayanagar Glory*, p. 8.

25   Wagoner, *Tidings of the King*, pp. 81–82, 166–67.

26   Ibid.

27   Ibid., pp.84–85.

28   Ibid.

29   *Manu Dharma Sastra* (The Laws of Manu), tr. Georg Buhler, *Sacred Books of the East*, vol. 25, London: Oxford University, 1886, IV, pp. 1–3, 8, 20, 22.

30   Wagoner, *Tidings of the King*, p. 85–86. Discussion of the ritual foundation is also on pp. 188-189.

31   This ritual act of laying out the grid of the *vastumandala* is the first of all the archetypal actions involved in constructing a temple, laying out a town and in preparing to build all the other important Hindu structures. It symbolizes the primordial sacrifice described in *Rig Veda* hymn X.90 in which the cosmic person is divided up to make existence. To found an enduring kingdom the knowers of the tradition proceeded in the archetypal way. 'Every big activity means a renewed conquest of disintegration … a restitution of integrity.' Stella Kramrisch, *The Hindu Temple*, vol. I. New Delhi: Motilal Banarsidass, 1980, p. 97. See also my website 'Hindu Temple Fractals' at http://liberalarts.iupui.edu/~wijackso/templefractals/

32   A *manuvu* was also called a '*maund*'. In 1900 it was the equivalent of 25 pounds weight. In earlier times it was as much as 75, or 82 pounds.

33   Kramrisch, *The Hindu Temple*, vol. 1, pp. 7, 66–67, 70–71.

34   Plato in *The Republic* suggested that, if the state starts out well, it proceeds in a cycle of orderly development. Various traditions note the principle of the importance of initial conditions: 'What is muddied at the source will be muddied all the way through,' and 'A small cause can lead to a big result.' See *Tibetan Proverbs*, 60, 51. Other cultures have proverbs such as a bent twig will produce a bent branch, and you can know the end by observing the beginning (Taoist).

35   Balasundaram, Relics of the Vijayanagar Glory, p. 8.

36   There are actually more than nine gates, but there were nine ritually placed gates in the ideal plan laid out on the land.

37   *Rig Veda* X.90.

38   Michell, *Splendours of the Vijayanagara Empire* - Hampi, p. 22.

39   Paraphrased from Wagoner's verse translation in *Tidings of the King*, pp. 125–26. Another poet wrote that the whole city was like Goddess Lakshmi's eternal lotus throne of prosperity and well-being – the suburbs were its petals, elephants its busy bees, the hills were mirrored like stems in the shining-sky water of the moat.

40   *Mysore Archeological Report*, 1916, p. 56, cited in Venkata Ramanayya, *Vijavanagara: Origin of the City and the Empire*, p. 54.

41   Ibid., pp. 9–10.

42   Stein, '*Vijayanagara*', p. 1. The Varaha emblem, and the copying of the ways of their sovereigns is discussed by Venkata Ramanayya, *Vijayanagara: Origin of the City and the Empire*, pp. 102–103.

The prestige of power, seen in the idea that whatever a great man does provides a model (*pramana*) that sets the standard, is found in *Bhagavad Gita* III.21.

43   Stein, *Peasant State and Society in Medieval South India*, p. 367. For more on the segmentary character of South Indian society see pp. 100–101. For a very useful discussion of scholarship on the founding of Vijayanagara and questions about its structure see pp. 373 ff.

44   Cited in ibid.

45   Ibid., p. 391, citing Hocart, *Kings and Councillors*. John M. Fritz writes: 'King and god [Rama] were the focus of the city: they paid homage to each other, and by radiating their energies outward they gave form, harmony, and plenty to the empire. Just as the god sat on the boundary between distinct aspects of the king's life (and the structural relations that they implied), the king sat at the centre of his realm. His actions maintained the appropriate relations between the distinct and often conflicting elements of his world – Hindu and Muslim, the powerful and the weak, the castes and so on … . See Fritz, 'Vijayanagara: Authority and Meaning of a South Indian Imperial Capital', *American Anthropological Association*, 88 (1), pp. 44–55.

46   Fractal geometry is a useful way of picturing relations of organic wholeness reflected in the parts at different scales. Other explorations of this concept follow in the chapters of this book.

47   Stein, *Peasant, State and Society in Medieval South India*, pp. 367–68.

48   Madeleine Biardeau, *Hinduism: The Anthropology of a Civilization*, Delhi: Oxford University Press, 1994, pp. 13–14 . Biardeau's thinking is a good corrective to the overly linear, narrowly historicist and Western-biased approaches in Indology. To develop such a holistic understanding of Hinduism's continuities amid such a plethora of views that are sometimes rather authoritarian and myopic is truly a feat. Burton Stein has also depicted the social organization in patterns that sound like fractals. From kingdom to village all the units resemble each other in organization. Not only villages and kingdoms are important in this scheme of things, but also (and often even more so) the *nadu* (locality) and *periyanadu* (supralocalities) are important and self-similar, structurally resembling each other on different scales. Sophia Diaz wrote an article entitled 'Bharata Natyam: A Hindu Fractal', *Anthropology of Consciousness* 1 (3–4), October – December, 1990, pp. 19–23 in which the fractal concept is used suggestively to frame the contents of the whole piece, and not discussed in detail.

49   'Islamicate' is a specific term defined by Marshall Hodgson, a great scholar of Islam, as referring 'not directly to the religion, Islam, itself, but to the social and cultural complex historically associated with Islam and the Muslims, both among Muslims themselves and even when found among non-Muslims'. Marshall Hodgson, Venture of Islam, Chicago: University of Chicago Press, 1975, vol. I, p. 59.

50   Since Hinduism is eclectic and adaptive, how does a title or stylish dress – matters of fashion, and technology of warfare – necessarily deny or dissolve a simultaneous sense of Hindu identity? Is there necessarily a loss of Hindu identity, a lessening of concerns in making a Hindu kingdom because there is no evidence of conversion? It was a Hindu rule, cosmopolitan and eclectic. It organized in ways necessary to preserve itself. There were signs of rulers honouring Hindu religion and allowing Muslim soldiers simultaneously to pay tribute to the Qur'an and the king. Motivation is hard to prove. Did Bukka only want power and to fit in with the dominant Muslim Islamic style? How was *smarta* Vidyaranya thrust to the centre of the foundation story? Kings obtained legitimation from brahmans, and in later times from religious authorities associated with the Tirupati temple. What are the clear signs they were not Hindu-motivated, that their purpose was something other than to re-establish their people's power? The truth lies between tradition and expedience.

51   'The edge of chaos … is now one of the lodestar concepts in the theory of complex adaptive systems. It proposes that the boundary between chaos and order is the most fruitful place for complex adaptive systems to emerge … that is where they can thrive … some scientists believe that cells, brains, organisms, ecosystems, corporations and economies all exist at the edge of chaos – in a regime not so orderly as to be sterile and not so chaotic as to be meaningless.' Thomas A. Bass, 'Black Box: What Happens when Maverick Physicists in New Mexico Set out to Predict the Markets?', *The New Yorker*, 26 April 1999, p. 117. Also available at http://www.columbia.edu/~dj114/btofc.htm.

52   In contemporary biological research literature and in chaos science, heart rhythms and brain activity are called 'chaotic systems' because chaotic systems are unpredictable yet ordered, with a deeper order inherent in the turbulence. In other words, the seeming chaos is not randomness but has subtle structures in it.

One writer on the topic wrote: 'While your pulse may feel perfectly regular, you actually have a great deal of subtle variability from one beat to the next. These fluctuations are produced by the normal functioning of the involuntary nervous system, which can cause your heart to slow down or speed up. The normal heartbeat, therefore, "is more a dance than a march".' 'Music of the Heart' at http://polymer.bu.edu/music.

53   *A Tagore Reader*, ed. Amiya Chakravarty, Boston, MA: Beacon Press, 1966, p. 100.

54   Frank Kermode, *The Sense of an Ending: Studies in the Theory of Fiction*, New York: Oxford University Press, 1967, p. 64.

55   See the introduction to Wagoner's *Tidings of the King*, p. 45.

56   Paradoxically the tone that this image sets at the outset of the Vijayanagara empire is hopeful for success in this-worldly terms. The empire begins with the blessings of a Shaivite sacred power (Virupaksha, the local Shiva temple deity is the patron deity of Vijayanagara); a little over two centuries later the empire declines under protection of Vishnu, with Vaishnavas dominant. From the outlook seen in their lyrics we might say the Haridasas favoured by the king upheld world-transcending values. It is interesting to compare this image of the aggressive hare, giving confidence in the underdog spirit facing larger forces, with the next-worldly image of 'the lion shall lie down with the lamb' in Christian symbolism.

CHAPTER 2

Vidyaranya: Sage, Political Adviser, Music Theorist, Philosopher and Biographer

*'Doesn't philosophy ... consist in pretending not to know what one
does know, and to know what one does not know?'*   Paul Valery[1]

*'The investigation of truth is in one sense difficult, in another easy. A sign of
this is the fact that neither can one attain it adequately, nor do all fail, but
each says something about the nature of things ... '*   Aristotle.[2]

The Multifaceted Vidyaranya

According to legends, Madhava Vidyaranya Muni was the mysterious fourteenth-century brahman philosopher whose presence was so important in the founding and early growth of the Vijayanagara kingdom that he has been called the chief architect of the empire's plan. In terms of Western archetypes we could say that Vidyaranya played a role like the wizard's in Camelot: Merlin advised King Arthur and his knights on the quest for the Holy Grail, giving wisdom and spiritual vision to men whose forte was physical strength and martial skill. Like the mysteriously knowledgeable Merlin, Vidyaranya had the whole programme in his mind, founded on the highest ideals and realizations of the past, and through Vidyaranya, as through Merlin, the passionate and practical men of muscle and blood could access the programme and work to attain its goal. Vidyaranya had the vision, knew the secrets, saw the connections and revealed the pathways. According to tradition, Vidyaranya served as chief minister to the first king, Harihara, and then to Bukka I and Harihara II. Thus he would have been the most important and influential religious thinker of his time in that region of South India. Some questions arise when we look at the dates of events. Probably born between 1280 and 1285, Vidyaranya seems to have spent a significant part of his life as a married householder, and there are references to his role in conducting a number Vedic sacrifices. He had a son named Mayana.[3] The empire was founded sometime around 1335, give or take a year or so. Vidyaranya became head of the Shringeri *matha* in 1377. This is much later than some traditions would have it – they say he was already the authority at Shringeri in 1334.

Besides having brothers named Sayana and Bhoganatha he had a younger sister, Singambika, who was the mother of Lakshmidhara, who became a minister of the Vijayanagara court. Vidyaranya was initiated into the sannyasin brotherhood, renunciate status, in 1331 and lived until 1386. Some say he died in the proximity of Virupaksha temple in Hampi, where a *brindavan-samadhi* still exists commemorating his life, but a *stotra* verse says that his life ended in Kanchipuram, a holy city to the east of Hampi where he seems to have spent considerable time.[4] Nevertheless, uncertainties exist on this and other points when one begins to look closely and ask questions.

In fact, the identity, name and background of Vidyaranya, the traditionally acclaimed first *rajaguru* of the Vijayanagara empire, has been called into question by a number of scholars. T.N. Mallappa in his book, *Kriyasakti Vidyaranya*, offers an example of dissenting Indian scholarship exploring these questions.[5] Mallappa argues against assertions by another scholar, H. Heras, that some Vidyaranya inscriptions were fabricated by the Shringeri monastery, and stresses the Shaivite, especially Kalamukha, background of the *rajaguru* and his associates at the origin of the empire. He maintains that Vidyaranya was the Kalamukha guru named Kriyashakti. The Kalamukhas were important in the educational systems of the region, he notes, and the differences among sects were not so great at that time; the three sects had not yet become such distinct groupings, because the followers of Madhvacharya were not yet so numerous as to be a rival group.[6] Mallappa also sees the two sects of Virashaivas, Lingayats and Aradhya brahmans as groups working in cooperation to help the ruler, Pratapa Rudra, resist Muslim invaders even before the origin of the empire. Mallappa believes that Vidyaranya was consecrated as the 'pontiff' or spiritual head of the Shringeri *matha* around 1381.[7]

Whilst the Shaivite presence (especially in its Kalamukha form) at the time of the empire's formation should perhaps be better appreciated, I find the work of T.M.P. Mahadevan, who discusses various aspects of the controversy regarding Vidyaranya's identity, to be valuable as well. Mahadevan shows the reasons for the confusion about the authorship of some of Vidyaranya's works, distinguishing between the sage with whom we are concerned (Madhava Vidyaranya) and his senior contemporary, whose name is Bharati Tirtha Vidyaranya. Mahadevan believes that the sage Madhava Vidyaranya succeeded Bharati Tirtha, a great scholar of Advaita, as head of the Shringeri *matha* from 1377 until 1386. Mahadevan cites an inscription dated 1386, which dramatizes with poetic images how Bharati Tirtha Vidyaranya was the pupil of Vidya Tirtha and teacher of sage Madhava Vidyaranya. Hence there are three generations of spiritual lineage represented by the three persons mentioned in the following verse:

King Bukka the swan enjoys himself near the lotus
named Bharati Tirtha which sprang from Vidya Tirtha

and is redolent with bliss-fragrance
emanating from non-dualist wisdom, blossoming
in the sunbeams of Vidyaranya's brilliance.[8]

Another scholar, Hermann Kulke, who independently reached some of the same basic conclusions as Mahadevan's findings discussed above, adds that no inscriptions about Madhava Vidyaranya mention his role in the early history of Vijayanagara. He also notes that, although Madhava Vidyaranya was extremely knowledgeable, he seems to have 'reached the highest level of hierocracy only in his old age'.[9] Like some other recent scholars he calls into question the traditional stories of Madhava Vidyaranya's role as chief cultural architect in the formation of the Vijayanagara empire. Thus the debate over the sage, the formation of the empire and motives of the founders is far from over. We shall return to these questions.[10]

Figure 2.1   Seated ascetic depicted in a sculpture in Vijayanagara

Vidyaranya's Texts on Law and Music

In any case, there is evidence that Madhava Vidyaranya wrote a number of books on philosophy, though some attributed to him are contested by scholars. He taught students whom he later entrusted with duties of leadership in Virupaksha and Shringeri *mathas*, he debated with thinkers such as Akshobhya Tirtha, and he invited the celebrated poet and philosopher Vedanta Deshika to the Vijayanagara court. He saw to it that a regional centre of learning which was important to *smarta* brahmans (Raghuttama *matha* of Gokarna) received honours such as ceremonial crown, throne, umbrella and musical instruments. As a *smarta brahman*, he was a member of the priestly caste of custodians of orthodoxy; the *smarta* community has been the source of many culturally creative and tolerant updaters of religion who preserved essentials and systematized the often rather unruly and sprawling collection of traditions known today as 'Hinduism'.[11] *Smartas* preserved the *smriti*, remembered authoritative texts. The *smriti* was something like the collection of cultural recipes – rules, customs, beliefs – for preparing the daily and perennial fare of the Hindu lifeway. Thus, as a *smarta*, Vidyaranya was at least eligible to be entrusted with the religio-cultural plan for the empire whose capital was sometimes called 'Vidyanagara'. (Some accounts say that this name was used in honour of him and the wisdom he embodied and disseminated.)[12]

Vidyaranya wrote important philosophical and legal works in Sanskrit, some of which are available in translation.[13] He wrote the treatise, *Parashara Madhaviya* – which is in fact a commentary on the traditional Sanskrit legal work entitled *Parasharasmriti*, so that the expanding empire would have a unified code of law. Because the *Parasharasmriti* did not have a chapter delineating the administration of justice in detail, Vidyaranya described the practice in the empire of his time. In this work, the emperor is the centre of justice, and ideally he settles disputes himself. A series of courts (*sabhas*, or assemblies) exists in all the provinces. There are two kinds of courts – regular (which can have both fixed and changing locations). If the court is headed by the emperor it is called *shastrita*, and if it is headed by an appointed judge with an official seal it is *mudrita*. The most important court is the one in the capital, dealing with civil and criminal cases, conducted by the judge (the emperor), his assistant and assessors, a recording clerk, accountant, and bailiff. The emperor is not the sole judge there, but appoints a representative to assist him.[14] The judge sits in the 'seat of dharma', the assistant examines the witnesses to elicit the facts of the case, and the assessors explain the law that is relevant to the case. Cases are brought by the parties involved in the dispute or by a government official, or the emperor summons the accused and witnesses. Sometimes victims would approach the king when he travelled and lie prone before him asking for justice. Because a victim could not always be present at every trial, he could send a representative, a *niyogi*, who was authorized to attend the proceedings in his place. The complainant could lodge a complaint by filing the proper document with the court, and then the defendant would be called to answer. With both sides of the argument present, the court would begin with the examination of both sides, the considering of evidence and the noting of findings. Human evidence involved personal testimony, documents and material objects. Divine evidence involved ordeals, proofs from supernatural signs, such as putting a hand in boiling oil without being harmed. (The court resorted to divine evidence only when human evidence was unavailable.) [15] Serious punishments, such as losing a foot or a hand, were doled out for serious offences, such as larceny and rape. Upper-caste traitors might be impaled. Lower-caste criminals might be beheaded in the marketplace.[16] Although the emperor on tour could be requested to settle disputes in provincial courts, most civil cases were settled locally without resorting to the government. The administration of justice in this system was decentralized, and the accused were judged by a jury of peers. Vidyaranya specifically states that people of the hills should be tried in courts made up of hill people; soldiers should be tried in courts of fellow soldiers, caste disputes should be worked out by courts of elders of the caste involved, and assemblies of elder villagers should settle village issues.[17]

Vidyaranya's treatise on music, *Sangita Sara* ('*Essence of Music*'), now lost, is said to have been the earliest text of the Vijayanagara empire. The treatise *Sangita Sudha*,[18] attributed to King Raghunatha of Tanjavur was written by Govinda Dikshita. In it the sage Vidyaranya is said to have been the first to distinguish between basic and generated ragas, and therefore was the original father of the *mela* system of classification. Surviving quotations from the *Sangita Sara*, also found in the later *Sangita Sudha*, show Vidyaranya, as the establisher of dharma, clarifying structures of order in his time. In writing the *Sangita Sara*, Vidyaranya was the tone-setter, distinguishing musical right from wrong, citing the faults of a poor musician (*kevalagayaka*), who would only create more disharmony and chaos. To distinguish the respectable from the inferior musician, he describes the skills that the good singer employs. It is noteworthy that these descriptions of the incompetent and the excellent singers are all matters of musicological knowledge and strictly empirical observations, not matters of philosophical debate or religious opinion. South Indian music is a very specific system of ragas, a practical discipline with set limits and known rules; it is not the same as philosophy, yet Vidyaranya's philosophical rigour enabled him to delineate essentials with clarity. To brand the incorrect and to present the objectives of singers, Vidyaranya lists marks of technical excellence and errors to avoid. Besides giving criteria for judgement, his writing gives an outline of topics that a teacher should cover in lessons, as well as guidelines for excellence. Among his guidelines, as we find them cited by Govinda Dikshita's text, there is no particularly religious idea mentioned, as later lists sometimes provide.

Vidyaranya, following the *smarta* outlook, took it for granted that retuning the Hindu lifeway after jangling years of disruptive chaos and destruction could not be accomplished by political actions alone. From Vedic times onwards, the correct performance of rituals had been held to be essential to order in the world. The connections between music and harmonious life may not be well known in our age, but ancient Chinese, Greek and Hindu traditions recognized music as a powerful force for refinement and order.[19] Music can be persuasive without the use of force; it posits an unconscious invitation to cooperation through beauty. It can bring one back to oneself when one is scattered, distracted or distraught.[20] Hindus often respond to deep feelings expressed gracefully in media such as music and dance; the Muslim mystics of the Sufi schools, with their inspiring songs and ecstatic dances, sometimes shared their spiritual fervour and found Hindus receptive, whereas stern Muslim legalists and fierce warriors left them cold or with a bitter taste.[21] Vidyaranya probably recognized this natural power of song and knew the necessity of working with it.[22] It is regrettable that we have access to only a few tantalizing fragments of his musical treatise.

Vidyaranya as Philosopher

Whilst I will not attempt to give an exhaustive account of Vidyaranya as philosopher – which would be too large an undertaking for this book – I do want to present some characteristic aspects of his rigorous thought, and at least indicate some aspects of his work in philosophy to convey its flavour. To reflect on Vidyaranya's highly developed philosophical mind I will briefly highlight selections on language, method and symbolism from his writings in the field of the Hindu philosophy of oneness (*advaita* – literally, the 'non-duality' of ultimate reality).

Ganeswar Misra, a renowned Indian philosopher of our times, has argued that Vidyaranya brought to his philosophy original insights which are comparable in their significance to some of Wittgenstein's. For example, Wittgenstein is credited with perceiving that 'the nature of philosophy is logico-linguistic'[23] Vidyaranya stated in no uncertain terms that 'the method of philosophical enquiry is the logico-linguistic analysis of all intelligible discourse and its object is also logico-linguistic'. Vidyaranya is known for four major philosophical writing[24] in Sanskrit: (1) *Panchadashi* (on the *advaita* theme '*Brahma satyam, jaganmithya, jivo Brahmaiva na parah*' meaning 'Only Brahman is real; the world is an unreal mixture; the soul is not other than Brahman'); (2) *Jivanmukti-viveka* (also on the *advaita* theme); (3) *Anubhuti-prakashika* (on interpreting the Vedas); and (4) *Vivarana-prameya-sangraha* (explaining the *vivarana*, or 'interpretation', of Vedanta as understood by the philosophers Padmapada and Prakasatman. It is especially in this last treatise that Vidyaranya rigorously argues for the view that philosophy is a logico-linguistic enterprise. The title of this work literally means 'Summary of the Vivarana', but it is really a large opus with many innovative interpretations and fresh ideas which he developed.[25]

It is significant that Vidyaranya's thought implies the intellectual discernment of bracketing philosophy, religion, music and other spheres as separate realms of inquiry and discipline. This strictness in differentiating this divisibility of life, thought and action raises questions about stereotypical presuppositions regarding India. It is commonly said that India's greatest singers and philosophers, poets and activists were often saints who mixed religion with every kind of thinking, perhaps rather indiscriminately. Vidyaranya seems very different; he seems to have made efforts to avoid mixing different kinds of thought.

Vidyaranya explained that the method of an inquiry and the object of that inquiry cannot be different. If the object is an empirical one, so must be the method; if the object is logico-linguistic, so must be the method. As Ganeswar Misra says 'the necessary form of the understanding and that of the intelligible world which is comprehended by it must be identical'.[26] Therefore ontological truth has no direct contact with empirical truth; philosophical knowledge and empirical constitute separate domains, independent unto themselves. Vidyaranya asserts that empirical disciplines stand by themselves, not needing borrowed strength to buttress them.

> Empirical disciplines do not look upon philosophy as being completely different from religion. The *brahman* [ultimate reality – consciousness which is formless, all-pervasive, blissful awareness in which yogis seek to be established]; which is worshipped in religion is different from the *brahman* of philosophy. The aim of philosophy is knowledge, but that of religion is happiness in another world.[27]

Vidyaranya retains a clarity through his careful differentiation.

The philosophical method of logico-linguistic analysis gives knowledge of 'the depth-grammar of our discourse'[28] showing us some of the presuppositions leading to our understanding of the world. Empirical knowledge is *vyavaharika* – practical understanding relating to relative existence. *Paramarthika*, on the other hand, is ontological knowledge of the ultimate structure of existence.

Vidyaranya's epistemology holds that *shruti pramana* ('the standard for knowing revealed teachings') has three parts.[29] The names of these three aspects are common to various traditions in South India, but Vidyaranya's interpretation of them is unique. First, *shravana* is not just listening to Upanishad texts, but means 'getting' the meaning of the statements on Atman – actually experiencing what is described. Second, *manana* is not cogitating or rolling the meaning over in the mind, but understanding the arguments of Vedanta's philosophical language in depth, following the logic of the language – not relying on mystic intuition or inferring the existence of such things as a Creator. (Thus relying on authority is not the be-all and end-all in Vedanta, which requires the application of reason to know the nature of understanding itself, as Misra asserts.) Third, *nididhyasana* means giving a clear idea of what one is going to investigate so that the mind will not become confused or be sidetracked, and end up saying something contrary to what it intends. This points to the need for every inquiry to start with a clear definition. The authentic inquiry must pursue an object to reach completion; it must also have a certain consistency and must not be self-contradictory.[30]

Vidyaranya, like other teachers of Advaita philosophy, lists four credentials for philosophical seekers of truth: (1) an ability to discern the eternal from the non-eternal; (2) an ability to be disinterested in the content of judgement; (3) mental calm and self-control; and (4) most importantly, an urgent desire to be liberated from bonds of false knowledge.

For *advaita* philosophy, Brahman, the absolute, is the basis of all intelligible discourse; it is not an entity, oversoul, universal consciousness, creator-maintainer-destroyer, object of adoration and so on. This strict view holds that philosophy seeks unconditional truth unconcerned with human purposes and interests (a view held by most modern and postmodern thinkers as untenable, since human purpose is always involved in thinking). Several times Vidyaranya asserts that *advaita* Vedanta philosophy does not teach the existence of a separate soul which survives the death of the body.[31] This is a view also found in Buddhism. The ground of consciousness is the ultimate reality in which the smaller existence finds its destiny, as a river finds itself entering a sea.

'I saw this same Devadatta in Pataliputra once before' is a well-known example used by Vidyaranya to illustrate what is knowable. In a sense this is a counterargument to Heraclitas' famous river-step sentence ('You can't step in the same stream twice'). If we put his views in a modern way, Vidyaranya is saying something like 'Devadatta stepped into the river of my sight in the town of Pataliputra once, and now again I see the same Devadatta, or at least there is enough identity that I can uphold it; the changes of place, time, personal characteristics (like becoming white-haired and wrinkled), are not so great that I must deny what I know. In fact I must affirm this sort of phenomenon to make intellectual understanding possible. The identity of an object is an ontological truth, not an empirical truth; existence is, *a priori*, a necessary condition for all knowledge. To know a Shankara is to locate him in space and time; to regard him as the same person at any point, even when he died eleven centuries ago, is to understand him as belonging to a region of space and time, in relation to his own situations, geography and so on.' Scepticism is 'buried' here, asserts Misra in his discussion of this point. If you deny continuity too much you can't rely on it when you need it to recognize your own coherence.[32]

Contrary to popular views, *advaita* philosophers do not all claim that world and body are mere illusions. Vidyaranya asserts that a person can't be 'conceived as having a real spiritual part which is immortal, and a mortal body which is illusory. To think of a disembodied soul is to enter the land of meaninglessness'. Also, *sat-chid-ananda* (like nirvana) is not to be understood as an entity in the empirical world. 'These are the end-points and supply the grounds of intelligibility to our entire conceptual system.'[33]

Vidyaranya also explains the terms *maya* and *avidya* along logico-linguistic lines, rather than religiously as divinely created illusory veils: '*Maya* and *avidya* ... signify the conditional character of our empirical knowledge.'[34] This usage constitutes a denial of the possibility of 'knowing a world independent of all its relations to the very necessary conditions of intelligibility'[35] as a chimerical enterprise. The term *adhyasa* is not about illusion but about the analysis of language: 'To be liberated is to know the limits and the very conditions of intelligibility and thereby to be aware of the chimerical character of the whole of absolute knowledge in the transcendental sense and also to be aware of the practical efficiency of our language of daily use and its incompetence to know its own organizational principle.'[36] Only wisdom able to see through the *samsara*-generated ignorance realizes the unknown on which the known rests.

Philosophically, nothing can be said about the atman, the spiritual Self which is not different from Brahman, since it is not a part of the empirical world, even though it is the support of all meaningful discourse. Atman is not describable. Yet, if left at that, the vast multitude of human beings would have no hope. But Indian thinkers do not cut off hope – they offer makeshift equivalences, skilful means to guide the seeker.[37] For a language-careful philosopher such as Vidyaranya, strictly speaking, '*Moksha ...* is *liberation from the illusion* created by knowing the concrete by means of the abstract'.[38] Illusion, in this view, is a confusion caused by taking a symbol system for the reality. (It is interesting that this matter of taking metaphors for realities is also a recent concern in the perceptive works of Donald Miller and Jacques Derrida, as they seek to examine the tacit infrastructures of world-views and the limits of conventional symbolisms.)[39]

Philosopher P.T. Raju (considered by many the leading modern authority on *advaita* Vedanta philosophy) sees Vidyaranya's remark that 'practical activity decides whether an epistemological object is real or illusory'[40] as crucially important. This *advaitin* observation, holding that the world is an arena meant for action, made up of activities and created by acts, and that *maya* includes both form and intellectual order, is of profound significance. Thus in the *advaita* view the world is more than mere illusion and it includes mind. Vidyaranya also presents the concept that the term *maya* signifies both magical order (as in 'Vishnu's veil of *maya*') and rational order or reason (mental constructs as involving *maya*, although they seem absolutely real). The empirical experiential becomes pragmatic in this way. Vidyaranya's goal-oriented purposive clear-cutness was a useful strategy for his time, necessary to survival, to keep the goal and the way clear – it was admirably rational in method. Today's thinkers are likely to ask whether one can always keep realms conveniently separate.[41] For his own time and place he ranked as one of the most important Andhra thinkers, alongside Buddhist thinker Nagarjuna and Vidyaranya's own brother Sayana, who commented on the *Rig Veda*.

In his philosophical writings Vidyaranya shows a flair for using archetypal images. In his *Panchadashi*, for example, he employs the great repertoire of classical metaphors – seed and tree, sea and rivers, spider and web, beads and thread, charioteer and driver, stage and actor, puppeteer and puppet, dream, dance, and *lila* to explain philosophical views. He had a deep awareness that the great images which people remember and live by are transformative. He wielded them as dynamic complexes that resonate in the soul, leading development onwards. He wrote with a poet's strong sense of accurate and vivid images being the link between the power of religious imagination and spiritual maturity. In his *Panchadashi* text, Vidyaranya says that *prakriti* is the reflection of Brahman, not a reality, as the Sankhyas say; the *jiva* is deluded, identifies with the world and then grieves – all caused by the duality which Ishvara creates. The ultimate answer in Vidyaranya's text is meditation on the attributeless Brahman, the ultimate consciousness which transcends the green and juicy world.[42] It is probably no coincidence that legends picture the sage as meditating in solitude before he was called into the active life by an empire seeking to be born.

Vidyaranya uses memorable expressions to assert that continuous focus on the ultimate is the ideal: 'Just as a profligate woman, even in the midst of her household work, mentally dwells on the pleasure experienced in company with her lover ... so does a man of faith ... internally taste the supreme felicity of Brahman.'[43] Thus, an image of a woman astray, preoccupied in the midst of mundane activities, serves in Vidyaranya's poetic sensibility to illustrate the practice of a man who has found the way to dwell in an awareness of higher consciousness beyond the world's troubles. The image vividly portrays the *jnanayoga* goal of having one's attention on the ultimately real in the midst of the merely relatively real world.

Elsewhere in the same text Vidyaranya's metaphor for the shame of pre-enlightenment ignorance is vivid: as a woman with cancer of the uterus feels uncomfortable and ashamed during the act of intercourse, even so, a knower of Brahman is painfully ashamed at the mistaken notions which he entertained prior to gnosis of the spiritual self.[44] Both are uncomfortably aware of what is outside the norms because there is a new self-consciousness when habitual conditions are gone. Yet if all is one, and illusion is a passing phase, discomfort cannot be eternal, but just another part of the drama of time.

Vidyaranya in his *Jivanmukti-Viveka* cites the Sanskrit text *Yogavashishtha* to shame feelings of attraction to seductive beauty by associating negative images of vulnerability and disgust, perhaps of scenes he himself observed in Banaras. Woman's beauty tends to distract the yogi from his goal and so has become a synechdochical cypher for the world. Negative images are used by yogis and other seekers to counter worldly attractions, like anti-advertisements about enticement. Vidyaranya speaks from that tradition when he writes that even the once lovely breasts of a dead woman become no better than dogfood as matter decays in the inevitable changes of timebound existence:

> Replete with flowing pitch-black hair (therefore, like lampblack, best left untouched), though so alluring to the eye, women, who kindle indeed the flame of desire's fire, are able to consume men as if they were mere straw. Is it not women who, though appearing to be as juicy and green as vitality itself, are in actuality devoid of grace and who, by their attractive looks, allure men to their destruction and feed the fires of hell raging in a far off region ... . Woman is the treacherous bait, attached to the hook on the line of impure latent desires, to catch men, who are, in a manner of speaking, so many fish swimming in Birth-and-death Pond, wallowing in the mire of the mind ... . Whoever has a woman near him is bound to feel the desire for intercourse. But what temptation is there for such enjoyment when a man has no woman? Abandoning woman you abandon the whole world; abandoning the whole world, you reach Supreme Bliss.[45]

This passage cited by Vidyaranya is an exercise aimed at dissuading the yogi from becoming enamoured of bodily pleasures. Its warnings of burns and loss are calculated to destroy the pitfalls of worldly life. It seeks to inspire revulsion in world-renouncing yogis, who have chosen to transcend the lures of earthly pleasures. To modern ears which fortunately have been educated and sensitized by feminist intelligence to criticize wholesale complaints about women, it seems harsh and hostile. Whilst I do not wish to defend nastiness towards women in any way, perhaps we should recall the text's aim – a serious concern of the medieval world – liberation, limitless bliss and freedom of *moksha*. The illusory world, harmony between sexes, the demands of society and attraction to pleasures were of no concern to seekers of ultimate freedom in medieval India. There, seekers of *moksha*, sannyasins, were in a different social order with different expectations from householders – an order liable to be disrupted by proximity to allurements of the flesh. Hence the stern warning.

Whilst the text is a strong sermon for renunciants it also sets up a standard even for family householders to look beyond indulgence in pleasure to a spiritual ultimate – attainable someday in a later phase of life or in another lifetime. It holds up a life of focus on *moksha*, not *dharma*, *artha*, or least of all *kama (pleasure)*. The way in which Vidyaranya sets up opposing poles, equating the female with the world of death and decay, delusion and misery, and the yogi's ideal transcendence with bliss, eternal life and perfect being sounds especially objectionable to moderns. It seems extreme in our age; it seems to be a viewpoint fraught with its own *maya*. Nevertheless it is a historian's responsibility to understand people in their historical context. We live in a time during which great thinkers – Rabindranath Tagore and Octavio Paz, for example – have rightly tried to reconcile the life of body and soul, matter and spirit. But to understand better why this view is cultivated we need to know more of the ancient world-views which took a very different approach. And we need to remember that Vidyaranya (and India in general) during the whole of his lifetime encompassed, by turns and with 'context sensitivity',[46] both aspects– celebration of woman, as well as anxiety about her attractiveness. A one-sided approach would miss the dynamics of the whole situation. The four goals of life, the *purushartha*s, include *kama* as a legitimate goal for those at the appropriate stage of life.

When it came to the beauty of women, while in his philosophical mode Vidyaranya was quick to ask after a brief reductive analysis: 'Where is the beauty in a woman? She is made of flesh and tendons, fickle in nature, and in her wonderful organ there is nothing very exquisite.'[47] In such arguments he routinely presented a negative view. Yet, as we shall see, Vidyaranya knew how to sing positively of the female body when his purpose was to argue for another value in an appealing way.

Figure 2.2   Depiction of an ascetic from a sculpture in Vijayanagara

Another Side of Vidyaranya: Biographer of Shankara

Vidyaranya in his biography of the great philosopher Shankaracharya, *Shankara-Dig-Vijaya*, 'The Conquest of the Four Quarters',[48] is remarkably free in his description of feminine physical charms, not as cudgels to break men's attachments to worldly life, but as enticing charms to stir their religious imagination alluringly. In this work Vidyaranya's imagery gracefully brings together the earthy and the ethereal in telling the story of Shankara, a saint well known as an ascetic philosopher. One wonders if he was merely following poetic conventions, or if someone else wrote the story and it was attributed to Vidyaranya. (Vedantadeshika, the prolific Vaishnava author who was Vidyaranya's contemporary, was similarly able to please *rasika*s, connoisseurs, with vivid erotic images in service of significant religious narratives.)

Early in his narration of Shankara's life Vidyaranya confesses that, by previously praising kings when he did not sincerely mean what he was saying, he had dirtied and diminished his inspiration:

> 'Flattering kings' goodness and magnanimity (virtues which actually exist no more than the son of an infertile woman or the horn of a hare), my poetic inspiration has become very polluted. But now I'll turn it pure and aromatic by rubbing into it the sweet-smelling and skin-cooling sandalwood paste which has fallen from the body of the dancing girl who is none other than my Master's holy fame and greatness.'[49]

Vidyaranya knows how to convey the beauty of his guru's glory in a way that dry scholars cannot. From the note of disillusionment with royalty it would seem that Vidyaranya wrote this after his involvement in political activities. His regret at praising kings who conquer earthly territory will be superseded, he hopes, by telling the story of a renunciant's spiritual conquest.

Vidyaranya's biography of Shankara is a traditional telling, drawing on previous narratives, detailing the legendary accomplishments of the great reformer and philosopher-saint, carrying them forward with poetic flair. Evidently people of that time could not only handle, but expected and relished, a permissive, openly sexually frank discourse style in which the coexistence of body and spirit, heart's desire and philosophy can be put before the reader with some fidelity to real life. It's as if the *purushartha*s ('goals' of life – *kama*, *artha*, dharma, *moksha*) allowed an inclusive spectrum. Thus, religious imagination would not be relegated to stuffy abstract terminology but *kama*, pleasure, will be given its due, dispelling dullness, enriching dharma and helping on the path to *moksha*.[50]

Vidyaranya, though a renunciant in later life, was married for quite a few years before he took sannyasin vows. His life of Shankara shows a candid poet's touch. He boldly uses charming uninhibited imagery of attractive female anatomy coupled with, and promoting, the attractiveness of renunciant values. For example, the downy hair that grows on a woman's belly and darkens around her navel is put to imaginative use as a *danda*, or staff, one of the few possessions a monk may own:

She had a line of mossy hair which ran like a radiant rivulet flowing to her bellybutton after meandering around the curves of her hillock breasts, and that line was shining like a unique staff of a renunciant, placed there on purpose by the creator for the special use of the divine child inside her, as if to indicate that the boy was a renunciant – even while inside the womb.

The creator had disguised two jugs full of a new kind of nectar that is actually *mukti* – release – to take the form of her two charming breasts. And those two motherly breasts stood out sharply, as if for the theory of difference (*bedha*), and the cleavage in between them for the doctrine of *shunyata*, and the child inside her was refuting those theories, by making her breasts swell together and her belly grow, as her pregnancy filled her with rounded oneness.[51]

Vidyaranya was ever the philosopher, even when considering the ripe body of an expectant woman. Thus, implied in the symbolic logic of female shape and motherhood, the poet depicts the unborn Shankara in his mother's womb as a persuasive presence for *advaita*, silently winning debates even before he could speak or write commentaries. To traditionalist brahmans such delightful images may be amusing and fetching, an ingenious mixture that compels attention with charm; to others they may seem rather far-fetched.

When the child was born, auspicious signs of the reconciliation of old enmities appear, including animals who are natural enemies helpfully scratching each others' itches.[52] Oddly, Vidyaranya does not include the following legend of Shankara which is current in South India today. His father was away, and the boy Shankara, as he had promised, was performing *puja* to the Goddess. He placed a milk offering before the image, and wept so sincerely the Mother consumed all the milk. Knowing the custom was to distribute the milk as *prasad* (remains of an offering to God) to family members, Shankara feared that he would be blamed for taking others' shares for himself. Weeping more, he caused Devi to squeeze the milk from her own mothering breasts, filling the cup with her sweetness. 'Because you expressed your yearning for my grace, I'm expressing this milk prasad for you,' she said, illustrating the flowing mutuality of bhakti.[53]

In this version when the boy was about eight years old his father died.

However, Vidyaranya does relate one of the most famous episodes of Shankara's early life in traditional Hindu narratives, the story of the crocodile clutching Shankara as he bathed and his use of this threat to his life to obtain his mother's permission to become a monk.[54] According to this story, Shankara's mother, fearing the youth was near death, agrees to let him take the spiritually beneficial vow, but the trick was against her; the threatening crocodile unclamped its jaws and the young man was released and went free, released from all family entanglements. Though Shankara did not die as a boy he did die as a rather young man, at 32, as had been foretold to his mother by the sage Agastya.[55]

The text describes Shankara's religious fervour in terms of a woman in love:

> As a bashful young bride, pushed by her friends' gentle persuasion, tiptoes into
> the nuptial chamber and gradually loses her natural shyness and embraces her
> husband, and at last, forgetting herself entirely, oblivious to all else, becomes
> one with him, even so did the sage Shankara withdraw his mind deep into the
> inner depths with the help of the process of practicing discernment cultivated by
> Vedanta teachings, and gradually losing his egoism, his sense of separate
> individuality, he sought the Lord's embrace, and at the summit of communion
> sought to lose his identity fully in union with the ultimate.[56]

Though in modern times Shankara is usually associated with philosophical
abstraction and spiritual transcendence, this is a poetry of spiritual enthusiasm,
useful to a religion of poetic imagination. It has to do with seeing imaginally,[57] with
following urges to feel with the mind's body, to think with the embodied mind.

Vidyaranya on Shankara's Excursion into Erotics

In one intriguing section of Vidyaranya's *Shankara-Dig-Vijaya*, the author does not
avoid a ticklish conflict as less complex and less skilful storytellers might. In this
episode, Shankara, because he has claimed to be the master of all learning, finds
himself in a situation where he must somehow learn about loveplay – the realm of
kama and the *Kama Sutra* – and since knowledge has an experiential component, he
at first appears to be caught in a corner, since he is a renunciate. Sex has long been
his area of unconsciousness, but now he urgently needs to know all about it so that
he can speak expertly with genuine knowledge.

The dilemma erupts when lovely Ubhaya-Bharati, wife of Madana (and said, in
the story, to be Goddess Saraswati incarnated to help bring out the Veda's meaning)
calls Shankara's bluff after he had defeated her husband in debate.[58]

Madana acknowledges that Shankara has protected the crownjewel of the
Upanishads, which is the word *eka* (one without a second), the unity of all existence,
by wielding his weapon of *Tattvamasi* (the *mahavakya* 'great utterance', 'Thou art
That' – the Self of the individual is the all-pervasive spiritual consciousness).
Shankara is pictured as illuminating many lives – his very gaze can grant release to
samsara-bound men. 'Let those who enjoy the embraces of women waste their days
in whatever love-sports they like, while they seem to be noble and learned souls, they
really just pretend; only those whose boat of life rocks and rolls in the ocean waves
of your teachings deserve to be called wise and great men,' Madana compliments his
opponent – as if setting Shankara up for a fall through hidden vulnerability due to
his unconscious area, his non-expertise.[59]

Then Madana's wife, Ubhaya-Bharati, steps in and tells of a monk's prediction
that she would one day meet Shiva incarnate (which is the traditional understanding
of Shankara's incarnation). Furthermore she cleverly tells Shankara that since she is
her husband's 'better half', Shankara has not totally defeated Madana because he has

not debated with her. At first Shankara objects to the impropriety of this, but eventually he agrees to the contest. For 17 days they argue the fine points of Vedic lore, philosophies and Hindu holy books, stopping the marathon debate only long enough to take care of life's mundane necessities. At the end of that time, during which Shankara seems to know everything, Madana's wife gets a new idea: Shankara has been a renunciant since boyhood, he's never lived with a woman, so he couldn't know the techniques of making love. Knowing that this is his blindspot – the area of knowledge where his experience is not just shallow but virtually non-existent – she throws down a challenge. 'Debate with me the science and art of lovemaking. Enumerate its forms and expressions, its nature, and speak of the focus spots of pleasure. Discuss the differences of the genders during bright and dark fortnights, and explain the embodied manifestations of sexuality in men and women.'[60]

The ensuing episode is a storyteller's *tour de force*, a scenario which allows Vidyaranya, Shankara and the reader to have it both ways – as a detached ascetic above it all, and also as one skilled in the illusory pleasures of erotic arts.

Thus challenged by a low blow, Shankara baulks and ponders his dilemma. What might he be willing to do to win the debate? The dilemma is clear. If he refrains from answering this challenge, his claim to 'mastery of all learning' will be seen for what it was – partiality claiming completeness. On the other hand, if he directly discusses the topic it will be contrary to sannyasin dharma; a renunciant is expected to be above sexual relations. Though he does possess some theoretical knowledge, he tells her he is ignorant of sex, because he is a true renunciant. Having admitted this, he asks for a month's recess before proceeding, telling her, 'Then you will lose your pride at knowing all about the science of lovemaking.'[61]

Thus, in this story, it takes a woman to prove that knowledge includes the body, that the flesh has its own organic ways and that human life naturally includes passionate pleasure, just as it takes bhakti to give life to religion dry with rites and wordy debatable philosophies. But Shankara is up to the challenge. He conceives of a way he can learn. He uses his yogic powers – always a magical possibility in Hindu stories – to fly about the region and discover a dead king's body. King Amaruka Raja has recently died, and his still warm body is surrounded by grieving wives – more than 100 of them – just what Shankara's mind needs to learn about making love.[62]

One disciple, Padmapada, realizing what Shankara was contemplating, cautions his master that it may be dangerous to leave his own body unattended. He recalls a story: 'Once a yogi named Matsyendra left his body in the care of a disciple named Goraksha and entered a dead king, and good fortune spread through the land. But sly ministers suspected what had happened and they persuade the king's consorts to use all their skill in lovemaking to keep the king absorbed in erotic pastimes, to get the yogi attached to that life so he would not abruptly leave. The yogi soul in the king grew so immersed in the affectionate feelings and charms, seductive allure, gentle-voiced giggles, pretty songs and attractive dances, that he forgot his previous states of spirituality and *samadhi*, behaving like a simpleton absorbed in debauchery. His disciple, disguised as a dance instructor, gained admittance to the living quarters of the king's wives, and surreptitiously taught the king, reminding him of spiritual truth, deadening his hunger for sensual enjoyments.' Thus, by recounting the story, the disciple Padmapada cautions Shankara that sensual attraction is a mighty trap; if he fails to take care, even a skilled yogi will be caught. The flesh must be given its due, but must neither be overestimated nor underestimated.[63]

Shankara replies that the disciple has left out part of the situation in his assessment – the important fact that, to a truly detached person such as himself, a personal desire for sensual pleasure will not grow – just as Krishna was detached, full of self-control, even while he was in the midst of the *gopis*. *Sankalpa*, the brooding imagination with its impulse and associations, causes desires. 'But I', Shankara asserts, 'am without that flaw. A being with true knowledge is not affected by his actions, so even if I engage in all the pleasures of lovemaking with this body I'm in now, no evil will accrue. But to avoid misleading the world I will use the dead king's body, not this sannyasin body.' Padmapada and the disciples are thus reassured.[64]

And so Shankara leaves his own body in a cave, to be guarded there by disciples, and his disembodied *prana* or life-force enters the dead king. Reviving physically, the king causes his wives and subjects to rejoice, and the whole kingdom prospers – flora and fauna flourish, good weather and social harmony ensue. Ministers to the king suspect that a great yogi's soul may have entered the ruler. Wanting to maintain the status quo, they pass a decree to be announced throughout the kingdom: any dead bodies found in the realm are to be burned without delay.[65]

The king, meanwhile, entrusts the public affairs of the kingdom to his aides, and withdraws from the routines of the state, spending all his time sequestered inside the palace, the better to enjoy his beautiful wives and learn the art of lovemaking.

The text describes in detail the intensive researches made by the king, who is the vehicle for Shankara's foray into courses of self-educational erotic virtual reality:

> In clean and cool crystalline halls he dallied, continually enjoying all the forms of lovemaking with those charming and responsive women. He shook dice with them, betting on erotic stakes, winning couplings in various positions. He drank wine from golden cups held by their hands, and had them drink wine too. He tenderly squeezed them, pressed kisses on their eyelid-lowered faces, and smelled their warm fragrant breaths and delighted in listening to their honeysweet voices. He hugged their soft bare bodies in close embraces, oblivious to all else in the thrill of intense joy. He served them well, pleasuring the bodies of these women, playfully fondling their breasts, and they were his tutors in the lessons of lovemaking, as he stood as a witness within the king's body, perceiving closely all the pleasure centers to be kindled, and the varied expressions of amorous gratification. By living there in their midst as their companion he came to understand well the nature of the pleasures which lovemaking can give... .[66]

As he predicted, although Shankara is vicariously present in the midst of enjoyment of pleasures, he is free from worldly attachments. His activities, however thorough and absorbing, are spiritually motivated – for educational purposes only.

Figure 2.3 Image of Latasundari from a sculpture in Vijayanagara

The story goes on to explain that to casual observers it seems that the king is enjoying the company of the women as he always had before, but in reality the detached sage in the king's body is carefully studying the principles of eroticism. In a very organized way, with definite objectives, assisted by learned experts in the field, he is conducting research on sex. At the same time he is also studying the sage Vatsyayana's *sutra*s on the erotic arts and all the commentaries, and he himself writes a new text to convey his knowledge and insights, entitled *Amaruka*. But as the weeks pass, Shankara's followers become anxious.[67]

> Disciples guarding Shankara's body which was in a state of suspended animation in the cave after a month of inaction grew restless. They went to the palace in the guise of musicians, where they were invited to perform. There, inside the palace music hall, they saw the king within whom their teacher's life-force was residing, surrounded by a cluster of gorgeous women, like the moon thronged by stars. Behind him lovely women waved a royal fan with petal soft hands, acccompanied by the melodies of their jingling bracelets, and in front of him other beauties, fine musicians, were filling the whole hall with dulcet tones from their instruments ... he looked like the love god ... . When they came all the way into the music hall the king indicated where they should sit with a glance; so ordered, they sat and started to sing with melodious voices, closely observing all the rules of musical science.[68]

The song's lyrics are about waiting for Shankara's return. Hearing the pointed reminder in the lyrics of the song, the alert ascetic in the king's body is made more conscious of his situation, reminding him of his mission and teachings.

Knowing that he needs to return to his own precarious flesh, Shankara as the king gives the musicians gifts, withdraws his subtle body from the king's physical form, and re-enters his own body – reviving just in the nick of time. The poor body he has left behind is about to be cremated. Shankara recites a hymn to Lakshmi-Narasimha, who escaped the fate of being burned to ashes by the fire and 'emerged from the cave as the moon comes out of Rahu's mouth when an eclipse has occurred'.[69] Yoga is 'skill in action', as the *Bhagavad Gita* says,[70] and Shankara, when challenged, rose to new heights and proved he could perform his dangerous mission with its unfamiliar tasks and exquisite demands with aplomb.

The episode teaches that the pulls of pleasure are so powerful that even Shankara had to be reminded of his higher calling by his lessers before he snapped out of it.[71] One has to respect something that strong, and pay the dues it demands. In all fields one cannot know unless one experiences and explores, in some way or other; and the most detached high consciousness can find a way of learning from earthy experience, when necessary. This is part of the vision of life in Hinduism – acknowledging the various parts in the drama of creation.

As Ubhaya-Bharati, the woman who challenged him, is about to leave the debate, knowing that she cannot beat Shankara, the sage says to her, 'I know that you are Saraswati, Consort of Brahma, sister of Shiva. You who are of the nature of pure consciousness, have become Lakshmi to protect the worlds. In the future I will establish temples for your worship in Shringeri[72] (Rishyashringa) and elsewhere. Please, manifest yourself in all those temples, and accept the devotees who will worship there, give them the boons they deserve.' She agrees and disappears, merging in Brahmaloka.[73] In divine *lilas* the various forces honour each other and work together; ultimately, all are forms of the divine, part of the cosmic play.

Vidyaranya's telling of Shankara's life is a cumulative restatement. It is composed partly of previous tradition and partly of new writing. Tradition was malleable enough to allow Vidyaranya to say what he wanted, and he entertainingly allowed tradition to say what seemed to be demanded by his times. Although Vidyaranya was a philosopher and a renunciate, he also had a mature knowledge of the world. He could exercise mental freedom in writing about the spectrum of human life – he was not cramped or bound in some small corner of existence. It was a good match; both Shankara's and Vidyaranya's agility in thought, word and deed makes the narrative succeed. Vidyaranya needed to become a Shankara who could re-establish tradition (putting Shringeri on the map). As we shall see, in so doing, Vidyaranya probably helped create our view of Shankara by telling his story in such an unforgettable way – as a spiritual conqueror's creatively written conquests.

Though he was not known for his devotion as much as Vaishnava saints were, bhakti played a part in Vidyaranya's total scheme of things. It is interesting, too, that even if it were to turn out that he did not write this Shankara biography, Hindu tradition has had no trouble in accepting him as able to write rigorous philosophy, law, music and human interest stories too. Perhaps, in its overall trajectory, Hindu tradition wanted to imagine Shankara as free as the atman, yet flexible enough to cavort in the body of a king when duty demanded, unattached to any one *guna* or condition, engaged in the pleasures of sexplay, knowledgeable in the deepest philosophy, beyond all the limits of *sattva*, *rajas*, and *tamas*. And perhaps we can say that Vidyaranya also seems to have shared that quality: enjoying the freedom to know the realms of *kama*, *artha*, *dharma* and, of course, the realm of *moksha*, which is freedom and peace in transcendence itself.

Vidyaranya could be supremely rational (and many Hindu intellectuals are proud of that), but he was also a man of his time, and he shares similarities with the culture that he and others helped to survive. He was not just a rational philosopher, not just a misogynic yogi, not just a lyrical poet, but an enigma like the rest of us. Some other thinkers may see him as no greater or less than other scholastic thinkers in other traditions, such as Thomistic thinkers from medieval times onward, finding nothing especially to cause pride or embarrassment.[74] Nethertheless, memorial verses celebrating his life indicate how members of Vidyaranya's own tradition sought to remember him and sing his praises:

> May the auspicious glances of the sage Vidyaranya,
> like camphor-dust showers, and garlands of *kahara*s,[75]
> like cool moonrays and soothing sandalwood paste,
> like waves on the Milk Ocean – glances which taste

like refreshing showers of compassion's nectar –
May they make you happy forever.
                              Several sages mulled it over:
'It could be he is Brahma'. 'But he hasn't four heads'.
'It might be he's Shiva'. 'But we see no third eye'.
Debating like this the sages came to the conclusion
'Vidyaranya must be Supreme Light's incarnation'.[76]

But, as we shall see, there are troubling questions about Vidyaranya's life and work.

Notes

1   Paul Valery, 'Man and the Sea Shell', in *Aesthetics*, tr. Ralph Manheim, New York: Bollingen/Pantheon, 1964, p. 18. (Also published as a book under the title *Seashells*, tr. Ralph Manheim, Boston: Beacon Press, 1998.)

2   Aristotle, *Aristotle's Metaphysics*, tr., Hippocrates G. Apostle, Grinnell: The Peripatetic Press, 1979, p. 35.

3   *Sri Vidyaranya* (Publication No. 3), Hampi: The Vidyaranya Vidyapitha Trust, 1983, p. 10. (No author's name is given.)

4   Ibid., pp. 16–17.

5   T.N. Mallappa, *Kriyasakti Vidyaranya*, Bangalore: Department of Publications and Extension Lectures, 1974. These issues are also discussed by S. Shrikantaya in 'Vijayanagara and Vidyaranya', *Vijayanagara Sexcentenary Commemoration Volume*, Dharwar: Vijayanagara Empire Sexcentenary Association, 1936, pp. 161–68.

6   'The division of Brahmins into what is known as "thrimathas" did not exist prior to the 14th century A.D., as Madhvamatha must have taken, to come to a form, a hundred years at least after the death of Acharya Madhva early in the 14th century A.D. Before that time they were all Smarthas, i.e., persons who followed the Smritis. They were divided into Vaishnavas and Shaivas ... ' (Mallappa, *Kriyasakti Vidyaranya*, p. 31).

7   Ibid., pp. 30, 34.

8   T.M.P. Mahadevan, *The Philosophy of Advaita with Special Reference to Bharatatirtha-Vidyaranya*, Madras: Ganesh, 1969, p. 8.

9   Hermann Kulke, 'Maharajas, Mahants and Historians ...' in Anna Libera Dallapiccola and Stephanie Zingel-Ave Lallemant (eds), *Vijayanagara – City and Empire*, vol. 1, Stuttgart: Steiner Verlag Wiesbaden GMBH, 1985, p. 132.

10 Phillip Wagoner's recent work in this area is very interesting. Sometimes the more one delves into evidence about a figure such as Vidyaranya the more questions arise. See Phillip B. Wagoner, 'Harihara, Bukka, and the Sultan: The Delhi Sultanate in the Political Imagination of Vijayanagara', in David Gilmartin and Bruce B. Lawrence (eds), *Beyond Turn and Hindu: Shaping Religious Identities in Islamicate India*, Gainesville: University of Florida Press, 2000.

11 Probably the earliest use of a word like 'Hindu' was in 1645 in a phrase in a letter of Shivaji, '*Hindavi swarajya*', meaning independence from foreign rule, 'self-rule of Hindu people'. See Wilfred Cantwell Smith, 'The Crystallization of Religious Communities in Mughal India', reprint from *Yad-Name-ye Irani-ye Minorsky*, Tehran, Tehran University 1969, p. 21.

12 The role of *smarta*s has often been overlooked in India's cultural history. Many great sages and saints were of this community, which is trained in the perennial order of Hinduism. Certain artistic personalities were stimulated by the fine frenzy of bhakti, the frisson of Vaishnava love, and this chaotic disturbance of creative excitement crystallized in the shape of new literature, songs and philosopical works. These creative people are sometimes bridgers of classes and

communities, including lower-caste and women, extending bhakti's hope to all. They embody a dynamism, as conservative progressives, passionate intellectuals, rooted in patterns of the past, but branching with new fruits of Hinduism. They are alive to the time, responding with arts improvisationally, reaching for transcendence with what's at hand. Being ultraconservatives, Sanskrit ritualists, wanting control, initially resisted the Hindi Ramayana of Tulsidas, for example, but some of the more open-minded *smarta*s asked: 'Why shouldn't inspiring spiritual potentials be available to ordinary people?'

13 Some of his writings include: *Vedanta Panchadesi, Vivarana Prameya Sangraha*, and *Jivanmuktiviveka*. These are all philosophical works. The *Parasara Madhaviya* is a legal treatise.

14 N. Venkata Ramanayya, *Studies in the Third Dynasty of Vijayanagara*, Madras: University of Madras, 1935, pp. 268–70.

15 Ibid., p. 272.

16 Ibid., p. 273.

17 Ibid., p. 276.

18 *The Sangita Sudha of King Raghunatha of Tanjore*, ed. P.S. Sundaram Aiyar and S. Subrahmanya Sastri, Madras: Music Academy of Madras, 1940, Chapter 3, verses 35–39. See also S. Ramanathan's 'The Sangita Sara of Sri Vidyaranya', in *The Journal of the Madras Music Academy*, LI 1977, vol. LI.

19 See Confucius' *Analects*, for example. Also the Greek saying 'When the mode of the music changes the walls of the city shake.' See *The Analects of Confucius*, tr. Arthur Waley, New York: Vintage Books, 1938, pp. 68–69.

20 Each level of existence – physical (organism and ecosystem), social, emotional and so on – has its order and tonality, and the inspired charismatic person who is empowered to influence order may have an effect on several levels, disrupting, exciting enthusiasm, retuning and refining them. Sometimes the great musician is a leader subconsciously active in peoples' inner lives, just as poets are said to be 'unacknowledged legislators'. I am aware that some take only political authority and economic power seriously, but in my view Aretha Franklin, John Coltrane, Bob Dylan and the Beatles have also swayed lives, as have rap artists in more recent times. Other ages had their own charismatic musicians.

21 See Vasudha Narayanan, 'The Strains of Hindu–Muslim Relations: Babri Masjid, Rituals, Music, and other Areas where the Traditions Cleave', in Arvind Sharma (ed.), *Hinduism and Secularism: After Ayodhya*, London: Palgrave-Macmillan, 2001; also idem, 'Religious Vows at the Shrine of Shahul Hamid', in William Harman and Selva Raj (eds), *Dealing with Deities: Promising Gods in South Asia*, Albany, NY: SUNY Press, 2004. We need better models for the dynamics of mutually indebted cultures, to picture the shared commonalities that bridge them, the order in the entanglement. Towards that end see the article by Carl Ernst and Tony Stewart entitled 'Syncretism' in Margaret Mills, Peter J. Claus, and Sarah Diamond (eds), *South Asian Folklore: An Encyclopedia*, New York/London: Routledge, 2003, pp. 586–88.

22 As S.K. Thyagarajan, in *Nadhopansana*, (Palni: Sarada Publishing House, 1968, p. 21) writes '*Svarajnana* is the establishment of communion between *nada* manifested in the individual self and unmanifested *nada* in the universe or the realization of Brahman in oneself. This is the end and aim of Carnatic music and the life of Saint Tyagaraja is its glorious example.'

23 Ganeswar Misra, *Language, Reality and Analysis: Essays on Indian Philosophy*, ed. J.N. Mohanty, Leiden: E.J. Brill, 1990, p. 57.

24 In fact there are more. For example, in addition to the four listed here, he wrote a brief philosophical work teaching the essence of *advaita* in the form of a blessing: *Brahmavidasirvadah*, Hospet/Hampi: Vidyaranya Vidyapitha Trust, 1981. On the other hand, T.M.P. Mahadevan wrote that only two texts are definitely attributed to Vidyaranya – the *Panchadashi* and the *Vivarana-prameya-sangraha*. See Mahadevan, *The Philosophy of Advaita*, p. 2. Venimadhavashastri admits that it is difficult to make a definite list of works by Vidyaranya and Sayana, but presents a list of 16 works he thinks Vidyaranya wrote. See 'Works of Vidyaranya in G.S. Dikshit (ed.), *Early Vijayanagara: Studies in its History and Culture*, Bangalore: BMS Memorial Foundation, 1988, pp. 113–17.

25 Traditional men, such as Vidyaranya and the other creative *smarta*s who from time to time helped Hinduism as a whole system update as necessary, seldom call attention to their own originality, preferring to cover their tracks by appearing to follow the ancients. Taoist sages of China also practised this kind of non-egotistical wisdom, attributing insights to the sages of earlier times.

26 Misra, *Language, Reality and Analysis*, p. 58. Another way of putting this – one favoured by V.V. Raman – is 'To elucidate any aspect of the phenomenal world, we need to adopt an observational rather than a speculative methodology'. Personal correspondence, May 2003.

27 This is like the note Pascal wrote after a mystical experience: 'Fire! God of Abraham – not of the philosophers' – distinguishing experiential from theoretical. See Blaise Pascal, *Pensées: Thoughts on Religion and Other Subjects*, tr. William Finlayson Trotter, New York: Washington Square Press, 1965, p. 285.

28 Misra, *Language, Reality and Analysis*, p. 59.

29 Ibid., p. 60.

30 Ibid., p. 59–60.

31 Ibid., p. 68.

32 Ibid., pp. 67–68.

33 Ibid., p. 68.

34 Ibid.

35 Ibid.

36 Ibid.

37 For example *prema*, love, is a way to conceive of the atman in everyday life. Sathya Sai Baba explains: 'The sages of India ... sought to know that which if known all else can be known. The Upanishads lay down the process of this discovery. The expression of that discovery, in practical life, is Love; for it is Love that creates, sustains and engulfs all. Without Love, no one can claim to have succeeded in deciphering God and His Handiwork, the Universe. God is love; Live in Love – that is the direction indicated by the sages.' According to this perspective realization is won through a purification accomplished by repeating a holy name, by *jnana*, by service, or by all three paths integrated together. *Sathya Sai Speaks*, vol. VII, tr. N. Kasturi, Bombay: Sri Sathya Sai Education Foundation, n.d., p. 13.

38 Misra, *Language, Reality and Analysis*, p. 70.

39 Donald Miller, *The Reason of Metaphor*, New Delhi: Sage Publications, 1992; Jacques Derrida, 'The Retrait of Metaphor', *Enclitic* (2) 1978, pp. 6–33; idem, 'White Mythology: Metaphor in the Text of Philosophy', *New Literary History*, Baltimore, MD: Johns Hopkins University Press, vol. 6, 1974, pp. 5–74.

40 S.S. Rama Rao Pappu (ed), *Perspectives on Vedanta: Essays in Honor of P.T. Raju*, Leiden: E.J. Brill, 1988, p. 4.

41 In physics today the both/and wave/particle or 'wavicle', and other concepts of ambiguity, mutuality and paradox such as space/time and mind-and-body seem to be at the bedrock of human understanding, the deeper probes go. The radical rationalist separation serves an important purpose, but also seems to block the way to some forms of reasonableness and insightful discovery in non-linear modes. Does it give enough room for the way things work together, the way in which, historically, discoveries that are useful often came from play, from non-purposive responsiveness and so on? Arthur Koestler has shown how matrices, dimensions and different levels can be interconnected in unexpected ways. See Arthur Koestler. *The Act of Creation*, London: Pan, 1964, 1970, pp. 37–38, 45–46, 96–97. Without openness to possibilities of mutuality and a sense that there is always more to explore, a thinker may avoid recognizing realities. Vidyaranya's radical strictness produced interpretations unexpected by modern minds; but it sometimes seems that he had little or no interest in the unexpected, the non-purposiveness which creatively hits on an objective which is significant.

42 Vidyaranya, *Pancadasi*, vol. I, Calcutta: Society for Resuscitation of Indian Literature, 1899; Vol. II, 1900, pp. 60–61.

43 Ibid., X.121, p. 274. Some poets picture the *gopis* and Krishna in a similar way, but, in the South, Krishna is usually a little boy, not a man.

44 Ibid., VII.238, p. 193.

45 My paraphrase of a passage cited by Vidyaranya in *The Jivan-Mukti-Viveka, or the Path to Liberation in this Life*, ed. and tr. S. Subramanya Sastri and T.R. Srinivasa Ayyangar, Adyar: The Theosophical Publishing House, 1935, pp. 100–101, in the chapter 'On the Obliteration of Latent Desire'. See also Andrew O. Fort 'Liberation in the *Jivanmuktiviveka*: Vidyaranya's "Yogic Advaita"' in Andrew O. Fort and Patricia Y. Mumme (eds), *Living Liberation in Hindu Thought*, Albany: State University of New York, 1996. Fort writes of Vidyaranya's 'yogic advaitin' views as differing in some ways from Shankara's, in a passage on p. 155. Vidyaranya's *Jivanmuktiviveka* is influenced by the eleventh-century text, *Yogavashishtha*.

46 A.K. Ramanujan, "Is There an Indian Way of Thinking? An Informal Essay', in McKim Marriott (ed.), *India through Hindu Categories*, New Delhi: Sage Publications, 1990, pp. 41–58.

47 Vidyaranya, *Pancadasi* VII., 140, p. 174. Compare Shankara's *Carpatapanjarika Stotram* VI.8: 'Eager to fondle the breast of a woman, brimming with foolish infatuation, think to yourself repeatedly: "This is merely a form of flesh, fat, etc"'.

48 There are ten *Shankara Vijayas* listed in T.S. Narayana Sastri's *The Age of Sankara*, Madras, 1916. See also David Lorenzen's article in Frank E. Reynolds and Donald Capps (eds), *The Biographical Process*, The Hague: Mouton, 1976, pp. 87–107.

49 Madhava Vidyaranya, *Sankara-Dig-Vijaya: The Traditional Life of Sri Sankaracharya*, tr. Swami Tapasyananda, Madras: Sri Ramakrishna Math, 1986. p. 2, verse 8.

50 This is an example of Hinduism's non-linearity; it reveals the complexity, not simple one-dimensional linearity.

51 My paraphrase of a passage from Vidyaranya's *Sankara-Dig-Vijaya*, pp. 15–16, Canto 2, lines 66 ff. The vertical line of downy hair growing from the navel downward (in Sanskrit, *romavali*) is a sign of beauty found in other Sanskrit poets' works also.

52 Ibid., p. 16.

53 *Sathya Sai Speaks*, ed. N. Kasturi, Bombay: Sri Sathya Sai Education Foundation, (n.d.), vol. III, p. 3.

54 Vidyaranya, *Sankara-Dig-Vijaya*, p. 44, Canto 5, verses 59–74.

55 Ibid., p. 43, Canto 5, verses 36–49.

56 Ibid., p. 52, Canto 5, lines 125–26.

57 A term used by James Hillman for the power of images and imagination – the adjective 'imaginary' tends to devalue these experiences.

58 The debate is detailed in Canto 8; the challenge is in Canto 9. Vidyaranya, *Sankara-Dig-Vijaya*, p. 110.

59 The praise of Shankara is extensive in Canto 8, lines 24–44. Ibid., pp. 107–10.

60 Ibid., p. 112. Canto 9.

61 Ibid.

62 Ibid., p. 115–16, Canto 9.

63 Ibid., p. 113–14, Canto 9.

64 Ibid., p. 114, Canto 9.

65 Ibid., p. 118, Canto 10, lines 9–10.

66 Ibid., p. 118, Canto 10, lines 12–16. My paraphrase of the passage.

67 Ibid., p. 118, Canto 10, line 18.

68 Ibid., p. 121, Canto 10, lines 40–44. My paraphrase.

69 Ibid., p. 123

70 *Bhagavad Gita*, II.50.

71 There are stories of Indra in which he comes to earth and becomes so engrossed with the pleasures of being a pig that he has to be reminded of his exalted status, showing that, when immersed in worldly life, even the sky god can forget his identity.

72 The origin story told here gives Shringeri's Lakshmi temple an aura of sacredness going back to this encounter.

73 Vidyaranya, *Sankara-Dig-Vijaya*, p. 124.

74 V.V. Raman, for example, who wrote about this in personal correspondence, May 2003.

75 Some sources suggest that the *kahara* flower is a kind of lotus.

76 My versification of this inscription of Harihara II. cited by Mahadevan, *The Philosophy of Advaita*, p. 5.

CHAPTER 3

Reflections on Vidyaranya, and the 'Hinduness' of Islamicate Vijayanagara[1]

Dissonance/(if you're interested)/leads to discovery.
William Carlos Williams[2]

... history isn't really history/until it's rewritten
Lawrence Ferlinghetti[3]

Debates about Vidyaranya

For decades debates raged over the question: were the founders of the empire whose capital was Vijayanagara speakers of Telugu or Kannada?[4] At present there continue to be differences among scholars regarding the origins, originators and original motives of the Vijayanagara empire. Hermann Kulke seems to think that the sage Vidyaranya and the founders were so able in reshaping a resurgent Hinduism and asserting a Hindu identity opposed to the forces destructive of Hinduism that they actually created some of the great traditions now assumed to have come from earlier times. For example, Kulke thinks that it was not Shankara (in the ninth century) who put the Shringeri *matha*, the regional monastery of orthodox Hindu tradition, on the map as a major centre of South Indian spiritual life but, rather, the activities of Vidyaranya's teacher and Vidyaranya himself, along with the support of the early Vijayanagara kings.

Philip Wagoner, on the other hand, seems to conclude that Vijayanagara rulers were so eclectic – using a title of prestige such as 'Shah among *raja*s' and wearing cloth cut to Islamicate fashions, and so adaptive to prevailing modes of Muslim warfare using cavalry and the like, that they had little of Hinduism on their minds when they set up their empire. Instead, Wagoner prefers to emphasize 'a larger process of fundamental cultural change' which he refers to as 'Islamicization'.[6] Wagoner seriously questions the continuing notion that 'Vijayanagara's purpose was to contain the spread of Islam and preserve Hindu institutions in the southern peninsula'.[7] (In his denial of a sense of Hindu defensiveness against Islam as the primary motive of Vijayanagara founders, Wagoner agrees with assertions made by historian Burton Stein.[8])

But why do Kulke and Wagoner disagree on this? I will suggest some reasons. An important starting point for Wagoner – the story of the conversion of the founding brothers to Islam and then their conversion back to Hinduism – involves giving 'political expression to this act of apostasy by founding the Vijayanagara kingdom', thus allowing Vijayanagara to be 'construed as a great counterpolity to the Delhi Sultanate'.[9] Since Vidyaranya's part in this founding, and the story of the founding itself, are not found in the earliest available inscriptions,[10] Wagoner doubts the interpretation of the role of the founders as Hindu 'Saviours of the South' and points instead to evidences of convergences of Hindu and Muslim culture during the time when Vijayanagara was a great capital.[11]

Although Kulke would agree that Vidyaranya's legendary role in the inception of the kingdom in 1336 cannot be proved textually because only spurious inscriptions and later texts relate it, he does accept Vidyaranya's importance in the ministry of the early kings Bukka, Narihara II, Kampa and Sangama II.[12] As we saw, part of the problem of Vidyaranya's identity involves a confusion of names. (A man named Madhva Mantrin was a minister on the Western coast; he should not to be confused with the Madhva whose name became Vidyaranya later in his life when he became a sannyasin; these two Madhvas had different parents and gurus, as various reliable documents have recorded.[13])

Shringeri, the site of the *matha* not too far from Vijayanagara, which for many generations has been traced to Shankara's establishment of centres of *advaita* teaching in the four cardinal directions of regions of the subcontinent, became more important and well endowed as the Vijayanagara empire grew. Vidyaranya, records show, most probably became head of the *matha* sometime between 1356 and 1375.[14] In fact, some modern scholars have argued that there is no textual evidence connecting Shankara to Shringeri from before the time of Vidyaranya.[15] Some scholars, such as Kulke, consider Vidyaranya, who wrote the *Shankara-Dig-Vijaya* biographical text, where we first find the story of Shankara establishing the four *matha*s, to be the originator of the Shringeri *matha* tradition.[16] In that case, Vidyaranya, and the royal patrons who supported him, shaped Hindu traditions creatively and decisively by putting Shringeri on the map and endowing it with prestigious associations with the past. This conclusion regarding the shaping of tradition impresses Kulke with the significance and greatness of Vidyaranya's abilities; but it is probably the kind of evidence that makes Wagoner less impressed with Vidyaranya's and his royal cohorts' actual contributions and all the more dubious of our knowledge of them.

The Vijayanagara leaders may have built up the Shringeri *matha*'s tradition in such a way that they covered their tracks – because it is not originality but tradition that is typically affirmed in India. In fact there may be several aspects of Hindu style involved in the confusion regarding Vijayanagara origins, motives and policies. First, Hindu eclecticism is old and pervasive – from the Vedic prayer, 'Let good thoughts come from every side' to Gandhi's use of knowledge and wisdom from various traditions. Second, there is a practice of hiding innovations, or not drawing attention to them. Tradition often favours blending in rather than sticking out as an individual, not trumpeting one's own originality but masking it with faces of the past. This involves a favouring of the archetypal; for example, the portraits of kings are often very similar and the stories of saints bear resemblances. Third, observing silence about awkward, embarrassing and ritually impure matters is a time-honoured custom (for example, the founders' conversion to Islam, then their return to Hinduism would not be carved into stone inscriptions). The Hindu sense of discretion dictates that it is in bad taste to bring up in public historical incidents which have left a bad taste in the mouth, so to speak.[17] In this view it is better to put the face of order on disorder. 'Don't look back' is a response to traumas of the past, a way of not wallowing in sad memories. Traditionally Hindus have often preferred the timeless, trying to rise above history and not become attached to terrible events. This classic philosophical approach of deliberate silence forgets unpleasant historical matters as painful timebound *maya*, distractions from enjoying the possibilities in the present and the ultimate beyond time.[18]

Whilst there are some signs of convergence and assimilation of Islamicate fashions in the lives of the rulers and their officials, in my view to give the impression that defence against Islam was not at all involved in the formation and development of Vijayanagara seems extreme. Unless generative motives were Hindu-preservation-oriented, some other set of rituals, laws and cultural outlook would have become the norm in Vijayanagara. But characteristic Hindu systems, such as the conservative system of Hindu music in the South, remained largely intact. Even today, North Indian music is much more Islamicized than Karnataka (classical South Indian) music, which preserved old standards and regulations more strictly.

Certainly, in architecture and sculpture the capital of Vijayanagara was a place where artists and traditions tried new combinations and developed a new aesthetic which then spread to other parts of the kingdom.[19] The monumental elephant stables in the capital offer an example of the impressive improvisations which developed in the Vijayanagara style. These stables have ten domed chambers in a row, with a central tower, showing a combination of Hindu and Muslim designs.[20] Hindus readily incorporated such external fashions and techniques of the times. Thus both strict orthodoxy and eclecticism seem to have been vital parts of Vijayanagara culture and ethos.[21]

Further Speculations on Vidyaranya

We have seen how Hindu tradition revered Vidyaranya as both an ascetic philosopher and a biographer who could write interestingly about sexual matters. Worldly-wise and spiritual, Vidyaranya seems like a conundrum, or a postmodern medley of qualities. How far can we stretch the possible extremes in Vidyaranya's character and still explain how the tradition held it all together?[22] *Kama* and *artha*, *dharma* and *moksha* are the goals of classical Hinduism – tradition pictures Vidyaranya as one intimately familiar with them all.[23]

To resume the issue. According to traditional Hindu accounts constructed by historians such as S. Krishnaswami Aiyangar, N. Venkataramanayya and Nilakanta

Sastri, it was the desire of the founders of Vijayanagara (Harihara and Vidyaranya) to re-establish Hindu rule and rid the South of Muslim domination which inspired the formation of the empire.[24] As I have indicated, this view is being challenged by recent scholarship as biased – as too derivative of communal concerns of the twentieth and twenty-first centuries, not accounting for personal ambitions and the eclectic assimilation of non-Hindu elements. This is a very complex issue. Creative adaptation to the challenges of the changing times has formed a large part of Hinduism's genius for survival. Perhaps the new empire was not created solely as a Hindu bulwark against the dominating forces of Islam. As I have mentioned, a crucial point for some critics is the lack of a conversion story in the oldest narratives and inscriptions. But there are reasons why writers may have omitted that; V.S. Naipaul refers to one: 'There in the south, far from Delhi, the converted prince had reestablished his independence, and unusually, in defiance of Hindu caste rules, had declared himself a Hindu again, a representative on earth of the local Hindu god [Virupaksha – the one with strange eyes].[25] In a formal official document it would probably have been awkward and socially incorrect to bring up loss of caste and the expiation of that state; avoidance of the topic could be a deliberate shying away from chaotic and dangerous, or at least inauspicious, ritual impurity – one of those things about which Hindus seem to feel 'the less said about it the better'. Those who reject Krishnaswami Aiyangar's idea – that the Vijayanagara mission was the defence and protection of Hindu society and culture – sometimes do not bother to discuss the evident Hinduness of the kingdom. This background is evident in the Hindu rituals, in the rulers' support of brahmans and vice versa, and in the Vijayanagara leaders' veneration of their ancestors' achievements. It is also evident in their upholding of the Hindu order of rule, continuing highly valued cultural advances by funding educational institutions, traditional artists, cultural projects and other signs of cherishing the Hindu past.

In the usual Hindu view, because the five Hindu brothers (Harihara, Bukka and the others) had been part of the new Muslim order, then experienced a conversion and repented the chaos which Hinduism was suffering, they sought out Vidyaranya and his brother Sayana. These learned men were *smarta* brahmans whose training in the Hindu traditions, written in Sanskrit, had prepared them to be, as it were, microcosms of 'Hinduness'. Others tilled the fields, defended the kingdom, engaged in business, but they were responsible for studying the time-honoured teachings – *shruti* (revealed Vedic scriptures) and *smriti* (remembered customs). They were carriers of the patterns, trained in the learning and lore of tradition, gatekeepers who could give boundaries to a Hindu way of life and re-establish the security, the *sanatana* or 'ancient' order, able to incarnate its latest authentic version. In the large-grain view of historical cycles, dissipation can be an agent of order, as Lorenz suggested. After the devastating loss a reinvigorated structure can re-emerge.[26] The founders of Vijayanagara, whichever of the brothers and others did most of it, accomplished their plans. The founding resisted decay, rebuilding a clearer and stronger, more resolved form of Hindu order: perhaps, as some say, it was the last great old-style Hindu kingdom to emerge in India's history. The lawbook for the kingdom, written it would seem by Vidyaranya, was an updated Hindu code of conduct adapted to the region.[27] It would be logical or natural to assume that re-establishing Hindu dharma to counter the chaos caused by Muslim invaders was a main motive of the founders of Vijayanagara. Perhaps modern thinkers are more ready than is justified to read an ethos of individualism and personal motives back into a culture and time of traditional roles in families and communities.[28]

But Burton Stein helps us nuance our understanding of the situation:

> To view this disruption and competition as some sort of inter-imperial political chaos – as the disorder that followed the fall of older regimes such as the Hoysalas and Kakatiyas or the Cholas and an anticipation of the new imperial order under Vijayanagara – posits a false telos.[29]

Instead, Stein asserts that the founding must be seen within a set of political processes that existed through a large part of the medieval era. Stein admits that there was a new factor – the fierce and expanding Muslim power in the fourteenth century – but suggests that Muslims had already been part of South Indian society for a long time before the Vijayanagara empire was organized. He notes that the Muslim soldiers employed by Hindu kings – such as Hoysala King Jagadmalla – had no connection with the Turkic warriors from Delhi. These Turkic warriors were a destructive element in South India for over 50 years, but Stein says they did not create the pervasive disorder of the fourteenth century. That chaos also involved Hindu rulers' movements from riverine centres to upland dry zones, where less food could be grown and more plundering and military activity was generated.[30] Stein sees the Sangama brothers in this complex context. Perhaps this helps us understand some of the differences of interpretation among the previously mentioned historians. We might consider that not one or the other, but both, have some insights.[31]

Reflections on an Image, and Non-linearity

The issue of dealing with complexity is one we should not avoid. After reading about India for many years one may arrive there and see things one has never read about, as various researchers have attested.[32] If one allows oneself to follow intriguing clues rather than settling prematurely on an oversimple answer, new vistas keep opening up. We may commonly think of 'systematic' as having to do with linear systems – a one-way linear sequence – but in fact there can be a non-linear systematic style too, which has to do with repeated return, reconsideration from a new angle, exploring recursive variations, considering relevant aspects from new points in time and sensing from many points things about both the whole situation being discussed and the relations of parts in that whole situation. It is sometimes useful to 'run with the hares and hunt with the hounds', to be in one position for a while and look around, loop back and see what you have found, not censoring the unexpected but living with it awhile, observing.

The 'hare and the hounds' incident in the stories of Vijayanagara's origins (in which Vidyaranya sees a hare chase a hound, and takes this as a sign that this will be a protected place) – an event which signalled the auspicious place of beginnings – is capable of multiple interpretations. It was a convenient archetype. If you know the *Rig Veda*, you can find a passage that has a somewhat similar pattern, in which a riddle describes backward-running rivers, a jackal driving a wild boar from the brushwood, a hare swallowing a razor, and the *rishi* singing the mantra and sundering a distant mountain with a clod.[33]

T.M.P. Mahadevan writes of copperplate records dated 1336, narrating how Harihara, while hunting on the southern bank of the Tungabhadra, saw a hare and a hound together in proximity, despite their natural enmity.[34]

In a verse narrative described in *Sri Vidyaranya*, an official publication of the Vidyaranya Vidyapitha Trust, the episode is described a bit differently: Vidyaranya asked the princes to build a new city on the spot where 'hares chased the hunting dogs'.[35] All these contradictory hare-turning-on-hounds stories are variations on a theme: the display of unexpected power, a non-linear turn of events.[36]

It is a basic principle that non-linear systems are sensitive to initial conditions, which give a trend or thrust – a trajectory repeated with variations. (This is like Eliade's characterization of the power of origin myths, which are replayed in a society when it needs to regenerate itself – for example, annually at New Year festivals or Christmas, or the hajj, or Passover.) Another principle is that free will is reconciled with determinism: determinism (like the British Queen) rules but doesn't govern; a formal pattern exists within which life is possible. The creation of organization is seen as a two-sided coin – order, with randomness emerging, and then, a step further, randomness with its own underlying or incipient order.[37] Things do not take random shapes, nor do they disclose their true shapes or patterns to those with preconceptions out of tune with the context and locked into other meanings. At the origin of the empire significant patterns take shape: 'Just where a chaotic dynamical system will end up on its attractor is exquisitely sensitive to initial conditions, but that it will be pulled onto its attractor, [38] regardless of initial conditions, is certain.'[39] As yet, historians have no way of speaking easily about 'attractors' of empires and civilizations, but perhaps that is what, in other words, they have been concerned with in their final analyses. The stories of the 'anomalous' unlikely turn of events – the weak, hunted creature becoming the pursuer – held an archetypal memory, an image enshrining the hope of the new Hindu empire which eventually thrived, then over three centuries later lost its charmed life.

Vidyaranya as a *Smarta*, Rememberer of Hindu Order

How was Vidyaranya chosen for his fateful role, according to tradition? Stories picture him as a meditative learned man, a sage. He had a reputation for wisdom, which is a knowledge of enduring patterns. The founding ruler, Harihara, was impressed and sensed that Vidyaranya knew what a genuine foundation-layer needed to know and, as a sannyasin, was without worldly attachments. In the necessary marriage of spiritual wisdom and earthly power which classical Hinduism visualizes and dictates[40] there was a wisdom in selecting skilful sage and entrusting the founding to him. There was prescience in knowing that the initial conditions augur, accurately predict and provide the seeds for later developments, whether disaster or viable polity. If inaugurated well, with the lifeway of a whole people organized in proven dharmic patterns, the kingdom could last a long time. If the tone was not set right at the outset, if heaven and earth failed to connect, if chance or what a strong man idiosyncratically happens to think were to prevail in the pattern-setting origin, all would fall apart and the people of the realm would end up worse off than before.

The Hinduism reconstituted in the Vijayanagara era was a faith that had passed through the fires of trial and loss. It had undergone ordeals and survived those hard times, and therefore did not take its own identity or future for granted. The culture was summed up in a fractal-like pattern of dharma, each part containing the whole in condensed form. To use an organic metaphor, the seeds of past culture were cultivated to sprout into present and future culture. Hindu survival through revival would seem to be the tacit mission of certain *smarta* brahmans of each succeeding generation.[41]

Smarta refers to a training, an orientation and faith in traditions, a code of knowledge of the orthodox classics, but also a community of specialists in memory harbouring the seed of retranslation, new gestalt reconfigurations depending on the incorporation of the new. Since tradition means transmission and memory means re-*member*-ing – reconstituting the past anew – *smarta* brahman renewal involves a simultaneous screening out of old non-essentials, 'forgettery', to use a playful term coined to pair up with 'memory', the preserving of essentials in an expansive renewed form. Culturally creative *smarta*s under the right conditions could be eclectic and yet also observe strict limits. They could be counted on to be concerned with the return to roots (*shastras*, rule systems) and renewal of fresh shoots (in arts and commentaries). Examples include the Purana authors, and Shankaracharya, Ramanujacharya, Ramananda, Narasimha Mehta, Tyagaraja, and many others.[42]

Metaphorically speaking, *smarta*s, because of their training in the *shastras*, are like the DNA code programming the growth of an organism; their informed memory of past patterns is like the genetic identity in a molecule. Harihara and his brothers were military men with some governing know-how and the ability to use fighting forces garnered from their service with the Muslim powers, and they found their purpose in the sage Vidyaranya, whom they encountered in an uncivilized area with a great potential to become a new centre. This convergence of *kshatriya* energy and skill, forces and temporal power resources, and brahman knowledge of the Hindu world-view led to a classical incarnation of the whole Hindu system.[43] The reformation was like the tradition passing through the eye of a needle, retrieving essential ideals from the 'seed realm of the densely packed'[44] tradition in brahman knowledge coded in texts. Then came the elaborate full bloom of the empire's expansion in embodied actuality, thriving for over three centuries. Then followed the decline of the system, devolving into separated segments, ripe for new organizers (the Maratha kings with their military and political ability and unifying force of bhakti inspiration) and vulnerable to European colonizers.

The intermittent activity of certain key *smartas*, serving as feedback loops and reconstituting updated versions of old traditions, is a significant phenomenon. *Smartas* function like thermostats in Hindu history; when chaos reaches a certain level their activities kick in and they resystematize the whole civilization, updating life with new conditions, using adaptive intellectual reflections in accordance with time-honoured standards.[45] The founding king needed the official sanction of the religious authority. On the social, practical level the king needs the trust of the people; they need to believe that he has all the answers, the valid *shastra*ic knowledge needed to run a kingdom, the advice and consent of the wise priest, to give him tradition's seal of approval, to be legitimate at every level, endowed by earthly and spiritual authority.

On the individual level the king, to overcome the stain of his previous conversion to Islam, would need to atone and purify himself. He had betrayed his original Hindu faith and had sided with outsiders who were subjugating his own people. To cleanse that pollution and re-identify with Hinduism, to accomplish something even greater than merely surviving and then breaking away, Harihara needed the sage, Vidyaranya. That alone could affirm a stable Hindu identity after the disequilibrium caused by trying to be another and renouncing one's previous identity. Together, the ruler and the religious leader could radiate a needed energy and order, an ethnic identity. They could spur a resurgence of religious fervour, promoting a unity among people. Bhakti promotes this,[46] as does asserting that cosmic dharma is the way needing to be reinstituted. The people could feel invited to participate in this venture, which is a different experience from being commanded to do something. The compulsion must be inner, a compelling leadership of men of heart and soul, wisdom, tradition and strength, in the Hindu lifeway. Thus the situation was a positive challenge, a high vision worth fulfilling rather than a forced march through self-denial for the betterment of higher-ups. The dharmic kingdom gave Hindus of the region a sense of belonging to a larger whole, of the fulfilment of integration, participatory self-transcendence for which they presumably longed, especially when suffering from menacing adharmic chaos.[47]

All cultures and world-view systems surviving in time go through 'bottlenecks', critical times of 'threading the needle' again and again; these are cycles of growth and dwindling, patterns of proliferation, then crisis, and the loss of many and the survival of few. A plague is a bottleneck; an invasion is a bottleneck. *Smartas* preserve the seeds of religious and social order, provide the vision of cohesion, lay out programmes with ancient principles, depth and creative potential, offering stability through selective repetition in the face of bewildering complexity.

All organisms alive today reached this present moment in time by going through crises and responding with successful defences and brilliant artifices enabling them to survive and regenerate against very great odds. Though we acknowledge that there are differences, why should we not think of cultural products also as struggling to survive in the – in some ways – parallel system of human culture?[48] The meanings of the *Rig Veda* barely survived the bottleneck of the loss of Hindu autonomy. If Sayana, Vidyaranya's brother, had not written a voluminous commentary explaining or paraphrasing every word of the *Rig Veda*, many traditional meanings would be unknown today. This alone was a remarkable revival of Hindu knowledge, even if only on the textual level. 'As Sayana's commentary constantly referred to ancient authorities, it was thought to have preserved the true meanings of the *Rig Veda* in a traditional interpretation going back to the most ancient times … [Sayana] has been of the greatest service in facilitating and accelerating the comprehension of the Vedas'[49] even though, with much labour and time-consuming searching, much could have been retrieved from various other sources in India and pieced together by others if Sayana had not done it. His work was an accumulated data bank on the *Rig Veda*, referred to by all modern Vedic scholars. Sayana's universally respected work was dedicated to his brother Vidyaranya and was composed with his help.[50]

How was a *smarta* guardian of the Hindu past, such as Vidyaranya, thrust into the centre of the story of Vijayanagara's formation, if, as Wagoner asserts, the founders had no concern for defending and preserving Hinduism? Though the matters of the rulers' style – imported goods, Arabian horses, Muslim clothing and architecture – show changing tastes of the times and eclectic adaptability, the ritual authority of brahmans, and the continued importance of Tirupati seem to bespeak Hindu values. Other signs that the rulers intended a purpose other than re-establishing their people's power are needed to make a convincing case that Hindu identity was unimportant to the Vijayanagara rulers. Determining the personal motivations of people who lived hundreds of years ago is a complex process. Those who deny the Hindu defence motive also need to explain why Vidyaranya wrote a legal treatise for the rulers, based on Hindu texts and customs, and synthesized the chapter on administrative justice from existing regional practices and Hindu legal writings from elsewhere. It would seem that the accomplishments of Vidyaranya and Sayana and others like them, promoted by the rulers, kept the overall Hindu outlook and identity in the empire stronger than the Muslim elements being incorporated.[51] From a precarious situation they instituted and preserved a strong Hindu realm. The interreliant roles of brahman and kshatriya were typically Hindu – the ruler needs the priest to anoint ritually his authority, and the priest needs the king and warriors for protection, order and social status.

Conclusion: Other Patterns

The emergence of biology … to the point where it threatens the status of physics as the archetype of scientific enquiry; the epistemological and ontological problems besetting physics … the return of cosmology as a general cultural concern … the growth of computer-mediated 'sciences of complexity' (negative

entropy, fractals, and strange attractors …) suggest that the withdrawal of the
natural sciences over the last 120 years or so from connections with any
discourse but their own, is not the permanent condition of things.

Clifford Geertz[52]

Other scholars continue to problematize the Hindu sage Vidyaranya. Which side's interpretation is correct? Perhaps the truth lies somewhere in between the view of Vidyaranya as a Hindu Merlin guiding a revitalized Hindu Camelot, on the one hand, and of Vijayanagara rulers fully conforming to Islamicate styles and ways because those were the prevailing forms and fashions in the region at that time, with no thought of preserving Hinduism from the Muslim invaders on the other hand. It is difficult to explain the later 'Hinduness' of the kingdom if it was not a concern to begin with, and absorbing prestigious and successful styles and methods seems quite natural to the Hindu outlook. In that case Vijayanagara can be seen as partly traditional and partly progressive – a kingdom demonstrating Hindu inclusiveness, able to learn from and employ Muslims, Westerners and other non-Hindus, yet insisting on some core identity with key values in the long tradition of India's 'Sanatana Dharma', or ancient way of life.

In the Indian folk mind the resolve of two small groups of brothers made a great difference in South India in the fourteenth century. Their founding Vijayanagara turned out to be far-reaching, having a 'butterfly effect', as the realm grew. For three centuries Vijayanagara stimulated a large-scale creative surge, composed of smaller, but sustained, creative surges in successive generations and smaller creative urges in individuals, embodying a new empire incarnating the generative order in the society.[53] Today, we are coming to a new understanding of order and hierarchy – one in which:

> … the general principle is immanent, that is, actively pervading and indwelling, not only in the less general, but ultimately in reality as a whole. Emerging in this fashion, hierarchies are no longer fixed and rigid structures, involving domination of lower levels by the higher. Rather, they develop out of an immanent generative principle, from the more general to the less general.[54]

Strong men, seeing the need to build upon tested patterns of the past, to structure society in a way that was known to be enduring, called upon the spiritual knowers of the past to renew and legitimate the system, giving it a classical Hindu form. Vidyaranya is remembered as chief among these sages; he had been around, he had 'drunk from the water of 36 wells', he had studied with a guru, lived in Banaras, offered sacrifices, raised a son and had acquired wisdom. He had become a master who knew the past and held it all together for the present founding of the future. Vidyaranya and his brothers, and others like them, re-established the familiar attractors that patterned great Hindu kingdoms of the past.[55] Like the Western archetype, Merlin, the part he plays in the legends is that of protector and guide who, with his knowledge, helps both the ruler and the kingdom. His power is mysterious and far-reaching; like Merlin's it is unknowable, not unspecific and unpredictable, a non-linear element in the world of governance and dominion. I emphasize the systemic patterns not to condone any injustices, but to avoid a narrow oversimplification that focuses only on politics or economy. The people 'remembered' themselves – put their members back together. As one more local example of a universal ordering process, they 'self-organized' a state, and the empire grew and flourished – although this is not to say that this was an unconscious instinctive process of nature any more than any other such human activity is. In any case, 'the rise of Vijayanagara as a champion of Hindu revival led to a spurt of musical activity all over the South'[56] and a burgeoning of bhakti creativity in the fine arts in general. Vidyaranya, and/or some other creative personalities, able to reinvent themselves according to life's demands, helped bring order out of the chaos of the times by reinventing or reinstating the cultural codes and authorities. Some thinkers stress the point that in history it is often the misfit who shows an ability to adapt, take risks and innovate. The five converted brothers, who had known weakness as captives fugitives and underwent other 'misfit' experiences, founded a new empire.[57] Vidyaranya and others who could uphold *smarta* standards were able to lend a traditional order to channel the energetic activities of the creative 'misfits' of the first dynasty.[58]

Parts and wholes are often dynamically interrelated rather than static. We can see a fitting pattern of symmetry at the beginning and end of the Vijayanagara empire. According to historians, in the beginning it cannot be determined whether there was one kingdom or five – each of the five brothers (sons of Sangama) ruled as governor (*mahamandaleshvara*) over a *rajya*, a kingdom on the frontiers of Karnataka, and there was no absolute sovereign. After a while Bukka emerged supreme, and his sons and their descendents formed Vijayanagara's first dynastic royal line. And, in the end, there were five Nayaka kingdoms with capitals in Madurai, Tanjavur, Gingee, Ikkeri and Mysore. But this progression is more of a conceptually constructed continuity than a real one; likewise, it would be mistaken to view the continuity of Vijayanagara and Maratha rulers as simple and without dissonance.

Further Reflections on Hindu/Muslim Relations

The special central quality and potential knot of meaning of Vijayanagara, with its capital in the Deccan plains, involves on the way in which this empire both reaches back and flows forward, as a nucleus of Hinduism rooted in the ancient, which blossoms into the modern era. Vijayanagara came into existence, according to some scholars, after the crash of two great tectonic plates of religious civilization: Muslim civilization, with its origins in the Islamic Crescent, collided with the civilization of South Asia – the Hindu lifeway on the Indian subcontinent. The Vijayanagara empire ended as the next great crash of metaphorical 'tectonic plates' of civilizations began to reverberate: the arrival, during the sixteenth century and onwards, of European traders, colonizers and rulers to make their impacts on traditional patterns of Hindu life, and

India's response. V.S. Naipaul seems to think that Vijayanagara rulers tried to preserve their archaic ways and, because of this, were unable to thrive. Phillip Wagoner and others take the opposite view, observing that the Vijayanagara elite emulated Muslim fashions and titles. This view is comparable to other recent scholars' observations about the absorption of invading conquerers' ways in other cultures.[59]

I think Wagoner's logic is this: if the five brothers did not convert to Islam (as he deduces from the lack of mention of their conversion in documents) then the kingdom they founded was not primarily about defence against Islam, but was more about (as Stein said) warriors looking for a realm to rule. Only then, having gained a realm, did Hinduism enter the picture, as an almost incidental background or afterthought. This argument reasons that, since some of the forces which Vijayanagara rulers battled against were also Hindu and some of the manpower in the kingdom was Muslim, the defence against Muslims was not primary. In that case, we might ask, why did Hinduism flourish, and how else can we construe the growing wealth of Shringeri *matha*, the Hindu temples and other Hindu institutions if not as signs of a hopeful attempt to preserve Hindu identity? Was not Vidyaranya the architect, or the chief knower of the orthodox recipe, for the renewal of the classical traditions of Hindu culture? Wagoner's and Stein's point is that the Vijayanagara rulers – especially the last fragmented rulers of Vijayanagara – were not so much bearing the torch of Hinduism as trying to survive in a demanding new world. But in that case, if it was such a non-Hindu venture, why did it fare so badly at the hands of the Muslims in 1565? Why did the Muslim coalition from the North spend six months looting and vandalizing the Hindu culture there? Would the Muslims show such sustained vehemence in attacking a citadel of civilization unless they felt divinely sanctioned and had considered it incontrovertibly 'other'? Why would they display such animosity if they did not see the capital as populated by mere infidels?

Historians, like news reporters, must ask: who, where, when, what, why, and then come up with news. This is very different from the tellers of origin stories. While '[h]istory ... is a fictive substitute for authority and tradition, a maker of concords between past, present, and future, a provider of significance to mere chronicity',[60] origin stories concern human life in the cosmos. In thinking about Vijayanagara, Hindus have their own identities and futures at stake, whereas Western historians have their historical sense at stake. My guess is that we have to realize that there are two differing orientations – one towards cosmos and one towards history – and we need to tread carefully if we are to avoid one-sidedness in our expectations and our conclusions.

In this study of Vidyaranya and the empire centred at Vijayanagara I am attempting to evoke a semblence of the past by presenting salient and resonant points rather than launch a tit-for-tat argument. I like Borges' statement:

> perhaps the human mind has a tendency to deny a statement. Remember what Emerson said: arguments convince nobody. They convince nobody because they are presented as arguments, then we look at them, we weigh them, we turn them over, and we decide against them.[61]

Often, the mind is more receptive to well-hinted things. Shifting perspectives enriches the imagination but is inconvenient for historical certainty. For Hindus, the Vijayanagara story is one of seduction, repentance, regret and restitution. Hindus naturally interpret the story as the seduction of one culture by another, a loss and a retrieval. The Muslim ruler who employed five brothers made it worth their while to work for him. For Muslims, it would be a story of becoming part of the true faith and then betraying it. As scholars of our time, we can see it as a multifaceted story.

Going back to the beginnings always stirs up questions about what we do and do not know, and what patterns may be discernible in the earliest memories and records.[62] There is a South Indian proverb which advises the hearer not to inquire into the origins of a river or a sage, presumably because they are usually illusorily unimpressive.[63] Perhaps the same might be said about origin stories of empires. Origin stories are told by traditional people in order to avoid further questions about origins. They are told to answer archetypally the question once and for all, to chase away the snooping hounds enigmatically and get on with the demanding business of living. In any case, the actions of the hare and the hounds, the sage and the renegades renewing the Hindu polity of South India, make a good story – one which people who are not historians know how to remember, more or less.

Notes

1 Parts of this chapter and the previous one were presented at the Twelfth International Congress of Vedanta, at Miami University, Oxford, Ohio, on 16 September 2000, as a presentation entitled 'Questions about the Sage Vidyaranya', on a panel with the topic 'Vedantic Philosophers'. My thanks go to the discussants for their helpful questions and suggestions.

2 William Carlos Williams, *Paterson*, New York: New Directions, 1963, Book IV, p. 207.

3 Lawrence Ferlinghetti, *A Far Rockaway of the Heart*, New York: New Directions, 1997, p. 11.

4 See T.V. Mahalingam, *Administration and Social Life under Vijayanagara*, Part 1, Administration, 2nd edn, Madras: University of Madras, 1969, p. 2, n. 2. It would seem that scholars associated with Dharwad University often asserted Kannada origins and scholars from Warangal University asserted Telugu origins. As other scholars have noted, it is not clear today whether such a strict division on the basis of language would have seemed meaningful to the people of the region in the 1300s.

5 Kulke sees the popular image of Vidyaranya as a conflation of two different historical figures. One was named Madhava Vidyaranya (born to Mayana and Shrimati, of the Bharadvaja *gotra*, disciple to Vidyatirtha, Bharati Tirtha and Shrikantha, and head of the Shringeri *matha* from 1374 to 1386. The other was named Madhava-mantrin, son of Chaunda, of the Angirasa *gotra*, pupil of Kashivilasa Kriyashakti, a member of the Kalamukha sect, serving as minister under Marappa during the emergence of the Sangamas in the late 1340s. See Hermann Kulke, 'Maharajas, Mahants and Historians … ' in Anna Libera Dallapiccola and Stephanie Zingel-Ave Lallemant (eds), *Vijayanagara – City and Empire*, vol. 1, Stuttgart: Steiner Verlag Wiesbaden GMBH, 1985.

6 Phillip B. Wagoner, '"Sultan among Hindu Kings": Dress, Titles, and the Islamicization of Hindu Culture at Vijayanagara', *Journal of Asian Studies*, 55 (4), November 1996, p. 853.

7 Ibid., p. 852.

8 ' … defence of Hindu society and culture [as] the mission of the Vijayanagara kingdom. That ideological framing of Vijayanagara history is rejected here,' Burton Stein writes in 'Vijayanagara', *The New Cambridge History of India*, 1.2, Cambridge: Cambridge University Press, p. 146.

9   Phillip B. Wagoner's recent work in this area is very interesting. Sometimes the more one delves into evidence about a figure such as Vidyaranya the more questions arise. Phillip B. Wagoner, 'Harihara, Bukka, and the Sultan: The Delhi Sultanate in the Political Imagination of Vijayanagara', in David Gilmartin and Bruce B. Lawrence (eds), *Beyond Turk and Hindu: Shaping Religious Identities in Islamicate India*, Gainesville: University of Florida Press, 2000, pp. 300–326.

10   Inscriptions often constitute a reliable source of information for historians.

11   Wagoner in the bibliography of 'Harihara, Bukka, and the Sultan' omits mention of Robert Sewell's *The Historical Inscriptions of Southern India*, New Delhi: Asian Educational Services, 1983 (reprint), and B. Lewis Rice's *Mysore and Coorg from the Inscriptions*, New Delhi: Asian Educational Services, 1986. Both refer to inscriptions about early Vijayanagara kings' involvement in supporting Hinduism and defending against Muslim invaders. Sewell includes reflections such as 'It may be due to the fact that the whole mass of Hindus in the Hoysala dominions were roused against him that Muhammad Tughlak refrained from marching across Mysore against his rebellious subjects at Madura' (p. 185).

12   Kulke, 'Maharajas, Mahants and Historians ... ' p. 128. Even beyond the first two generations of Sangam rulers, Harihara's son, young prince Virupaksha venerated Vidyaranya. See p. 141, note 66 for the inscription citations for this.

13   Ibid. For a presentation of the traditional view of Vidyaranya and his role in the empire and at Shringeri see S. Shrikantaya, 'Vijayanagara and Vidyaranya', in the classic compendium of scholarly essays, *Vijayanagara Sexcentenary Commemoration Volume*, Dharwar: Vijayanagara Empire Sexcentenary Association, 1936, pp. 161–68.

14   Ibid., p. 130.

15   Ibid., pp. 134–35.

16   Kulke follows Paul Hacker in this conclusion.

17   In recent decades politicians in India have sometimes flouted this sensibility to stir up passions and gain support.

18   Mircea Eliade used the term 'the terror of history' in *The Myth of The Eternal Return, or, Cosmos and History*, tr. Willard R. Trask, Princeton, NJ: Princeton University Press, 1974, pp. 139–62.

19   Anna Libera Dallapiccola, *Sculpture at Vijayanagara: Iconography and Style*, New Delhi: Manohar Publications, 1998, p. 6.

20   John M. Fritz, 'Vijayanagara: Authority and Meaning of a South Indian Imperial Capital, *American Anthropologist*, Vol. 88 (1), 1986, p. 47.

21   George Michell, *The Vijayanagara Courtly Style: Incorporation and Synthesis in the Royal Architecture of Southern India, 15th–17th Centuries*, New Delhi: Manohar, 1992.

22   Odd accounts are not easy to reconcile: J.N. Mohanty in a letter told me of a Bengali edition of the *Vivarananaprameya sangraha* with an introductory essay by Pramathanath Tarkabhushana, in which it is said that Vidyaranya played not only a major part in politics of Vijayanagara but also in wars fought by the empire. (Personal correspondence from Germany, 15 June 1993.) 'States make wars, and wars make states [by the exercise of organizing, taxing, governing, and so on.]' is a political science axiom.

23   *Kama* is love's enjoyments, *artha* is success, *dharma* is righteousness, and *moksha* is liberation from cycles of birth and death; they encompass a large spectrum. I believe India, because of yoga's depth exploration of consciousness, developed a wider 'weirdness threshold' – that is, a larger pool of possible experiences and views, an expanded repertoire of known existences and acceptable behaviour. Witness naked *sadhu*s, ash-smeared *tantrika*s with a human skull for an eating bowl ('I've gone so far I don't care – I'll eat out of a dead man's head!'), dramatic iconography of fierce goddesses, multiheaded many-armed beings, and so on. Hindus inherit an awareness of the high snow-cold Himalayas in the back of their minds, with deep dark caves, and white hot heat of tropical sun and the seething ocean all around, with monsoon clouds of feast or famine. This is the Hindu geospiritual background, with vivid links between environment and soul and vast cosmic energies to be leashed and released. Miguel Serrano remarked that Hindu mythology is commensurate with Indian landscape: 'These very mountains were united to their soul. One summit was the throat of

Siva, another the throne of Visnu ... . Each mountain has its history and is a living symbol ... . We in Chile also have magnificent mountains, but we have not interpreted them yet, and we have not incorporated them into our souls. We have not discovered the Gods and titans which the Hindus have found in the Himalayas.' Cited by K.R. Vaidyanathan in *Pilgrimage to Sabari*, Mumbai: Bharatiya Vidya Bhavan, 1996, p. 1. See also A.K. Ramanujan, *The Interior Landscape*, Bloomington: Indiana University Press, 1975, pp. 105-115.

That said, there is still the problem of how traditions are able to endure, how people select from the many possibilities in the flow of time, deciding what cultural elements should endure for posterity sake, how to survive amid the flux of time, how to keep the pattern of life continuous, viable and secure, with supportive 'feedforward'. Cycles of renewal, replenishment, reordering are required. Each age has its contests with time's forces of decay and havoc, in which order is elicited from chaos. The Vedic age sang of strong Indra and Vishnu overcoming Vritra, holding up the archetype of the Controller of the Abyss conquering *asat* or non-being. The *Bhagavad Gita* age uplifted the values of work, to maintain the order which Krishna, avatar of Vishnu the Expansive Preserver, affirmed. The Gupta age saw *smartas* systematizing and ordering in response to the disruptive Hunas, who were invading barbarians. Shankara's age faced the heterodox and the sprawling uncoordinated Hinduism. Ramanuja and Madhvacharya rallied the Hindu lifeway in the face of a new era. Vidyaranya embodied a spectrum of life-urges and Hindu dharmas.

24 S. Krishnaswami Aiyangar, 'Foundation of Vijayanagar', in *Ancient India and South Indian History and Culture*, 2 vols, Poona: Oriental Book Agency, 1920. N. Venkata Ramanayya, *Vijayanagara: Origin of the City and Empire*, New Delhi: Asian Educational Services, 1933 edn reprinted in 1990. K.A. Nilakanta Sastri and N. Venkata Ramanayya (eds), *Further Sources of Vijayanagara History*, 3 vols, Madras: University of Madras, 1946. vol. I, pp. 22–53.

25 V.S. Naipaul, *India: A Wounded Civilization*, New York: Knopf, 1997, p. 6.

26 Lorenz suggested that dissipation can be an agent of order; see James Gleick, *Chaos: Making a New Science*, New York: Penguin, 1987, p. 314.

27 This contribution of Vidyaranya's deals with such matters as the organization of law courts, the appointment of judges, giving proper punishments and so on.

28 Western individualism is taken for granted as the universal standard, but 'context-sensitivity', feeling a part of a group, family, community and so on is a traditional pervasive Indian aspect of the Hindu world-view. See A.K. Ramanujan, 'Is There an Indian Way of Thinking? An Informed Essay', in McKim Marriot (ed.), *India through Hindu Categories*, New Delhi: Sage Publications, 1990, pp. 41–58.

29 Stein, '*Vijayanagara*', p. 20.

30 Ibid., pp. 20–23.

31 A historian encounters a series of dissonant views of the past and, realizing that the version on which he has begun to found his views is only one of several, finds that it is like surveying the landscape during an earthquake or like walking through a labyrinth whose dimensions shift and rearrange themselves with each step taken. This image is suggested by Gleick in *Chaos*, p. 24.

32 A researcher in chaos science in discussing his research experience of anomalous behaviour as an opportunity to explore more deeply similarly noted: 'We had no concept of the real difference that non-linearity makes in a model. The idea that an equation could bounce around in an apparently random way – that was pretty exciting. You would say "Where is this random motion coming from? I don't see it in the equations". It seemed like something for nothing or something out of nothing ... . It was a realization that here is a whole realm of physical experience that doesn't fit in the current framework. We had a chance to look ... and understand something'. Gleick, *Chaos*, p. 151. Soon they were delving into questions of determinism, the nature of intelligence, the direction of biological evolution and so on.

33 Ralph T.H. Griffith, *The Hymns of Rg Veda*, Delhi: Motilal Banarsidass, 1986 (reprint), X.28, p. 550.

34 T.M.P. Mahadevan, *The Philosophy of Advaita with Special Reference to Bharatatirtha Vidyaranya*, Madras: Ganesh, 1969, p. 4.

35 *Sri Vidyaranya*, (Publication No.3), p. 34.

36 Perhaps we can take this as a reminder to expect the unexpected, the non-linear. Nothing is simple, and every person, as a centre of consciousness, may have its own perception of, or relation to, events in a society. But things are part of a whole web. It is not the rabbit–hound event or other wonder stories or signs that are crucial. It is not the embarrassing question: did Harihara and Bukka convert to Islam or not? Memories can vary, and the points people wish to remember vary. Specialists concern themselves with politics, economy, military aspects and the like, but it is the whole of the system of Hinduism and its renewal that is involved in the most significant activity of Vidyaranya and his helpers. Why not see humanity's doings and the workings of the cosmos both as a vast non-linear system of systems? What does 'non-linear system of systems' mean? Examples of non-linear systems include art forms in which levels connect – music, dramas, dance, poetry, dreamlike religious myths, rituals and other alternative worlds. Ecosystems, caste systems, nervous systems, single cells are non-linear, as is the totality. What are some of the implications of this? For one thing the fact that 'non-linear equations must be solved by iterating, or recycling, the end result of the equations is to see whether processing the equation pushes that end value toward a stable number, a periodically returning number, or a number that fluctuates randomly … implies processes of nature have some kind of dynamic recycling that leads to stability, periodicity or chaos …'. Gleick, *Chaos*, p. 45. Few Western people in the past 'thought of non-linearity as a creative force', yet non-linear dynamics can lead to mysterious beautiful patterns (reminiscent of the Taoist principle that the 'way the Tao works is by return') through recursion. This is not to say that it is an unconscious instinctual process. (In his book *African Fractals*, New Brunswick: Rutgers, 1999, Ron Eglash discusses this concern.) The point is not to imply that human life is merely determined by uncontrollable unknown instincts, but that, by recognizing such patterns as attractors or fractal wholes, we may see that such an order is crucial to surviving in a recurrent form, following a way attempting to be 'true to life'. The implication is that to live and thrive in the universe as an integral part of the thriving universe means to follow some underlying cosmic patterns through traditions.

37 Gleick, *Chaos*, p. 252.

38 An attractor is the recursive pattern the process is drawn into; it has variations and yet gives a trajectory of predelictions, a likely unfolding path with its own unique or defining characteristics.

39 Gleick, *Chaos*, p. 98

40 See A.K. Coomaraswamy, *Spiritual Authority and Temporal Power in the Indian Theory of Government*, New Haven, CT: American Oriental Society, 1942.

41 See V.S. Pathak, *Smarta Religious Tradition*, Meerut: Kusumanjali Prakashan, 1987. See also Jan Gonda, *Change and Continuity in Indian Religion*, New Delhi: Munshiram Manoharlal Publications, 1985, pp. 400–401. Some researchers suggest that memory is hologramic or fractal-like, in that the whole pattern is found in a number of the parts.

42 I have written about *smarta*s in *Tyagaraja and the Renewal of Tradition*. New Delhi: Motilal Banarsidass, 1994. For a discussion of the importance of *shastras* – the view that the new is merely the older truths rephrased and so on – see Sheldon Pollock's 'The Theory of Practice and the Practice of Theory in Indian Intellectual History', *Journal of the American Oriental Society*, 105, 1985, pp. 499–519.

43 Kulke also believes that his new interpretation points to 'the most intricete mutual relations between *brahman* and *ksatra*, the sacerdotal and secular realms in Indian history. Though being intricately interwoven, they both follow their own *svadharma*'. Kulke, 'Maharajas, Mahants and Historians', p. 136.

44 This is a Buddhist phrase, but it evokes a sense of DNA-like coded information brought out by culturally creative renovators of tradition.

45 See V.S. Pathak's book *Smarta Religious Tradition*, Meerut: Kusumanjali, 1987. See also T.K. Venkateswaran's 'The Radha-Krishna Bhajanas of South India: A Phenomenological, Theological, and Philosophical Study', in Milton Singer's *Krishna: Myths, Rites and Attitudes*, Chicago: University of Chicago Press, 1971, and the essay 'Questions About the "Rememberers"' in my book *Tyagaraja and the Renewal of Tradition*. *Smarta*s systematized the sacred regional stories which they

put into the preservative Sanskrit language in the Puranas, systematized the sacred geography in pilgrimage manuals, systematized regional festivals and were involved in systematizing the six *darshana*s. They are usually characterized by universalism, 'catholic' tastes and inclusivist synthesis. The *smarta* concept of *ishtadevata*, one's favourite form of God, and *panchayatana puja*, is an ingenious way of accomodating inevitable diversity.

46 Later Maratha regimes were more democratic because of bhakti values they upheld, which tend to diminish differences in shared ideals of devotion.

47 See Sewell, *The Historical Inscriptions of Southern India*, pp. 184–85 ff.

48 Steven J. Gould rightly cautions us about the differences between natural evolution and cultural change, and reminds us of the limits of the similarities. See Steven J. Gould, *Full House*, New York: Harmony Books, 1995, p. 219.

49 Arthur A. Macdonell, *A History of Sanskrit Literature*, Delhi: Motilal Banarsidass, 1976 (reprint), p. 50.

50 Ibid., pp. 49, 51, 232. Macdonnell notes that Sayana usually confines his commentary to the meaning of single words. This means that the explanation is not holistic or very concerned with interrelations of terms and image. See pp. 50-51.

51 I fail to see why the situation was mutually exclusive. Could not the founders have used current Muslim terms and clothing fashions and simultaneously reinstated a Hindu system? Since Hindus are famous for eclecticism that seems more likely than picturing them as pseudo-Muslims or accommodating to Islam in all things, or as largely secular and motivated mostly by personal desires. They were known to have supported Hindu institutions, but were also realistic enough to be sensitive to the needs and sensibilities of Muslims in their army ranks and so on.

52 Clifford Geertz, *Available Light: Anthropological Reflections on Philosophical Topics*, Princeton, NJ: Princeton University Press, 2000, pp. 147–48.

53 See David Bohm and F. David Peat, *Science, Order, and Creativity*, New York: Bantam, 1987.

54 Ibid., p. 164.

55 The structure of the system of government and society shaped by Vidyaranya was based on the record of past functioning – how Hindu kingdoms of the past had worked for centuries. The brahmans were the repositories of the groundplan, and so they and the other elements of society had no choice – democracy had not been introduced, and would not be for another 600 years. If a Hindu empire were to speak it would sound like the epics and folksongs of India, Vedanta and *dharma shastras*, and if an empire founder would begin he would have to know those and other expressions of Hindu lifeways.

56 R. Rangaramanuja Ayyangar, *History of South Indian (Carnatic) Music*, Madras: Author, 1972, p. 34.

57 Eric Hoffer asserts that adaptability in the human species is tied to the weak: 'the role the unfit play in human affairs should make us pause whenever we are prompted to see man as a mere animal and not a being of an order apart … . It is often the failure who is a pioneer in new lands, new undertakings, and new forms of expression.' Eric Hoffer, *The Passionate State of Mind*, New York, Harper and Row, 1955, pp. 37–38, 102. Compare the *Tao Te Ching* teaching that Tao works by weakness. See *Tao Te Ching*, tr. Stephen Mitchell, New York: Harper Collins, 2000, chs 30, 41 etc.

58 Eric Hoffer, in *The Passionate State of Mind*, suggests a useful idea: 'There is perhaps in all misfits a powerful secret craving to turn the whole of humanity into misfits. Hence partly their passionate advocacy of a drastically new social order. For we are all misfits when we have to adjust ourselves to the wholly new' (p. 64). The desires of the founders were tempered by the desires of the traditionalists; Hinduism had ways of combining the expansive innovative warrior caste urges and the traditional forms of order transmitted by the priestly caste.

59 For example, the dynamics in Judah when Hellenistic power was dominant had a double-edged impact on Jewish identity; there was some cultural absorption (Jews becoming like the Greeks) but also reaction against that foreign power (Jewish identity shaped by resisting the other – by seeing Antiochus as archetypal threat). When Vidyaranya and Harihara founded the empire, the centre Vijayanagara was laid out like a cosmic person; the empire extended from that capital. There are

parallels also between authority vested in the priest and the Torah, and Vidyaranya and the Veda. Mircea Eliade wrote: 'Palestine, Jerusalem, and the Temple severally and concurrently represent the image of the universe and the Center of the World. This multiplicity of centers and this reiteration of the image of the world on smaller and smaller scales constitute one of the specific characteristics of traditional societies', Mircea Eliade, *The Sacred and the Profane*, New York: Harvest, 1959, p. 43.

60   Frank Kermode, *The Sense of an Ending: Studies in the Theory of Fiction*, New York: Oxford University Press, 1967, p. 56.

61   Jorge Luis Borges, *This Craft of Verse*, ed. C. Mihailescu, Cambridge, MA: Harvard University Press, 2000, p. 31.

62   An evocative example of the articulation of this situation at the cosmic level: '[Stare at] what looks like the chaos from which God created the world – night and day swirling around each other in an inchaote mass ... patterns begin to emerge. One sees vortices of night curled into whirlpools of day, and these starry patterns repeat endlessly, like a mirror reflected back on itself. For centuries scientists have known that patterns exist in turbulent fluid flow.' Thomas A. Bass, 'Black Box', *The New Yorker*, 26 April / 3 May, 1999, p. 120.

63   'Enquire not into the origin of a Rishi, a river or a woman'. Proverb 285, M.W. Carr, *A Selection of Telugu Proverbs*, New Delhi: Asian Educational Service, p. 29.

CHAPTER 4

The Goddess' Sword: Queen Ganga Devi's Rousing Story; and the Archetype

Then the woman drew from her belt a brilliant sword...

Ganga Devi[1]

The Story of King Kampana

An entrancing voice of fourteenth-century Vijayanagara, that of Ganga Devi, offers a woman's perspective in the form of classical Sanskrit poetry, or *kavya*. Ganga Devi was the wife of Prince Kumara Kampana, second son of Bukka I, who ruled various provinces during the 1360s and 1370s. Her long poetic narrative, *Madhura Vijayam*, is the story of her husband's accomplishments, his life as a king called upon to defend dharma. The Karnataka empire, with Vijayanagara as its capital, was spread over South India laterally to the east more than to the south at that time. Kampana was in the second generation of the Sangama dynasty which was begun by five brothers and the sage Vidyaranya.

The poem begins with Bukka, brother of Harihara, reigning at Vijayanagara,[2] making gifts, furthering cultural life there, reviving dharma, and bringing prosperity to the people. Then Prince Kumara Kampana was born to Devayi, queen of the king of Kuntala.

The prince was born on an auspicious day at the time astrologers had determined was most auspicious, and happiness spread all over the kingdom, because everyone felt sure that the child would grow up to become a famous king able to be a great guardian of the earth, a protector of brahman sacrifices and a generous giver of gifts.[3]

Cheering multitudes rejoiced throughout the city, auspicious horns were sounded, filling the air with excitement, and wandering singers chanted words of praise. The king wanted to give away everything he owned, even himself, to the messengers who came with such a joyous announcement. By royal command the prisons were unlocked and the inmates were freed. Ganga Devi says that Bukka let the prisoners loose, as if anticipating the need which would soon arise for new space to hold the many Muslim prisoners who would be captured during the frays in the times to come.[4]

The king bathed and dressed in silk and, after handing out great wealth as gifts to brahmans, went into the inner palace, his heart happy, wanting to gaze upon the auspiciously marked baby lying there on the lap of the queen.[5]

(Another work which describes the occasion includes these details: The brahman chief minister accompanied the king on this grand occasion. Having been blessed with a son to carry on the line and family traditions, the king was released from his debt to the spirits of his ancestors. Hundreds of kettledrums rumbled in celebration and the dance of the *devadasis* enhanced the festival atmosphere. Attendants sprinkled camphor all about as the news was being spread to noble houses, and coloured kumkum powder was sprinkled in the ten directions. Elderly chamberlains joined in the festivities, holding hands with hunchbacks and dwarves, jumping for joy, cavorting with crowds boisterous in their merrymaking.[6])

Ganga Devi's poem follows the prince as he grows up, and depicts his impressive prowess, his great natural talents and shining valour. We are told that Kampana goes to fight against the country of Champa and seizes a hill fortress. He overcomes the Champa army with many arrows, but loses many men in doing so. After winning the fort, and the war, he rules wisely, enjoying culture, poetry, learning, loveplay with ladies of the zenana, and pleasures appropriate for the six *ritus* (seasons), including water sports and flower-gathering. Ganga Devi's poem celebrates the beauty of nature, moonrise, and tender moments of eros.[7] But then images of decay are brought to the king's attention, by a figure with a magic sword from the Pandyan dynasty, somewhat like the image of Joan of Arc in European history. I will paraphrase some of the key parts of the narrative.

The Voice of Ganga Devi: The Stranger of the Southland's Lament[8]

Madhura Vijayam

A woman of extraordinary presence, whose identity no one in the region knew, arrived one day at the capital, and stood before Kampana raya, describing how the Southland was harrassed by 'Turushka' (Muslim or 'Turkish') invaders. At first the king and his court did not realize she was a Goddess. She told them:

'O Raja, Vyaghrapuri has reverted to its namesake! Yes, now it's literally a "town" where "tigers" roam! And Chidambaram, and Perumparrapuliya! The whole region is truly becoming a wilderness again. Long ago, people civilized that land, but wild beasts run free again there now.'

'The main shrine of the Shrirangam temple, including the superstructure, has pathetically fallen apart, so much that the only roof which covers the image of Shriranganatha, Lord Vishnu reclining on the world stage, sheltering him from the tumbling debris and crumbling masonry, is the hood of Adisesha, the cosmic serpent with coiled energy under whose protective presence the Lord always rests.'

'Shiva, Lord of Gajaranya [Tiruvanaikka, Jambukeshvaram near Shrirangam] who was mighty enough to slay an elephant to use its skin as a loincloth, is now naked again, stripped of his clothes.'

'The *garbhagriha*s [sacred inner sanctums], the very womb-rooms of many other temples there are also crumbling, their *mantapa*s [pavilions] are now overgrown with jungle leaves; their solemn wooden doors are honeycombed by white ant holes.'

'In temples where the joyous drumbeat rhythms of *mridangam* drums echoed resonantly, now there's just the desolate sickening howl of scavenging jackals who've moved in and taken over the dilapidated buildings.'

'Even the womanly river Kaveri, once channelled with sturdy dams and bunds, flowing with life-sustaining order, now has begun to lose her discipline, randomly breaching her banks and sprawling anywhichway, as chaos of all sorts, caused by the invaders, spreads.'

'Even in *agrahara*s [neighbourhoods gifted to brahmans as places to do their sacred work], where smoke used to rise from Vedic rites [*yagadhuma*] now people gag from the stench of the Muslim fires roasting flesh; solemn Vedic chants have been replaced by the foreign invaders' gruff voices.'

'The graceful coconut trees, which used to flourish in gardens scattered all around Madurai, have been felled by the invaders; instead, iron spears stand in their place, decorated with hideous garlands of decapitated heads.'

'The Tamraparni river, which used to run bright with sandalwood paste rinsed from the breasts of young women bathing there, now flows red with cow blood as the invaders slaughter herds of cattle.'[9]'

Gift of the Indomitable Sword and The Goddess' Call to Restore Order

Kampana listened carefully to the stranger reporting the way the Southland had been suffering. Then the woman drew from her belt a brilliant sword, held it up high and said to him:

'O King, long, long ago the cosmic artisan Vishvakarman gathered together particles from of all the gods' weapons; he melted them down and from that metal with hammer and tong he forged this fabled blade. Then he gave this sword to Parameshvara,[10] to conquer the destructive *daitya*s [demons].'

'Later, one of the Pandya kings, through long *tapa*s (austerities), won this sword from Lord Parameshvara. The offspring of the Pandya, wielding this great sword, ruled their kingdom unopposed for generations. Then, as time passed, unfortunately the Pandya dynasty scions lost the family's vigour and virility, becoming weaklings.'

'Agastya [the great holy man of ancient times who settled the Southland, civilizing and sacralizing the South for later generations] is the one who saw this happening, and he is now passing this extraordinary round-bladed sword, through me, to you.'

'You will find that when you wield this sword, you will have peerless strength that does not dwindle, and the weapons of your foes will be weak and useless when they are raised against you.'

'Just as Krishna went to Mathura and killed wicked Kamsa long ago, so too, O King, must you now go to the southern town of Madhurai, and kill the Muslim ruler, the enemy of the world, and set up victory pillars along the bridge of Rama [in the water by Rameshvaram].'

'During your rule of the Southland, you will also build a dam, to channel the Kaveri river, and improve the irrigation system, benefiting farmers who grow the grain upon which the whole Southland's prosperity depends'.

So spoke the Divine Protectress of Madhurai during that time of disaster to the able Kampana, who now knew what he had to do.[11]

In this story of the arousal of resistance the king enjoys dalliance with his harem while en route to the battle with the sultan, and there are metaphorical correspondences between Kampana's power as a lover and his prowess in combat. In the climax of his adventure he duels with the sultan and, even beheads him, although the headless body still keeps a tight grasp on the reins of the horse it is riding and strikes out at Kampana before finally being finished off. Whilst Richard H. Davis calls this story of restoration an 'epic of resistance', Rao, Shulman and Subrahmanyam point out that this is not exactly an epic but, rather, elegant poetry, with few historical facts.[12] The intention of the poem is a celebration of the king's greatness, through lyrical bursts of poetic images.

Significant Themes of the Story

Ganga Devi, Prince Kumara Kampana's wife, thus enacts in her poetry, in thought and story, the entrusting of a mission to her husband. To show the urge to win the South as a divine desire, a mandate from heaven, the Goddess with the sword gives the right and responsibility, the power to prevail, entrusting the king with the means to undertake the righting of vast wrongs. Though this is a fight for survival, not aggression for colonization, it brings the ability to annex land and extend an empire that will last for over two centuries. Driving the sultan out of Madurai, reopening the Minakshi temple, and the Ranganatha temple in Shrirangam, the reconquest will change the destiny of South India.

According to an ancient story about the deity in Madurai's great Minakshi temple, the goddess Minakshi was born into the royal family. She was born with three breasts, and it was foretold that she would lose one when she met her destined mate. It was also foretold that she would be a great warrior, able to conquer any force in the world, except Shiva. With her sword she conquered all, but when she met Shiva, she could not defeat him, one breast disappeared and she married him. This story, and the wedding of Minakshi, is celebrated in a great annual festival. The poet Ganga Devi used the image already in the collective religious memory – the goddess and the sword – to express the need for defence and to evoke the efficient power which was desired. (In a later Telugu work of the early sixteenth century, Ekamranath's *Prataparudracharitramu*, the king Madhava Varma as a child is so fearless that the goddess Padmakshi offers him any boon he wants. He asks for the power to vanquish an encroaching king's forces and to retrieve lost herds of cows. Padmakshi gives him a divine sword and shield with which he can rule for 2000 months.) [13]

The religious dimension in the story's archetypes appeals to the pervasive devotional tradition. India's bhakti spirit is a large pool of worshipfulness, a resourceful attitude of dependence and fealty, giving an easy acceptance to the king as lord, showing a Taoist-like humility. In traditional Hinduism the self-abnegation and acceptance of a greater power has sometimes been interpreted by individualist-minded Westerners as a lack of good sense and self-esteem. Traditional Hindus think of it as submission to a higher order, acknowledging actual dependence. Bhakti channels the drives which are latent in the psyche, releasing them in the dedicated acts of sublimation, which is another word for spirituality.

In Ganga Devi's poem the shining sword made by the celestial blacksmith is a composite made of all the gods' swords, showing that heaven itself wants the king to be victorious. Images of charmed weapons figure in many Hindu stories. Similarly, in the *Siddheshvara Charitramu*[14] the goddess Padmakshi gives a magic sword and shield to Madhava Varman, and there is a well-known episode in post-Vijayanagara stories describing how Bhavani gives a blessed sword to Shivaji. The magical sword motif is found in other cultures as well. In Quest stories Arthur receives a sword from the Lady of the Lake,[15] and a sword figures in the story of Joan of Arc, as we shall

Figure 4.1   Sword, boar, sun and moon: emblem of Vijayanagara rulers

see. The sword has many precedents and associated archetypal meanings; it seems to be an attractor for patterns of empowerment and stories of help coming from on high.[16]

The court poet's 'reasons of the heart' for rejoicing in the story of defeating invaders are not hard to find; there is a tension mixing material purposes and spiritual needs. There were real armies and not just illusionary phantoms to fight. History may be full of delusive clashes, as poet Allen Ginsberg suggests: 'Fighting phantoms Egyptians mummied pharaohs ... Fighting phantoms David picked up his sling ... Fighting phantoms Siddhartha meditated under a Bo tree' and so on.[17] Fighting phantoms, poets wrote satires, people committed suicide, planned excesses and spent the wealth of nations, no doubt; but at Vijayanagara the fighting was against 'phantoms' who were quite real. The Hindu king had a dharmic obligation to reclaim provinces lost to the Muslim invaders, and, through this action, Vijayanagara developed into a great empire governing much of South India in provincial segments for the next 250 years. The sword and the boar emblem impressed its meaning: power and rescue, the strength of protection, fighting non-phantom occupiers of a traditionally Hindu land.

In classical Hinduism the four goals of life (*purusharthas*) are dynamically interactive. It is a system to satisfy desires: *kama* absorbs hungers, and *dharma* absorbs rages. It is a system to dissolve despairs: *artha* gives hope and meaning, and *moksha* gives the ultimate reason. Thus the aims of life are conceptualized as a system of attractors in a rising order. They are goals for seekers, imposing certain limits in the expending of pent-up energies. Bhakti is another unifying concept and programme which holds the ways of dedicated action and spiritual wisdom together. But these are classical Hindu formulations. Further back in time, in the Vedas (the fountainhead of Hindu outlooks), and in pre-Vedic oral traditions, there is a primal myth upon which later historical conquests, and many sorts of meaningful accomplishment are patterned. This myth is an archetypal image of the way things happen in the universe, a primal event often referred to in the Vedas. Even when the archetypal image is not mentioned it often lurks in the background, somewhat as the image of St George and the dragon constitutes an emblem that stands for England. The image of an original divine heroic conquest is paradigmatic for many acts in the human realm.

The Oldest Story Ever Told: The Hero Overcoming Chaos

The original cosmogonic myth of Indra conquering Vritra, which is often glancingly referred to in the Vedas, is a paradigm for many longstanding Hindu patterns. I follow A.K. Coomaraswamy in his thinking about this myth. Mythic thinking asserts a view, saying, 'this is the way things happened at first, and so, the way they are always bound to happen, when things run down, and start up again. This is the same old story, though it takes endless forms.' The Vedic myth reveals the concept that, in the timeless beginning, only the supreme being, the One, (*Eka*) exists – the single reality without any differentiation. And the original All is imaginable as an endless serpent of eternal energy (or, alternatively, in other mythic images a cosmic tree or a vast mountain), and the alter ego of the same principle, the dragon-slayer, is born to take the place of the father (the One) and take over the existing kingdom, handing out its resources and treasures to his followers, inaugurating a new era.[18] Thus, the cosmic warrior god, Indra of the Sky, wielding a thunderbolt, overcomes the cosmic serpent Vritra, the power that has been confining the rivers and preventing the free flow of life, with its beauty and order. Indra defeats Vritra and divides up the hoarded energies and materials into a harmonious cosmos. Note the rapid transitions from sole to dual, from son of serpent to generous king with an obligation to those who reside in his kingdom (creation). In the narration there are hints to the effect that, although there is a primal conflict, a split-up differentiating two beings, a difference which makes the first big difference in the coming-to-be of the universe, the serpent-slayer and the serpent are ultimately one behind the scenes, where there is no polarity of contraries. Yet, they are mortal enemies on the stage of appearances in order that the story may happen, suggesting that it's all a play, a dramatic *lila*, sport or amusing trick. The Indra of the Sky who comes with the thunderstorm and rain frees the rivers; the serpent is a sleeping sun – from the darkly enclosed, the daylight of creation is released. In this cosmology no devil falls for all eternity, doomed to be an outsider; instead, chaos is a necessary part of the process of creation, according to the Hindu perspective.

The relationships become fairly clear to us: The serpent is the original primordial energy – chaos to be ordered by the creative Lord of the Abyss.[19] The dragon-slayer inherits the power of the being he sacrifices. Philosophically one is called upon to befriend the dragon-slayer and also the dragon, the original being, 'That One', *Tad Ekam*.[20] Vishnu reclining on Adishesha, the serpent of primal energy, points to this philosophical view of reconciled mutuality, dynamic relations of part to whole. The image has to do with chaos as potential and original oneness and the basic matter we're made of, not just as the opposite of order and light, not just an eternally demonic 'other' to be controlled by reason (which is how Greek thought saw chaos). That view (of chaos as a negative other) is too linear to satisfy the sense of the depth of the universe with which we now view life processes. Chaotic processes are basic in weather, social change and individual organisms (in heartbeats and brain patterns, for example.) As an *Upanishad* envisions it: 'When fullness is taken from Fullness, fullness remains'.[21]

Thus the creative metaphor found in the oldest story has inexhaustible uses over many generations of time.[22] As Coomaraswamy puts it, 'there is thus an incessant multiplication of the inexhaustible One and unification of the indefinitely Many' in an endless cosmic process of existence, evolution, spiritual realization. The beginnings and endings of whole worlds, entire civilizations, multitudes of individual beings follow this pattern, expanding 'from a point without position or dimensions ... accomplishing their destiny, and when their time is up, returning "home" to the Sea in which their life originated'.[23] Potential order is attained by overcoming chaos which is also the One, following what Indra and Vishnu did originally, finding the order already inherent in what is given. That ancient myth is referred to in a very large number of the Vedic hymns or mantras. The gift of the sword in the *Madhura Vijayam* by Ganga Devi, and the call to subdue the alien holders of the South, both recall the old paradigm. It would be a mistake to leave the image of the divine weapon out of the whole ethos of Hinduism,[24] which includes karma and ahimsa. Thus, bhakti religious life presupposes that a serious spiritual seeker can handle adult imagery, and uses loveplay, the symbolism of human body and its nature and beauty, to follow the archetypal attractor in the cultivation of practices to win oneness with the Supreme, which, in much of Hindu thinking is understood to be a vast, subtle consciousness at one's base. The spiritual–psychological level is a deep aspect of the mythic images. The story works on several levels: imaging origins and primordial relations of the components of reality; serving to rouse energetic resolve; offering a model for rituals and customs; and presenting a way to conceptualize processes of spiritual victory. It is an archetypal model for realizing the envisioned order.

Another Woman with a Sword, Another Culture: A Comparative Note on Saint Joan of Arc

The illiterate peasant girl who came to be known as Joan of Arc, the Maid of Orleans, was born in 1412, to poor and devout parents in France. Before her birth there were prophecies connected to a healing spring and a May Fair Tree near her home; it was foretold that some day a girl would step forth from that place and perform miracles. Perhaps the pre-Christian religious importance of the place of the tree is more significant than most historians have acknowledged.[25]

At the age of 13 Joan heard voices, telling her to leave her father's house, whispering that her presence was needed to break the siege which the king of England was imposing on the seemingly helpless Dauphin (eldest son of the king of France). Joan believed that the archangel Michael had promised her his aid. Joan dedicated her virginity to God and heard the voice of Michael promise that Saints Catherine and Margaret would also help her in times of need during her mission. Her mission grew clearer: to drive the English from French soil and to place the rightful ruler, the eldest son of the French ruler, the Dauphin Charles, on the throne.

In 1428, trying to get the help of Robert de Baudricourt, a supporter of the Dauphin Charles, Joan, in a threadbare red dress, told him of her voices. He took her to a duke, who was sobered by his contact with Joan and gave her a horse; Robert gave her a sword and took her to the Dauphin. (Joan had tried to warn the Dauphin not to attack the English before the middle of Lent, saying that her Master, the King of Heaven, would send her to help him. No one had listened and the French army fought and suffered defeat. She had then cut her hair off and dressed as a boy.) When Robert brought Joan for her first meeting with the Dauphin, Charles was in disguise, hidden anonymously among 300 knights. Joan went directly to him and told him what his secret prayer was, and mentioned secrets known only to Charles and his confessor, impressing everyone with her inexplicable abilities. Clergymen questioned her and doctors examined her closely, and she was declared to be a virgin. Passing these tests the fervently pious Joan received a lance from the Dauphin. Armourers fitted her woman's body with a good suit of armour. At this time Joan received the sword of St Catherine, which was engraved with five crosses. It is said that she mysteriously knew that this sword could be found hidden behind the altar of Tours Cathedral. When the old blade was polished, the rust magically fell off and it gleamed as if new. Joan had a banner made according to instructions from Saints Catherine and Margaret, and in white armour, with her shining sword, she rode on a white horse with a force of 6000 fighting men. She enjoyed being with soldiers and disliked formal assemblies of officials meeting to discuss important matters. For their part, the aristocrats felt some animosity towards Joan in the beginning, because she was a mere commoner presuming to lead – clearly an anomaly in the feudal hierarchy. Accounts describe her as small in stature, graceful and lightfooted, pious and generous, brave and goodhearted.

She fought the English after unsuccessfully offering them a way of enjoying peace; she was wounded, but she prayed and persevered confidently, and charged again, this time winning victory. She won the Battle of Orleans in 1429, and became famous as Joan of Arc, Maid of Orleans. She urged the Dauphin to be crowned in Rheims in 1429, saying that she would only live a year or two longer. She led him on 17 July, 1429 to his coronation ceremony in Rheims.

After Charles' coronation he disbanded the army, feeling that Joan had now accomplished all that was necessary. She, with loyal followers, continued to fight the English whom she had vowed to drive from France, and she suffered some defeats. She defeated a great army at the battle of Patay, was wounded again, and was warned by Saints Catherine and Margaret she would be captured soon. She was captured in 1430 by Burgundians and subsequently tried by an ecclesiastical court of the Inquisition, consisting of English sympathizers. They judged her voices to be lies or Satanic. The Burgundians sold Joan to the English. One spring day in May of 1431 at the tender age of 19 she was slowly burned on a high scaffold as a heretic. Her judges had been angered by her masculine appearance, seeing it as a wilful transgression of divine law and order.

Some scholars suggest that Joan drew strength from European religious traditions older than Christianity.[26] Burned at the stake as a witch by the English, she was loved by French peasants possibly as a leader of the Old Religion, archetypically appealing to their love of the powerful Goddess, the Victorious Feminine.

Old hagiographic accounts suggest that, as she died, Joan repeated the name of Jesus three times, a mantra-like prayer dating from early Christianity. George Bernard Shaw ended his play about Joan with a question. He asked if a Christ had to perish in torment in every age to save those who have no imagination. The maiden with a sword is an image of the beckoning soul, the anima figure leading one into the deeper waters of the unknown, demanding exertions for a higher good. Those who silence the appeal of the psyche to take up a new challenge are, Shaw suggests, imaginationless rigid old drones, whose rage may try to rid the world of creative risk-takers, colourfully disguised eccentrics and flowing souls following their inspirations. But the human spirit has its ways of rising up again and overcoming obstacles.

Notes

1   Ganga Devi, *Madhura Vijayam, or Vira Kamparaya Charita*, ed. G. Harihara Sastri and V. Srinivasa Sastri, 2nd edn, Trivandrum: Sridhara Power Press, 1924, VIII.2.2.
2   The brothers seem to have shared the rule in different parts of the kingdom from 1334 to 1354.
3   Devi, *Madhura Vijayam*, II.15–17. I am indebted to T.A. Gopinatha Rao whose 1916 paraphrase forms the basis for my telling of the story.
4   Ibid., II 21–23.
5   Ibid., II 24–26.
6   *Vemabhupalacarita* III provides the details in this paragraph. See D. Sridhara Babu, *Kingship: State and religion in South India, According to South Indian Historical Biographies of Kings (Madhuravijaya, Acyutarayabhyudaya, and Vemabhupalacarita)*, Gottingen: [n.p.], 1975, pp. 113–14.
7   Devi, *Madhura Vijayam*, Canto V.
8   This narration is based on the work in the book cited above, Ganga Devi's *Madhura Vijayam*. I thank Rajanikanta Rao for helping me locate this text. The passages are from Canto VIII.
9   A good discussion of this part of the *Madhura Vijayam* is in Richard H. Davis, *Lives of Indian Images*, Princeton, NJ: Princeton University Press, 1997, pp. 116–118.
10   Parameshvara is a name of Shiva.

11 Devi, *Madhura Vijayam*. VIII.21–29.

12 Davis, *Lives of Indian Images*, pp. 113–122. Velcheru Narayana Rao, David Shulman, Sanjay Subrahmanyam, *Textures of Time: Writing History in South India 1600–1800*, New York: Other Press, 2003, pp. 261–63.

13 Phillip B. Wagoner, *Tidings of the King*, Honolulu: University of Hawaii Press, 1993, pp. 41–42.

14 *Kase Sarvappa, Siddheshvara Charitramu, Kakatiyarajula Caritra – Pratapa Caritra*, ed. K. Lakshmiranjanam, Hyderabad: Andhra Racayitala Sanghamu, pp. 55–56.

15 Arthur received a sword from the Lady of the Lake in the Quest stories. See John Steinbeck, *The Acts of King Arthur and his Noble Knights*, New York: Farrar, Straus and Giroux, 1976. pp. 44–45. Constantine, in the history of Christianity, is supposed to have seen a sword-like cross and heard 'In this sign conquer'. The sword of ordained defence and destiny is an attractor in the minds of people with the knowledge of metalurgy and swordsmanship and a theology of divine guidance. It is a focus helping to sublimate potential martial energies for a high cause. Muhammad is sometimes pictured as praying with a sword by his side. Sikh men keep a small sword in their hair as a symbol of being armed by the divine. For an exploration of how archetypes function as attractors, see J.R. Van Eenwyk, 'Archetypes: The Strange Attractors of the Psyche', *Journal of Analytic Psychology*, 36, 1991, pp. 1–25. See also R.Robertson and Allan Combs (eds), *Chaos Theory in Psychology and the Life Sciences*, Mahwah, NJ: Lawrence Erlbaum Associates, 1995.

16 The sword in the story comes from Madurai, from Pandyan times. It calls to mind Goddess Minakshi's sword, the sword with which she conquers even the gods in all directions (as celebrated in Madurai festivals today). To re-use the sword to reconquer Madurai is an archetypal event with a divine paradigm. Wendell Beane has shown how the goddess's victory is a transposition of Indra's primordial victory. See his *Myth, Cult and Symbols in Sakta Hinduism: A Study of the Indian Mother Godess*, Leiden: Brill, 1977. Though to modern Western people the woman with a sword image may look odd, it is a theme going back a long way in India. The Indus Valley figurine of a thin dancing girl with bangles may have been a fencer, with the bangles used as armour. In Bharata's *Natya Shastra*, fencing with a sword is one of the 64 arts in a dancing girl's course of study. The Goddess Kali in various forms is a destroyer, holding a sword and a severed head. Life's pain, diagnosed in abstract analysis by Buddha is imaged in the nightmare appearance of the hag Kali, who cuts tentacles of attachment to free the soul. She is the bringer of bewilderment, depicted as drunk on blood, shown nude in paintings and sculptures, representing primordial chaos and reminding people of life's source, a transcendent, formless state far removed from human structures. She offers people a chance to renew themselves by remembering the transcendent mystery and reordering their lives inspired by the primordial chaos which only the divine can control. One cannot be indifferent to her image. The American 'Battle Hymn of the Republic' also pictures 'the glory of the coming of the Lord...with His terrible swift sword'. Xena the Warrior, and Buffy the Vampire Slayer are examples of women with swords in popular culture today. Robert Bly writes of the fierce goddess in 'I Came Out of the Mother Naked', in *Sleepers Joining Hands*, New York: Harper and Row, 1973, pp. 29–50.

17 Allen Ginsberg, *White Shroud: Poems 1980–1985*, New York: Harper, 1986, p. 42.

18 A.K. Coomaraswamy, *Spiritual Authority and Temporal Power in the Indian Theory of Government*, New Haven, CT: American Oriental Society, 1942 p. 24.

19 The chaos serpent represents potential energy to be ordered, turbulence mastered or transformed not only in Indra–Vritra stories, but elsewhere in Hindu myths: Vishnu reclines in peaceful repose on the serpent of primal energy, Adishesha, on the sea of eternity, coming to life when need arises, to restore balance. Garuda overcomes serpents. Shiva, who has a serpent ornamenting his neck, and takes poison in his stride, is the yogic master of cool amid craziness. Krishna dances on the head of the dangerous serpent, taming it, making life livable. Buddha overcomes the *naga*, converting it to a devotee, making use of opposing chaotic forces.

20 *Rig Veda*, X.129.2.

21 *Isha Upanishad*, I.1.

22 Some, like Jean-Francois Lyotard, proclaim that we who live in the postmodern condition no longer have recourse to the grand narratives which formed the framework for traditional peoples. But

others, like Alexander Argyros, argue that newly emerging chaos science and systems theory may give us good reason to affirm the desirability, usefulness and good qualities of great narratives. Great narrative is found in myths, epics and scriptures of the world. Scriptures are examples of narrative *par excellence* – they tell origin stories, they narrate expositions of teachings, injunctions, lyrics and wisdom. Why is narrative in all its many forms so ubiquitous? Where is a coherent life that is not shaped by some story? Argyros speculates that the patterns involved in narrative are biologically hardwired into the nervous system (as the capacity for language seems to be). He argues that the universality of narrative around the world shows how it reflects a neural substrate in the human constitution, or a set of 'epigenetic rules' which seem to predispose people to configuring their experiences in narrative modes. Attempts to do without narrative therefore may end up blocking the great ones and substituting unconscious narratives. (Think of communist hero worship, devotion to entertainment idols, fascination with demonic supernaturalism.) There are also environmental and societal reasons why narrative is so pervasive. Just as language is a system reflecting reality, narratives are also symbol systems, Argyros points out; narrative matches well the significant features of the world around us, especially the ways in which our landscapes, both natural and social, are not static but involve dynamic, causal interrelations. Even more basically, narrative seems akin to the force for order which is universal in galaxies and life-forms. Argyros believes that the global dynamics of narrative are able to serve as a cultural attractor, or a self-adjusting algorithm, by means of which all known cultures have developed their vision of the cosmos. Scriptures thus can be seen to function as 'attractors', dynamic system patterns channelling human energies, reminding people of their place in the scheme of things. They hold sway and channel the passions. At their worst they promote unthinking irrational behaviour. On the positive side, sacred narratives are important as revered repositories storing religious wisdom and reasons of the heart. Thus they seem to mirror life and generate order. They provide recognizable structures (enduring answers about life's meanings) yet allow some flexibility for new interpretations and applications as needs arise. They store information about ideals and yet make the meanings available and applicable to a great variety of situations by different people over the centuries. They are kept relevant by commentaries, new translations, and adaptive reiterations. See Alexander Argyros, *A Blessed Rage for Order*, See pp. 318–19: *Deconstruction, Evolution, and Chaos*, Ann Arbor: University of Michigan Press, 1992. Also Steven Johnson, 'Strange Attraction', in *Lingua Franca*, March/April 1996, pp. 42–50.

23 A.K. Coomaraswamy, *Hinduism and Buddhism*, New York: Philosophical Library, 1943, p. 9. It is not by chance that I refer to Coomaraswamy's remarks here. Though often neglected, his work has not only a sense of what is perennially significant in Hindu symbolism, but also a depth and complexity that gives it pertinence in the study of complex dynamical systems.

24 Where do the yogas of work (karma yoga) and worship (bhakti yoga) and wisdom (jnana yoga), taught in the *Bhagavad Gita*, fit in with the Indra/Vritra scheme of things, and how does it chime with the four *purusharthas* of classical Hinduism? In the Vedic vision of archetypal origins, Indra conquering Vritra, there is a wisdom teaching meant to establish the human being in the consciousness of the One behind the many, the spirit in all, not identifying with any smaller part or temporary manifestation. And yogic work is activity done to dissolve the rigid mental delusions of separateness and ego which people commonly take for granted as reality – to become free of the concern for aggrandizement which will come from fruits of action which people normally crave, free from shame felt at being blamed and so on. Conditioning's rigid infrastraucture is not the ultimate reality. The ego is not ultimate reality; the self is a temporary part of the whole. As Coomaraswamy wrote, bhakti means a given 'share', giving God his share, giving of ourselves to reach and share in transcendence. The deepest worship involves inner sacrifice, *manasa puja*, the subtle offering of mind and self. For many Hindus the spiritual process takes care of itself, independently of official authorities; hence Hinduism is rather decentralized and formless, with milling pilgrims, no fixed schedule for worship in a temple, and with incense lit in a home shrine. In Vedanta it is said that action or sacrifice will not enable one to reach the Supreme, but only the personal experience of gnosis, knowing silently within, self-realization. Letting go of externals, experiencing deeper

consciousness, finding the grace of peace, *moksha*, release; freedom comes from reaching beyond the swirling fluctuations of samsara.

25   For a full account of Joan's life story see Marina Warner, *Joan of Arc*, London: Weidenfeld and Nicholson, 1981.

26   Margaret A. Murray, *The Witch-Cult in Western Europe*, Oxford: Oxford University Press, 1971. Also, T'ang Sai-erh, a Taoist sorceress or shaman of fifteenth century China, roused her followers in a sedition by saying she had been given a magic sword and a secret treatise. Again, the invincible sword which suddenly appears is a familiar attractor in the imagination. It is an archetype which exerts a power over the psyche, an unexpected call to arms and a promise of victory. The weapon offered by the anima image involves its would-be wielder in alluring destiny. The specially forged weapon of special knowledge and blessing is a power from beyond, a sign of following the lead of divine will. The enigmatic helping woman with a magic sword is like a *dakini* ('sky-goer' in Tibetan Buddhism) who opens the way to the pilgrim's progress and people's fulfilment. The pointed sword she offers points in a direction and clears the obstacles, or leads to catastrophic loss, being swallowed by wrathful forces of chaos.

CHAPTER 5

Two Poets of the People: Shripadaraya and Atukuri Molla

'What Suffices?' : Shripadaraya's Answer

Shripadaraya was born in 1422 and grew up in a poor family in Abburu village of Chennapattana taluk, which is now in Bangalore District. His father, Seshagiriappa, was a village accountant. Svararnava Tirtha was the guru who initiated him. According to traditional stories, the boy who was to grow up to be Shripadaraya made good use of spare moments while taking care of the cattle entrusted to him, sedulously reading Sanskrit texts. Yet it was his knowledge of the life and the vernacular language common to the farmers and merchants which played a distinctive part in his cultural work in later life. When he became a sannyasin his name was Lakshminarayana Tirtha, but eventually people began calling him Shripadaraya in honour of his achievements in spreading knowledge and serving as guru to a Vijayanagara emperor, Saluva Narasimha.

Shripadaraya was a leader of the Madhva school, a member of the *Dasakuta*[1] in the line of Padmanabha-Tirtha, who was a direct disciple of Madhvacharya himself. Shripadaraya founded a *matha* (monastery) in Mulbagal in what is now the Kolar District of Karnataka. As a scholar he has been respected for centuries for his knowledge of Vedanta and logic. His Sanskrit text *Vagvajra* gives evidence of his philosophical profundity.[2]

But Shripadaraya's uniqueness and creative originality also have to do with his love of the people and his ability to compose works in the vernacular, giving voice to folk expressions. He was the first *acharya* or Vaishnava teacher of the Madhvacharya school to use colloquial Kannada language in songs and poems, teaching *dvaita* concepts to believers in the common man's regional tongue, opening access to those who did not know Sanskrit. He composed many devotional songs and poems for use in the nighttime worship at his *matha*. Shripadaraya is well known for the personal voice of sincere feelings resonating in his lyrics. Shripadaraya was the first to compose *suladi*s (a musical-lyrical form employing a medley of different ragas and rhythmic tempos (*tala*s) in succession to give a series of moods to one narrative structure). The *suladi* is a form later popularized by Telugu lyricist Annamacharya and Kannada composers Purandaradasa and Vyasatirtha.[3] In musical performance Shripadaraya also composed forms such as *vrittanama*s, *ugabhoga*s and *prabhandas*, besides the everpopular *kirtanas*, colloquial songs sung with cymbals and *tambura* accompaniment with several choruses and a rousing refrain. His lively works were certainly powerful bhakti expressions, probably influencing the prolific Telugu *kirtana* composer Annamacharya, among others.

During the period when Shripadaraya was the guru of Saluva Narasimha, the Vijayanagara emperor (1485–1493), who was impressed with the monk's spiritual, intellectual and creative powers, he achieved widespread prominence. Legends say that Saluva Narasimha sprinkled Shripadaraya with diamonds.[4] Saluva Narasimha was the founder of the second dynasty of Vijayanagara rulers, (the Saluvas, literally 'Hawks'), bringing rebellious provinces back under the central order of the empire and re-establishing hegemony, according to tradition.

Shripadaraya was also the guru of a disciple named Vyasatirtha in Mulbagal, later to become known as Vyasaraya, a great guru during the reign of Krishnadevaraya. Vyasaraya headed the *haridasa* movement, which included the singer-saints Purandaradasa and Kanakadasa, and is recognized as one of the most important spiritual leaders of the late fifteenth and sixteenth centuries.

It was with Shripadaraya that music increasingly came to be used as a powerful vehicle to communicate religious, philosophical and social ideas, though Narahi Tirtha, the successor and disciple of Madhvacharya had already made a start in that direction. In the *haridasa* tradition[5] of devotional singing, the first salutation in the singing programme consists of a poem dedicated to the earliest *haridasas*; significantly it invokes the name of Shripadaraya. It may be that Achalanandadasa or Narahari Tirtha actually began the movement, but Shripadaraya is often called the progenitor of the *haridasas* and he is remembered fondly for the many songs he composed in Kannada. Although they have some archaic features, these songs still have a contemporary feel and style, with mellisonant lyrics. Shripadaraya composed 133 *suladis* which are known today, at least three *ugabhogas*, and many *kirtanas*.[6]

After a long life of teaching, composing and singing, and serving Vaishnava devotees, Shripadaraya died in 1480, in Mulbagal, where his gravesite memorial *brindavan samadhi* is still visited by pilgrims.

The Voice of Shripadaraya

'It'll do'

Why should I go on worshipping you
if you won't show me this least little bit of grace?
All this time with your lotus feet as my refuge
I've offered all to you – my whole being's faith, why should I go on...

I haven't come here to wheedle and tease you
complaining that I have no food, no clothes.
O Vasudeva – it's enough if you do me the favour
of letting me serve your servants' servants, why should I go on...

I haven't come for the sake of abundant riches
to make my wife and children feel comfortable.
It will do if you just allow my mind to listen
to your nectar lifestory, not stray into joys of the world, why should I...

I have not come to you craving like some pauper
crying, 'I've no jewelry, no golden belt!' It will do
if you grant me the favour of never blocking the bliss
I get whenever I bow down at your feet, O Ranga Vithala
but why should I go on if you won't show me a little bit of grace ...[7]

Who Else?

If you won't protect me now in the depths of my disgrace
Why did you bother to create me in the first place?

It is said that you are really the world's sole protector
if so, then is it right for you to act like this and neglect me?

I can't get enough cloth to keep warm; see, I shiver
I left my wife, mother, brothers, became a forlorn creature

Who's to give me clothes, who's to care what I say or think?
This poverty has forced me to this desperate brink.

I see not a soul who can show me the way out of here
so please don't forsake me in the deeps of samsara
please, Lord Ranga Vithala, show me the other shore.[8]

Mistaken Identity

You've got it all wrong, calling me a 'Vaishnava'
Obviously I have no knowledge of Parabrahma.

Alright, I marked my forehead after washing up
but did I study Madhvacharya's *shastra*?
I only wear this *tulasi* garland
to make myself look good, but
have I immersed myself in the ocean of bhakti?
You've got it all wrong...

I wore myself out wasting too much time
with village gripers and gossips
but did I ever take shelter
at the feet of Lord Narayana?
I was seduced by the sweet words of women
but did I pay heed to true words of noble souls?
You've got me wrong, I'm not much of a Vaishnava.

Have I experienced the realization that the Lord
is only known by way of the sacred scriptures,

saying 'the world is real', knowing
the fivefold difference of Madhva's philosophy[9]
leaving the eight,[10] listening to the Bhagavata
and mulling over truths it teaches; have I done that?
You've pegged me wrong, classing me a Vaishnava.

Did I see how the Lord Shri Hari is of a higher status
than the goddess Lakshmi, who excels Brahma, who
himself excels Rudra, who in turn is superior to Indra,
who is up above the Gandharvas, who themselves
are higher than we mere human beings – did I
ever understand this order of greatness?
No, you've made an error, calling me Vaishnava.

Did I, when I ritually bathed in the sacred Ganges
merely to clean the dirt from my skin
really perform the kind of bathing that's holy?
Did I spend my time participating in Satsang,
travelling in the supportive good company
of the devotees of Shri Ranga Vithala?
You've misidentified me as a Vaishnava –
I am not worthy of knowledge of Parabrahma.[11]

Give Me Shelter

Shall I throw myself into flames and let my body burn?
Shall I tumble down from the mountain top into the valley,
or hang myself by dangling a rope from a tall tree's branch,
or slit my own throat with a sharp blade, or let
myself be dragged by a rope pulled by an elephant,
or should I take into my bloodstream
the fatal venom of a serpent?
  If you won't protect me, give me safe shelter,
  Oh Ocean of kindness, who else is there? so please protect me!

I've forced my adult body to bow as low as it will go
I've ardently called at bad folks' homes for a few mere crumbs,
all just to placate this nasty belly of mine[12]
but now I can't fawn and flatter, praising repulsive folk.
Now that my life has turned so desolate, where's the reason
to go on living in this world? So, Shri Krishna,
you will win great fame if you come save me without delay.
 So please protect me...

What's the reason the Vedas speak of you as 'Lord of Wealth'?
What do you get out of treating me this way?
Each moment passes more slowly that a *yuga*
I see no way out of this, Govinda, there's no doubt.
If you don't rescue me it will surely be held against you
when your devotees in the future come to hear of this
  So be my Lord and protect me, give me safe shelter
  Ocean of mercy, there's no one else, there's only you to protect me![13]

Who's Great?

Are you the one who's great, O Shri Hari
Or are the great ones your devotees?

If one looks with care one can see
that you have become the servant of devotees;
though the Vedas always praise you as Lord Supreme
and the Ultimate Being, you, living in the palace
with Dharmaja and Arjuna, followed them gladly
whenever they called you, therefore, who is great?

You are considered to be Lord of the whole cosmos;
because of that you are extremely great.
If you are pleased with someone you can grant *moksha*
but if you turn around and serve as King Bali's gate man
how can we honestly say you are the most great?

On the big battleground, when Bhishma the great
shot his arrow at your forehead you responded
by picking up your discus, but when you saw the great
Bhisma take refuge in the protection of your name
you quietly went back to what you had been doing, so
are you the one who is most great?

You leaped right out of a solid stone pillar
in the Narasimha form, all for a small boy's sake;
so, Ranga Vithala, kind protector of devoted souls,
since you are found to be under the sway of those
who meditate on you – say who is the one
who should really be called great?
Are you the one who's great, O Shri Hari
Or are the great ones your devotees?[14]

Gopis, Enchanted by Krishna, Sing to a Bee

O Bhramara, Bumblebee,
seeing you we feel we see
our Lord, who is the beauty
of all beauties; tell me
is he happier there
where he lives now?
We've known the Uplifter
(who is the turtledove[15]
to those who love him)
ever since he was a baby.

O Bhramara, Bumblebee
our eyes feel tipsy
we've heard melodies

from the flute of Krishna,
foe of Madhu, entrancing
Madhukunja forest, and we
have forgotten our homes.
We're used to chasing
his musk-scent anointed body
glancing at the love-god's Lord.

O honey-guzzler Bumblebee,
how we were in love abuzz
feeling so overjoyed
when with our heads bowed
looking down at the ground
with Krishna embracing us
saying sweet words, feeding us
the nectar of his delicious lips ...
but he who always was
at play here in our midst
has turned so harsh-hearted
and didn't stay, he went away
he left us in this dust.[16]

Available to All

Can anyone obtain for nothing
the holy name of Rama?
Only those who've rid themselves
of the sins of birth after birth.

Only those who have held tightly
to the holy name of Hari
controlling their minds with
the *rasa* of bhakti, the flavour of
the soul's love.

Can anyone obtain for nothing
the holy name of Rama?

Only those with a free serene mind
forgetting their worries, planting
the form of the love god's father
deep inside their hearts can win it.

Can all and sundry obtain for nothing
the holy name of Rama?

You must keep before your eyes
the holy form you've planted inside
remembering Lord Purandara Vithala
who embodies overflowing bliss.

Can anyone at all obtain for nothing
the sacred name of Lord Rama?
Only those who have shed the sins
which in birth after birth they committed.[17]

Thus, in the songs of Shripadaraya, we find bhakti's promise that love is enough, that love is the necessary price. Logic may vary, times may change, failures and difficulties, trials and horrors may beset the bhakta, but with the basic bhakti flow of *prema*, the primary reality of spirituality, everything is still alright. Bhakti is the *sine qua non*, the wisdom in which grace (*daya*) and surrender (*prapatti*) meet in love, a melody engaging the members of life. Bhakti is non-linear, non-material, as are the neutrons breezing through us. Shripadaraya is one of the South Indians who, when asked what is the answer to life's problems, responded with confidence: it is love.

Shripadaraya's Most Celebrated Disciple: The Great Guru Vyasaraya

The story of Vyasaraya, who was Shripadaraya's great disciple, living from 1478 to 1539, is very instructive. When childless parents-to-be Lakshmi Bai and Ramacharya of Bannuru village by the Kaveri river were blessed by a sannyasin they soon had a child for whom they had prayed. The boy, who was later to be called

Figure 5.1   Shripadaraya (left) and Vyasaraya (right) in traditional iconography

Vyasaraya, pleased his parents in every way as he grew to manhood. Shripadaraya flourished during the time of Emperor Narasimha, who asked him to perform daily *puja* of Venkateshvara at Tirumala, Tirupati. Therefore both the guru Shripadaraya and his disciple, who was to become the sage Vyasaraya, went to the holy mountain to live. They served there for a dozen years. Vyasaraya was said to be so conscious of the purity of the mountain that he would climb downhill to relieve himself on less sacred ground – he could not bear to pollute in any way the sacred heights.

When Vyasaraya went to Vijayanagara after the 12 years at Tirupati, Krishnadevaraya, impressed with his piety and wisdom, asked him to be his guru. According to legend, when astrologers warned Krishnadevaraya that whoever occupied the throne at a certain inauspicious time would die, the king entrusted Vyasaraya with the role of temporarily occupying that dangerous position at the unpropitious time. In one miracle story Vyasaraya threw a robe on to the throne at the critical moment whereupon it burst into flames, absorbing the misfortune. The famous throne is preserved at the Vyasaraya *matha*. Vyasaraya taught Purandaradasa, Kanakadasa and other bhaktas; he also wrote Sanskrit texts, songs and verses. His debt to Shripadaraya is seen in their similarities; both sannyasins were composers and leaders inspiring others with fervour, and both were *rajagurus*, teachers of kings.[18] Like begets like. Tradition holds that Madhva was an incarnation of Hanuman, and Shripadaraya was an incarnation of Dhruva, and Vyasaraya was an incarnation of Prahlada.[19]

A Woman's Voice: Atukuri Molla, Self-assured Poet of the Weaver Caste

We have seen how Shripadaraya, the erudite religious leader from a priestly caste and humble economic background, expressed his piety in the common man's language and won admiration. Similarly, legends say that the lower-caste woman, Atukuri Molla, who may have lived in the sixteenth century or earlier, exalted herself through her literary flair to win the love and respect of many Telugu-speaking bhaktas.[20]

Molla, according to tradition, was born after her parents prayed to Shri Kantha Malleshvara for a child. She was the daughter of a *lingayat* potter named Kesana of Gopavaram village in what is now Nellore District, on the bank of the Pennar river. Molla means 'jasmine'. In one narration of her life it is said that she may have received this name through an astrologically-based custom. It is also said that her name was an auspicious indication of the fame she would have, spreading like fragrance. Also as a consequence of astrological signs any marriage plans for Molla were postponed, and she remained single. In this narration it is also said that astrology foretold the death of Molla's mother while Molla was still a child.[21] Molla took her studies seriously when she was sent to the village school, and showed piety in her daily visits to the Shiva temple. When she was 12 years old her father took her to Shrishailam for initiation rites, and there the family priest told Kesana that his daughter was destined to be a saint who would bring honour to the family. It may be that, although her father and mother were devotees of Shiva, worshipping him as Mallikarjuna and Mallikamba of Shrishailam, Molla probably worshipped Vishnu as well, in the avatar form of the dharmic ruler Rama.[22]

In a folktale it is said that Tenali Ramakrishna, the legendary philosopher-buffoon in the court of Krishnadevaraya, once challenged an old poet from Gopavaram: 'I bet you can't write a great work, and no one in your village can.' When she heard about this, Molla was outraged at this presumption about her village and vowed to compose a whole Ramayana in five days. When he heard about this vow Tenali Ramakrishna, always the clown, laughed wildly at the idea that a woman from a family of potters should have such a big ego. Nonetheless, tradition has it that Molla was inspired while drying her hair after her bath[23] – she would write Rama's story in a form which could be appreciated by the Telugu-speaking people. She sat in the temple, dedicated her mind, and found inspiration to tell the story in verse in just five days, showing the virtue of honest perspiration and untutored inspiration. The daughter of the potter could chant the language as well as any upper-caste poet, improvising her new telling of the ancient epic in 138 stanzas in six chapters.[24] Her Ramayana, which uses the minimum of Sanskrit words, was the most popular version in Telugu, pleasing nearly everyone with its natural flavour and its clear and down-to-earth eloquence.[25] Soon, it was considered a classic, quoted by grammarians to illustrate proper usage, and used by teachers to introduce students to the beauties and structures of the Telugu language.

Figure 5.2   Statue of Molla, one of 33 prominent figures of Teluga culture represented at Hussein Sagar Lake, Hyderabad, South India

The Voice of Atukuri Molla

Kesana, my father, was a very pious man,
amicable, dedicated to his guru,
and devoted to the Lord
in all the shapes the sacred takes,
stable and fluid.

He was deeply devoted to Shiva, and was a guru.
I'm known as Molla, the one
the gracious Lord gave him to be his daughter.

Now I make no claims as to linguistics,
that field for minds fully focused upon
sorting out indigenous words from foreign ones.

I never specialized in the exact laws
which govern the linkage of consonants and vowels
depending on their adjacent sounds,
and I have no vast vocabulary hoarded anywhere.
I'm neither grammar authority nor rhetorician,
I couldn't tell you the method of organizing a speech
and then getting up and orating even if I had to.
I'm not well versed in the finer points of style
and the subtle nuances of comparative distinction.

I have no credentials in the field of phonetics,
I can't spout declensions and root derivations,
I'm unschooled in tropes, or rhythms; the artifice
of prosody isn't my thing either.

I lack the formal training in writing poetry
and composing long narratives,
and I haven't scanned handbooks of style
or familiarized myself with lexicons of grammar

But only by the grace of the renowned Lord
Shri Kantha Mallesha, somehow I've been blessed –
I find that I am able to write these verses.

As immediately as the tongue tastes honey
– the sense of poetry should be that direct.

Obscure references and clutter-buried meanings
have about as much point
as a deaf person talking
 with a lifelong mute – why bother?

To write in the naturally mellifluous language
of Telugu, studded with folklore tidbits and proverbs
is to prepare a delectable banquet, able to please

the ears and minds of discerning folk
who have the good taste to enjoy this sumptuous feast.

The sun worked his way
slowly across the sky
progressing from East to West,
all the livelong day.
When he arrived finally,
sweaty and exhausted,
our eyes lost him as he dove
into the sea, where he bathed.

Molla celebrated Sita's beauty and self-sacrifice in verses of vivid imagery. The following passage compares her features with other known things.

Guess – lotus petals or love god arrows?
Sita's eyes make it hard to say

Guess – sweet birdsong or *apsarasas* singing?
her words confuse the brain.

Guess – the radiant moon or a gleaming mirror?
her face could be mistaken for either.

Guess – Two *chakravaka* birds or golden smooth jugs?
Her breasts inspire dizzying love.

Guess – gracefully contoured dune
or cupid's nuptial pavilion *mantapa*?
Her curved thighs look a lot like both.

Thus the senses of ordinary people were bewildered,
stunned by her natural elegance.

The following series of verses is in the voice of tribal women who look with sympathy upon Sita trudging through the forest, describing her hardships dramatically.

Look – how poor Sita's feet are bruised – she's not used
to walking through rough forests bristling with thorns.

Her graceful hands have lost their soft pale aura.
On this rough trek they've turned a shade more like pink sapphire.

Like a dried up vine tossed helplessly in a withering wind
Sita's delicate body trembles and quivers in this heat-wave.

Like a full moon on the wane, so gradually dimming,
Sita's face has begun to lose its usually charming glow

As she tried hard to keep up with Rama and Lakshmana's pace
Sita's breasts are heaving as she gasps, she's out of breath.

See how Sita glances scouting about for any patch of shade
to find some relief from the relentless sun's scorching rays.

The *phala-shruti* verse at the end of the epic poem tells of the fruits one reaps by reading and hearing the poem recited:

Listeners who are always hearing this story about Lord Rama,
who himself caused this story to be written,
as well as those who devotedly study this sacred narrative,
will gain the merciful grace of Lord Rama
and they will also reap earthly benefits.

The Molla Ramayana and the Rama Story as a Fractal Pattern

That description of Sita gives a small taste of the way in which Sita is depicted in the Molla Ramayana – with great vitality. It is, some scholars suggest, as if the author put some of her own life into the personality she wrote about. And, just as in the story told by Valmiki in which a washerman maligned Sita, casting aspersions on her chastity, some stodgy traditionalists (of the sixteenth century and later) said that, since Molla is the name of a flower, it must be a code word or a nickname for fallen women. These critics were suspicious on account of the fact that Molla never mentioned having a husband in her verses, wondering if she was perhaps a prostitute. Those who cannot imagine devotion's pull often fail to recognize it as a real force in the lives of others. The mean-spirited and envious often begrudge creativity which they cannot account for or control; they feel at a loss and lash out blindly. But whatever we might conjecture about Molla's obscure background, she was an inspired traditional poet fabricating a literary vision in story form which connected with the folk imagination and won an enthusiastic response.

Some say that when friends suggested she dedicate her work to the king and earn wealth she responded: 'Would a tongue used to praising the great Lord Rama ever stoop to flattering an ordinary human ruler? Would anyone who enjoys the rich sweetness of brown sugar (jaggery), be tempted to chew on a chunk of raw ginger root?' (According to other stories, the poem was dedicated to King Pratapa Rudra.)

The whole corpus of all the *Ramayana*s, the different versions, in different languages and dialects, with their different scales of length, in their various extensions and elaborations, in summaries and condensations, performances and depictions, might well be conceptualized as a great fractal. Considering it like this avoids the rigid linear view of some Oriental scholarship which assumed Valmiki was the definitive touchstone text, and that 'later interpolations' and the like existed merely as false subsequent versions to be discredited. The trend in recent scholarship[26] has been to consider non-Valmiki Ramayanas as important in their own right, and performances, debates, puppetry, songs and icons as important reflections of issues in the story as well. It seems useful to think of the Ramayana as a vast fractal which is not limited or defined by any one text of group of texts, but exists over the centuries as a system of multivalent signifiers which can be configured and elaborated in various ways, both heterodox and vernacular. The poet Kalidasa in his *Raghuvamsha* emphasized Rama's traits; later, Murari, in his own way, wrote verses to reiterate and extend our sense of Rama's greatness.

For those who love it (and even for those who despise it) the Ramayana has often been a second language, a communication resource to affirm, deny or reshape the existing social order. Each telling is a replay, adapting basic aspects of the story-fractal, conveying human feelings and religious ideas through the characters, geography and action. Although this flexibility may seem like 'white noise' in its ability to become any sound to any listener, each telling also has organic dimensions of creative processes and cultural migrations – growth of form follows function. Use of the story in Bali or Thailand was shaped according to certain needs in the cultures of those geographic regions. The Rama story is a fractal *darshan* of fertile images, as creative religious imagination reaches beyond old limits to synthesize needed reflections of experience within limits of recognizability in given communities.

In Telugu literature the *Ranganatha Ramayana*, written by Kona Buddharaja, was the first summary of the Ramayana in the *dvipada* metre, a comparatively simple form of couplets popular in Andhra in the thirteenth century. This version later attracted Kings Kacha and Vithala, who supplemented it. With such literature in the language of the people, devotion to Rama and his story expanded.

Shri Natha (1365–1420) translated the *Ramayana* into Telugu in a way that incorporated more Sanskrit words into the language, and this Sanskritized Telugu became a standard form towards which later great works aspired. The *Bhaskara Ramayana*, which many in Andhra Pradesh would say is the best and most widely read, is about three-fifths the length of the *Valmiki Ramayana*. It is in the *campu* form, a mixture of prose and poetry, follows the Shri Natha mode and was influenced by Nannaya who translated the Mahabharata epic in the eleventh century. Several authors worked on the *Bhaskara Ramayana*, including Bhaskara's son Mallikarjuna Bhatta. Hullakki Bhaskara's grandson, Tikkana, wrote a Telugu *Mahabharata* and the *Nirvachanottara Ramayana*, developing an episode not explored in other versions. Since there was no sense of a fixed and finished story – a closed canon – regional poets who were open to inspiration could create new spin-offs and sing the story in their own words; hence the *Ramayana* of Errapraggada, Molla's *Ramayana* composed in the 1500s, the Ramayana of Chitrakavi Ramakavi, the *Accha Tenugu Ramayanam* of Kuchimanchi Timmakavi, the *Vichitra Ramayanam* of Velpuri Venkateshvara Kavi, *Vepakshi Ramayanam* of Gopinatham Venkatakavi, *Ramabhyudayam* by Ayyalaraju Ramabhadra Kavi, as well as those which are lost, such as Vemalavada Bhimakavi's *Vashishtha Ramayanam*. These are only some of the Telugu *Ramayanas*.[27] There are also brief versions, song cycles, dance-dramas, puppet shows and singer-saints' songs which celebrate the story in a small-scale epitome form.

In various ways traditional poets enact time-honoured stories and sacred facets of human experience in lively 'language-games' that are repeated in a new way, evoking the unity of self-similarity to other versions of the Rama story systematically and vividly in fresh styles. The best tellings are both familiar and distinct, repeated and new, fractally self-similar and in flow with the whole body of literature. Read from a great distance in terms of time and place, their voices seem related, of a whole; they are like varied timbres of one voice and echoing countervoices as they invoke the same mythos from various points of departure. Looked at closely, they are divergent, with different personalities. Molla herself, although she maintained that the earlier poets were an inspiration to her,[28] captured the Rama story in her own way, and in so voicing it she attracted the imagination and gratitude of Telugu-speaking people for many generations.

Molla Today

Modern readers may find it strange, but in India old stories live on, and the poets seem to live again and yet again. The past is not simply past in India, because devout people celebrate the saints, enact their stories, sing their songs and recite their poems. Belief in reincarnation also plays a part in this ongoing recycling of the religious past. For example, Molla is now considered in the newly originated Sambhavi Tantrism to have been an incarnation of the Goddess Sambhavi, first mentioned in the *Kaula Upanishad*.[29] Some South Indians believe that when the Vijayanagara empire fell to invaders, Molla asked Vishnu for help, and Vishnu assured her that the Molla Ramayana would survive.[30] They also believe that Vishnu's Kalki incarnation was born in the mid-twentieth century in South India (in Nemam near Chennai) and that Sambhavi was born as his daughter. (Given the choice of birth as a child or as a 400 year-old lady, Sambhavi chose the latter and opted to live in Gopavaram where she is cared for by children in the neighbourhood.) Seekers petition Sambhavi, with the help of her devotee, Bhrithya, for health, material benefits and relief from various vexations. Bhrithya regularly chants the Molla *Ramayana* in a previously unknown raga, the Sambhavi raga.[31]

One last point, regarding the philosophical source and 'democratic' results of bhakti poets using their mother tongues in India, ought to be made. There have been great poets in all of the various schools of Hindu thought. Though they differed on the soul's ultimate relationship with the Absolute – on whether it remains in nearness or merges into sameness – *the three major Hindu schools of theology – advaita* (ultimate non-duality of soul and God); *dvaita* (eternal duality of soul and God), and *vishishthadvaita* (qualified non-dualism of proximity and mingling without identity of soul and God) – *did not dispute the nature of consciousness behind all existence*: it is infinite, subtler than the subtlest, and therefore more complex than the most complex and simpler than the simplest. The Upanishads had spelled that out; *dvaita*, which does not envision the soul ever merging absolutely in pure divine consciousness, recognized its existence; *advaita* held it in high regard, yet still had a place in the total scheme of things for bhakti, which bespeaks a dualisim. (Even if the authorship of certain songs attributed to Shankara is disputed, Hindu tradition as a whole has tended to think of him as encompassing bhakti as a stage on the way to ultimate liberation.)[32] Thus there are underlying unities among the various schools and their poets.

Ramanujacharya's influence stopped growing in the South after its initial impact, but it took root, spread and grew in Northern India by way of the bhakti saint Ramananda who, after failing to see eye-to-eye (on the issue of monism?) with his own guru went to Banaras and taught many *bhaktas*.[33] Madhvacharya's influence, along with the inspiring religious imaginations of poets of passionate love imagery such as Chandidas and Vidyapati, seems to have made an impression on Chaitanya. Vallabha influenced the bhakti of Gujerat, land of saints Narasimha Mehta and Mirabai. Thus, '[f]rom the philosophical schools arose a Democratical Mysticism which laid stress upon the vernaculars as the media of mystical teaching... property of all', as R.D. Ranade has noted.[34]

The two poets discussed in this chapter, Shripadaraya and Molla, vividly illustrate Ranade's point. Bhakti at its best, offers a spiritual path of devotion and comradeship open to the many – a path of individuals singing their own experiences in their very own tongues.

Notes

1   *Dasakuta* means junction or association (*kuta*) where servants (*dasa*s) or devotees of Vishnu (especially in the form of Krishna) from the four directions congregate together. Shripadaraya was the guru of Vyasaraya, who established the 'family of Haridasas' on a firm footing. Known as the Haridasas these devotees of Vishnu followed a system of Vaishnavism according to the teachings of the great *dvaita* leader, Madhva. *Dvaita* means dualism, referring to the soul and God being ultimately separate, rather than merged in union, as *advaita* holds. The *dasa*s were initiated by a Madhva guru, and a number of famous *dasa* composers were devoted to Vishnu as Vithala. They were usually married men, rather than monks, but they owned no property and lived on what they gleaned on their wanderings, singing and receiving alms. The *dasakuta* can be traced back to a series of *smarta* devotees, according to V. Raghavan, starting with Achalanandadasa. It was carried on by generations of Madhva-school *bhakta*s – Narahari Tirtha (thirteenth century), Shripadaraya (fifteenth century), Vyasaraya, Purandaradasa and Kanakadasa (fifteenth–sixteenth century).

2   Hulugur Krishnacharya, 'Music Under the Vijayanagara Empire', *Vijayanagara Sexcentenary Commemoration*, Dharwar: Vijayanagara Empire Sexcentenary Association, 1936, p. 375.

3   The seven *talas* of the *suladi* are *dhruva, mathya, rupaka, jhampa, triputa, atta,* and *eka tala*. See Salva Krishnamurthy (tr., ed. and comm.), *Tunes of Divinity: Sankirtana Laksanamu*, Madras: Institute of Asian Studies, 1990, p. 54.

4   K. Appannacharya (ed.), *Karnataka Haridasas*, Tirupati: Tirumala Tirupati Devasthanams, 1984, p. 4.

5   Not to be confused with Svami Haridasa of North India.

6   G. Srinivasan, *The Haridasas of Karnataka*, Belgaum: Academy of Comparative Philosophy and Religion, 1972, pp. 17–19.

7   A.P. Karmarkar and N.B. Kalamdani, *Mystic Teachings of the Haridasas of Karnataka*, Dharwar: Karnatak Vidyavardhak Sangha, 1937, pp. 31–32. My renderings of Shripadaraya's songs are based on texts in this book.

8   Ibid., pp. 32–33.

9   Madhva's theory of difference is very important to his system. God, souls and matter are the three main realities in Madhva's view, and the differences are explored in a very nuanced way. The creed consists of five dualisms: God and matter; God and souls; souls and matter; one soul and another soul; various objects of matter. See B.N.K. Sharma, *Philosophy of Sri Madhvacarya*, Delhi: Motilal Banarsidass, 1986, pp. 92–101.

10 'The eight' probably refers to the *ashtadurguna*, the eight faults: lack of compassion, anxiety, jealousy, lack of cleanliness, fatigue, inauspiciousness, wretchedness and violence.

11 Karmarkar and Kalamdani, *Mystic Teachings of the Haridasas of Karnataka*, pp. 33–34.

12 This kind of confession about humbling oneself for support is found in Purandaradasa's songs as well.

13 Karmarkar and Kalamdani, *Mystic Teachings of the Haridasas of Karnataka*, pp. 34–35.

14 Ibid., pp. 35–36.

15 'Chakora' is equivalent to the nightingale or turtledove, according to C.P. Brown's Dictionary: Telugu – English, 2nd rev. edn, Madras: Asian Educational Services, 1979–80. First published 1905.

16 Karmarkar and Kalamdani, *Mystic Teachings of the Haridasas*, pp. 37–38. Jnaneshwara (1274–1296) wrote a bhakti song with this imagery of the bee, as did other Hindu singer-saints.

17 *Dasara Padagala Samgrahavu*, vol. III, Belgaum: Sriramatattva Prakasa Printing Press, 1947, p. 8. This kind of question is found in a number of later South Indian singer-saints' songs: Purandaradasa, Tyagaraja and others.

18 K. Appannacharya, *Sri Vyasarayalu*, tr. V. Suryanarayana Rao, Tirupati: TTD, 1983. See also B.N.K. Sharma, *A History of Dvaita School of Vedanta*, vols I and II, Bombay: Booksellers Publishing, 1960.

19 Hanuman, Prahlada and Dhruva are famous archetypal devotees of Vishnu in Vaishnava mythology.

20 Susie Tharu and K. Lalita (eds), *Women Writing in India: 600 BC to the Present* vol. I, New York: Feminist Press, 1991, pp. 94–98.

21 V.S. Srinivasan, 'Molla: The Saint Poetess of Andhra', at http://www.tirumala.org/sapthagiri/112002/molla.htm.

22 A number of other South Indian authors from Shaivite backgrounds including Potana, Bilva Mangala, and Tyagaraja, are also famous for their verses to forms of Vishnu.

23 This part of the story, about Molla's moment of inspiration, is from Udaya Rao's translation from Kesavapantulu Narasimha Sastry's introduction to the *Molla Ramayana*. See note below.

24 According to Udaya Rao the poem is in 900 verses, in a variety of ten metres used in Telugu poetry. These stanzas are from two to eight lines each.

25 *Mollaramayanam* ed. *Rentala Gopalakrishna* India: n.p., n.d., 1969. This Telugu edition of Molla's *Ramayana* is in the original Telugu and is 184 pages long. There is also an edition of the *Molla Ramayana* published in Kurnool and Madras: Balasaraswati Book Depot, 1987.

26 For example, Paula Richman (ed.), *Many Ramayanas: The Diversity of a Narrative Tradition in South Asia*, Berkeley: University of California Press, 1991.

27 Much of the information in this paragraph is based on parts of T. Rajagopala Rao's *A Historical Sketch of Telugu Literature*, New Delhi: Asian Educational Services, 1984, pp. 48–63, 120–125. Thanks also to Udaya Rao for his translation of Molla's story, and information about *Ramayanas*.

28 She mentions Nachana Soma, Bhima, Nannaya, Shrinatha, Ranganatha, and Tikkana. Introduction to *Molla Ramayana*, translated by Udaya Rao.

29 *The Kaula Upanishad*, tr. Mike Magee, London?: Worldwide Tantra Project, 1995.

30 Molla *Ramayana* is one of the first classical Telugu works which is now accessible via the internet. The entire Telugu script text is at http://www.andhrabharati.com/itihAsamulu/rAmAyaNamu/avatArika.html

31   This information is from a lecture given by Udaya Rao of Pittsburgh, Pennsylvania, at the Twelfth International Congress of Vedants, Miami University, Oxford, Ohio, 16 September 2000. These devotees of Molla believe she was born through the deity Shrikantha Malleswara. They say it was astrologically predicted she would remain single, and she did. The *Molla Ramayana*, intro. K. Narasimha Sastri, Chennai: Balasarswati Book Depot, 1987, is available in Telugu. Udaya Rao has translated and written about this topic in English.

32   Mrudula M. Marfatia, *The Philosophy of Vallabhacarya*. Delhi: Munshiram Manoharlal, 1967; J.G. Shah, *Shri Vallabhacharya: His Philosophy and Religion*. Nadiad: Pushtimargiya Pustakalay, 1969.

33   Besides the impact made on the expansive guru Ramananda's bhakti movement, Ramanuja's vashishthadvaita teachings also influenced Vallabhacharya's *suddhadvaita* teachings, and Chaitanya's *achintya bhedabheda* (simultaneous difference and identity beyond logic).

34   R.D. Ranade, *Mysticism in India*, Albany, NY: SUNY, 1983. First published Pune 1933.

CHAPTER 6

Popular Worldly Wisdom in the Oral Literature of Vemana and Baddena

Unforgettable Eccentric: The Life of Thoroughly Disillusioned Vemana

During the Vijayanagara era some Telugu poets seemed to be revolting against artificial formalities, falseness and pretensions, seizing on the language of everyday life as a means to reveal truths, criticize and rejoice. Folklore, proverbs and other colloquial expressions had a great vitality. Stilted grammar, Sanskrit terms and old-fashioned formalities lacked the zest and flavour of everyday life. Why shouldn't a poet sing in the living dialects of spoken language? Potana, who was born around 1400, put the gist of the Sanskrit text *Shrimad Bhagavata Purana* into his own Telugu. Annamacharya (1408–1503) sang Telugu lyrics of devotion which echoed expressions used by his contemporaries on the backroads of the countryside, rather than using classical Sanskrit. Shripadaraya (1422–1480) did the same in the Kannada language, and others did it in their own regional languages as well. Works which become an enduring part of a living folk tradition are often based on, and built from, already existing folk elements and patterns. Vemana was a poet who probably lived in the fourteenth–fifteenth century or later.[1] His poems became proverbial among Telugu-speaking people because he put his sharp observations, trenchant criticism and wary wisdom in colloquial verse in Telugu. He was a master of a short form of verse called the *ataveladi* (literally, 'dancing girl' meter) in which he composed over 400 poems. Through these, which voiced curt critiques in a humorous way, he became widely known as a madcap folk poet.

The traditional picture of Vemana, the one found on the paper covers of booklets of his verses, shows a naked man sitting on the ground, surrounded by the ultimate debris of life – skulls and bones – under a tree, in the midst of jungle leaves with a serpent hanging down from a vine. There Vemana sits alone, contemplating existence. It is the archetypal image of a thoroughly disillusioned solitary yogi. Sometimes the same pondering figure is seated on an animal skin under a tree with a bowl of fruit before him and stream flowing nearby. In both cases he is portrayed as the timeless thinker gazing into eternity, saying what he observes, not caring that some may dislike his message, just as Kabir did in the North. The common people learned his words by heart; the ideas he tossed off in a catchy metrical form danced with a generative life of their own, spreading by word of mouth, and soon were translated into neighbouring regional languages – Kannada, Tamil and Malayalam.

Some say that Vema was born in Moogachintapalle, in Chandragiri Taluk, in what is now Chittoor District in south-eastern Andhra Pradesh. The poet-yogi probably came from a Reddi family, a community of agriculturalists and merchants,[2] and some of his verses seem to reflect his background: '... This farmer Vemana engaged all men's minds and was good at teaching people, and so he became famous.'[3] An unusual number of verses pertain to the customary measurements of land and disputes about boundaries – a concern of farmers.[4] Others are about alchemy:[5] in some tales it is said that, in the early stages of his career, Vemana sought the secrets of alchemy, desiring to transmute base metals into gold. He was also born into a family with a name sometimes associated in legends with this quest.

His ancestors are traceable to a merchant named Vema who lived centuries before Vemana came along. According to legend, the merchant Vema once went to Shrisaila, the mountain which is a pilgrimage site, a place sacred to Shiva as Mallikarjuna, 'Lord white as jasmine', from ancient times. In those days it was a wilderness, and the temple tank, according to folklore, had the power to change iron into pure gold. When the other pilgrims had left for home, Vema scouted around. The temple elders told him to leave the premises, but Vema pleaded, 'I came a great distance to worship Lord Shiva. Please don't try to stop me now.' The priests said, 'Avoid the north side of the temple; fierce creatures live in the jungle there. No one is allowed into that area.' Vema suspected that this was a ploy to keep him away from the temple tank. Leaving a trail of mustard seeds (rather like Hansel and Gretel in the European fairytale left a trail of breadcrumbs), risking all, Vema went in search of the sacred water. Finding it, he filled two vessels with the magical fluid to take with him.

Searching for his mustard seed trail, he discovered that the seeds had sprouted. He followed the path of sprouts, left the mountain and went to Hanumakonda, a nearby village. Hungry, Vema hid the waterpots in a farmer's shed and went to find people of his own caste to try to get something to eat.

When the farmer who owned the shed, Donti Aliya Reddi, came to realize there was magic water in his shed, he lost no time in taking the pots into his home. Not long after that, the shed burned down, and Vema came running to save his pots of water. He ran right into the flames and smoke, and perished.

Donti Aliya Reddi gradually became a wealthy man. But as he grew richer, his children kept dying. When just a single son was left, Aliya Reddi saw Vema in a dream. He cried for forgiveness, and Vema said, 'Have an image of me made, of pure gold. Put the image in your shrine room and faithfully offer devotion. When your wife delivers boy children name them Vema. Your family will grow and will one day rule the whole region.'

Aliya Reddi followed the instructions heard in the dream, and his son, Prolaya Vema Reddi eventually became ruler of nearby Kondaveedu province. In the fourteenth century members of the family ruled Kondaveedu one generation after another, and in 1382 Komaragiri Vema became king. He had two sons – one a merchant named Venka Reddi, and the other Anavema Reddi. Vema Reddi was to become Vemana the poet. Such is one legend of his ancestry. Other stories link Vema to other centuries, both earlier and later. Some say that he was born in 1652 and that his mother died when he was quite young. When his father married again, Vema's stepmother mistreated him. In these tales Vema became infatuated with a *devadasi* when he heard her singing in *Todi raga*. She was also attracted to him. Her mother, a faded beauty, encouraged the couple's mutual affections only as long as it brought her a new source of income.

When the couple began spending lots of time together, and the mother found herself no better off than she was before, she insisted that Vemana bring her some valuables. Unless he could bring her jewellery of his brother's wife, which the girl's mother had admired from a distance, Vemana would no longer be welcome.

Vemana went home, pined and felt pained for a couple of days. His sister in law, noticing that he was not eating, asked him what his problem was. 'The mother of the woman I'm in love with has asked me to bring her jewels like yours. I don't know what to do.'

His sister-in-law laughed at his problem, shook her head, and gave him some of her jewellery. When he gave the jewels to his lady love she greedily grabbed them, her eyes full of crazy hunger. Vemana thought of his sister-in-law's sweet generosity: her virtue was so much more meaningful than the ugly avarice of the girl he was ready to die for. He felt like a fool. Out of his confused state, a new clarity and understanding of his fate came into focus.[6] (In some tellings, the courtesan asked for the sister-in-law's nose ring. She agreed on the condition that the courtesan let Vemana see her wearing nothing but the nose ring. She agreed. When Vemana saw her with nothing else on he was repulsed, lost all attraction to her and became the wandering 'naked one' himself.[7])

In one story Vemana's elder brother was ruling a province in which there was a jewellery, ornament and decoration and industrial centre. A man named Abhiramacharya was a goldsmith there. When Vemana was given a job as supervisor of the jewellery workshop he noticed that Abhiramacharya was always late for work. Though warned, he continued to be late, and finally informed Vemana that he could not come in any earlier, and that he was working later to make up for lost time. His curiosity aroused, Vemana decided to spy on the goldsmith to learn his secret. He followed the goldsmith one day and observed him washing and performing *puja*, before he entered a cave carrying fruits and flowers. In the cave a *yati* (holy man) was performing *tapas*, acts of austerity. The *yati* blessed the goldsmith: 'I am happy with your dedicated service to me. Tomorrow I enter *samadhi*, so please come before dawn.' Hearing this, Vemana devised a trick.

He told Abhiramacharya to stay in the workshop, not letting him out because 'The palace has demanded certain items be made immediately'. Then, the following day, before dawn, Vemana took flowers and fruit to the *yati*'s cave.

'Abhiramacharya is not coming today?' asked the *yati*.

'Because so much work had to be done for the palace, he sent me, his disciple', Vemana explained. 'Bless me with your mantra.'

The holy man looked right through Vemana and then gave him the blessing on one condition: 'When you have realization of the truth of my blessings, you must first pass the wisdom to Abhiramacharya and then receive it from him again. It's the just order of things.'

Vemana received the wisdom from the teacher, but to have gained the power of the sacred *mantra* through trickery felt wrong in his conscience. He ran to Abhiramacharya and fell at his feet, blurting out his offence and asking forgiveness. The goldsmith knew that what was done was done. Trust means vulnerability to betrayal; forgiveness releases both betrayer and betrayed. Bitter rancour does not yield wisdom. So Abhiramacharya forgave Vemana, and, receiving the *yati*'s last words through him, gave them back to Vemana, as a teacher would.

Disillusioned with dreams of love and wealth, and now guided by a spiritual wisdom which allowed him to observe the ways of the world for himself and to discern the deepest truths, Vemana became indifferent to conventional householder life and wandered the roads as a mendicant. He became a yogi concerned with transforming his life into spiritual gold, rather than accumulating shiny metal.[8] While on the road, he used his energetic mind to compose pithy teachings in verse – or so the legends which villagers have kept alive tell us. Some who encountered him thought him mad. Occasionally in verses he even calls himself *verri* Vema, 'mad Vema', or refers to his reputation in other ways: 'The discerning words which Vemana speaks/and his outrageous madcap ways/sting the real fools with sharp critiques/while wise men smile with what he says.'[9] In one verse he says that the rituals and prayers, meditation and veneration of ancestors he performed enabled him to become a poet.[10]

Vemana was an eclectic folk philosopher who drew on ideas from Virashaiva concepts, Tantric Shaivism, Buddhist teachings, Vedanta and yoga, and from proverbs and other aspects of the collective wisdom of India from five or six centuries ago. Not a strict sectarian or systematizer, in his verses he simplified and popularized esoteric teachings. He was eclectic, like Gandhi in the twentieth century and New Age people today, gathering from various sources the vocabulary and views suiting his own spirituality. In Vemana's view all humans share mortality, so arguing over differences is foolish; Shiva and Vishnu are different names for the same being, so broad-mindedness is called for.[11]

The usual ending of each of his verses was 'Vishvadabhirama *vinura* Vema', meaning, according to some, 'What Vishva (my guru) and Abhirama (*acharya*) told Vema'. Others, however, interpret the ambiguous alliterative words as, 'Vema, who is able to amuse the whole world with his meaningful verses',[12] and they are also commonly interpreted as 'You who are dear to the giver of all, listen, O Vema', or 'that's the way it goes in the world'. As a man of solitude his bemused dialogues were with himself, and this is reflected in his lines.[13]

It is interesting that a poet named Sarvajna, living at approximately the same time as Vemana, was writing similarly trenchant and memorable witty verses in the Kannada language. In the Vijayanagara empire both Telugu and Kannada were important languages spoken by many people. Tamil, as the empire cumulatively continued to expand and move south, was also an important regional language spoken by a vast populace of the Vijayanagara empire, with its own great store of proverbs, folk wisdom and verses. Some people have likened Vemana to Tiruvalluvar, the Tamil author of the *Tirukural*, proverbial wisdom in couplets written over 1500 years ago.

Verses and sayings which live in everyday speech have a way of spreading and transmuting, so anyone collecting them from old manuscripts encounters some problems.[14] The collections of Vemana's verses often evoke the eloquent voice of someone who is perceptive, someone so self-confident and relaxed that he knows how he personally feels about things and is unafraid to say it – a rare combination. Below we consider some of his poems to get a sense of the images that attract him and the themes that he explores.

Figure 6.1 Typical depiction of Vemana in popular South Indian culture

The Voice of Vemana

> Desire's drive can turn one soul into a poet, another into the sun.
> The drive of desire impels the freedom-seeker's obsession.
> Desire creates poet and sun; affinity climaxes in the embrace of love.[15]

This frank acceptance of the libido as a deep force in nature and culture is expressed by Vemana in another verse depicting his honest appraisal of attraction to the opposite sex as a typically human vulnerability:

> Piety forgets its way when knocked out by the taste
> of love's lips. Beauty makes sharp minds seem dull.
> Even spiritual men sometimes go blank when faced
> with alluring charm, vulnerable to life's tidal pulls.[16]

> The wills of kings constantly lean toward war;
> Sages always bend their minds toward the sacred;
> Body-bound men passionately obsess on the sexy –
> Men's minds vary, they all think as they're inclined.[17]

> The drone is well acquainted
> with each layer of the honeycomb
> and the black honeybee knows
> where the most nectary flowers grow;
> just so, the devoted soul knows
> just where to find the heart's goal.[18]

Just as Vemana rejects formal grammar for the living language, so he rejects formal religious exercises done without deeper attention and intention: 'Dishes without clean utensils, and worship of Shiva without mental purity, are useless.' He makes the same point again and again, mocking pretensions in different ways:

> Why waste your time in a temple built lovingly of mere stone
> when you can see for yourself living Shiva directly on your own?
> Fools worship stones, imagining that the stones are Shiva;
> Can't you see ultimate reality in your heart where it lives?[19]

> If folks could achieve *moksha* just
> by bobbing their bodies in a sacred river
> shouldn't a duck who never sins, always
> dipping in the same water, likewise be delivered?[20]

> One does not become a true wandering sage
> merely by shaving one's head, and smearing lots of ash
> all over one's body, or by practising yoga;
> it's more essential to have inner purity, O Vema.[21]

It's possible to pulverize a huge boulder;
even whole hills of stone can be crushed into fine dust.
But a man can have a mind so stubborn
that nothing can melt it or even make it budge –
That's what I call true hard-heartedness.[22]

A man who owns up to his ignorance has intelligence;
one who claims omniscience is really stupid.
The most excellent person knows when to shut up
And avoid dead-end tangles, not aloof but prudent.[23]

The lowly wretch envies the great.
Like dogs who explode into barking
whenever a noble man comes near
riding a fine horse: the two co-appear.[24]

In slinging barbs Vemana was a non-sectarian equal-opportunity critic – everyone was
fair game, rich and poor, priest and king, Vaishnava and Shaiva. He felt secure enough
to ridicule the orthodox and conventional, the pious performing their rites by rote:

O asses rolling balls of rice, offering them to crows,
thinking you're linking up with your departed loved ones –
answer me, if you know: are your ancestors dung-eating crows?
Hear me, Vema, the one who gives the world bliss.[25]

When folks hear a lizard make an auspicious chattering
they are thrilled at the sign their undertakings will work out.
If things go wrong they blame it on destiny. Hear me,
Vema, giver of joy to the world; they've got it all figured out.[26]

Brahman priests gather, chant gobbledeegook just right
and it becomes official; presto! the two are man and wife.
If priests *really knew* how to pick the best time
why would hubby then die leaving his widow all alone?
Listen to me, Vema, giver of joy to the world.[27]

Like unforgettable folk tunes, the wit of these colloquial verses often produces a
surprise that tickles the (often suppressed) critical sensibility in the listener and
generates a chuckle. In the original there is a rhythmic play of drumbeat words
conveying a sudden flight of images and connections:

If a Turk trekks to Tirupati
that doesn't make him a Vaishnavite.
If a whore visits the sacred city of Banaras
she doesn't turn lily-white.
If a dog bathes in the auspicious Godaveri
does he become a great lion?
Hear, O Vema, the world's delight.[28]

> In creation everything's equal, none is worth more or less.
> Claims of superiority in a religion have no meaning.
> What's the point of saying Shaiva or Vaishnava is best?
> Shiva *bhakta*s die and are buried; Vishnu *bhakta*s are cremated.
> Does this make any difference in divinity?[29]

The rebel poet Vemana seemed to say 'To each his own', and no doubt some of his barbs stirred resentment amongst some custodians of taste. It is said that some irritated higher-ups in the hierarchy of Andhra society tried to suppress his ideas and keep them from gaining currency, but the verses seemed to have a life of their own. Enough people spontaneously responded to the points he made, and the way he made them, that the verses eluded censorship and stayed alive in conversations, even if official scholarship denied them entry into the ranks of great Telugu writing for centuries. Ordinary people liked his frank observations and sceptical wisdom, and during the 1800s Europeans also collected his verses and published them.[30] Here are some more examples of his trenchant verses which speak up for the sincere soul's magnanimity, and against caste stereotyping and hypocrisy.

A good title for this one would be: 'Consider the Source':

> A little spoon of sacred cow's milk is deemed precious;
> a whole bucket of jackass milk is worthless.
> A humble little handful of food offered with reverence
> is a worthy gift: its pure source makes it a treasure.[31]

Some of Vemana's verses reflect on the world's injustices and meanness of spirit:

> Think of the wise as the highest caste in any society;
> consider the ignorant as the lowest caste in any society.[32]

> Folks pay honour to men who are wealthy
> even if they're mean and nasty
> even if they're ignorant,
> and act like people's enemies.[33]

> People are seldom generous to the poor
> compared to the way they give to rulers;
> A ruler stays happy if they give him his due.
> Otherwise he extorts it; none give much to the poor.[34]

> In the world as we know it if you desire
> to kill a miser no poison will be required;
> another way exists, and it's sure to satisfy –
> ask the miser for some money, he's sure to die.[35]

> It's good for people to have some money
> but better to have also a generous mind
> which enables them to see and to give freely
> to worthy causes and not pretend they're blind.[36]

Some verses remind us of deep principles such as one's inevitable dependence on participation in one's environment:

> Virtuosity isn't everything – a crocodile in his home waters
> makes short work of an elephant; on dry land even a dog
> can take that crocodile without even breaking into a pant –
> one's domain, and one's position in it, also play a big role.[37]

Vemana offers a view from outside the tender trap of family, and from beyond the cells of caste hierarchy, professional investment and religious sectarianism. As a yogi, Vemana wanted to dissolve the scars of his memories, his *vasanas* and *samskaras* (impressions made by experiences, which determine future experiences). In this way he desired to transcend his mind and reach the formless – *moksha*. As a folk poet wandering through the lives of South India his aim was to make a mark, create memorable impressions, have his voice heard and cause spiritual echoes.

> There are so many varieties of jewellery but only one gold;
> though cows are of different colours milk is one and the same;
> numerous kinds of flowers are all used for the same worship;
> multiple religions exist but ultimate reality is one – hear, Vema.[38]

> Though there are different castes, and personalities vary,
> human beings are all of one and the same race.
> All cotton shares a basic sameness, though pillows vary.
> Spiritual consciousness is affirmed by all faiths, Vema.[39]

> To remedy illness one requires medication;
> the condition of darkness is dispelled with light.
> To solve substantial problems takes imagination;
> to get rid of ignorance one needs a learned guide.[40]

Vemana harps on the issue of discernment: disasters threaten when the genuine and the fake, the valuable and the unworthy, cannot be distinguished:

> If even agreeable water buffaloes well fed with bran
> will sometimes kick and refuse to be milked
> isn't it understandable that courtesans baulk
> at pleasing their johns unless they're paid in advance?[41]

> The lowly are adored if they're wealthy,
> the high, if they're poor, get no respect.
> Therefore, even more important than birth,
> what brings fame and glory is a man's wealth.[42]

> A person boasting membership in a great lineage,
> a proud scholar who has mastered much knowledge,
> a high-caste man – all these are mere children of the servants
> of the man who has gold – hey Vema, beloved by the world.[43]

Serve as much as you will, strive as hard as you're able,
You can't trust royalty. Contact with them is dangerous.
It's like making friends with poisonous snakes. Hear, Vema.[44]

A family's reputation can be destroyed utterly
if only one member's behaviour is unworthy.
If a single insect burrows into the sugar cane
its sweetness will be drained out entirely.[45]

Though knowledge be as small as a nail,
if it is honestly won by a virtuous man
by dint of his decency it can grow big as a hill.
A man without the least bit of virtue will
be blind to all of the good done to him, and
won't appreciate knowledge even if it's big as a hill.[46]

Once a courtesan always a courtesan –
she must be kept in her place. She can never be a queen.
The thief of rice offerings intended for the dead
does not wish you well, but looks forward to your end.
Listen to me, I know what I have seen.[47]

Valmiki the transgressor by repeating Rama's name
became wise as a brahman priest, though he had been a robber.
The status of caste is not what brings true fame
but one's inner truth, one's genuine character. Hear Vema.[48]

Face it. Neem will always be bitter,
even after a millenium steeped in milk.
A traitor can try what he will,
but lose baseness, acquire nobility?
I say he'll never leave his ilk.[49]

A person looks at the world with the power of eyesight –
a person can only see himself with the help of a mirror.
But to realize the true nature of the soul deep inside
one must cultivate a deeper vision of the inner Self, the spiritual 'I'.[50]

There's no need to speak of a decent man's caste.
Having virtue gives a man boundless worth.
Lack of virtue is what determines lack of worth.
Birth in a caste doesn't matter as much as virtue's birth.[51]

Vemana, like the Italian poet Dante, lost the love of his life early on. Both Vemana and Dante were unable to entertain the court; they had no desire to cater to worldly conventions. Both wandered without solace from this world, absorbed in their own reflections, composing unforgettable verses. Neither of these two poets could look at folly without seeing its consequences and saying something about it in memorable concise poetry. This trait was not likely to endear them to fools, but it was useful to those who wished to make a point sharply – they could quote trenchant verses to make their points. And both poets appreciated true spiritual worth and celebrated it musically.

Rough talk, critical thinking, and depictions of the underside of society and unconscious activities gave Vemana's verse the power of realism. Like Alexander Pope, Vemana hurled well-honed insults at guilty parties and hit many of his targets with his well-aimed barbs. His verses form a hectoring pulpit from which he made direct hits on those who took for granted the easy ways of the sensual world, conformed to fashion and blindly lived for mere likes and dislikes. Are his verses humorously frank realism, jaundiced cynicism or misanthropy? Perhaps it all depends on the reader's viewpoint.

The following verse probably expresses a rather traditional sentiment:

> A true wife never contradicts her husband;
> one who always contradicts him is like a big curse.
> Better he should leave her to her own fate,
> And go live alone, wandering in the wilderness.[52]

But some of Vemana's verses go too far, and would be offensive to a modern audience. We might title the following verse 'Lowly Sources'.

> From the part of the body made for taking a leak
> humans are born. From the union of wife's and husband's
> places of taking leaks all human beings are conceived.
> Why all this affection for life, which is born a kin of piss?[53]

Vemana's thoughts on the human body are often quite negative. In verses like the following one Vemana represents a strain of South Indian asceticism that devalues the body, showing no amazement at its abilities, no celebration of what it makes possible, but focusing only on its limits and lacks.

> Stomach equals garbage bag.
> Fact: the whole human body
> equals a structure of bones
> and ephemeral skin and flesh.
> So how did you get so fond
> of your own pile of rubbish?[54]

Yet Vemana also speaks of the identity of the human body and *hiranyagarbha*, the golden egg of wholeness from which all creation arises, with the air being *prana*, sun and moon being eyes. Hence the universe and body are one – the abode of ultimate reality.[55] In the tantric world-view, the human microcosm is a smaller-scale reflection of the macrocosm, the six chakras (energy centres in the human body) are like six worlds, the nerve channels are like rivers and the five *prana*s are winds.[56]

Vemana pictured human existence as a quest to quench a deep thirst:

> You drink the milk of the first breast you see,
> and run after another breast before too long.
> It is this breast that dilutes liberation's quest;
> a true yogi is a man who dares to leave the breast.[57]

Although an ascetic, always wary of *maya*, Vemana does not discount the importance of food. We could call the following verse 'It's Up to You':

> If you overeat it can kill you; if you don't eat enough,
> the soul becomes famished, impoverished, dull.
> For killing or strengthening one, food is powerful.
> Vemana, food can kill you or make you grow.[58]

> From nutritious food one produces seminal fluid
> and *bija* ['seed' and mantra syllables related to
> the primordial sound]. The difference between *bindu*
> and *bija* can teach you how to find out the truth.[59]

In some verses Vemana refers to ideas about subtle energies which are part of the Hindu world-view and go back to the practices of yoga and the Upanishads. Vemana declares that the yogi knowing mystical sound vibrations (*nada*) and knowing *bindu* (concentrated energy from the original self-existent sound at the source of creation) and the 16 visually experienced splendours seen in the chakra at the top of the head, is able to still the rambunctious mind and achieve the highest 'opening', realizing Brahman or formless consciousness.[60]

Perhaps some comparisons would help us place Vemana and his contributions into some sort of context. Probably, the proverbs spread in America by Ben Frankin have enjoyed a currency in spoken language somewhat similar to the popularity of Vemana's verses in South India. But, in some ways, voices of loss, disappointment in romance and total disillusionment are in some ways more like Vemana's. American poet Edgar Allen Poe (1809–1849) found death the most melancholy subject of all, and he felt that it was most poetical when allied with beauty. Consequently, it was the death of a beautiful woman he cared for that launched Poe into poetry with works such as 'Tamerlain' and 'Annabel Lee' and 'Ulalume'. Poe was haunted by death, and drank excessively. He seems to have experienced the sensations of being a lost soul during significant parts of his life. He worked out his haunted psyche's anxious troubles and macabre obsessions in his writings, and left memorable imaginative narratives. It would seem that his intuition and ability to use the unconscious gave him prescient insights in his psychological and cosmological speculations. His wounds were windows on the human condition.[61]

Another man whose life was changed by the experience of a loved one's death was Bengali Vaishnava bhakti saint Chaitanya (1485–1533). At the death of his young wife he became a renunciate *bhakta* just as Vemana became a yogi when his hopes of love were dashed. Repulsed by the worldly life of the senses after that loss, he developed his ecstatic devotion to Krishna to such an extent that people thought of him as embodying the milkmaid Radha as well as the avatar Krishna – the devotee and the divine in one. Vemana also gave voice to impulses in his unconscious, and many people responded to his words.

However ecstatic spiritual devotion was not Vemana's way. How reductively simple it seems for Vemana to have renounced all feminine allure – presumably after rejection turned him towards bitterness. (Though we must always remember that this is a view based on legends and the sentiment of his verses.) Some of his verses seem like insults directed at the finer sex – brash verbal attacks on women who, in India, more often than not toil endlessly to keep their families' lives thriving and do many other good things. These verses shock with their cynical exuberance and aggressive world-weary disgust:

> If you really look close at her shapely rear end
> what do you find but a garbage disposal system?
> Take a gander at the front, you find a dirty hole.
> Yet looking at women causes men to run after them!
> So it goes in the world, Abhirama; listen well O Vemana.[62]

Is this a voice meant to encourage ascetic non-sensual spirituality? Is it sour grapes – dejection caused by rejection? Does he use words of contempt as a charm against the attraction of sirens? Wouldn't serene indifference be the wiser path? Women cannot help but take his repudiation of females as a wholesale condemnation of their very existence. Obviously a spirituality which alienates half the population is not acceptable in the age of equal rights. Nowadays, such misogyny would be countered by voices pointing out how men are the ones who more accurately should be derided on account of their troublesome body parts. As a means of ridding themselves of desires for women, mystics, monks, yogis, sufis and others have often tried to tell themselves that women are not desirable. Yet, clearly, it is because women are so attractive and sex is such a strong drive that such denials and propaganda had to be manufactured.[63] Only the devastation of a hopelessly jilted passion could explain the poisonous bitterness of Vemana's words about women. He is unforgiving and unforgetting, taking out his terrible anger in his coldest verses. Today, most would see Vemana's arch vitriol in his anti-female verses as too extreme, too relentless, too resolute. We see such verses as humourless rather than humorous. They seem prejudiced and psychologically unbalanced.

In some of his verses Vemana reveals the suppressed, though obvious, shadow sides of life – the rear end of a human is a garbage disposal drain, no matter how many glamorous youthful ones wiggle in audiences' faces as fashionable dancers gyrate. The self-disgusted self-exiled outsider speaks openly of the hidden and forbidden. He mutters sometimes obscene comments from the sidelines. He looks down on realms less enduring than the spirituality he is trying to attain. He is subversive, and those who dare to look along with him sometimes recall his outrageous views with a fascinated chuckle. Here is a lone wolf voicing what no-one in conventional society could think or speak. Vemana is never afraid to spank or slap, never too engrossed in his pilgrimage to mock or kick or curse the fool. Like a loud-mouthed comedian he brings up the embarrassing shadows which his society casts and refuses to see.

In any case, although not all of his words are equally popular, Vemana lives on in his verses. Vemana's verses are unforgettable and remain part of the Telugu

Figure 6.2   **A sati stone commemorates a woman who ended her life by fire
when her husband died. It shows the appearance of a woman in
Vijayanagara times and refers to a custom which cut short some
widows' lives and which has since been made illegal**

vernacular, pulled out when a shock or laugh is called for. Furthermore, as far as I
have been able to determine, no-one really knows which of the verses are spurious,
or which are corrupted by changes introduced by oral repetition or by anti-female
extremists seeking to use 'Vemana' as a vehicle for their own rage. But, to be fair,
we should note that some of his verses are positive and are written in an appreciative
tone. For example, on the beauty and wisdom of a good marriage he wrote:

> Affectionate bonds of marriage, formed of cooperation,
> open up like a lotus flower, blossoming
> to reach fulfilment in a wonderfully mellow fruition,
> so it goes in this world, tell me about it, Vemana.[64]

Here are a few more of Vemana's verses. These were recited to me by a physicist who had learned them in the original Telugu by heart when he was a child in school in Andhra Pradesh more than 50 years ago. He easily recited them *ex tempore* as we sat one night at a banquet table at an Indian philosophy conference, and I jotted them down on a napkin as fast as I could:

> Take a rat by the tail and whack it against a rock
> [like a washerman at a river] all year –
> it will still be black. Take a doll and spank it –
> it will never speak. Don't fool yourself with illusions,
> know what is possible and what is not –
> this is the way of the world Abhirama, hear O Vemana.[65]

> Why expect good behaviour from your in-laws?
> Or assume shepherds have literary knowledge?
> Why presume you'll ever get the truth from a woman,
> or imagine you'll get rice from pounding empty husks?
> These things, and white crows too – they don't exist
> in the world, O Abhirama, take this to heart O Vemana![66]

Vemana's cynicism regarding women is shared by some in Andhra Pradesh, but many would respond to hearing such verses today with a nervous laughter and vehement disavowals. Yet it must have been men who preserved such expressions of anti-woman sentiment, and women have suffered them for a long time. It would be an interesting sociological study to look into the specifics of who spread and repeated Vemana's verses, but at this point the evidence and clues would no doubt be very difficult to track down and analyse. Thus we must wonder 'Who was Vemana?' and 'How many Vemanas were there?'. But this, too, proves that he was a poet, for the true poet stirs people to recognize their own poetic truths. Vemana causes South Indians to say not only 'I know what you mean', but also 'I have ideas like that myself!'.

The Voice of Baddena from *Sumati Shatakam*

Another popular poet of Telugu-speaking South India was Baddena, also known, from the signature he used, as Sumati. Like Vemana, and probably living before him (1220–1280 / 1300?) Baddena wrote many verses which became proverbial among Telugu-speaking people. While Vemana as a renunciant had left the three lower *purushartha*s (goals of life) – *kama* (pleasure), *artha* (success), *dharma* (duty) – for the fourth, *moksha* (liberation), Baddena was a man of the world, not averse to pleasures or worldly social roles. Indeed, he is thought to have been a minor Chola prince and he wrote a text on political theory.[67] Baddena's 'moral verses' (*niti*) were very popular and current during the period when the Vijayanagara capital was flourishing. Rhyming like the rappers of today, playing with familiar images and turning out memorable phrases, such poets entered into the rhythms of everyday life, drumming their impulses into the heartbeat and bloodstream of the regional culture. Their witty words became a currency shared by everyone from childhood, when they first heard the clever jingles, to old age, when they would apply the verses to situations in their own grandchildren's lives with uncommonly eloquent common sense. It is a popular literature of worldly wisdom and wary warnings, cautions against betrayals, which are the lot of the naive.

The *Sumati Shatakam*, or collection of a hundred of Baddena's verses, exhibits a reasonableness via parallel metaphors, and a viable system of values to support traditional life, with a hard-edged realism. Perhaps the author built on existing proverbs, crafting folk traditions into more fully realized verses. Baddena upholds the caste stereotypes which Vemana explodes. The best of Vemana's and Baddena's verses have a depth that keeps them relevant over the centuries. Telgu speakers remember and apply them when they face certain situations in their lives, times of observing life's curious dilemmas and times of making evaluations and decisions. The verses ridicule sham, raise a warning, and 'tell it like it is' in a society where social and other hierarchies often made spontaneous frankness impossible.

The Voice of Baddena

To the dhobi who ties various clothes into one bundle –
the wealthy man's silks with the poorest slob's rag –
it's all the same, no one's any better than another.
Same with a whore; given a coin she'll pleasure all comers.[68]

You might be an expert in erotics,
handsome and dashing, a noble prince of men
but you'll have to lay out the going price –
you won't enjoy the courtesan's favour until then.[69]

Faith is a delicate matter – you'd better believe it.
The merchant's honesty, the serpent's friendship,
a kept woman's love and loyalty, the sweetness of gall
a Brahman's promises – these are fictions one and all.[70]

Give her wealth heaped in a pile high as her head –
a woman who sells herself won't be faithful or content.
Even if she vows with sincere pretty face, freshly bathed
in a sacred river, never trust or confide your heart to her.[71]

Making love with a wife who never spontaneously
embraces her man in time becomes disgusting, awful
to him – hideous as hugging a corpse that's ravaged
and half chomped to pieces by a team of jackals.[72]

The very soul of speech is candid truth:
an army of strong soldiers is the soul of a fort;
the soul of a letter is there in its signature;
modesty is a good woman's spiritual keynote, Sumati.[73]

If an impatient self-centred man pounces on a woman
before passion has been roused in her heart, know
that she will be dismally dry; it's like trying to grind
sandalwood paste without first watering the stone.[74]

A mouth that doesn't savour chewing betel,
a mouth which hasn't enjoyed the nectar of woman's lips,
a mouth which is a stranger to singing
all these are desolate graves – they know only ash.[75]

Studies which do not bring a man to happiness,
a song without graceful gestures or sweet tones,
an embrace of clutching and clinging without any feeling
and speech which the court considers too uncouth –
all these are lifeless and insipid. What are they worth?[76]

You should live in a village where the following are found:
a generous man who lends money to those in need,
a skilled physician who helps the unwell to heal,
a non-stop stream of fresh water, and a pious priest, O Sumati.[77]

A snake's venom is concentrated in his head;
a scorpion's poison is secreted in his tail.
the slanderer has poison in his tongue;
poison in a proud Velama chieftain is spread
from head to toe, without fail. O Sumati.[78]

Say the appropriate thing at the right time.
Don't hurt others and don't hurt yourself.
This is the way to manoeuvre through life,
So may you be skilful and thrive, O Sumati.[79]

If someone you invited to your celebration stays away, let him go.
If you worship a deity and plead for gold and don't get it, let that god go.
If in an emergency you jump on a horse and it doesn't move, hop off.
You have to know when to cut your losses, so says Sumati.[80]

Reflections on Functions and Form: The Fractal Geometry of Language

Some critics may compare the folk verses of Vemana and Baddena unfavourably
with the lines of a poet such as Pingali Surana, whose works brought out the unique
genius of the Telugu language without formulaic oversimplification. Yet it was the
memorable clarity of Vemana and Baddena in their almost haiku-brief poems which
gave their ideas longevity in the ongoing conversations of Andhra. Their power was
in their sharp bold brush strokes, rather than subtle nuances which would have found
no resonance in the hurlyburly worlds of marketplace banter and village debate.
Their terse versified thoughts became part of the folk mind, linking levels of society,
and integrating members of many generations. They have entered pan-Indian life,

influencing many conversations, songs and sets of values. Until the mid-twentieth century, children in the primary schools of Andhra Pradesh learned some of Vemana's and Baddena's verses by heart. Which would be more relevant to their lives – rhymes like "Jack and Jill went up the hill" from collections of verse written in England, or the following Telugu poem?

> Water is the one element all living beings depend on;
> the mouth is the single organ to let one's feelings be known;
> woman is the best masterpiece in the whole human race –
> The finest jewellery she can wear: modesty veiling her beauty.[81]

Verses like those presented above, and proverbs and songs, function as imagination-stimulating fractals imaging proper and improper behaviour. They are like the art of Chinese ink paintings, or Escher's graphics, or Borge's stories – they allow the landscapes of inner life (the soul's experience) to be called up suggestively in their essential features. They are brief memorable messages that retain their ability to startle and are easily reproducible in household, village, town and court. Reiterated in a new situation a cleverly crafted line takes on a life of its own. A growing child can learn by heart a quatrain of such lines in singsong rhythm, delighting in the rhyme and reason. Mature people accrue collections of such quatrains in their memories over the years. Thus literacy or cultural fluency can be found among the illiterate. As fractals (or, since, strictly speaking, fractals have three or more scales of similarity, as iterations or recursive patterns) dealing with, portraying and formalizing the roughly chaotic yet patterned aspects of nature in ways Euclid's lines could not, many of these expressions bring an insight of clarity to a world blurred by habits of ignorance and reducing everything to a short-term purpose. Take, for example, this stanza of Vemana's on the Humpty-Dumpty-like irreparable fragility of minds:

> When iron cracks, a blacksmith fires it up red hot
> a few times, then hammers it into a single piece again.
> But when the mind breaks down it's much harder
> – who can take it and make it normal again
> supple, responsive, and smoothly ordered?[82]

The soul needs such wisdom to know wholes – the psyche seeks wholes[83] – and the saints' visions and wise people's admonitions keep the larger pictures in mind with complexity and simplicity. Memorable verses such as those composed by Vemana and Baddena cast a subtle net of images in social discourse and subtly set up patterns to be followed by the generations of people who repeat them (for example, to avoid hoarding and to practise generosity.) Thus the memorable verse creates invisible behavioural dynamics by knitting a fractal network of thoughts, words and deeds.

We could reflect further on the fractal geometry of language. The verses above serve as examples. An apt image can conjure up a situation, as one proverb-like line calls to mind the whole rhyme-jingling rhythmic quatrain, or a fabric of others seems to be of a piece or contrary lines argue an opposite stance. A whole thought is often expressed in a line, and a larger whole thought is expressed in the whole quatrain. It is like mantras in the hymns of the Vedas, like phrases in ragas and like the multiple meanings of the Sanskrit terms *shastra* and *sutra*. *Shastra* has a number of meanings. First, *shastra* can be used to name any teaching – for example, the *Bhagavad Gita*[84] uses the term in describing Krishna's 'most secret teaching' (*guhyatamam shastram*). Second, it is a term used to denote a consecrated number of teachings, revealed tradition (*shruti*), the six philosophy systems and so on. Third, *shastra* can mean a specific work, and the composition of it might be described in the following manner: 'The *shastra* is a group of words characterized by a particular arrangement and stating such things as means of knowing rightly. A word is a group of sounds, and a group of words constitutes a *sutra*; a group of *sutra*s makes up a section; a group of sections constitutes an *ahnika* (subchapter); a group of *ahnika*s makes up a chapter; and the *shastra* is a group of five chapters'. Finally, individual *sutra*s of the *Ashtadhyayi* are called *shastra*: 'Patanjali speaks of a multitude of *shastra*s because each single *sutra* is a *shastra*.'[85] Whole parts make up wholes; organically composed entities are made of bundled bundles of bundles.

A way of better understanding these associations and recursive patterns – that a *shastra* is made up of *sutra*s and yet a *sutra* can itself be a *shastra* – has been suggested by David Steenburg.

> Perception is shaped (or made possible) by bringing order to complexity, and … fractal patterns are an efficient way of encoding this order; it is easy to believe that this kind of patterning arises again and again in the products of human consciousness [including writings, oral traditions and stories]. As we seek to make sense of our individual stories, or our cultural and religious narratives, I think it would be likely that the pattern would be capable of a fractal description. Indeed, I suspect that the different 'feel' of words themselves – some are shallow and some deep, some are merely indicative and others marvelously evocative – has something to do with them being rooted in a conscious process that has different degrees of 'roughness' or complexity. I assume that the emergence of an insight or a concept is the emergence of a stable pattern or process in consciousness, and that process can have varying degrees of roughness … .[86]

For example, Baddena's poem about a mango oozing nectar when squeezed, as a woman held tight by a passion-enflamed man offers him the soul of enjoyment's sweet flavour, is an invitation to learn more, to expand the glimpses afforded by those lines. The lines do not exist in isolation, but as part of a life made up of those kinds of experience.

Vemana's and Baddena's verses offer many such examples of a stable pattern with degrees of roughness or variations on a theme. They are verbal reflections using memorable images to posit a set of relations and are sufficiently open that a large number of everyday life-situations can be projected into them. Steenburg continues:

> 'In short, because I believe words themselves are fractal, I think it follows that narratives, too, would be fractal. I'm thinking here of the recurrence of self-similar patterns at different scales. And I would expect also that theories, stories

and ideologies can be variously smooth or rough, depending on their level of generality (which I see as a matter of scale). Newton's law of gravity is smooth and large scale (universal) ... . Theology ... is large scale, and it is strong when it captures patterns across all scales, when it can reach into individual experience (which itself is capable of increasingly fine scales of self-awareness and self-understanding), elucidating experience in a way that recapitulates the patterns of the larger whole.[87]

The verses of Vemana and Baddena, like the proverbs[88] of folk wisdom which they feed into and also grow out of, and the songs that live on people's lips for generations, all capture patterns across several scales, and remain (as long as they are called into use) a part of many lives. At their worst they may become clichés, rigidly imposing verdicts on situations in a way that does not help us understand; at their best they encourage alertness, common sense, conscience, honesty, and they rebalance distorted views. They provide common bonds of shared references and lend spicy flavours to a regional language. They deepen the pool of concepts and shared insights. And, of course, at their worst they condition bigots to believe more firmly in their harmful hostile prejudices.

As to the form, (the genre, the metrical pattern and other recognizable aspects that are fairly stable in music, poetry, religion and imagination,) it might well be conceived of as another kind of attractor, or holding pattern, in which different thoughts can be communicated by rhythmic and resonating words and images. The form is conducive to repetition, like a song brought into play in the memory in certain moods and on appropriate occasions. Richard Dawkins has developed the concept of 'memes',[89] identifying culturally shaped neuron patterns in the brain with the unusual ability to replicate themselves by spurring other brain cells to fire similarly. Rhyming proverbs and rhythmic verses can be likened to these memorable units in their ability to help give traditions their continuity. Such forms, like all tools, can obviously be used either for constructive purposes or aggression. No doubt tyrants have their catchphrases and mottoes, just as self-sacrificing heroes of humanity do.

Poetry's form (rhythms, length limits, rhyme schemes) 'is crucial to its power to persuade' us that the vulnerable part of our consciousness has its own rightness despite the evidence of wrongness all around it. It has 'the power to remind us that we are hunters and gatherers of values, that our very solitudes and distresses are creditable, insofar as they too are an earnest of our veritable human being'.[90] Jingles of conscience can sometimes be powerful attractors in the mind, able to persuade us with their arresting voices, which seem to ring true and cut through all the dross. Despite overwhelming massive forces for conformity, by refusing the lameness of sameness, attractive verses can be quirkily fresh forces pointing to forgotten or hidden truths. Thus they sometimes come into conflict with convention's simple-minded forces which cannot abide wounding criticisms or the strangeness of anomalies. But if deep in the heart there is some value of noble impulse to be encouraged, the best of Vemana's and Baddena's unsentimental yet soulful observations can help people stand their ground. (Of course, in such a set form the poet also sometimes pads the verse with extra words to fill out the form and make the meter work, so that the memorable rhythmic sound is kept.)

Vemana in some of his *Shatakams* ('Hundred verse series'),[91] including many of those represented above, wrote four-line poems in the *Ataveladi* meter, a Telugu meter simpler than the *Kanda* meter, in which Baddena often wrote.[92] In *Ataveladi* there is *yati*, which is a scheme of initial syllable rhyme (or near-rhyme) which must agree with the sound in the penultimate *gana*. In general Vemana wrote miniature poems in a language and form that anyone could grasp. (In the *Kanda* meter there is not only *yati* but also *prasa*, another internal complexity involving an alliteration pattern in which similar sounds chime with each other in the second syllable of each line. Both *yati* and *prasa* are Dravidian language poetic devices. *Kanda* also features two short lines (1 and 3) and two long lines (2 and 4)) These rhythmic cycle patterns are memory attractors working in synchrony with images and mental patterns.[93] They are selected for survival from the mass of verbal expressions generated over the centuries.

Like Emily Dickinson's or William Blake's or Kabir's memorable fresh-languaged little verses, Vemana's and Baddena's verses show that a great deal of richness can radiate from a simple structure. Poet and critic Seamus Heaney rightly notes that 'poetic form is both the ship and the anchor. It is at once a buoyancy and a holding, allowing for the simultaneous gratification of whatever is centrifugal and centripetal in mind and body... [the poet's effort is to] repose in the stability conferred by a musically satisfying order of sounds.[94] In terms of the interactive vitality of a poem being recalled or spoken, the melody of the order of the words is a dynamic contour, an edge of chaos, not still but strong and vibrant, not still but rough and moving with a lasting power. Creativity strives toward a strain where dynamic configuration is brought to life in the reading or reciting. Vemana's and Baddena's verses are made from the materials at hand – words of the spoken and written Telugu language, relevant themes, items and events of everyday life. Familiar situations are put in a dramatic way that snags the pattern-conscious brain. Such verses have a neat bite-size limit – a couplet or quatrain format tight enough to help the poet focus well and assert, argue and clinch a case with memorable aplomb. Their patterns stay in the memory naturally for years and travel like the seeds carried by waters, winds and migrating creatures. They playfully entertain and instruct in rice paddies and bazaars, tea stalls and pilgrims' resting places, and they forcefully remind people of hard facts and criticize hypocrisy in kitchens and public gatherings. Their cleverness of style invites repetition, memorization, recitation and translation. Their verses sometimes resemble today's stand-up comics' wisecracks – potshots at social foibles and human habits. Sometimes, too, they seem to be instruments made by yogis to encourage the yogic reach for freedom and transcendence.

Reflections of wide-angle consciousness, when well condensed in rhyming proverbs by a Vemana or a Baddena, can thrive for centuries with a life of their own. Sometimes they are not only repeated, but are transformed, generations later, into new variant verses by the minds that try to recall them. The output of these two masculine personalities may have attracted stray verses by anonymous authors, which have been incorporated into their bodies of work. Vemana, like Buddha and the Haridasas, a confirmed renouncer, wary of the world's pulls, and Sumati, the royal lover of women who celebrates the ecstasies of eros which Vemana shuns and mocks, both have their realms and their fans. I'm told that a popular Telugu book discussing Vemana asserts that '[t]here are no poems that can challenge the poems of Vemana'. Except, perhaps we should add, the poems of Baddena, (whose pen name 'Sumati', means 'good mind,') and other voices expressing the irrepressible and wryly wise folk mind. But such voices are not exactly rivals; they are similarity-sharing parts of a greater whole, and lines of their verses are sometimes confused, one for the other.

Notes

1   Some say that he lived in the latter part of the fifteenth century, others say the sixteenth or even the seventeenth century. For example, G. Gnanananda in *Vemana*, Bangalore: Bharata-Bharati Pustaka Sampada, 1982, says that Vemana was born in 1652; P.T. Raju in *Telugu Literature*, Bombay: PEN, All India Centre, n.d., places both Vemana and Baddena (or Sumati) in the fifteenth century. C.P. Brown dates Vemana later: 'He lived in the beginning of the eighteenth century. It is said in a verse ... the date of birth is ... 1652 ... Many verses ... prove satisfactorily that he wrote in the latter part of the seventeenth century when the Mohamedans were governors of that part of India.' Brown's book collects 1215 verses attributed to Vemana. If those who say Vemana lived in the 1600s are right, then he is the outcome nevertheless of South Indian learning and experience, culture and creativity, collecting and summing up myriad strands from Vijayanagara times and before. See Vemana, *Verses of Vemana*, ed. and tr. C.P. Brown, New Delhi: Asian Educational Services, 1986 (reprint of 1829 edn.). Excerpts of this can be found at website http://india/.bgsu.edu/telugu/Bio/vemana/html.

2   C.P. Brown, in the above-cited *Verses of Vemana* wrote: 'He was not a Brahmin but a capoo, or a farmer; a native of Cuddapah district and born, I believe, in the neighbourhood of Gandicotta' (p. ii).

3   Ibid., no. 691 p. 169.

4   Ibid., pp. 177–83.

5   Ibid., nos 681 and 682, p. 167.

6   Gnanananda, *Vemana*.

7   Vemana, *Selected Verses of Vemana*, ed. and tr. J.S.R.L. Narayana Moorty and Elliot Roberts, New Delhi: Sahitya Akademi, 1995, p. 4.

8   In some folk traditions Vemana produced gold magically – his urine and faeces turned to gold in the homes of those who welcomed him as a mendicant; when he grew melons, the seeds were golden and so on. There are some other strange tales told of Vemana, too: about his urinating on a coin and causing it to turn to gold, about curing his sister's cobra bite by scratching her breast, about opening his stomach while bathing and washing his innards, about being hit by lightning while ploughing, dying and reviving seven days later, about his tomb being hit by lightning, and his appearance there holding a lightning bolt. See ibid., pp. 5–6.

9   My versification from lines in Vemana, *Verses of Vemana*, ed. and tr. Brown, no. 717, p. 175.

10   Ibid., no. 598, pp. 147–48.

11   Ibid., no. 887, p. 214 and no. 952, p. 228.

12   Gnanananda, *Vemana*. Some of the lore about Vemana's life which I reflect in this piece is based on stories in that popular pamphlet. Charles Philip Brown collected Vemana's verses and published

them in 1829. There is also a Telugu volume entitled *Vemanapadyamulu*, Madras: N.V. Gopal and Company, 1981, which contains over 3000 verses in a variety of meters. I thank Jonathan Goldberg-Bell for his information on this and on questions of meter discussed later in this chapter.

13 This is also dicussed in Vemana, *Selected Verses of Vemana*, ed. and tr. Narayana Moorty and Roberts, p. xii.

14 Brown in *Verses of Vemana* discusses the errors and confusions in the old manuscripts he worked with, which were sometimes caused by the transcribers' imposing their own sense of propriety (pp. iv–v).

15 In this chapter I have drawn on several sources for Vemana's verses, which I have footnoted accordingly. Some of the collections have both Telugu original and rudimentary English translation, some are only Telugu and others only English. In each case I have tried to put the basic ideas into a lively English. See *Vemana's Moral Verses (Vemana Satakam)*, ed. and tr. G. Rana Reddy, Cuddapah: Sumithra Publications, 1976, no. 126, p. 58.

16 Vemana, *Vemana's Moral Verses* ed. and tr. Ranya Reddy, no. 125, pp. 58–59. On this topic Marilyn Monroe, the American actress known for exuding an aura of charismatic sexuality, said 'We are all born sexual creatures, thank God, but it's a pity so many people despise and crush this natural gift. Art, real art, comes from it – everything' (*Life Magazine*, August. 1992, p. 78). Compare American poet William Carlos Williams' thoughts on desire: in the mature artist 'mastery... shows itself more and more as the type of all his desires... more expressive of what he is himself' (*The Embodiment of Knowledge*, New York: New Directions, 1974, p. 73). In writing about his work 'Desert Music' this theme is also important: desire as the source of specific acts of creativity. See also James Hillman: 'To desire and to see through desire – this is the courage that the heart requires' (*A Blue Fire*, New York: Harper Perennial, 1991, p. 128). D.T. Suzuki in *Mysticism: Christian and Buddhist*, London: Unwin Hyman, 1979, writes of the necessity of *tanha*, cosmic desire, for existence, and Plotinus, in his commentary on the *Song of Songs*, and Augustine also, discuss desire's relative place in human life and in the scheme of things.

17 Vemana, *Verses of Vemana*, ed. and tr. A.L.N. Murty, Kakinada: Sripathi Press, 1978, p. 13. (This collection includes Telugu originals, and is divided into subjects; it includes some verses not from the *Shatakam*, because they are in *Kanda* and other metres.)

18 Ibid., p. 73.

19 C.R. Sarma, *Ramblings in Telugu Literature*, Madras: Lakshminarayana Granthamala, 1978, p. 9.

20 Gnanananda, *Vemana*, p. 43.

21 Ibid., p. 44. Inner purity meaning integrity of conscience, wholehearted sincerity, being completely established in deepest self-knowledge, presumably.

22 Vemana, *Vemana's Moral Verses*, ed. and tr. Ranga Reddy, pp. 44–45.

23 Vemana, *Verses of Vemana*, ed. and tr. Murty, p. 72.

24 Ibid., p. 70.

25 Raju, *Telugu Literature*, p. 104. This verse is also found in Narayana Moorty and Roberts, *Selected Verses of Vemana*, p. 77.

26 Raju, *Telegu Literature*, p. 104.

27 Ibid.

28 Ibid., p. 105.

29 Gnanananda, *Vemana*, p. 33.

30 V.R. Narla (ed.), *Vemana Through Western Eyes*, Madras: Seshachalam, 1969. See also C.P. Brown, *Literary Autobiography of C.P. Brown*, Tirupati: Sri Venkateswara University, 1978, pp 48–49.

31 Vemana, *Vemana's Moral Verses*, ed. and tr. Ranga Reddy, no. 7, p. 11.

32 Vemana, *Verses of Vemana*, ed. and tr. Murty, p. 7.

33 Ibid., p. 25.

34 Gnanananda, *Vemana*, p. 42.

35 Dr Pariti Suryanarayana Murthy of Vijayawada recited this verse to me in Telugu and translated it into an English paraphrase when I met him in Indianapolis on 9 April 2003.

36   Ibid.
37   Vemana, *Vemana's Moral Verses*, ed. and tr. Ranga Reddy, pp. 32–33. Cf. Gracian Baltazar's sayings of worldly wisdom: ' … the fool fails by behaving without regard to his condition, position, origin.' The unit of survival, as Gregory Bateson says, is organism-in-environment. This verse is also found in Narayana Moorty and Roberts, *Selected Verses of Vemana*, p. 44.
38   Vemana, *Verses of Vemana*, ed. and tr. Murty, p. 9.
39   Ibid., p. 11.
40   Ibid., p. 14.
41   Ibid., p. 20.
42   Ibid., p. 22.
43   Dr Pariti Suryanarayana Murthy of Vijayawada recited this verse to me in Telugu and translated it into an English paraphrase when I met him in Indianapolis on 9 April 2003.
44   Vemana, *Verses of Vemana*, ed. and tr. Murty, p. 29.
45   Ibid., p. 34. Cf. Sarma, *Ramblings in Telugu Literature*, p. 67. Sarma attributes this verse to *Sumati Satakam*. He discusses various manuscripts and translations of Sumati, with some mention of Vemana.
46   Vemana, *Verses of Vemana*, ed. and tr. Murty, p. 39.
47   Ibid., p. 47.
48   Ibid., p. 57.
49   Ibid., p. 58.
50   Ibid., p. 64.
51   Ibid., p. 66.
52   Gnanananda, *Vemana*, p. 22. The book of Proverbs in the Old Testament has similar sayings about a disagreeing wife.
53   Vemana, *Verses of Vemana*, ed. and tr. Brown, no. 380, p. 98.
54   This verse was recited by Venkata Subbayya, Indianapolis. I believe it is in Vemana, *Verses of Vemana*, ed. and tr. Brown.
55   Vemana, *Selected Verses of Vemana*, ed. and tr. Narayana Moorty and Roberts p. 161.
56   Ibid., pp. 164–65.
57   Vemana, *Verses of Vemana*, ed. and tr. Brown, no. 799, p. 194.
58   Ibid., p. 20.
59   Ibid., p. 34
60   Vemana, *Selected Verses of Vemana*, ed. and tr. Narayana Moorty and Roberts p. 24 and p. 195. See also p. 161.
61   See, for example, Emily Eakin, 'What Did Poe Know About Cosmology? Nothing. But He Was Right', *The New York Times*, 2 November 2002, Arts and Ideas Section, p. A19.
62   Vemana, *Verses of Vemana*, ed. and tr. Murty, p. 14. The same and similar verses are found in Brown, *Verses of Vemana*, no. 463 p. 118, and nos 379 and 380, p. 98.
63   See Annemarie Schimmel, *The Mystical Dimensions of Islam,* Chapel Hill: University of North Carolina Press, 1975, pp. 428–29, for a discussion of Muslim examples of equating the world with women, and emphasizing the repulsive attributes of women.
64   Vemana, *Selected Verses of Vemana*, ed. and tr. Narayana Moorty and Roberts, pp. 104–105.
65   Related to me orally by B.D. Nageswara Rao, Physics Department, Indiana University-Purdue University at Indianapolis, 14 September 2002.
66   Ibid.
67   T. Rajagopala Rao, in *A Historical Sketch of Telugu Literature*, New Delhi, Asian Educational Services, 1984, p. 50, places Baddena in the thirteenth century. Some say he was a pupil of Tikkana. Some think, like Sarma, *Ramblings in Teluga Literature*, p. 66, that the author was a Jaina or a ruler of the 'Southern Six Thousand' country. Whoever he was, it seems he also wrote *Nitishastra Muktavali*, a handbook on the obligations of kings. See Rao, *A Historical Sketch*, p. 50.
68   C.R. Sarma, *Sumati Satakam*, ed. C.P. Brown, Hyderabad: Andhra Pradesh Sahitya Akademi, 1973, 27.

69   Ibid., 35.
70   Ibid., 37.
71   Ibid., 47.
72   Ibid., 49.
73   Ibid., 76.
74   Ibid., 79.
75   Ibid., 80.
76   Ibid., 83.
77   Ibid., 68.
78   Ibid., 46.
79   Related to me orally by B.D. Nageswara Rao, Physics Department, Indiana University-Purdue University at Indianapolis, 14 September 2002.
80   Ibid.
81   Sarma, *Ramblings in Telugu Literature*, p. 70.
82   Vemana, *Verses of Vemana*, ed. and tr. Murty, p. 29. See also Vemana, *Selected Verses of Vemana*, ed. and tr. Narayana Moorty and Roberts, p. 97.
83   According to C.G. Jung and others. I find this to be a promising idea.
84   *Bhagavad Gita*, XV.20.
85   George Cardona, *Panini: His Works and Its Tradition, Vol. I Background and Introduction*, Delhi: Motilal Bararsidass, 1988, pp. 666–67.
86   Personal correspondence from David Steenburg from Woodstock, Ontario, 31 March 1997.
87   Ibid.
88   In South Indian languages such as Tamil, Telugu and Kannada, there is usually a rhythm – the first half of the proverb is the same as the second half. Sometimes the two halves rhyme.
89   As genes are to DNA, 'memes' are to culturally learned identities. The term was introduced by Richard Dawkins in *The Selfish Genes*, New York: Oxford University Press, 1976.
90   Seamus Heaney, Nobel Prize acceptance speech, *Crediting Poetry*, New York: Farrar Straus Giroux, 1996, p. 54.
91   A *Shatakam* is a string of one hundred or more (e.g., 108, 110) stanzas. There are over 6000 *Shatakams* in Telugu, on many themes: devotional, satirical, legendary, celebrating love, expounding philosophy and morals. Often the author repeats a refrain or *makuta*, including his own name. Series of verses like these are part of an ongoing tradition, not just a relic of the past. In newspapers and magazines, clever verses continue to be popular. Mallikarjuna Panditaradhya in the twelfth century wrote a *shatakam*-like work in Telugu. See Dr S.V. Suryanarayana Rao, 'Sataka Literature in Telugu', at http://www.mihira.com/mihmay99/SATAKA%20LITERATURE%
92   Vemana wrote many of his verses in *Tetagiti* ('simple song) and *Ataveladi* ('dancing girl') meters. These two metrical forms are specific to Telugu literature. In the recent past V.R. Narla composed hundreds of reform-themed Telugu poems in this meter. *Tetagiti* has four equal lines, each consisting of one *Surya* foot, followed by two *Indras* and two *Suryas*. The first and fourth feet of each line rhyme in *yati*. There is no *prasa*. (*Indra* feet or *ganas* are collections of syllables. There are six Indra *ganas*: long/short/long, short/short/short/long, long/long/short, short/short/long/short, long/short/short, short/short/short/short. *Surya ganas* are: long/short, short/short/short). In the *Ataveladi* meter, the first and third lines consist each of three *Suryas* and two *Indras*: while the second and fourth are each formed of five *Suryas*. There is no *prasa*. *Yati* rhyme is between the first and fourth *ganas*. Vemana also uses the *Sisa* meter on occasion. It consists of four similar lines, each of which may be conveniently divided into a couplet, having four *Indra* feet in the first half, with two *Indras* and two *Suryas* in the second. Six varieties of the *Sisa* are described by the Telugu prosodians, but a fundamental rule explains all of them. Each of these eight half lines has a separate *yati*, which falls in the middle. The third *gana* rhymes with the initial. The other verse found regularly in Vemana is *Kanda*. *Kanda* uses only such feet as equal four short syllables. The *Kanda* verse consists of four lines. The first and third have three *ganas*, while the second and fourth have

five, thus each half has eight *gana*s. There are various rules about specific *gana*s, *prasa* and *yati*. Thanks to Jonathon Goldberg-Bell for this information.

93   See also Vemana, *Selected Verses of Vemana*, ed. and tr. Narayana Moorty and Roberts, p. xii.
94   Heaney, *Crediting Poetry*, p. 51.

CHAPTER 7

Krishnadevaraya in the Night Kitchen: Realizing his Power at the Peak of Chaos' Edge

The Greatest King of Vijayanagara

Reigning at the peak of glory in the Vijayanagara empire, Krishnadevaraya (of the Tuluva family, the third dynasty) was the most famous of Vijayanagara emperors. During his rule (1509–1530) the prosperous realm expanded to its all-time utmost reach.[1] In his time the population of the Tungabhadra heartland was about 2 million. The capital city of Vijayanagara numbered about 100 000 households.[2] The population of the peninsula south of the Krishna river was about 25 million.[3] Krishnadevaraya was described by his European contemporary, Domingo Paes, as a man 'gallant and perfect in all things'.[4] Well respected and admired by his own people as well as by travellers from afar,[5] he made a strong impression on those who knew him. By all accounts, most of his contemporaries saw him as a king of rigorous mind and body, creative and capably responsive in his dealings with the world. Many written stories and many folk memory voices have tried to portray his life and accomplishments, his character and his kingdom.

Two dramatic legends depict Krishnadevaraya as a wily survivor. In one his stepmother tried to prevent him from becoming the ruler. She asked her dying husband, King Viranarasimha, to have Krishnadevaraya blinded, as a prince without eyes would be unfit to rule. When Krishnadevaraya heard of this he said that he had no interest in being a king, but wanted to become a wandering yogi. A minister showed the dying king two goat eyes, and he died believing he had done as his wife had asked.[6] In another legend, one of Krishnadevaraya's wives-to-be had been told he was not really a *kshatriya*, and on their wedding night she tried to murder him. His wise minister Appaji came to know of the plan and he had a skilful artisan make a realistic dummy, filled with a sweet red liquid. When the wife's golden dagger pierced the dummy as it lay in the bed in a dark room, the liquid spurted and hit her lips, and she tasted its sweetness. She then repented and became frightened she had killed an extraordinary man. Appaji, who had concealed himself under the bed came out and consoled her, convincing her that the king was a fit and proper ruler.[7]

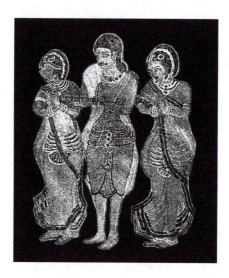

Figure 7.1   Krishnadevaraya and two wives worshipping at Tirupati, from a painting of bronze images representing their visit to the temple

His chief queen was probably Tirumalamba, and his penultimate queen Chinnadevi, but the *Amuktamalyada*, a text attributed to Krishnadevaraya,[8] mentions three queens, Tirumala, Annapurna and Kamala. Paes wrote that he had 12 queens.[9] And Nuniz recorded that, immediately after his accession, Krishnadevaraya married a courtesan of his youth, Chinnadevi.[10] Nuniz also mentions a son, Tirumalaraya, who was anointed as king at the age of six, but died of poison in a court intrigue. As a result, Nuniz wrote, Krishnadevaraya had his minister Saluva Timma and his sons blinded and imprisoned, suspecting them of murdering the boy.[11] But Nuniz's account is not respected by many historians. Mulk Raj Anand interprets Krishnadevaraya's marital relationships as a lifestyle of drawing on the Shakti (cosmic energy) of women: 'The belief was current that every virgin queen would transmit new energies to the Raja. The will to power inspired by the victory over woman was often transformed into urges for prevalance and creativeness.'[12] In this way, the theory goes, the king lost the loneliness which men at the top often feel, and forged, through bodily contact, deep bonds among the people, 'in the affirmation of the mating of Shiva and Shakti'.[13] He found in his wives and *devadasi*s fulfilment, grounding and inspiration.

'The Wisdom of Insecurity': Tidings of Krishnadevaraya's Kingship

One of the narratives of Krishnadevaraya's career was written (according to modern textual scholarship) by the minister of a Nayaka in Madurai, around the end of the sixteenth century or the beginning of the seventeenth century – the Telugu

Rayavachakamu (Tidings of the King). The text, which forms the basis for my shortened paraphrase in contemporary English, depicts a man's world of inventories of horses and elephants, strategies concerning enemies, plans for staying in power, issues of real politics and historical specificity.[14] It is the story of the growth and prowess of a dynamic ruler. Though one of its purposes seems to have been the legitimization of later Nayaka rule, the text is valuable as a legendary ideal reflection of memories about a real king's rule.

The genre of *karanam*, historiography in Telugu, as Rao, Shulman and Subrahmanyam show in their book, *Textures of Time: Writing History in South India 1600–1800*, is a rich form of traditional memory. *Tidings of the King* is an example of the *karanam* form which usually contains certain kinds of reflection and information. It is a book about statecraft. Typically, the *karanam* is a means of communicating certain kinds of knowledge, such as how to think about political situations, different customs and personalities, sexuality, strategies for dealing with conflicts, and how to understand and act in the public arena. These texts helped provincial people become men of the world. They illustrated situations and showed how causes and effects, and intentions and results, might unfold in unexpected ways. Typically in these texts the self-effacing assistant or adviser is wiser and more capable than the actual power-wielders on the thrones.[15]

Tidings of the King. describing how Krishnadevaraya became king, tells us that he distributed appropriate gifts and that he was anointed from golden vessels with water from four oceans and all the great rivers at an auspicious time, while the air was vibrating with the tones of 18 royal musical instruments, with brahmans chanting Vedic *mantra*s. He was given a shower of gold and gems, and then was freshly dressed and perfumed. With such auspicious rituals, including the chanting of brahmans, at the beginning, Krishnaraya was ready to reign.

In the course of his daily activities, the king heard a verse from the codes of conduct for kings,[16] describing how a king should rule, warning that a king's army should be greater than the armies of his feudatories. Krishnadevaraya began to realize that his forces were not as numerous and strong as they should be.

Disturbed by this, feeling anxious about the security of the entire political system of which he was head, the king began to go out and inspect the capital city surreptitiously by night, spying on everyone, including his own spies. It would seem that he trusted only himself at this point. His words to an inspector who seemed to be falling short in his duties were sarcastic: 'You're fine–and I'm perfect.' The king's mistrust of everyone even led him at first to underestimate his excellent minister, Appaji. (At times the whole narration seems to be a paean of praise not just to the shrewd Krishnadevaraya, but also to his wise and loyal minister Appaji, who always seems to know best.)

In short, the king was all alone, pulled this way and that by his personal dilemma of insecurity, looking out upon his kingdom, seeking to get control of his destiny and feeling inadequate, ignorant and impotent. So he was active each night, sneaking around in the hope of learning everything he could about his realm, seeking ways to improve his methods of protecting himself. The days occupied him with official public duties; at night he personally sought out the edge of chaos – an understanding of unknown, lurking challenges and dangerous problems – so that he could better define a system of order to counter risky chance and control unstable forces. It was not just his mind, capable of being soothed by the order of court and custom, nor just his body, able to be satisfied by exercise and pleasures, but his whole being – body and mind and destiny – which sought deeper genuine competence. His inner fire of restlessness and flaring imagination impelled him to discover what was happening, to learn for himself and to grow in his ability to rule. So he became acquainted with the night.

One night after scouting around the kingdom in disguise, he failed to return to his quarters. Appaji, his trusted minister, was alarmed. From scouts sent out to report back when they found the king, Appaji found that the king was at a temple on a hill 16 miles north of the capital. He went to meet him there, along with a retinue of the king's men and his forces. When he arrived at the vantage point where the king was thinking about his capital, Appaji approached him, and Krishnadevaraya pretended to be asleep, although in reality he was awake and worrying about his enemies, working out strategies to build defence bulwarks up to an adequate state and, further, to a condition of superiority.

Appaji waited until the king sat up and asked, as if surprised, 'Why are you here?'

Appaji explained how the king's absence caused him to take precautions and send out scouts and then asked, 'Is it wise to go out alone?'

The king gave an answer that seemed disingenuous, as if he were winking to someone who really knew better, or as if covering his doubt with a thick coat of sarcasm: 'Since I have great men like you there to carry the burden of the Lion Throne, how could any untoward events, such as losing the city, ever possibly happen? I'm sure you're so capable you could pluck a stalk of grass and turn it to cosmic Mount Meru, and no doubt you could change Mount Meru into a wavering blade of grass. You're a great man; who else could perform such deeds?'[17]

Appaji replied in all sincerity, 'I can accomplish things because you entrusted me with my position; a real sapphire attracts grass when it's rubbed,[18] a fake one doesn't; a servant rises in importance only through the greatness of his master, and only a master surrounded by the best servants can reach out for fame and glory. Shall we return home now? Day dawns and you're not at your throne.'

The king was not ready. 'No. I really doubt my ability to rule. Does anyone bow to my wishes? How would I respond to people who don't obey me? I'm not even able to punish them. How can a king rule if he doesn't have the ability to command and lead? How will he hold up *dharma*, punish wrongdoers and protect the good? Until I resolve this I feel I'm better off staying right here.'

Appaji agreed with the king and told him, 'Give me the word. Just tell me your wishes and I'll carry them out.'

The king replied, 'I've been thinking about verses on the proper conduct of kings. One aphorism in particular struck me as very profound and it made me think I should gather a military force more powerful than all my feudatories, and stop the momentum of the Turks. We need a big standing army, with elephants, horses, infantry – get it together; when you've done that I'll come back to the city.'

'Please wait here while I assemble such an army immediately,' Appaji said.

Appaji had ordered the king's forces to attend him, and now he went out to see them.

Having decided for himself how to accomplish what he needed, the king now waited all alone for the decision to be carried out. Now his feeling of being a lone man made him feel independent and strong, not vulnerable. He had rediscovered his *svadharma*, his own duty (as the five brothers of the first dynasty had discovered theirs). He had rediscovered a trust that clarity of resolve can be found beneath murky anxieties.

His minister Appaji went around to assess the king's resources. He spoke with the attending forces. The *nayaka* feudatories apologized for neglecting their duties of paying all the revenue they owed, and offered elephants and horses in lieu of cash. There was a great treasury in the capital, to be used only in time of great need. And, according to legend, long ago when the Vijayanagara capital was founded, *rajaguru* Vidyaranya had buried treasure for the use of rulers. Drawing on all these sources the minister returned with more forces and resources, sooner than the king had thought possible.

Appaji explained how, through negotiations, he had made ready 500 elephants, 12000 horses, 100000 foot soldiers and the appropriate numbers of officers to take charge of them. The king was pleased and gave his minister a cap, shirt, necklace, pearl earrings, shawl, musk and *pan* to chew, and, leading the way in a gold howdah, the king brought the splendidly assembled forces into Vijayanagara.

Krishnadevaraya then appointed a new accountant to oversee the payments from the treasury, so that all the people in his employ would receive their fair share. And he felt relieved: 'Finally, today, I can say my rule is resting on solid ground.'[19] Another minister, Ayyamarasu, congratulated Appaji as well: 'You're an extraordinary administrator – one in a million. Well done. You've done well.'

Before long, the other forces to the north of the capital got wind of Krishnadevaraya's plan to fight them, so they began to worry and build up troops, preparing and mobilizing their armies.

On hearing about this development from his spies, Krishnadevaraya asked if his enemies were really ready to attack him or would be able to defend themselves.

His adviser, Ayyamarasu, explained to the king the character of the threatening forces, whom he identified as Turks: 'These Turks are just a bunch of drunks and opium addicts, and they're so stoned all the time they can't filter out the noise of their own anxieties. They drink themselves loony and next day can barely even recognize their own bodies when they see them – they're that hung over. Obviously in that wasted state they don't know how to act. If a person gets in their way they just chop him down, hack him to pieces and move on. They act like some kind of Kali Yuga demons, if you ask me. Then, when they come to their senses, they stop a second and think: "Now these are our people's characteristics, right? That's just the way we are. But brahmans, they're different;[20] they're careful what they eat and drink, have a strict diet of rice, salt and sambar. So they're calm, they aren't afflicted with blind arrogance, rage and meanness.' After thinking it through like that, the

Turks get a bright idea: employ brahmans exclusively to work in the palace, and let these hired brahmans do the governing for them. So you see, it's only the advice of the brahmans that gives the Turks the sense to appoint the right commanders and organize the government's administration well. No doubt it's just because of the brahmans' cool heads and good judgement that the Turks are able to get away with it; they keep the realm in order, everything is done just as their advisers guide them. If the advisers start any infighting the master threatens their lives. (Little does he know he'd be undermining his own position if ever he really did kill the brahmans off.)'[21] In light of this new information, the king began to re-evaluate his enemies.

The minister assured the king that his boldness would overpower the three Turkish rulers. 'Wherever there is courage, there is Lakshmi; where she is, Vishnu follows; wherever you find Vishnu, *dharma* is present, and where dharma prevails victory rules.'

Krishnadevaraya's spies reported back to him after infiltrating the towns of Ahmadnagar and Golconda, saying that all was not well; they described horrible tortures meted out in punishment. They had overheard discussions of reports that Vijayanagara planned to attack Bijapur, Ahmadnagar and Golconda – the kingdoms of the three clans (of Muslim forces). 'If the Three Lion Thrones together joined forces, like Shiva going against the demons of the three cities, then we would fall.[22]

The rulers of Ahmadnagar and Golconda sent many spies to Vijayanagara and they also asked fortunetellers, both Muslim and Hindu, to predict the future. The soothsayers told them, 'A king has been born in Karnataka, who embodies an aspect of Vishnu. He will conquer your kingdom and those of the Ashvapatis and Gajapatis. After planting his victory pillar he will make a pilgrimage to worship Kalyana Venkateshvara, and to the 108 Vishnu temples, and the 72 Shiva temples and the shrines of the 18 Goddesses. He will worship Ramanatha at Setu, far on Southern tip of India and wash his sword at Dhanushkoti. Sitting on the Lion Throne in Karnataka he will rule unopposed for 64 years.'

Spies from Vijayanagara who were present in Ahmadnagar and Golconda and heard these words returned to Krishnadevaraya and told him of this prediction, and the king rewarded them handsomely.[23]

Rumours spread and tensions grew as both leaders and common people wondered exactly when war would occur. The Turks were suspicious and worried, having heard reports of the king's strengths.

The king summoned princes, leaders, government officials, sons and sons-in-law and asked about the numbers of elephants, horses and footsoldiers in the Turkish armies. Satisfied with the answers he got, he held court and spoke to two men familiar with Bijapur, asking how the leaders there rose to power.

Ayyanamalaka told Krishnadevaraya the following story: During a war which lasted 15 years between the Sultan of Delhi (who, among the kings of the Three Lion Thrones was the Ashvapati) and Prataparudra, the Kakatiya king of Warangal, Prataparudra was wounded in the hand by the sultan. The sultan took Prataparudra captive and brought him back to Delhi. There, when the sultan's mother was shown Prataparudra while he slept, she asked to her son, 'Is it right for you to take such a king captive? He's not a human being – he's an embodied aspect of Shiva; looking on him as he slept I could see Shiva, trident and drum and all.'[24]

The Sultan told her, 'I want you to take a look at me when I'm asleep.'

And when his mother looked upon him sleeping it seemed to her that she saw Lord Vishnu there, sleeping on the cosmic serpent Adisesha, with Lakshmi. Seeing this she was even more disturbed. 'For shame! If really and truly you are so great, can it be right for you to have captured poor Prataparudra?'

Next day she told her son, 'I know how great you are. Spread out a feast, let Prataparudra enjoy it, treat him with honour and then send him back home. That way your glory will be sung forever.'

Some time after that incident a man named Barid of Bidar conquered territory and captured forts, and, having established himself as a strong man, began to rule. Three of his men were put in charge of provinces. His hawk-keeper became known as Nijam Shah and ruled Ahmadnagar. His water-jug carrier became known as Adil Shah and ruled Bijapur. His dog-keeper became Qutb-all Mulk, ruler of Golconda. And Barid of Bidar promised them that their governance would last a century. This was how those rulers to the north got their power.[25]

Ayyanamalaka, after telling the king this story also told him that the Turks would be no match for Karnataka forces, since the Turks did not know the battle techniques and the strategic organization of armed forces; though they had a strong cavalry, they were unaware of the importance of foot soldiers which Krishnadevaraya's kingdom used to good advantage.[26]

'The Turkish style is not one of caution and calculation, but bravado and advancing in wild massacre; they charge ahead and flail about, unless their opponents are massively strong – in which case the Turkish soldiers beg to retreat. The Karnataka style is to plan carefully, to calculate well beforehand what is really possible, and to rule out what is clearly impossible.' The adviser encouraged the king to have no qualms. 'Your people will rise to the occasion – yours is the power of true mastery.'

Krishnadevaraya decided to launch an attack. 'Go, all of you, wash your hair, get ready to march!' (Hindu tradition holds that the warrior's long hair, tied with topknots, held their heroic power and valour; to wash it in an oil bath was a means of re-energizing them with fresh strength.)

Spies reported their findings in the Gajapati kingdom. They told of the king's daily routines there, his ceremonies and his fears. One morning while bathing in a river, guarded by his 16 *patra*s ('worthies'), the Gajapati was charged by Mughal horsemen. An amazing number of enemy horsemen were held at bay by the few defenders of the king. To escape, the king hurried on horseback across the river to safety, and his *patra*s fought valiantly in the skirmish. In the flurry of events all forgot the Jagannatha deity they had with them for their religious rituals – they had not had time to put it in the sacred *puja* container where it belonged. One of the four *patra*s who had been absent from the battle volunteered to retrieve it. When he was chased he turned and cut his pursuers to pieces, then crossed the river and joined his companions. Twelve of the other *patra*s told the king, 'You may not have understood

how strenuously we were engaged in fighting. We killed a lot of horses and riders.'
    The king was grateful to the 12 and gave them gifts.
    Three of the elders who had the misfortune of not having had an opportunity to
show their heroism at that time were disappointed; they had not been able to
demonstrate to the king their abilities and receive gifts as tokens of his appreciation.[27]
    To show their abilities, they performed three feats which were marvels – with a
sword one hacked off a huge branch which blocked their way; another was able to
remove a big tamarind branch obstacle by grabbing it while his horse leaped like a
gazelle; the third, on horseback, leapt over a canal 64 feet wide. For these various
feats the king gave all 16 *patra*s some gifts. Spies who witnessed these events
described to Krishnadevaraya the Gajapati wrestlers' amazing feats, and acrobatic
and other tricks which could be useful in battle. The king thus came to realize that
the Gajapati king was powerful and that the *patra*s and warriors were very brave and
admirably skilled and knowledgeable about warfare tactics.[28]
    At a feast for the lords of the 18 districts the king told his allies, the 'sons of the
eating dish', to penetrate the Turks' border and pillage the lands, and made
arrangements with his supply officers. He told Saluva Timmarasayya to stay and
protect the capital city. The king's men took forts and cities, one after another in
Bijapur and Golconda territory, destroying villages, taking cattle to sell to their own
people and devastating the territory.[29]
    Ramalingama Nayadu received a token gift from the king and used it to rally the
Kamma caste troops: '... This is your gift, so all I expect from you is virility – you
will be the basis and vitality for posterity in our Kamma community, and you will
have immortality in the praise which people will sing of you. Come here, we're in
this together – everyone who joins me to embrace heaven's joys!' And, dancing
around, he enthused them with his stirring words. Eighthly thousand soldiers came
forward as bridegrooms for the battle. Leaving the hopes and worries of this world
they eagerly joined Ramalingana Nayadu in battle, each considering himself as
fortunate as a groom approaching a waiting bride.'[29]
    When the leader and his men neared the Turkish camp they jumped on elephants'
backs with their swords and shields, and sported there graceful as lion cubs
frolicking on a mountainside.
    There was a flood at that time, and it brought bad luck to the Turks, who lost the
battle. Those who could get away, fled.
    When it was over, poet Muku Timmana described the victory:

> O Krishnaraya, you Man-Lion! You destroyed the Turks
> From far away with just your great name's power!
> Oh Lord of the elephant king, just from seeing you
> The multitude of elephants ran away in horror![31]

Others also praised the king after his great victory, and then Bacharasu suggested
that they take other Turkish forts south of the river, until the flooding subsided. This
was agreed and they began performing the *puja* of the war drums.

Enjoying the sweet reveries of conquest
the king at last can not restrain himself;
the earth-lord gives the command: 'Thunder
the war drums!' His foes' hearts burst asunder.

The drum-roars quake and convulse the earth;
releasing behemoth waves to wrack sea shores
uprooting Lokaka mountains; three worlds without
anchor now, waver, whirl, rock and spin about.

This is the awesome roar of high thunderheads
when the rains at last let loose all their fury,
This is the rumble when the cosmic embryo
breaks at the origin and time's becoming flows.[32]

The king's armies marched on; they took possession of forts and then marched further. After demolishing enemy fortifications, his men planted castor-beans in the fields.[33] The king kept marching relentlessly towards the Gajapati realm.

Appaji came and met the king, telling him: 'You've wrought much havoc in the kingdoms of the Three Clans, taking forts, sowing castor beans. You've won all the Gajapati hill forts, water forts, woods forts and open plain forts. But I must warn you now, you've reached the limit and it would not be wise to go any further on this campaign. You cannot go further. To do so you would need to cross the mountain passes next, and if you get to the other side, the Gajapati's allies will surely stop all your supplies from reaching you. Now it's time to stop.'[34]

Figure 7.2 Krishnadevaraya on horseback

But Krishnadevaraya stubbornly ignored this good advice which went against his desires, and continued his advance. As his men proceeded through the Gajapati's passes they were ambushed by archers, whose arrows poured down like a monsoon shower, and wild chaos ensued – some men ran, while some decided to stand their ground. The resistance proved effective and many of the ambushers died and retreated. Then the Gajapati king summoned his advisers, asking them, 'If the Adil Shah, Qutb-ul-Mulk and Nizam Shah couldn't take this king on, how can I? This is the first time a Karnataka king has presumed to invade our lands, thanks to the courage and power of the 16 *patras*. But remember that when your predecessor Pedda Gajapati ruled, once when he was on pilgrimage to holy shrines en route to Rameshvaram, some of his unruly soldiers ran amok and ransacked temples, disturbing brahman settlements and villages and groves in the Rayas' territory. Krishnadevaraya no doubt wants revenge. He has beaten the Turks, taken forts no one else could win so fast. He's no ordinary man – he must be an aspect of Vishnu embodied.[35]

The Gajapati then called his 16 *patras* together, and asked what they thought about the danger of attack.[36]

They told him that when the Turks couldn't withstand Krishnadevaraya's advance this gave the king a false sense of excessive confidence. 'We should send word to the Turks to mass a big force at their border, so he can't retreat that way; then we can march right up on him. He's in over his head, not listening to his advisers. We can take all he has: treasury, elephants, horses – everything; we'll bring you his chiefs in person.'

Pleased with this advice the Gajapati ruler gave gifts to his men, and they promised to meet him at dawn next day, to do battle.[37]

However, a spy who had been present at this meeting sent a letter to Krishnadevaraya describing all that had happened. Krishnadevaraya read it and began to fear he was on the verge of disaster. Seeing all his plans coming to ruin he cursed the way he'd rejected Appaji's advice. Seeing the king distraught, the army began to panic.[38]

When Appaji learned of the letter describing the Gajapati's plans, he immediately thought of a counter plan – a trick based on the strategy of gaining advantage by sowing dissension. He told the king to gather money and valuable jewels, putting them in 16 chests. He had a letter written and planted among the treasures, as if the 16 boxes were part of an agreement, and as if the *patras* had made secret arrangements without the Gajapati's knowledge. The 16 chests were sent towards the Gajapati's residence and the carriers were intercepted by the Gajapati and the carriers ran away. On reading the letter, the Gajapati lost faith in the *patras*, and fled to the north. The next day, when the *patras* came, they were astonished to find their leader gone. Feeling that it would be a disgrace to follow him, they all went home. This was exactly what Appaji had hoped would happen.[39]

Krishnadevaraya, taking advantage of the enemy's disarray, marched into the capital and set up a victory pillar. But he announced that he had come to increase his renown, not to annex the kingdom, and that he would soon return to his own territory. When the Gajapati king returned, he realized that he had been duped – that the 16 *patra*s had not really betrayed him. Acknowledging and respecting Krishnadevaraya's power and craftiness, he handed his daughter in marriage to him, and gave as dowry not only the kingdoms under his control south of the Krishna river, but also many gifts, including gems equal to 16 chests of treasure. From that point on, the three chiefs from Golconda, Bijapur and Ahmadnagar no longer fought Krishnadevaraya. They went to see him, to make peace, and they bowed to him, worshipping his feet.[40]

Krishnadevaraya then went to Tirupati, taking time out on the way there to win back a fort from rebels at Gulbarga. At Tirupati the king saw the sacred ritual of Lord Venkatesha and his consort Alamelumanga's wedding, and made offerings there, and also had a copper image made of himself and his two queens worshipping the Lord. He pilgrimaged and worshipped in many temples, going to Kalahasti, Chidambaram and Madurai, making gifts, bathing in holy waters and performing rites, and having pilgrim shelters built. At an auspicious time he returned to Vijayanagara, worshipping Vithala and Virupaksha. He held court, showered Appaji with jewels and gold, garments, ornaments and scents, and gave gifts to others too, in generous gratitude. He commissioned works of literature to be written by Allasani Peddayya, Mukku Timmayya, and Madanagiri Malayya, including the masterpieces in Telugu *Parijatapaharanamu* and *Manucharitramu*. The *phalashruti* ('fruits of listening') given at the end of this story promises that those who listen will become clever and wise, gaining the power of discrimination, as well as material and spiritual wealth and happiness, as long as the sun and moon shine high in the sky.[41]

Reflections on *Tidings of the King*

The story just recounted seems to illustrate a theme: even imperilled by unprecedented dangers one can survive and thrive with wisdom anticipating crises. In effect the story shows the qualities of a person who can prevail against loss. Though solitary, Krishnadevaraya had a knowledge of the whole system, as well as a valued network of helpers. He listened within, but also had the guidance of the profound and wily Appaji. Admitting his naivete to himself he initiated himself into a more nuanced realism, facing his fears in the night. As a result of Krishnadevaraya's worrying, his empire became the most militaristic and expensive South Indian state that the capital of Vijayanagara was ever to head. His rule was the empire's heyday. Shunning sleep and dreaming, he worried and spied, at least during the first part of his career, moved by the wisdom of insecurity. Staying up all night, agitated and bothered by thoughts of vulnerability, he caused his ministers to reorganize his forces, march all his troops, elephants and horses out, unlike any previous military leader before him. Worry-driven, he accomplished a practical dream in that region of South India. At the 'edge of chaos', where there is a struggle to redefine order and make the most of circumstances, one finds the optimum conditions for achievement[42] – the energies needed to face the dangers, the wisdom to keep balance and be both stable and daring, finding the power of vital endurance, enduring vitality. One must be adaptive – not too lax, not too rigidly aggressive. In situations where one is challenged and feels that survival is endangered and triumph demands full use of one's faculties and resources, order emerges out of necessity. Turbulent disorder can stimulate order, just as the challenges of life, 'the moral equivalent of war' can galvanize resolve, increase efficiency and expand productivity.

In the first half of Krishnadevaraya's career he is pictured as anxious and energetic in the marshalling of forces and the launching of wars. In the story narrated above, his experience of error concerned not listening to a warning – a purposive, unresponsive, male mistake. He was aggressively assertive beyond necessity, rigidly fixed in his stance, not knowing when to stop or accept limits or shift to a new mode. The wise man, Appaji, instead of taking, tried to surprise by giving (16 treasure chests) and saved the day. For a long time Krishnadevaraya was a continuous campaigner, but in the second half of his career he is pictured as being satisfied with his military achievements and concerned instead with culture and the arts of peace. He had eight great poets associated with his court, including Allasani Peddanna. He built temples, suburbs and reservoirs and sponsored great religious rituals and festivals. He seemed to know that his glory would endure if he was associated with immortal literature, great architecture, prosperity and beauty, and the encouragement of religious activities. Respected for his strength and generosity, his leadership skills and promotion of culture, he is remembered for his colourful combination of 'romantic and practical' qualities.[43]

Krishnadevaraya's Own Writing

Amuktamalyada, is a book in verse attributed to Krishnadevaraya. The text describes Vishnu as worshipped at Shrikakulam (in what is now the Kistna District) appearing before the king in a dream and telling him to write a Telugu poem on the marriage of the *alvar* Andal with Ranganatha. When the king tells his advisers and court poets about this the following day, they praise his literary gifts and speak of the Sanskrit works he has already composed. In the poem the king says, 'The language of this poem is Telugu, for in this land Telugu is our language, and I am king of the people here, and everyone praises this language. Of all the languages of the land Telugu is the best one.'[44] Although nationalist fervours have since caused all hyperbolic enthusiasm about regions and mother tongues to be suspect, there have been times when colloquial language has needed to be defended, and uplifted in the face of other values – as a counter to the exclusive use of Sanskrit in literature, for example. During Krishnadevaraya's time, as well as that of Achyuta Raya, Kannada and Telugu were both appreciated and encouraged and were mutually influential. This poem (which has sometimes been attributed to Peddana) seems to be the first Telugu work dealing with *vishishthadvaita* philosophy.[45] It is the most difficult and the greatest of the five traditional Telugu *kavyas*.[46] The poem tells how a king became a devoted Vaishnava, under the influence of Vishnu Chitta, the inspired debater who was the father of Goda (also known as Andal). Both father and daughter were *alvars* ('divers') – members of a revered group of South Indian Vaishnava saints whose lives were characterized by deep diving in bhakti consciousness. This following passage, from the First Canto of the book, is the poet's candid description of the simple natural delights of everyday life in Villuputtur, the village where Vishnu Chitta lived:

The Voice of Krishnadevaraya – The Atmosphere of Village Life

Dravidian women, before they have their baths
gather around the village well and rub turmeric
on glistening stones, then slosh and wash it away.

The splashed-down golden water flows along
and dyes the geese asleep downstream and they
awake transformed with shiny yellow wings
and flap and flutter, conjuring up images of geese
who would be at home in the lake of Vishnu's heaven.

Making their early morning rounds, village watchmen
spot the geese asleep, heads tucked under their wings
along the canal of irrigation water which folks use
to wash their clothes; confusing the geese with heaps
of laundry left by forgetful brahmans who came there for
morning ablutions, and hoping to return the clothes
to their rightful owners, watchmen reach for the bundles
and what a shock it is as the birds flap to glory and
the village women who are keeping an eye on their crops
can't help but laugh at the poor bewildered watchmen.

The brilliant Rajana crop proclaims it is best;
tickled here and there by cranes it seems to ripple
and giggle with pride, looking down on flower gardens
where jasmine blossoming vines and dates grow in rows,
where mangoes ripen, and chrysanthemums and other buds
puff up their own exquisitely clustered petals.

The rice crop is ripe; each stalk droops down
under the weight of sharp-point ears. When the wind
from the nearby forest shoves and shakes them
their prickly points rough up the lilies thick beneath;
when the paddies are drained of their water
the rice plants seem to be upside down – bent
all the way over in the sun, trying to quench their thirst
by drinking in the nectar of the flowers.

At the foot of the jackfuit tree a ripe fruit bursts
and it gets soiled. The juices flow from it and the bees
are swarming over it, drinking sweetness.
The jackfruit's as big as a boulder, and almost
looks like a springtime elephant in rut, his temple
burst, covered with dust, drunk with wine,
making passionate music, rhythmic twangs,
when he pulls and pulls on his strong chains.

In Villuputtur village ripe-fragrant hefty bunches
of bananas decorate orderly rows of plantains;
some of the fruits are so full and mellow
they have burst at the seams, hanging down and rubbing
against the earth. The clusters of fruits look like
huge garlands of chrysanthemum blossoms
bunched tightly together. The black noses of the bananas
look like bees who have passed out
from the overpowering chrysanthemum fragrance.

In this village the betel nut trees shed their leaves
which dryly drop down on the sugarcane stalks, and
(as folklore has it) are always knocking sugarcane pearls
into the oven where the juice is boiled; there the pearls
dissolve into white powder, as if the betel plant winding
round their necks is whispering to them, 'The powder
of pearls is the only sure cure', the remedy to bring about
the vital hue of their sweet joining together in love.

In the village mango groves the ancient pools built long ago
covered so thickly with lotus petals you might think
you could walk right across them; aromas of camphor,
green leaves and moss, and lotus hearts rise up from them.
Little fishes chase each other around, and the ducks arch
their necks, reaching under the water with a splash
and a gurgle to catch those fish for their breakfast.

In the twilight and at night, pounding drumbeats resonate
from the old stone temple of Vishnu. The rhythm ricochets
echoing up through Buruga tree branches, in the arbours
of pleasant gardens, just as the call of white birds
with fluttering wings, flying back to their nests from ponds,
mimic the temple's chant and drum sound patterns.[47]

In a sense, the village life that *Amuktamalyada* poetically pictures is fractal-like. The scenes of women in water, for example, are a glimpse of what is happening on a vast scale in thousands of villages in India. The verses have resonance because they portray self-similar events that have been enacted all over the whole of the subcontinent for centuries. The depiction of nature, observations of villagers working, the atmosphere of village life provide an entrancing background for the story of Vaishnava lives. In the narrative the poet tells the story of Yamunacharya, guru of

Ramanujacharya, and introduces some historically impossible connections among characters in the story in order to weave a better plot and bring rulers and saints together. Another reason for this fabrication is to allow Yamunacharya, the Vaishnava leader, on the eve of renouncing the householder stage of life, to teach his son political aphorisms. He would need this teaching, since in the story a law of succession causes Yamuna's son to inherit the Pandya throne. The teachings on statecraft concern the conduct of a king, employment of ministers, army and officers, spies, the administration of temples and public endowments and charities, justice, punishments and rewards, foreign affairs, war, the treatment of brahmans and other political matters. Some of the maxims are similar to those found in other *niti* literature.[48]

The Voice of Krishnadevaraya – Speaking of Tribal People

A unique feature of the text is the enumeration of principles for dealing with tribal peoples in the kingdom. Some seem rather cynical, others simply seem to be an attempt to assess likely patterns in tribal behaviour, and to recommend a policy of understanding that encourages restraint, leniency, tolerance and cooperation:

> It is always advisable to entrust the governance of wild tribes inhabiting hills and forests to heroes who have fallen from higher positions of status. That way the king is not affected much either way whoever succeeds in the power struggle that might ensue between them.

> If the tribal people of the forest multiply in any state the trouble to the king and his people would not be small. The king should make such people his own by destroying their fears. Because they are people of very little advancement, faith and want of faith, anger and friendship, bitter enmity and close friendship, often result from insignificant causes.

> When a Bhilla forester went, carrying his bow, into another's house, and the other entertained him with food mixed in milk, the guest observed the bark of some trees used for making ropes in a pot boiling in the fireplace. He mistook this for flesh. Angry because he was insulted at not being served a meal, the forester resolved to murder his host when it came time to leave the house and return home. But on that occasion the host explained he could not walk with his guest because the fibre boiling in the fireplace would get spoiled. The guest realized his mistake and parted from his host with affection....

> When foresters promise to do something after partaking of food mixed with milk in any one's house, under no circumstance do they swerve from their promise. If they observe any wrong, however small it might be, they become angry and become enemies with the supposed offender without considering the probable results of their acts.

> The wild forest tribes can be brought under control by truthfulness – by being trustworthy and keeping one's commitments to them ... [49] Increase the forests

that are near your frontier fortresses and destroy all those forests which are in the middle of your territory. Then alone you will not be troubled by robbers.

Minding the small faults of the forest chiefs who have no extensive power is like trying to clean a mud wall by pouring water over it. If a king gets angry at them he cannot utterly destroy them. If, on the other hand, he attaches them to himself by kind words and charity they will prove useful to him in invading foreign territory and plundering enemy fortresses. It is inconceivably bad government for a king to try to correct a hundred faults with a thousand punishments.[50]

Excursion: Other Voices Singing of Tribals

The voice of Dhurjati on tribal women's beauty

Whilst Krishnadevaraya's position as emperor may have kept him largely distant from the tribal people, other South Indian poets of the time celebrated their beauty in their verses. The sixteenth-century Shaivite poet Dhurjati, for example, wrote the *Kalahastimahatmyam*, in which he celebrated tribal girls' charms:

> The Bhilla girls stationed above the fields
> on lookout platforms drive away the birds
> with their yells and their amazing slings;
> yellow waist-leaves breezed back reveal
> naked bodies beneath. And beautiful lines
> curve gracefully up from their armpits
> to their youthful breasts' tips.

Figure 7.3   Women folk-dancers, from a sculpture in Vijayanagara

The girls frighten away the flocks of birds
with such high-pitched calls
that the passionate male cuckoo thinks
his own kind are calling him, so he returns
the calls; and the Bhilla tribesmen hunting nearby
feel their hearts pierced by the love god's arrows
and their response is to approach.

The girls wander around with their stalwarts
who have barbed arrows and bows of tough bamboo
with taut strings made of sinewy inner tree-bark.
They tie peacock feathers in their knotted matted hair
and mark their foreheads with shiny fragrant kumkum.
They cover with smooth fresh leaves their breasts
where no kuruvinda beads dangle
and one ties the peacock's tail securely
to the rough belt wound round her waist.[51]

The Vaishnava singer-saint associated with Tirupati, Annamacharya (b.1408) composed many songs which still survive. He saw the charm of the tribal woman in love and turned it into a voice expressing bhakti. The body of bhakti imagination hungrily devours beauty wherever it finds it. Here, natural love is celebrated as preferable to civilized artifice of a formal suitor. The *Chenchu* girl finds her authentic being, her own heart and body, dress and lifeways too satisfying to abandon.

The voice of Annamacharya: singing with tribal imagery

What are these jasmine flowers for?
Tell him to wear them himself.
For what am I but a tribal girl (*chenchu*)?
My hairstyle's already naturally fragrant.

What would I do with this silk sari?
Shiny green leaves are good enough for me.
Tell him that he can wind it
as a sash around his waist – I'm a tribal.

What do I want with a canopied bed?
Tell him to keep it and sleep on it.
What am I but *chenchu* girl who'd
rather roll around beneath a tree?[52]

Tolerance and encouragement of a variety of religious traditions marked Krishnadevaraya's rule; because of his personal conversion, the Vaishnava faith became very important in his time, and *prapatti* (surrender) is one of its major tenets.[53] One story from the sixth and seventh chapters of *Amuktamalyada* depicts the power of faith in Lord Vishnu's ability to save. The Vaishnava devotee must put full confidence in Vishnu, and this egoless trust is the greatness of surrender.

The Voice of Krishnadevaraya – Verses of Spiritual and Worldly Wisdom

Dasari, an untouchable devotee of Vishnu, always used to rise in the predawn hours, and go to the temple and sing praise. He was so immersed in the ecstasy of the spiritual realm, he ignored the rising heat of the sun until noon, and didn't even notice his own hunger.

One day he went astray on the path and met a *brahma rakshasa*, a spirit under a curse. This hungry demon, upon seeing Dasari, was dying to devour him.

The Vaishnava *bhakta* said, 'I'm happy to offer my flesh to fill your stomach, but please let me go to the temple first, so I can sing my daily songs of praise.'

'No,' said the demon. 'If I let you go you'll be gone.'

'If you fear I'll vanish after worshipping, let me assure you – I solemnly swear to return after completing all my prayers.'

The demon reluctantly agreed, and waited for his feast to return... .

The demon was overjoyed when he saw the devotee coming back along the path, offering again to satisfy his appetite. But mysteriously impressed by the faith of the devotee and his self-sacrificing spirit, the demon had a change of heart and changed his mind. Apologizing for his earlier demands and previous demeanour; he begged to be saved. He wanted spiritual sustenance now, and he urged the *bhakta* to give to him his *punya*, to share with him the merit of his songs of praise. The untouchable devotee refused.

'But why?' the demon asked. 'Does the ocean lose its water if a small fish takes a gulp? Does your God lose any glory when his praises are sung?'

The *bhakta* finally agreed, but admitted they were dealing with an unknown factor: 'I don't even know what the *punya*, the reward of singing God's praises might be. How am I supposed to give you something I know nothing about? But regardless of all that, one thing is certain: Lord Vishnu will definitely protect you and save you. Therefore, be assured and feel consoled.'

The demon suddenly was transfigured from an ogre – it was like dense smoke bursting into flame – and was transformed into Somasharma, a Vaishnava brahman. Then he venerated the untouchable devotee, and praised him, grateful that through him he had come to know Vishnu's merciful love and his power to transform and save.

The *brahma rakshasa* is the unhappy ghost of someone cursed because he went against his dharma and so had to suffer and harass others as an ogre. Spirits of ancestors who are neglected, and so are stuck on some ungodly level haunting the living until they find release, are also *brahma rakshasas*. There are many stories of their deliverance to a higher level. Sometimes they are specifically described as former brahmans. It is as if brahman purity is hounded by a nightmare shadow. The strict brahman sense of ritual purity casts a shadow of unconscious anxiety, and impurity is externalized as the other: untouchables and the like. The shadow which brahman sensibility casts in folklore and literature sometimes seems like a ritualist's impurity reflected and embodied in the form of the *brahma rakshasa*. Love of purity and auspicious light, on the one hand, and aversion to impurity, fear of darkness and inauspiciousness, on the other, form a strong dual dynamic of bonds and polar relationships. Within the Hindu system such stories picture a way out of this demanding order: saints arrive at serenity beyond aversions and attractions, liberated from the play of opposites.

In another part of the *Amuktamalyada* Krishnadevaraya writes with worldly wisdom of ways in which a king can endear himself to friends on whom he depends:

> Let a king fix up the various docks in the port cities of his territory
> and thereby encourage the sphere of commerce so that horses,
> elephants, jewels, sandalwood, pearls and other commodities
> may be imported with ease. And let him work things out so that
> foreign sailors who take refuge in his ports during bouts of bad weather,
> sickness or fatigue, may be cared for appropriately, according to
> their own culture's customs. Let him make strong bonds with traders
> from afar who deal in dependable elephants and the finest of horses,
> by making himself available through daily interviews; let him
> give them gifts and allow them to reap good profits. The king who acts
> like this will never have his belongings parcelled out among his foes.[54]

Notes

1   According to Vasundhara Filliozat, it was during the reign of Devaraya II (1425–1446) that the glory of the Karnataka empire reached its zenith. A time of peace and order, literary productivity, town planning and temple support. See Vasundhara Filliozat, *Vijayanagar*, New Delhi: National Book Trust, 1999, pp. 38–40.

2   This is according to Domingo Paes. *The Vijayanagar Empire as seen by Domingos Paes and Fernao Nuniz*, ed. Vasundhara Filliozat, tr. Robert Sewell, New Dehli: National Book Trust, 1977, p. 68.

3   Burton Stein, *Vijayanagara*, New Cambridge History series, 1987, pp. 44, 50.

4   Robert Sewell, *A Forgotten Empire*, New Delhi: Asian Educational Services (1982, reprint of 1900 edn), p. 239.

5   K. Raghavacharlu, 'Krishna Raya the Man' *Vijayanagara Sexcentenary Commemoration*, Dharwar: Vijayanagara Empire Sexcentenary Association, 1936. pp.181 ff. Walter M. Spink, 'Vijayanagara – The City of Victory,' *Journal of Indian History*, Trivandrum, Dept. of History, University of Kerala, No. 1, 1973.

6   A.K. Balasundaram, *Relics of the Vijayanagar Glory*, Anantapur: Rayaseemla Krishnaraya Publishing Works, 1948, pp. 13–18.

7   Ibid.

8   The debate still goes on. If Krishnadevaraya was such a good writer why do we have no other writings by him? There seem to be some similarities in style with Timmana's *Parijatapaharanam*. Others argue the king was too busy with administrative duties to write more. One source says the *Amuktamalyada* was written 16 years after the battle of Raichur, which was fought in 1520. See A. Balasundaram, *Relics of the Vijayanagar Glory*, p. 19. Thanks to Rama Rao Pappu for his thoughts on this. Personal correspondence, 3 June 2003.

9   Domingo Paes and Fernao Nuniz, *The Vijayanagara Empire as seen by Domingos Paes and Fernao Nuniz*, ed. Vasundhara Filliozat, tr. Robert Sewell, New Delhi: National Book Trust, 1977, p. 29.

10   Ibid., p. 141.

11   Ibid., p. 137.

12   Mulk Raj Anand, 'The Rise and Fall of the Vijayanagara Empire' in George Michell (ed.), *Splendours of the Vijayanagara Empire-Hampi*, Bombay: Marg Publications, 1981, pp. 35–36.

13   Ibid.

14   I have largely based my telling of Krishnadevaraya's life on Phillip B. Wagoner's excellent translation of the *Rayavacakamu*, entitled *Tidings of the King: A Translation and Ethnohistorical Analysis of the Rayavacakamu*, Honolulu: University of Hawaii Press, 1993. In this part of the chapter I have selected certain parts for emphasis, summarized and retold the story in my own words, and supplemented parts with information from other sources. I have noted those places where I use direct quotes. In his introduction Wagoner discusses the likely author of this 'ethnohistory' as a writer patronized by Visvanatha Nayaka of Madurai who reigned from 1595–1602. For more details refer to Wagoner's fine translation.

15   Velcheru Narayana Rao, David Shulman and Sanjay Subrahmanyam, *Textures of Time: Writing History in South India 1600–1800*, New York, Other Press, 2003, pp. 115–29. This book gives valuable discussions of kinds of historical writing found in South India in the late Viyanagagara and post-Vijayanagara era.

16   *The Sukraniti*, tr. Benoy Kumar Sarkar, New Delhi: Oriental Books 1975 (reprint). See also *Canakya-raja-niti*, ed. Ludwik Sternbach, Madras: Adyar Library and Research Centre, 1963. The *Artha Shastra* by Kautilya offers realistic advice to rulers on seizing and holding power, not relying on chance or the good nature of others, but by forcefully controlling situations.

17   The 'Three Lion Thrones' are the kingdoms of the Ashvapati, the Gajapati and the Narapati, of which Vijayanagara is the last.

18   A real sapphire attracts grass when rubbed, because of what we now call 'static electricity'.

19   Wagoner, *Tidings of the King,* p. 107.

20   In Krishnadevaraya's *Amuktamalyada*, he writes of brahmans: 'The king can place his hand on his breast and sleep serenely if he appoints brahmans loyal to him to be in charge of fortresses. Brahmans' services are necessary; therefore it's appropriate to put them in charge of well-provisioned fortresses, and well-equipped military forces and land' (IV, 225 and 261). Also 'Entrust your forces to those brahmans with whom you are well-acquainted. Don't leave them in a weakened state, but give them sufficiently powerful forces so they will not fear foes... a brahman will persevere in his position even in dangerous times, and will persevere in his service to you even if he is made a subordinate of a *kshatriya* or even a *shudra*' (IV, 207 and 217). See T.V. Mahalingam, *Administration and Social Life Under Vijayanagar*, Part One, Administration, Madras: University of Madras, 1969, p. 150.

21   Wagoner, *Tidings of the King,* p. 118. After the nephew of Vidyaranya, Ahobala, who averted a revolution, for over a century there is no brahman on the lists of ministers and generals until the reign of Krishnadevaraya. Then, for his and his brother Achyutaraya's reign, most on the list are brahmans. See M.A. Rangasvami Sarasvati, 'Political Maxims of the Emperor-Poet, Krishnadeva Raya', *Journal of Indian History*, IV, pt 3, p. 85.

22   In Hindu mythology the 'three cities' of demons referred to in this statement had received a boon of mobility – the whole of the cities could fly about flexibly for 12-year cycles; they could meet in assembly for three and three-quarter hours, and then take off again with impunity. Finally, after a long time, the Earth-goddess grew weary of this and complained that the demons were excessive, and it was decided that a combination of all the gods would be necessary to vanquish all those demons. A mind-boggling mythological array of vast powers are then all brought into play. Under assault from a vehicle with the four Vedas as horses, the Goddess as chariot, Mount Meru as bow, cosmic serpent Adisesha as bowstring, Vishnu as arrow and Shiva as charioteer, the three cities of demons would come crashing down.

23 Wagoner, *Tidings of the King*, p. 118.
24 Ibid., p. 123.
25 Ibid., pp. 123–24.
26 Ibid., p. 124.
27 Ibid., pp. 130–32.
28 Ibid., pp. 133–35.
29 Ibid., p. 138.
30 Ibid., pp. 138–39.
31 Ibid., p. 141.
32 Ibid., p. 143.
33 Castor plants are highly poisonous and grow quite large, some having 30-inch-long leaves.
34 Wagoner, *Tidings of the King*, p. 145.
35 Ibid. p. 146.
36 Ibid., 147.
37 Ibid., pp. 148–49.
38 Ibid., p. 150.
39 Ibid., pp. 151–52,
40 Ibid., pp. 152–53.
41 Ibid., 157–60.
42 For a far more detailed and technical example of this concept see Steve Lansing and James Kramer, 'Emergent Properties of Balinese Water Temple Networks...', in *American Anthropologist,* 95 (1) pp. 97–114. Complex adaptive systems, whether the Balinese water temple system in which farmers cooperate to share water or the Vijayanagara empire with its resources and opposing forces, strive to survive. The concepts used in complex adaptive systems theory offer modes of analysis to find the ways in which the system under consideration can reach the situation of optimum biological fitness or economic profit. This is called 'the edge of chaos' because it is poised between order and the turbulent energies of the dynamic cosmos. Sensitive to change and able to learn from experience, complex adaptive systems, when functioning well, can embody variable patterns which endure a long time.
43 Cited in V.V. Raman, *Satanama: 100 Great Names from India's Past*, Mumbai: Popular Prakashan, 1989, p. 15, citing M.H. Sharma, *The History of the Vijayanagara Empire: Beginnings and Expansion (1308–1569)*, Bombay: Prakashan, 1978, p. 150.
44 T. Rajagopala Rao, *A Historical Sketch of Telugu Literature*, New Delhi: Asian Educational Services, 1984, (reprint of 1933 edn,) p. 78.
45 C.R. Sarma, *Ramblings in Telugu Literature*, Madras: Lakshminarayana Granthamala, 1978, p. 38.
46 Rao, *A Historical Sketch,* p. 82.
47 Krishnadevaraya, *Amuktamalyada*, Visakhapattanam: Varald Ticar Trust, 1978, verses 64–72. See also Papireddi Narasimhareddi, *A Linguistic Study of Amuktamalyada*, Tirupati: Srinivasa Murali Publications, 1987.
48 Sarasvati, 'Political Maxims of the Emperor-Poet, Krishnadeva Raya', pp. 77 ff.
49 Ibid., verses 221–25.
50 Ibid., verses 256–57.
51 Dhurjati, *Kalahastimahatmyam III, 10–15*. Parts excerpted in P.T. Raju, *Telugu Literature*, Bombay: PEN All India Centre, n.d., pp. 111–12. Dhurjati's *Kalahastishvarashatakam* was translated by Hank Haifetz and Velcheru Narayana Rao in *For the Lord of the Animals: Poems from the Telugu*, Berkeley: University Of California Press, 1987.
52 *Molla lele naku tanne* by Annamacharya, cited by B. Rajanikanta Rao in 'Some Raga Patterns of the 15th Century and Their Setting in Annamacharya's Lyrics', *Journal of the Madras Music Academy* **LIV**, pts 1–4, 1980, p. 186. Similar to Annamacharya's song are these verses by Potana. In Chapter Two of Potana's Telugu *Bhagavatam*, Shuka says: 'There are many lovely spots where one can recline upon the ground,/So who needs special beds of cotton?/When palm leaves are easily available,/ What's the use of owning many platters?/With bark, hides and woven grass to use,/Who needs to bother with

lots of cloth?/Since there are caves around to inhabit,/Who needs to possess fancy palaces?/Trees drip juice, rivers run with fresh water/And good women offer plenty of food,/ So why should spiritual seekers serve men/Blind with wealth and drunk with arrogance?' (*Bammera Potana Bhagavatamu*, ed. K.A. Krishnamacaryulu, Vishakapatnam: Andhra University Press, 1979, Chapter II).

53   Not everyone considers Krishnadevaraya to have had a profound Vaishnava connection; see T.K.T. Viraraghavacharya in *History of Tirupati (The Tiruvengadam Temple)* Tirupati: TTD, 1954, vol. II, p. 616 ('...he had no Shri Vaishnava *acharya* or *purohit* initiate him into the Sampradayas...') and p. 619: ('as a devotee he was half-baked.')

54   Versified from the words of Sarasvati, 'Political Maxims of the Emperor – Poet Krishnadeva Raya', pp. 70–71.

CHAPTER 8

Krishnadevaraya's Legendary Court Jester and his Dancing Women

Jokers Wild: Tales of Tenali Ramakrishna, Court Jester of Emperor Krishnadevaraya

Many folktales in Andhra Pradesh purport to relate episodes from the life of Krishnadevaraya, describing his court and the doings of his queens and companions. A favourite folklore figure in South India ever since Vijayanagara times is Krishnadevaraya's jester, the irrepressible philosopher-poet Tenali Ramakrishna or Tenali Rama Linga.

The historical figure Tenali Rama was an actual poet who wrote a text entitled *Panduranga Mahatmya*, considered one of the five greatest poetic masterpieces in Telugu. Some scholars consider him to have been a creative, almost saintly, thinker, involved in spiritual culture of the highest order. Perhaps the poet was also a humorist and practical joker, and so legends grew up around memories of his eccentric demeanour. Especially in Tamil Nadu folktales he became an archetypal buffoon the mere mention of whose name often still brings outbursts of laughter. Yet a deep theme in legends about him is wisdom disguised as foolishness.

In Tenali Rama's *Panduranga Mahatmya* a ne'er-do-well brahman, because he happens to die in the sacred town of Pandaripuram in Maharashtra, is saved by Vishnu's servants from the clutches of Yama, the god of death. (The religious influence and popularity of the Vithoba tradition of Vaishnavism was growing in Maharashtra at this time. In this tradition Vishnu is pictured standing on a brick with his hands on his hips.) The story illustrates how even ordinary people who have faith and surrender to Vishnu can win the highest goal. The good fortune of grace and quick wits save the day, as piety laughs at itself, recognizing its own 'magpiety' and even 'custard piety', and yet affirming the pied beauty of loving piety. The figure of the tricky winner is an engaging one for the humorous imagination.

The avatars Rama and Krishna are divine tricksters; in the Ramayana epic Rama tricked Vali, killing him to do a favour for Sugriva. Krishna as a child was the trickster outwitting *gopi*s and demons. As an adult, Krishna cheated, breaking the rules of war in the Mahabharata epic. 'I am the trickster's hoax,' Krishna says in the *Bhagavad Gita* (X.36). Krishna sometimes seems to suggest to Arjuna, 'You can outsmart your opponents at their own game. Instead of being their fool you can fool them.' Later, it was sometimes the devotees who seem like full-fledged tricksters, cheating their deity out of boons and winning liberation through loopholes. Shiva could also be an elusive trickster, showing up in surprising disguises, always remaining a mystery to easily fooled mortals with their rigid value structures. In many folktales, an example of the bold and adventurous *bhakta* who tricks God and wins big is the poet-philosopher Tenali Ramakrishna. Sometimes wise men smile through fools' disguises rather than hitting people over the head with their brainpower.

Four Tales of Tenali Rama

Tenali Rama Receives a Boon

Once, it is said, Tenali Ramakrishna lost his way when travelling through a dense jungle. When he saw an ancient sage he ran up to him and prostrated himself at his feet. 'How did you end up here?' he asked the sage.

'The same mysterious force which brought you here also brought me. One thing leads to another. I have lived in this body a long, long time, but now the moment has come for me to leave it all behind. First, however, I'll initiate you into the mantra I've recited all these years, my talisman and my treasure." With that, he whispered the mantra of Mother Kali into the eager wayfarer's ear.

Tenali Ramakrishna was thrilled to receive this boon. He went on retreat in a temple dedicated to Kali deep in the thick jungle. There he meditated deeply on the Goddess with the help of the mantra, which he recited countless times.

At midnight the tribal Koyas of the forest brought a goat to the temple to offer a sacrifice to the Goddess. Tenali Ramakrishna hid behind the image of the Goddess and, as the blade touched the goat's neck, he spoke: 'I am Mother of all beings alive, including you Koyas. If you dare to kill this child of mine I will curse you, not bless you.' Believing this was the voice of Kali, the Koyas ran off in dread.

Then Kali, pleased with the wit and warmhearted compassion shown by the impostor, appeared before him, asking, 'What boon do you want?'

In her hands she offered the two choices: one was a vessel of curd rice, and in the other a vessel of rice milk. Tenali Ramakrishna was uncertain. 'What happens if I choose one or the other?'

'The curd rice will give you riches; the milk rice gives wisdom. But enough of your quizzing – right now – make your decision.'

Tenali Ramakrishna did not like the either/or limits set by the Goddess. He thought to himself, 'A fool with great riches, or a scholar who is starving – both are far from ideal.' He could see that Kali was beginning to lose her graceful patience. 'Before I choose please tell me how each dish tastes?' he asked her.

Kali laughed. 'How could I describe for you in words the taste of this curd rice or this rice milk? I don't have all day to explain the subtle nuances and exact differences – are you a fool? Taste for yourself!'

So Tenali Ramakrishna shrugged, and then gulped down both. Kali was furious. 'You'll pay for this impertinence! You won't get away without punishment.'

'Alright, I made a mistake. What will your penalty be?' He trembled as he submitted, waiting to receive whatever Mother Kali decreed.

Everyone knows the Mother cannot discipline her child by destroying him. In mercy Kali said, 'My punishment will not ruin you but will save you. It is this. Become a "Vikatakavi", a clever clown with power at court, gathering wealth and influence, guiding those who seek advice with your ironic wisdom. Your unconscious foolery will be wiser than the careful logic of prosaic plodders.' [Vikatakavi is a symmetrical anagrammic series of syllables meaning 'contrary poet' or 'inspired buffoon'.]

His self-confidence, boldness, faith in himself had truly paid off.[1]

Krishnadevaraya Honours the Specialist-Clowns Who Learn Their Limitations

One time, at the height of the Vijayanagara empire, during the glorious reign of Krishnadevaraya, there were five great scholars – a logician, a grammarian, a musician, an astrologer and a physician – all of them expert in their respective fields. Their outstanding qualities came to the attention of the ever-watchful and excellence-appreciative chief minister, Timmarasu.

When Krishnadevaraya was informed about them, he asked that they be invited to the capital, to be honoured with gifts and titles. Timmarasu prepared a spacious house for them to stay in, and furnished it with utensils and conveniences. He also put some spies in charge of keeping an eye on them. After the scholars had arrived, and settled themselves, they were invited to a reception at the court. 'But first, please make yourselves at home, and select your foods of choice, and cook them and eat a meal together. Then you will meet the king.' He knew this was something out of the ordinary for them – they were not used to doing ordinary chores.

To get the food ready the experts divided the chores among themselves. The logician's task was to go to market and buy clarified butter, ghee. After acquiring it he was returning to the house, holding the ghee vessel in his hand when his expertise in logic took over. It occurred to him to ask the question: 'For its existence and identity, does the vessel depend on the ghee or the ghee depend on the vessel? I must think about this.' First, he argued the point one way, then he argued the other. Though highly rational, the debate of hypotheses was inconclusive, undecisive. It was only rhetoric and theory. He desired to know what the actual truth was, and he began to think that only an experiment could prove for certain what was factually true, so he turned the vessel upside down and the ghee poured out into the dust. Only at that moment, when it was too late, did the logician understand the actual relationship between 'the support' (the vessel) and 'the supported' (the ghee). Therefore, fully satisfied that he had arrived at the conclusive solution to his dilemma, he returned to the lodging, quite pleased with himself, barely noticing the fact that the vessel was empty.

Meanwhile, the grammarian's task was to go buy some curds. He heard a milkmaiden out in the lanes, calling out '*Salloy yamma salla!*' The correct pronunciation would have been '*Challoyamma challa!*' – I offer this buttermilk for sale!' The ungrammatical sounds jarred his nerves and, feelng rankled, he covered his ears. A little further along the lane another milkmaid called '*Perughoyamma perughu!*' whereas the correct pronunciation would have been '*Peruguyamma perugu.*' Unable to restrain himself he went up to her and berated her: 'You simple-minded country bumpkin. Correct pronunciation is very important. It is said that *shabda*, subtle vibration, is near the supreme consciousness. To corrupt it is to falsify, to taint the absolute; and, to misuse language so badly, you are guilty of sacrilege. The science and discipline of grammar forbids elongating vowels arbitrarily, and condemns aspirating them on sheer whim. Ignorance is no excuse. There are exact rules. One syllable is in no way interchangeable with another. If substitutions are allowed terrible anarchy ensues, misinterpretations, faulty transactions and awful calamities will befall us all. You must practise speaking correctly, with perfect attention, or else be silent.'

The milkmaid made a face and said, 'Somebody ask your opinion? Where you come from? You a wild man or somethin'? Where'd you get the right to dictate how I talk? You're sorta outta control, ain'tcha? You want some curds, buy! If not, shut your trap and leave me be. Quit wastin' my time with your idiotic speeches!'

The grammarian was indignant. 'If I were to purchase any curds from an uncouth wretch like this who speaks so poorly, I too would incur considerable blame, because of guilt by association.' And so he went back without any curd.

The astrologer's task was to obtain some leaves to use as plates for the meal. He went to a nearby forest and climbed up a banyan tree to pick leaves. When he was about to start collecting them, a lizard on a nearby branch clucked: 'Kurkur kur.' The astrologer was startled by this. He knew that a lizard making such a sound was a bad sign. 'I'd better not pick any leaves under such inauspicious conditions. I'll just climb back to the ground.'

But, as he started down the tree, another lizard beneath him started chirping oddly. 'A lizard chirping like that is a bad omen. What should I do now?' Thinking like that, uncertain, going back and forth, he was stuck. And when the day was done he gave up and went back without any leaves.

The doctor's task was to buy vegetables. He went to market and saw many varieties. He thought, 'There's bringal, but it generates heat. Those bottle gourds generate phlegm. Dumpakarula roots cause rheumatism. That Goruchikkudukaya produces bile, I don't know … ' It seemed that every single kind of vegetable had some drawback, so he drew back and returned to the house without any food.

The musician's chore was to cook the food. He boiled a pot of water and poured rice into it, covering it with a lid. As the fuel burned and the flames rose, the steam rattled the lid rhythmically, and with that, the musician tapped his fingers and started singing the tones of the scale: '*Sa ri ga ma pa*' and clapping his hands.

The rattling lid was somewhat offbeat compared with the musician's *tala*, so he held the lid down tightly. That stopped the rattling, though the simmering and boiling water inside kept up its rumble and was even more out of tune with his song. 'This is chaos!' he exclaimed, grabbing a big stick to give the offending pot a big whack, causing the pot to crack and the boiling rice to splatter. But he felt justified and relieved that the wrong rhythms and unharmonious tones had been silenced, even if it meant a broken pot.

By nightfall the five one-sided specialists were together again. Each used unkind words to blame the others that there was nothing to eat. When Krishnadevaraya learned of their problems through his spies' reports, he felt sorry for them and called them to court. There, Tenali Ramakrishna asked them: 'Good sirs, dear friends, what have you learned?'

The five humiliated 'experts' felt like sad clowns and stood speechless, hoping they would not be called on by name.

The king said, 'Honoured guests, specialist gentlemen, dear friends – it's useless to be so expert in a field if you have no common sense. If you are obsessed and overly purposive, you'll forget how to respond intelligently to what actually is there – you'll forget what you most deeply need. Your basic hunger will go unsatisfied; you'll be so brainy and dominant you'll starve to death.'

Cautioning them like this about narrowness and rigidity, he had his servants feed them, gave them gifts and sent them off to their respective homes.[2]

The King Learns About Parrot-style Devotion

Birds provided a form of entertainment in Vijayanagara: 'Birds, such as swans, doves and parrots were domesticated and taught to amuse [people in] the palace.'[3] According to a folktale Krishnadevaraya once trained a parrot to recite, 'Rama Krishna Govinda Achyuta Ananta'. The emperor and his queens liked to fondle and pet this parrot, and give her dainty morsels of food, fruits, nuts and sweets. In return the parrot faithfully recited the holy names, 'Rama Krishna Govinda Achyuta Ananta'.

Figure 8.1 Woman with a parrot, based on a sculpture in Vijayanagara

One day, when Krishnadevaraya was feeding the bird, he told Tenali Ramakrishna, 'Observe her great bhakti! She recites the names of the Lord with such heartfelt love. She has more bhakti than you do. Listen!'

The bird said, 'Rama Krishna Govinda Achyuta Ananta.'

Tenali Ramakrishna said, 'But majesty, this parrot is reciting the names of God out of gluttony, isn't it? To get more fruit and sweets out of you. It's not from true bhakti.'

Krishnadevaraya denied this angrily, saying, 'You're obviously wrong. If you think you can stop this sincerely devoted parrot from doing her *japa*, go ahead, try.'

'It shouldn't be difficult to do that,' Tenali Ramakrishna said, as the parrot said, 'Rama Krishna Govinda Achyuta Ananta,' again.

Next day, Tenali Ramakrishna brought a cat, and, putting a leash on him, let him get into the parrot's cage. He could control the cat with the leash fairly easily.

At first, the parrot said, as usual, 'Rama Krishna Govinda Achyuta Ananta.' But as soon as the parrot saw the cat she got flustered and fluttered about wildly, trembling and rushing from one side of the cage to the other, shrieking loudly with fear.

Krishnadevaraya felt sorry for the parrot and coached her, 'Say "Rama!" Call out to "Krishna!".' But the parrot just squawked shrieks of terrified panic, and nothing of the usual mantra was heard. Then the king had to admit, 'True bhakti is something that only humans with loving hearts can express in human languages.'[4]

The King Learns What Is Natural

One day Queen Tirumalamba, favourite wife of Krishnadevaraya, sent a messenger requesting Tenali Ramakrishna to come and visit with her. When he arrived, she seemed downcast. He asked her, 'What seems to be the problem?'.

The queen explained. 'O Rama Linga, there's been an error, a *faux pas*. And for this breach of etiquette I must make amends.'

'Tell me about it,' Tenali Ramakrishna responded.

'Recently the emperor came to see me. And as he spoke at length on a matter dear to his heart, I happened, unfortunately, to yawn. He saw my yawn and interpreted it as boredom, and he felt so insulted that he left in a huff and hasn't come back. It's tragic. I never realized what a great error it could be to yawn. If only you could persuade him to come back to me. You've heard the famous story of how Timmana was able to bring the king back to my co-wife Nagalamba, haven't you? When she made that mistake of touching the king's portrait with her feet when it was on a bed? He came back and they straightened things out, and Timmana wrote the *Parijatapaharana*, in which it is shown how even pushing at the head of her Lord with her feet was a blameless blunder since the queen did it in a mood of amorous anger. Can't you think up something along those lines to help me out?'

Smiling, Tenali Ramakrishna shook his head, saying, 'Your majesty, that was different. Your little yawn was not the stuff of immortal verse. But trust me. I'll get the king to realize that he is the one who is making a mistake. Have patience.'

And so time passed. Soon the king was busy managing a project to send relief to an area where famine was imperilling the very lives of his subjects. It was a serious problem and he was doubtful about accomplishing it. He was somewhat downcast, feeling frustrated that he could not orchestrate events to produce a huge harvest all of a sudden – it was just not in his control.

Tenali Ramakrishna approached him with a handful of rice. 'Your majesty, this paddy is a marvelous variety. When it is planted, it multiplies almost magically.'

The king seemed to brighten immediately.

'The only catch is this: it must be sown by a person who has never once yawned in his or her life – not once!'

The king scowled. 'That's stupid. Who in the world has never yawned? It can't be helped. Who could stop himself from yawning? It's uncontrollable.'

Tenali Ramakrishna began to walk away. 'Where are you going?' the king asked.

'I did not know that – that everyone yawns,' he said, like a fool. 'I'm going to tell poor Queen Tirumalamba. She's been fretting – she thinks she's the only one, and she's sad, inconsolable in fact. She feels helpless that she can't control her yawns.'

The king saw the point and felt foolish. He said, 'Very well. You don't need to do that. I'll go see her now.'[5] And so the queen's problem was resolved.

People in South India have delighted in Tenali Ramakrishna's stories for centuries: how he escaped the king's punishment of having his head crushed by an elephant by tricking a hunchbacked dhobi to take his place; how he used cleverness to avoid a beheading; how he got out of being whipped by promising to give two different sentries 'half of whatever I get'; how he got thieves to remove the water from a well when he wanted to water a garden; how he mistreated a horse and a kitten; how he outsmarted a man of great knowledge and a wrestler; and how he tried to wash a black dog white to show the king that a barber could not be made into a brahman.[6] Such a clown leads a charmed life, because he seems to be a foolish outsider who is inferior to his listeners, but he also has a power of surprise – turning the tables, going against ordinary preconceptions. Like the fool in Shakespeare's tragedy *King Lear* he spouts nonsense that, at a deeper level than surface logic, is somehow coherent.

There are also many stories of the king and his wise minister Appaji, in which the shrewd adviser anticipates the king's needs, and solves his problems or saves him from danger. It may be significant that so many of the stories have to do with the theme of learning lessons, facing self-education in unknown areas. This seems to reflect a need of the day – to confront one's own foolishness and limits of the known, and break new ground in understanding. Whereas in the South Indian folk memory Krishnadevaraya stood firm in his earnest endeavours, taking his royal responsibilities so seriously, Tenali Ramakrishna stood for delight in caprice, the uncontrollable elements of life that are most daunting to those who try to keep all things under control. Like King Lear's fool he reveals the hidden truths which lurk under everyone's noses. Even great leaders need to relax and remember their humanity – otherwise they follow ambition and ego to absurd heights, where only a fool would dare say, 'But the emperor is wearing no clothes'. Tenali kept his childlike naivete and its childish power delights the child in us. If one can make the powerful laugh they may be disarmed of their harshness. Even if Tenali Ramakrishna did not exist, his age would have to invent him, to keep in the people's mind the dynamic paradoxes and quirks of reality as they were actually experienced.

Considering all the King's Women and Auspicious Waters as the Unifying Spirit of Life

The archeological ruins of the octagonal royal bath[7] in the capital of Vijayanagara are very intriguing. The cool geometry evokes in the imagination scenes of relaxation and refreshment, even though there is no water there now, and no signs of the women and the kings who spent time here. It is easy to picture the king relaxing there with women, especially if one reads the European visitors' descriptions. Paes, who was in Vijayanagara in 1518–1519 describes Krishnadevaraya as a man of medium height, fair complexion, well built, with a smallpox-marked face and cheerful demeanour. His dozen wives each had their own apartments or homes, and each had 60 women attendants. The wives and attendants and dancers were said to be ornamented with dazzling jewels, showing their great wealth. The king was surrounded with 12 000 women – doorkeepers, swordfighters, musicians, attendants, carriers, wrestlers, washer women, astrologers, writers, cooks, judges, bailiffs, watchwomen. According to Nuniz, 4000 women lived in Krishnadevaraya's palace. Wearing white cloth with roses stitched in gold, and diamonds around his neck, the king ate on a three-footed stool of gold and was served food from vessels of gold.[8] The energies he took in were inextricable from the dynamic females surrounding him, who not only fed his physical being with rice and fruit, but fed his psyche being as well.

Women in classical Hinduism embody an abundance of beauties and energies; they embody a goddess power (in Sanskrit, Shakti) capable of being turned in many ways, and men have tried to limit, lock, and shape women's lives to their own benefit. From some of the artistic depictions surviving from that age – carvings and paintings – it is easy to imagine the *rasika* in the company of the courtesans. Like *apsarasa*s, the mythical heavenly women of waters, the courtesans disrobe, yawn, smile, rinse their long luxuriant hair, look in the mirror, remove a thorn from a foot, play with pets, write a letter, apply cosmetics, and amuse themselves with trained birds – everyday acts done with the gracefulness of dancers, ordinary yet cosmic, with a soulful nonchalance. The women are waves and the men sport among them, swimming in the fluid trance of sexuality. The soul loves moisture; this is a very ancient psychological observation.[9]

According to Paes, in Krishnapura, the suburb built by Krishnadevaraya, there were tall buildings decorated with figures of erotic couples.[10] In bedrooms of wealthy Vijayanagara citizens and in public places were depictions of the 84 positions of lovemaking.[11] This frank acceptance of sex as a natural glory or integral part of life, instead of branding it as shameful or offensive, is shown in the same methods and positions of lovemaking sometimes carved in stone at temples. For example, further north, Khajuraho's 84 temples[12] show a vision of lovemaking different from that of the West and one that is oddly disturbing to the psyches of some Westerners, like seeing a dream in broad daylight. It is not a Platonic sublimation, not Freudian libido's destiny of regression, and not an accountant's aberration of swarming proliferation.[13] It is *ananda* (bliss) and wonder in joyful coupling.

The lovers are like interlinking participants in the great chain of being, lives encircled, levelled and intoxicated by a season of heat and affection, rendered cosmic by tantric vision's experience.[14] It is almost like an artistic rendering of Raimundo Pannikar's philosophical concept of the 'Cosmotheandric principle' – connective similarities among the three levels of world, God and humanity. They form an illustration of the spiritual resonances and depth of community among existences in the universe. The *Kama Sutra* depicts how characteristics of bull and cow, stag and doe and other creatures should be manifested in lovemaking by lovers play-acting like them while showing affection.[15] And some artworks visually depict features of animals, vegetables and minerals in harmonious similarity to lovely female features.[16] Different species may share similar features and capacities within the same creation, which depends upon the sun. This vision can also be seen as a metaphor for the mystery of beauty itself. The poet Kalidasa suggested that the Creator selected the best aspects of various examples of beauty in the universe and joined them together uniquely in the creation of Goddess Parvati. Thus those things of beauty share an existence – they are in her, and she is reflected in them. And she is the archetype of the feminine, imaging the polymorphous ways of the soul. Cosmic beauty focuses in her form, an attractor in the religious imagination, a visualization of a vast and exquisite intermingling of energies.[17]

And, of course, the Hindu world-view pictures each person as having struggled up to higher consciousness, through stone to plant, through plant to animal, through animal to man. God is no other than animating energy, intelligent pulse circulating blood, brilliance, wisdom, 'negentropy' (the power of consciousness running contrary to disintegration) and the fluid play of life. God is the consciousness behind it all, *paramatman*, the juice of unity that ultimately gives life to every moment of experience in all. God has played, incarnated in all the levels – fish, turtle, boar, man-lion and so on. God is consciousness, and consciousness is the source of all order seen in the universe – elusive simplicity which conceals its operations, covering traces of its modality. Images of cosmic love suggest all this.

In Vedanta philosophy, nameless formless consciousness makes names and forms possible: the vocabulary of bodily beauties and graceful radiances is abundant in the art of dance. The ten *Deshi lasya angas*, which are the classical *Bharata Natya* poses, include one for bending part of the body into a bowlike curve (*angahara*) and the graceful moving of the breasts (*dhasaka*). *Tharahara* is also a term for with the proper dance gesture of breast movement, and *kittu* is the proper movement of breasts, arms and hips. *Dillayi* is the sweet abandon of limbs without loss of *sausthava* and with the dancer appearing to be soaked in the sentiment (*rasa*) presented. *Lavani* or *tavani* is bending the body with ease, even in difficult movements.[18]

Traditional Hindu physiology values fluid suppleness, tender stretchability, twistable, archable, bendable, knotable bodies.[19] The dancer, *apsarasa*-like, embodies the spirit of life. Without a vision of fertile love, men risk going beserk, or their lives are in danger of drying up. In the Vijayanagara empire the courtesans who practised the art of dancing were representatives of a role essential to society since the earliest known times, constituting a 'normal and necessary adjunct of both palace and temple. The *apsarasas* were their heavenly counterparts'. [20] Without the blessings of the power of fertility, represented by *apsarasas*, the land dries up barren as the wounded Fisher King's in the old story of the lost grail. Goddess Sarasvati is associated with waters, and is the guide blessing the graceful way in learning, music and arts.[21]

As Lee Siegal writes, ' ... *rasa* is love, the pleasure of savouring love and the heavenly elixir, the lifegiving honey of love'.[22] In Indian tradition, Angirasa is the God of Life, and *Angirasa bhuta* is the essence of life, protecting and vivifying all the organs in a person, and enabling people to live in the material world of different names and forms.[23] *Rasa* is the flowing sap, the living juice of supple plants. The season of spring is fluid with new beauty emerging, *sa-rasa* – beautiful, delicious, impassioned, the season of throbbing fluidity. In depictions of the 84 *asanas* of coupling, in the poetry of loveplay, in the coupling of flowers and features ('lotus eyes'), creatures and human functions, and in temple art, the pilgrim can see the world soul reflected and imagine participation in that spiritual wholeness.[24] To lose oneself, to loosen up and release oneself, to transcend oneself, to work and send oneself up into a fervor and say 'I love you' to the light at the core of all life means the liquification of ego, the glittering sweat of love, the coolness of evaporation. In the *Bhagavad Gita* (VII.8) Krishna says, 'I am the *rasa* in water' and the sound in space, the *paurashtam* – zest, aspiration, courage, daring creativity – of life'. Thus, Krishna identifies himself with the eros in woman, the rhythm in dancers, the unifying love in bhakti, the balance of work, worship, and wisdom. The embodied soul on earth is like a skilful woman who comes from the temple to court and returns; and then again comes to court. To paraphrase Goethe, 'The soul of the human is like water; it comes from heaven, and soars back to heaven, and then it again descends to the earth, always involved in transformations.'[25] 'Narayana', a name of Vishnu the Preserver, is playfully derived from the idea that the Lord has his abode (*ayana*) in the waters (*nara*), specifically the flowing generations of the human family, the river of humanity.[26]

The woman power of the dancer was a fertile energy which could be turned towards the secular or towards the sacred, like the ambidextrous quality of water: 'If you pour water into a conch shell, it becomes holy water; if you pour water into a potsherd it becomes ordinary water' (Telugu proverb). Water is a primary system, so simple, of one fluid substance, always following its own way. The ways of water are able to inform, help man 'metaphorealize', and serve as a comparative system for other processes of nature, including human life. Water, like a long-suffering woman, has the power to return in cycles, to slowly wear stone away with patience. Sanctified or secularized, adored or exploited, woman and water are basic power – shakti. In India the rivers are goddesses – liquid shakti. The illusion of men's strength, apparently firm and changeless, also depends on a fluidity. Krishnadevaraya built himself up daily with exercise, oil massages, horse riding and vigorous physical activities in the predawn hours, increasing his flexibility for his personal strength. Paes reported that the king daily drank three-quarters of a pint of gingelly (sesame) oil before dawn, took an oil bath and then worked out with earthenware weights and sword practice until the oil had been perspired. After this, he wrestled with one of the wrestlers, and then went for a fast ride on a horse, racing back and forth on a plain. After these predawn practices he washed, assisted by a brahman.[27] Then he performed *puja* (worship), and entered a many-pillared pavilion with two exquisite images of women on either side, where he met with his officials and advisers.

As mentioned earlier, Krishnadevaraya was constantly surrounded by women attendants, pananquin bearers, doorkeepers and dancers. The Lotus Mahal, with its intricate architecture, was decorated with paintings depicting various lifestyles in different places, used to teach the king's wives about different regions and cultures.[28] In a hundred-pillared hall there was a sculpture of the young woman saint Andal, in a dancing pose, and in the exercise area of this hall was a bar for the dancing women to hold while doing their stretching exercises. On one side there was a golden-walled and floored space where the king could watch the dancers. In the centre of the wall there was a golden image of a woman of the size of a 12 year old, with her arms held in the pose used to signify the ending of a dance,[29] reminiscent of the thin youthful dancer statue found in the Indus valley. In my view, this is an anima image – an inspiring picture of unfolding vitality. The graceful girl suggests life's forward flow, the glorious promise of fulfilling life, vibrancy. She stands for the beauty of fitness and the fitness of beauty – hope, the attractiveness of potential. Mulk Raj Anand has discussed how Krishnadevaraya was a great man 'who expressed himself with freedom and spontaneity'[30] with his women, and how the king needed to inspire the wills of many people, drawing on the power of Shiva's fearlessness for his army's bravery and Vishnu's abundance for his subjects' enjoyment. As the muse inspires poets and artists, so the courtesans of Vijayanagara inspired the rulers. With his rituals, festivals and processions, Krishnadevaraya 'inspired a collective spirit of aspiration to greatness, by evoking the unconscious urges of people ... . He made the sense of glory into an ultimate passion for himself and the people.'[31] I believe that this interpretation helps us understand the religious imagination of the age, the psychological power of the religious images and practices. In understanding the dynamics of attractions and fulfilments, Antonio Damasio's ideas are relevant: 'The mind exists for the body, is engaged in telling the story of the body's multifarious events, and uses that story to optimize the life of the organism.'[32] Such ideas help us consider the meanings of the king's many women in the arts and imagination of the day.

Woman's caring and loving body is like the molten platinum glimmer on dark water; her charm is incandescent, a fleeting moment at dawn, effervescent yet full of stamina, evanescent in bashfulness but enduring steadily unlike that of men. Woman has a steady charge, South Indians say, a constant flow of riverlike shakti, electric with energy, whereas man's strength often peters out.[33] She is like the many busy hands of a river's waves or currents; she is the water of serving, humble lowliness, helping all as it gracefully, majestically and invitingly flows along.

Apsarasas, the original archetype of many later attractive figures of women associated with water, are ancient figures, evoked in the Vedas – for example, 'the *apsarasa*, the Lady, sweetly smiling, supports her Lover in Sublimest heaven ... '[34] *Apsarasas* come from the waters, *apsu*, and the sunlight illuminates the waters, making *soma*, 'the depths of light become an aerial ocean'.[35] The play of language embodied in the term '*apsarasas*' is only surpassed by the playfulness of their being. As Kees Bolle points out, *apsarasas* arise from the ocean, but are a permanent aspect of the heavens and a continuation of the realm of the 'chaotic'. They belong to all, not exclusively to anyone. Yet, this quality of belonging to all seems wrong to conventional Western social morality:

> The *apsarasas*' behavior is different from the set forms and has a semblance of 'immorality.' As a matter of fact, their immorality is recognized and allowed and plays a great role in the Epics. They are, so to speak, a permanent feature of heaven in which the human opposites of morality–immorality are obliterated.[36]

Apsarasas form an archetype of divine play, of imagination's freedom – free lightness in motion. These celestial dancers with their hypnotic gracefulness have such lithe and airy bodies that they are said to be made not of the earth element, not of solid human flesh and bones, but of the playful breezy qualities of air – flowing, bending, extending outward, jumping up and running along.[37] Their dynamic activity is full of the subtle energies of life. Originally *gandharvas* (mythical musician-guardians of *soma*) and *apsarasas* were *yakshas* and *yakshis* – life-spirits, lovers, dissolvers and solvers of devotees' vital needs, meeting folks under trees on the roadsides of life and blessing them with abundance.

The delightful sound of rippling water is the music of *apsarasas*' musical instruments.[38] The *apsarasas* step out of their vaporous robes, their golden skin glowing, their faces dazzling. Some sing heavenly songs, others play on instruments, others hum, yet others dance and still others fan the face of God.[39] Leibniz (and no doubt other Europeans also) envisioned each waterdrop holding the whole universe, and a more recent European philosopher remarked:

> A pool contains a universe. A fragment of a dream contains an entire soul ... . Water is the mistress of liquid language, of smooth flowing language, of continued and continuing language, of language that softens rhythm and gives a uniform substance to different rhythms ... liquidity is the very desire of language. Language needs to flow. It flows naturally ... .[40]

Such a view evokes a Ganges of thought-forms sung in words, and a mind-lake of fluid light reflections. For the imagination all that flows is water, and 'every joyful drink is mother's milk'.[41] Water is naturally beautiful in many ways; it cleans away tropical sweat and sins, it washes off anxiety and regret, it flushes out the structures that force life into too narrow lanes and cramped spaces. When human lifeways grow too rigid with *idées fixes*, fresh water unfixes, clearing away stagnation.

Woman is associated with water; life's fluidity marks her feminine mystique.[42] In sculptures of women from the Vijayanagara era, still seen in Hampi today, the exuberance of their fully rounded breasts is striking. Some are dark and smooth from generations of pilgrims rubbing them in order to partake of the abundance they symbolize. In India the veneration of cows (like that of ancient Egypt) is also linked to gratitude for the abundant life fluid of milk, which is a gift of motherly substance; it is a prayer for protection from scarcity.

It is possible that the *ahimsa* of Buddhism, Jainism and Hinduism developed from the ancient veneration of the life-spirit as *yakshi*s or *apsarasa*s, (for fluid stands for spirit). Both veneration of the cow and *ahimsa* show sensitivity to reciprocity: 'The intellect itself will go dry if pressed too hard, and if you milk a cow like a tyrant you will draw only blood.'[43] Natural resources must be respected, for you can't extract blood from a stone. Affection must balance drily abstract exploitative logical mastery or else the *rasa* and heart-meaning of life as a whole will be drained away in waste and exhaustion.

Each world-view pays for its strengths by allowing other possibilities to atrophy. Consider the roots of Western civilization. According to V. Shekhawat, '[t]he future hides itself, perhaps maliciously,' from Greco-European culture, whose logic is based on geometry and maths, on differences, in non-paradoxical boundaries; it is a culture that is engrossed in history, with every hope in the future giving rise to 'futurist' rationality.[44] This is in deep contrast to the 'eternalist' rationality of India which is based on the model of language, generative grammar (as well as astrology and Ayurveda) and in which past, present and future mingle and time stands still, like 'transparent and still water in a lake for which the danger of getting frozen lurks every moment'.[45] Vijayanagara tried to return from the turbulence of Muslim domination to the still lake, even while welcoming the Portuguese and others who came with ships full of fast horses and a futurist outlook – welcoming the West and its ways to a prominent place in the waters of time in South India. Krishnadevaraya did not know what the consequences of European contact would be; he could not foresee what would dessicate in his kingdom. But he continued to cultivate the ethos of women and water. The king, nobles and wealthy merchants lived in well-built stone houses, as did the *devadasi*s (dancers).[46] The *devadasi*s had access to the king; they helped him bathe, dressed him, served him his meals in vessels of gold and entertained him with stories, music and dance. He was always surrounded by women, even when he went to war.[47] Symbolic of fertility, moisture, wealth and power, courtesans played an important role in society; in people's minds they were as important as the four castes into which society was organized. Some were attached to temples, others lived independently. No blame or shame was attached to the *devadasi* community.[48] Today, in secular societies, entertainers and celebrities may play a similar role in social life. Beautiful and wealthy entertainers and models enjoy great prestige and respect. They make a living through glamour, music and dance, they bare their bodies and excite strangers' imaginations, and they may associate with politically and economically powerful people with swimming pools and other appurtenances of luxury and affluence. Performers, with their tours and commitments to schedules and productions, often put strains on their family life, but they give pleasure to many strangers.[49]

Figure 8.2   Woman dancer, based on a sculpture in Vijayanagara

As a modern scientist said, 'If there is magic on this planet, it is contained in water'.[50] According to a Telugu proverb, 'Every man must dip in his own destiny's waters'.[51] A man, hard in head and heart, is still no match for the vulnerable weaker sex; Shakespeare knew that 'women's weapons, waterdrops' can douse his every spark of hope or moisten sprouts of desire to make him aspire higher. Man fails and uses force; woman succeeds slowly but surely. Goddess power prevails.

*Apsarasa*s play on, in Vijayanagara times, as women of watersports, *jalakrida*, which the king loves to watch. And the king has the luxury of choosing from among them, while they giggle and splash, and their flimsy silk saris cling like a slick film on their sleek bodies. In some stories, the king's pleasure pool had an underwater passage through which one could swim with a mate to an adjoining chamber, make love and then resurface later.[52]

The *devadasi* (literally 'servant of God') threads her way through life, sewing together several realms; and she gives access to others, through her knowledge and her body. She is linked to God, dances to please the image in the temple, and is trained in artful actions and graceful beauty. She is linked to powerful men, officers, through *kama* – the power of inflaming and satiating their senses when they visit her for pleasure. So the king could learn things from her, as he did from his spies, who float freely and intermingle more fluidly than the more publicly fixed and instantly recognizable throned crown could. Some *devadasi*s were the only women with direct access to the king.[53] As counterparts to the *apsarasa*s, the *devadasi*s were not forbidden the things that were forbidden to other earthly beings. Woman, source of life, like water, is a necessity under all circumstances for life's normal flow of events.

The dancer needed a graceful body to incarnate the graceful arts, to move freely as a dream above the earth. The *haridasa*'s energies and aims were different, although both *haridasa*s and *devadasi*s may be consecrated to the temple deity. The saint's service was spiritual whereas the dancer's was sensual, and yet both had the grace of proficiency in the musical arts and cultivated an aura of attractive friendliness in order to gain a smooth acceptance into people's lives and be welcomed. The king needed both for his kingdom: the cosmos-balancing renunciation of holy men, which stills the tyranny of the senses and says 'no', and the fruitful power of generation, which continues life with an indulgent 'yes', a radiant affirmation of vibrance. Both had a role in the kingdom of Vijayanagara in heartily affirming aspects of life – for beauty and order, prosperity and meaning.

The dancer's beauty and art were a sign of sacred and profane power – the power to go from temple to king, the power of eros. The best courtesans were refined, trained in the arts, cultured and witty, but was it rather euphemistic to call them 'the wives of the god'? Many, according to the popular poets Vemana and Baddena,[54] were probably venal and fickle.

On the other side of the spectrum that existed in Krishnadevaraya's time, the *haridasa* sublimated his sexual energies in bhakti, cultivating a deep yearning for Vishnu. The *devadasi* incorporated aspects of bhakti worship in her dancing for God. The *haridasa*, shouting warnings, telling people to pay attention to God, and the silent, knowing *devadasi* both played their parts in the kingdom. Both were servants who gave their all; both sang and danced, according to their calling. Both were needed, along with the worldly-wise advisers and the Nayaka regional captains and their forces.

The High Point of an Empire

In my view, one of the most enduring images of Krishnadevaraya is as the man who went out at night to grapple with his dangerous vulnerabilities – to seek the 'edge of chaos', so that he could know it and be a fit match for any threat. Krishnadevaraya showed a healthy instinct for thinking for himself, for avoiding complacency. Knowing that appearances can be deceptive, he sought a sure footing for his reign; he took a step back so that he could leap forward. He reached a bedrock of honest uncertainty and, from that position, made a fresh search for mastery, going on to take vigorous and aggressive action against his enemies. He also benefited from good advisers and appreciated their abilities to extend his knowledge of the rugged 'fitness landscape',[55] so that he could act accordingly. The comic side of human efforts at striving mightily to improve is illustrated by his shadowlike clown, Tenali Ramakrishna. Krishnadevaraya marked the peak of the Vijayanagara empire's greatness, but when a civilization reaches its most glorious height can the undertow and decline be far away? The whole person, the body-and-mind-together of the wisdom-endowed king at the peak, riddled by the clownish fluctuations of life, coped creatively with 'chaorder', preparing for potential disasters, trying to be as fit as he could. He was a great man ruling a great realm, focusing rich energies for optimal use. Lesser men followed his fit reign, bringing a dwindling of power.[56]

During his reign Krishnadevaraya defended his own territories, repulsed invaders

Figure 8.3   Portuguese horse-trader, based on a sculpture in Vijayanagara

and attacked enemies in their own lands. As a result, he continually needed more horses – shiploads of stallions for his warriors to ride – so he imported them from far-off Arabia, trading his empire's jewels to foreigners. On the long voyage to Cochin and on the battlefield many of these horses died, so each year Krishnadevaraya needed 2000 new horses to bolster the strength of his forces, to reduce his vulnerability. Horse-dealers thrived and grew wealthy on this trade. Portuguese ambassadors offered the king gifts and told him that they would help him eliminate the danger of Muslim invasion. With shiploads of horses they won the king over into friendship and alliance. They built factories and established settlements on the West coast on their way to taking Goa as their own territory. In 1565, 35 years after Krishnadevaraya's death, Muslim forces representing four of the five existing Deccani sultanates invaded Vijayanagara causing bloodshed and destruction. They surprised the *de facto* ruler Rama Raya (of the Aravidu family, fourth dynasty of Vijayanagara) who, despite his advanced age, insisted on directing military operations from his portable couch, enclosed in curtains and carried by bearers, or in battle on an elephant. Despite his vigorous attempts to fight for the empire, he fell. In landslides, aggregate groups of ground break off and fall, in fractal amounts of loss, until the whole is affected. Two Muslim commanders in Rama Raya's army deserted, each in charge of 70 000 men or more. Nizam Shah captured Rama Raya, had him beheaded and displayed the severed head on the end of a spear. In total, 100 000 men died, and the Muslims took the capital and cut it off. The former beauty of the now decapitated empire broke down into rubble as the capital city which had grown in strength for over two centuries, was now brutalized and robbed by soldiers and hordes of looters and vandals.[57] Krishnadevaraya's worst nightmares had come true. For want of sufficient defensive precautions – the multitudes of small details that form the safeguards and supportive web of a social system's existence – the empire was lost. Vandals defaced sculptures and monuments, pulled down pillars holding up roofs, gleefully destroying in minutes what had taken centuries to build. On the death of Rama Raya, his brother Tirumala loaded 1550 elephants with treasures, gathered the women of the royal family and abandoned the capital, taking with him Sadashiva, the nephew of Achyuta and supposed heir to the throne. Taking up residence in the town of Penukonda, he tried to build up an army. But, by then, Vijayanagara, where once pearls and rubies had been so plentiful that they were sold in the market place like grain, had had its day. After months of looting and vandalism, all the king's horses from Arabia and all the king's men could not restore Vijayanagara to wholeness. It was reduced to a dismembered order of scattered provinces and memories, ruins and legends.

Notes

1   Based on the tale told in *Sathya Sai Speaks*, ed. and tr. N. Kasturi, vol. VII, Bombay: Sri Sathya Sai Education Foundation, n.d., pp. 8–10. See also David Schulman, *The King and the Clown in South India*, Princeton, NJ: Princeton University Press, 1985, pp. 20–40, 95 ff. 152 ff, for a discussion of this within the context of brahman–king relationships in South Indian literature.

2   B. Rama Raju, *Folk Tales of Andhra Pradesh*, New Delhi: Sterling, 1974, pp. 84–87.

3   Swans are said to have walked freely about, doves lived in the eaves, peafowls stood on wooden planks on poles and dances, and parrots were kept in golden cages, according to N. Venkata Ramanayya, *Vijayanagara: Origin of the City and the Empire*, Madras: University of Madras, 1933, p. 368.

4   Ibid., pp. 50–51.

5   Ibid. See also Edward Jewitt Robinson, *Tales and Poems of South India*, London: T. Woolmer, 1885, pp. 342–56; Panchapakesa Ayyar, *Tenali Rama*, Madras, Madras Alliance Co., 1947.

6   *Indian Tales of Fun, Folly and Folk-lore*, ed. and tr. S.M. Natesa Sastri and T.M. Sundaram Aiyar, Madras: G.A. Natesan, 1920, pp. 3,4,8,10,12,13,15,17.

7   John M. Fritz and George Michell, *City of Victory: Vijayanagara*, New York: Aperture, 1991, p. 109.

8   Domingos Paes and Fernao Nuniz, *The Vijayanagar Empire as seen by Domingos Paes and Fernao Nuniz*, ed. Vasundhara Filliozat, tr. Robert Sewell, New Delhi: National Book Trust, 1999. Paes, pp. 29–31, Nuniz p. 159.

9   The Greek philosopher Heraclitus (500 BCE) noted that 'souls take pleasure in moisture'. Cited in R. Sardello and G. Thomas, *Stirrings of Culture*, Dallas: The Dallas Institute, 1986, pp. 203–205. An inscription from ancient Mohenjo Daro has been interpreted as a blessing: 'May the one with fish eyes when dying be happy.' Heras explained the inscription: 'To have fish eyes means to have the eyes of God, and to work always with the knowledge of God … only those who have fish eyes may be happy after death.' See A.P. Karmarkar and N.B. Kamdani, *The Haridasas of Karnataka*, Dharwar: Karnatak Vidyavardhak Sangha, 1939, p. xli. In this creative interpretation, being immersed in the auspicious waters of spiritual consciousness is blissful, and one is thus peaceful facing mortality.

10   Paes and Nuniz, *The Vijayanagar Empire*, ed. Filliozat, tr. Sewell, p. 69.

11   N. Venkata Ramanayya, *Studies in the Third Dynasty of Vijayanagara*, Madras: University of Madras, 1935, p. 365.

12   Twenty-five of these 84 temples at Khajuraho were built between 900 and 1500 ACE.

13   'These are not temples of love in that the culture knew nothing higher to enshrine than biological functions; they are temples in which sensuality itself reaches a supreme degree of intelligence, thoughtfulness, beauty, capable of entering into or assembling the cosmos. Indeed rarely has man assumed a more ennobled visage than in this rock. These men and women closed in passionate embraces have brows poised with respect and gazes emanating intelligence, mouths trembling with susceptibility and lips benevolent and responsive, fingers ungrasping and reverent. Here there is nothing guilty or crafty, nothing disfigured with leering and duplicity, nothing self-indulgent or self-ashamed. There is nothing servile. They are blissful with the freedom of gods who have understood everything.' Alphonso Lingis, *Excesses: Eros and Culture*, Albany, NY: SUNY, 1983, p. 61.

14   'In these hundreds of figures we see all that humans have found to be noble in the wingspread of eagles, in the langour of a tiger, in the coiling of a scorpion, in the watery freedom of fish, in the intensity of a cobra ready to strike … there is not in yoga which seeks to know and to stand, soar or creep with animal perfection the sense that one debases oneself to make love with scorpions, swans, bitches and boars … . Men pour their semen into [Ganga's] white sidereal river; women open their wombs to the moon, to the sun, to the lonely and perfect stars … . Here one neither descends, when one makes love with animals and trees, nor ascends, when one makes love with the moon, the rivers, the stars; one travels aimlessly or circularly about a universe eroticized' (ibid., p. 62). See also Gary Snyder on 'trans-species erotics'. He notes the worldwide stories of animal–human marriages and supernatural-human marriages as 'evidence of the fascination our ancestors had for the possibility of full membership in a biotic erotic universe.' Gary Snyder, *A Place in Space* Washington DC: Counterpoint, 1995, p. 210. This is another reflection of cosmic unity.

15   *Kama Sutra* II.6.

16   'The eyes of an *apsarasa* are fish … her eyebrows are taut bows, her buttocks swelling gourds, her lips a sesamum petal. Faces are lotuses; jewel strings are water birds … . Fingers are comets descending from the sky, the gauzy clothes ripple off in streams. Unlike in Plato, the erotic gaze does not move from the human figure to the universal forms, but to sequences of particular forms which, having no

common form, are metonymic and not metaphorical. A Gandharva's chest is the face of a cow, his arms are plaintain-tree trunks, his kneecap the back of a crab' (Lingis, *Excesses*, p. 63). Huston Smith writes of interspecies mimicry: 'It is as if nature, always more prolific and life-loving than we had supposed, first staked out distinct species and then decided to ring changes on these by having each reflect the forms of the others insofar as it could do so without transgressing its own essential limits. Seen in this light, variations are not generative links between species ... . They are rather, mimics; they show species imitating the ways and forms of species that in essence are foreign to them. Not solely for utilitarian reasons of adaptation and survival ... for *lila*, the divine play: sheer protean exuberance. *Esse qua esse so bonum est* (being as being is so good) that God cannot resist any of its possibilities ... . It is like Indra's net, each jewel reflecting the others and being reflected in them.' Huston Smith, *Forgotten Truth: The Primordial Tradition*, New York: Harper and Row, 1976, pp. 140–41.

17   A tale about Brahma illustrates another way in which Indian tradition has described the creation of woman's beauty. Brahma had no more solid substances left, having run out after creating earth and other matter. So he took clustering lines of bees, the splendid joy of sunbeams. clouds' tears, the whimsy of wind, the timidness of the rabbit, the vanity of the peacock, the unbreakability of the diamond, the sweetness of the honey, the ruthlessness of the tiger, the warmth of fire, the chill of snow, the chatter of birds, the cooing of kokils, the contrariness of the crane, the faithfulness of chakravaka birds and mixed them all up together to make woman. Thus, she has links with them all.

18   V. Raghavan, 'Bharata Natya', *Journal of the Music Academy,* Madras, **XLV**, 1974, pp. 241–43.

19   Lingis, *Excesses*, p. 64.

20   V. Raghavan, 'Bharata Natya', p. 234. In ancient Greece there were *hetaerae*, courtesans much like *devadasi*s. '[Hetaerae] are a lovely mystery – only veiled, not locked up. In an analogous way the philosophers' mystery attracts us ... . Each people, each time have their lovely woman-symbol ... . Only woman and love dissolve the intellect.' *Novalis: Pollen and Fragments*, tr. Arthur Versiuis, Grand Rapids, MI: Phanes Press, 1989, no. 184, p. 60. There is a comparison of *devadasi*s with similar dancers in ancient cultures in A.K. Singh's *Devadasi System in Ancient India (A Study of Temple Dancing Girls of South India)*, Delhi: H.K. Publishers, 1990.

21   Emma Jung in *Animus and Anima*, New York: Spring Publications, 1957, 1969, explores archetypal images of feminine beings associated with water. See also James Hillman's *Anima: An Anatomy of a Personified Notion*, Dallas: Spring Publications, 1985.

22   Lee Siegel, *Sacred and Profane Dimensions of Love in Indian Traditions as Exemplified in Gita Govinda of Jayadeva*, Delhi: Oxford University Press, 1990, p. 45.

23   Sathya Sai Baba, *Summer Showers in Brindavan 1974*, New Delhi: Bhagavan Sri Sathya Sai Seva Samithi, 1975, p. 53.

24   Octavio Paz, *The Monkey Grammarian*, London: Peter Owen, 1989, p. 89. Paz's analysis of this artwork is really not so far from the *Brihadaranyaka Upanishad* passage, repeating that "all things are honey for each other'.

25   Johann Wolfgang von Goethe, 'Spirit Song over the Waters', cited in C.G. Jung, *Psychological Reflections*, ed. Jolande Jacobi, New York: Harper and Row, 1961, p. 3.

26   *Manu Smriti* I.10. See also Diana Eck, 'The Dynamics of Indian Symbolism', in Peter Berger (ed), *The Other Side of God*, Garden City: Anchor, 1981.

27   *The Vijayanagara Empire*, ed. Filliozat, tr. Sewell, p. 31.

28   Ibid., p. 63.

29   Ibid.

30   Mulk Raja Anand, 'The Rise and Fall of the Vijanagara Empire', in George Michell (ed.), *Splendours of Vijayanagara Empire–Hampi*, Bombay, Mary Publications, 1981, p.35.

31   Ibid., p. 36.

32   Damasio is quoted in Emily Eakin, 'I feel, Therefore, I am', *New York Times*, 19 April 2003, p. A15.

33   See E. Valentine Daniel, *Fluid Signs: Being a Person in the Tamil Way*, Berkeley: University of California Press, 1987.

34   *Rig Veda* X.cxxiii.5, Ralph T.H. Griffiths' translation. *The Hymns of the Rg Veda*, Delhi: Motilal Banarsidass, 1986, pp. 629–30.

35 Or, as Walt Whitman says, 'seas of bright juice suffuse heaven'. 'Song of Myself', part 24, in *Leaves of Grass*, New York: Book of the Month Club, 1992, p. 41.

36 Kees W. Bolle, *The Freedom of Man in Myth*, Nashville: Vanderbilt University Press, 1968. Meaning and reasonableness meet and overlap in harmonizing archetypes, attractive images of the psyche. Deep archetypal attractors come in many variations all over the globe. Aphrodite the goddess rising from the sea, the water as source of life of all things. Mary is also connected with the ocean. Tammuz means 'vivifying waters' and is like Varuna (mate and son of Aditi) the 'son-consort of waters'. Some Chinese poems delight in the presences in waters, and American lyricist Stephen Foster wrote of the magical vapours over streams evoking mysterious presence – eerie, eternal, spiritual. Greek nymphs are semi-divine beauties living in rivers, fountains, trees or the sea, attending on deities. Woman at the water, washing clothes, bathing, oiling themselves, playing ball, dancing, running and playing are depicted in Homer's *Odyssey* VI.85. In India the Ahir people have a *basgit* (folksong) which goes: 'Slowly flows the stream/The golden girl is catching fish;/Both her young breasts/Are smeared with mud – /Seeing these who would gaze/anywhere else, even at her decorated hair?' The text on the reverse of a Basoli painting, *ca.* 1695, shows Mugdha as a youthful, inexperienced girl, innocently confused: 'Youth has come unknown. The Nayika with moon-like face stands drying herself beside the pool. Her full-blown eyes look like lotuses in the reflection, and thinking that perhaps the flowers have stuck to her ears, she moves her hands to brush them away. Next her eyes drift to the downy hair on her person which she mistakes for algae and tries to wipe off. Her hips feel heavy, and in virginal innocence she asks her companion again and again, "Can it be that I have tired?"' European painters and composers have found the theme attractive – for example, Renoir's *'The Bather'*. Wagner's Ring opera opens with water nymphs. Many poems and artworks could be cited. Goddess Sarasvati is 'one who flows', and is associated with auspicious waters.

37 *Garuda Purana* XV. 25. Cited by Stella Kramrisch, *The Hindu Temple*, vol. II, New Delhi: Motilal Banardissas, 1980, p. 343.

38 *Valmiki Ramayana* 3.11.12.

39 Ibid., 7.77.13.

40 Gaston Bachelard, *The Poetics of Reverie*, tr. D. Russell, New York: Orion Press, 1969, pp. 50, 187. 'You Are Every-where – Thorns of Thunder' by Paul Eluard also celebrates water and woman.

41 Bachelard, *The Poetics of Reverie*, p. 117. It is as if generous breasts say: 'You are loved and you will live off the fat of the land; despite the existence of harshness, this comfort is warm and sweet, a homey foundation of faith that life is worth living, that someone cares.' In terms of evolution, 'The new mammalian mode of nourishing the young in the earliest period of their existence outside the womb was immensely significant for the future psychological formation of the mammalian species. This bodily intimacy during pregnancy and after birth can be associated with the distinctive emotional qualities that develop in this line of descent.' Brian Swimme and Thomas Berry, *The Universe Story*, San Francisco: HarperSanFrancisco, 1992, p. 122. 'The Mother Goddesses... were always sculpted with their breasts bare, as if to say: I have breasts, therefore I am. Father consciousness [thinking with linear logic] tries to control mammal nature through rules, morality, commandments, and tries to reach the spirit as asceticism.' Robert Bly, *Sleepers Joining Hands*, New York: Harper and Row, 1973, p. 32.

42 Studies of this archetypal attractor, the anima or feminine image of the soul and its relations to waters of life, include such books as Emma Jung's *Anima and Animus*, and Gaston Bachelard's *Poetics of Reverie*.

43 Baltazar Gracian, *The Art of Worldly Wisdom: A Pocket Oracle*. tr. Christopher Maurer, New York: Doubleday, 1992, p. 46.

44 V. Shekhawat, 'Specific Cultures and the Coexistence of Alternative Rationalities: A Case Study of the Contact of Indian and Greco-European cultures', *Journal of Indian Council of Philosophical Research*, IX (2), January–April, 1992, p. 131. The theme of this issue of the journal is the nature of rationality.

45 Ibid.

46 Venkata Ramanayya, *Vijayanagara: Origin of the City and the Empire*, p. 363.

47   Ibid., pp. 384–85.

48   Ibid., p. 401.

49   On the archetype of the courtesan see Nancy Qualls-Corbett, *The Sacred Prostitute: Eternal Aspect of the Feminine*, Toronto: Inner City Books, 1988; also Susan Griffin, *The Book of Courtesans*, New York: Broadway Books, 2001. Bob Dylan in an interview said that in his view, a performer is a cut above a prostitute.

50   Loren Eisley, *The Immense Journey*, New York: Scribners, 1957.

51   M.W. Carr, *A Selection of Telugu Proverbs*, New Delhi: Asian Educational Services, 1986, no. 327, p. 33.

52   V. Raghavan in an article about mechanical devices in premodern India writes about this kind of inventive design involving water. See R. Raghavan, *Yantras or Mechanical Contrivances in Ancient India*, Bangalore: The Indian Institute of Culture, transaction no. 10, 1952, pp. 25–27.

53   Paes in Robert Sewell's *A Forgotten Empire*, New Delhi: Asian Educational Services, 1982 (reprint of 1900 edn), pp. 242 ff. V. Raghavan writes of *devadasi*s in 'Bharata Natya', *Journal of the Madras Music Academy, Madras*, XLV, 1974. See also Kay Kirkpatrick Jordan, 'From Sacred Servant to Profane Prostitute: A Study of the Changing Legal Status of the *Devadasi*s', dissertation, University of Iowa, 1989, and Frederique Apffel Marglin, *Wives of the God-King*, Delhi, New York: Oxford University Press, 1985.

54   Baddena, in *Sumati Satakam*, ed. C.R. Sarma, tr. C.P. Brown, Hyderabad: Andhra Pradesh Sahityam Akademi, 1973, p. 82.

55   The term 'fitness landscape' was first used by Sewell Wright in 'Roles of Mutation, Inbreeding, and Selection in Evolution', in D.F. Jones (ed.), *Proceedings of the Sixth International Congress on Genetics*, Vol. I, Menasha, Wisc.: Brooklyn Botanic Garden, 1932. It is used in evolutionary biology to refer to the study of evolution by charting the changes in a population during a given period of time as a landscape. In complex adaptive systems theory 'fitness landscapes' can be used to show the results of various possible alternatives as a way of better understanding the optimum conditions leading to success in survival.

56   Aliya Rama Raya, husband of Krishnadevaraya's daughter Tirumalamba was 'practically the ruler of the State during the days of Emperor Sadashiva'. He was killed at the decisive battle of Talikota in 1565. Vijayanagara, the capital, was invaded and sacked, and Sadshiva escaped to Penukonda with Aliya Tama Raya's brother. Tirumala later founded the Aravidu dynasty, ruling from 1570 to 1593. Ranga Raya ruled from 1573 to 1585. Venkata ruled in 1585. His successors were reduced to holding the small kingdom of Chandragiri. In 1639 one of these rulers made a grant of Madras to the East India Company. See M. Krishnamachariar, *History of Classical Sanskrit Literature*, Delhi: Motilal Banarsidass, 1989. p. 212.

57   K.A. Nilakanta Sastri, *A History of South India, from Prehistoric Times until the Fall of Vijayanagar*, Madras: Oxford University Press, 1976, pp. 295, 287 ff.

CHAPTER 9

Poet: Kanakadasa's Eloquent Responses to Caste Prejudice[1]

"I fled Him, down the nights and down the days;
I fled Him, down the arches of the years ... "   Francis Thompson[2]

The Life of Kanakadasa

When we consider the life and works of singer-saint Kanakadasa, who lived in what is now Karnataka state during the height of the Vijayanagara empire in the 1500s, we are confronted with signs of caste frictions and prejudices, birth status disadvantages and privileges, and we are forced to think about his struggle for the dignity of being accepted as an equal among upper-caste Vaishnava devotees. Perhaps his literary urges were partly stimulated by his desire to prove to his critics that a Kuruba (shepherd community) tribesman inspired by bhakti could be as eloquent as anyone else, or even more so. The recognition and respect that he won did not come easily, as the traditionally told story of his life reveals.

In Bada near Dharwad, in what is now Karnataka State, Birappa was a feudal chief[3] of a village of Kurubas, a herding and hunting clan. He was the local revenue collector for the Vijayanagara ruler. His wife was named Bacchamma. The pious Kuruba couple prayed to Lord Venkateshvara at the sacred mountaintop pilgrimage shrine, Tirupati, asking for a child to be born to them. When their prayers were answered and a baby was born to them, after 12 days they performed the proper ceremony and put him in the cradle, naming him Timmappa. Stories depict him as an energetic child, and he grew up enjoying an active boyhood, running races, playing children's games and thriving on vigorous sports like swimming.

Popular accounts say that, at the great pilgrimage destination of Tirupati,[4] Timmappa came in contact with the saintly teacher Tatacharya, an enthusiastic Vaishnava of the Ramanujacharya school, and Timmappa learned Vishnu bhakti from him.

Legends say that Timmappa once discovered a treasure of gold while digging a well, and local people started calling him 'Kanaka Nayaka',[5] meaning 'Gold Chief', Timmappa built a temple in the village of Kaginele (in what is now North Karnataka) to house the image of Lord Adikeshava, a form of Krishna, which he brought from a tumbledown temple in nearby Bada.[6] When Timmappa later became Kanakadasa, and composed his many songs of devotion and philosophy, Kaginele Adikeshava was the signature (*mudra*) he embedded near the end of each song to identify himself as author.[7]

Figure 9.1   Emblems of Vishnu: the disc which is his chakra weapon (left) and the conch shell (right), displayed prominently at Tirupati

As a young man, Kanaka Nyaka lived an active life in pursuit of *artha*, success and prosperity in life. Having taken over his father's duties he would sometimes go to the capital, Vijayanagara, in his official capacity as revenue collector. There he came into contact with the important Vaishnava guru of the Madhva school, Vyasaraya, although at first it was from a distance.

Traditional stories of Kanaka Nayaka's life relate how he saw the Lord Channakeshava in several dreams. Each time, the mysterious presence, before vanishing, requested him to become his servant. And, each time, Kanaka Nayaka resisted the call, saying that he did not yet want to renounce the world, or did not yet need to follow the taskmaster so closely.[8] However, the call kept coming back for Kanaka until at last he answered, and began a life of devoted service. The turning point, when it finally did overwhelm him, was very dramatic.

It is said that during a war[9] Kanaka Nayaka was wounded, and he fell from his horse in battle. Wounded, he was left for dead, but after hours of lying unconscious he recovered awareness. His rigid sense of self was defeated in this helpless state. He saw a dark form reaching for him, and heard the Voice around him 'like a bursting sea' ask 'Are you ready? Will you become my servant now?'[10]

According to tradition, Kanaka Nyaka, exasperated, answered: 'You again! Can't you see I'm dying?'

'I saved you from death, just so you could be my servant, my *dasa*.'

'How is it you keep seeking me out? Isn't there anyone else to serve you?'

'We have a special relationship. In past lives you were my dear servant, and you took this birth to serve me too – can't you remember? You drove away love from yourself when you drove me away.'

'If you really saved me from the realm of death, could you put an end to my suffering as well?'

**Figure 9.2   Image of Krishna dancing on the serpent Kaliya, based on a
sculpture in Vijayanagara**

'If with my touch I heal your wounds will you believe and serve me then?'

The name Krishna is related to the root *krish*, which means 'to draw to oneself,
to draw into one's power, to pull, to attract', and Krishna is the attractive dark lord.
In Kanaka Nayaka's life story it is as if a 'strange attractor',[11] a divine phantom, a
kind of insistent numinous voice kept calling on him to serve, to revolve his life
around Krishna. The recurrent request was ignored by the stubborn Kanaka until he
had been traumatized and reduced into a dependent childlike state – finally, the
insistent force could not be resisted. It was as if an orderly vortex in the midst of the
havoc of the battlefield set Kanaka on a different course. This branching of the ways
signalled a new beginning. In the margins between chaos and order during a near-
death experience, a renewed personality was born, committing to Krishna the inmost
core of his being, not with a superficial promise, but with a destiny-determining

commitment. The new direction and orientation was one of 'Vishnu-tropic' urgency, feeding on the bliss of the attractor, seeking more of the same. Thus, in all the stories that have come down to us, the inexplicable allurement calling to him from the shadows became his dazzlingly clear and irresistible destiny.

When Kanaka agreed to serve, he found that he was well, undamaged by the fray. Revived and enthused, energized and fervent with fresh faith, he left the destruction of the battlefield and ran to the temple to give thanks, only to find it locked. Then, it is said, he looked at the sky and realized it was the middle of the night. In his intense mood of spiritual desire he pounded his head against the gate and wept at being kept from his Lord. A famous song of his is connected with this part of his story, for he cried out: 'Open the gate, allow me to serve you, O lord why can't you hear my pleas? When ... When ... Why not now?'

Then, stories say, the gate burst open, bells rang in the sky, mysterious brilliant *puja* lights waved spontaneously before the sacred image. This inspiring vision was an experience of the radiance of God, and Kanaka Nayaka wept, his hair standing on end, his heart thrilled with love and reverent awe.

'Kanaka, will you become my servant now?' the voice asked.

'Yes', he exclaimed and in his mood of surrender sang a song praising the holy feet of the Lord. Lord Krishna accepted him as a servant, and then Kanaka sang some more, according to the legends.

Kanaka had been pursued by Krishna directly, but he had not been initiated personally by a guru; usually in Hindu traditions one needs a guru to attain a vision of the divine, but, according to tradition, Kanaka was unique in this respect.[12]

Inspired by his vision Kanaka went to the guru he had seen in Vijayanagara, the famous Madhva teacher who enjoyed the king's patronage, Vyasaraya. Emboldened by his vision, and despite the fact that he was a Kuruba and such people were normally not given initiation by royal gurus, Kanaka asked the sage for a mantra.

The guru Vyasaraya, knowing nothing of Kanaka's vision, surrounded by high-caste devotees and used to thinking in stereotypes about social classes, impatiently or snidely told the chief of herdsmen: 'Yes, you can have a mantra – just repeat the buffalo mantra "water buffalo, water buffalo ... (*yemme kona*)."'

Kanaka took the insult of the high-born guru as a literal instruction and went off to recite his 'buffalo mantra' religiously. Just like some other Hindu saints and ascetics whose faith was greater than that of their teachers, Kanaka's singular fervency in practice helped develop his spirituality far beyond what anyone could have predicted, and he acquired inward strength and outward powers.[13] According to legend, his faith was such that he was able to move a big boulder which was blocking a spring.[14] (There is a place called Kanaka Jubu in Andhra Pradesh which people still associate with this incident.) When Vyasaraya saw this, he knew that such intense bhakti could accomplish many things, and so he stopped fooling around with the sincere devotee. He gave Kanaka a real initiation and welcomed him into the community of *dasa*s. The guru's other followers were, however, less than welcoming, some nicknaming him Kunidasa ('Dog-servant'), others Kurubadasa

('Herdsman-servant'). To show these jealous disciples their own limitations Vyasaraya is said to have given each *dasa* a plaintain, saying, 'Eat this plaintain unseen by anyone.' They all scurried off to secret nooks' but Kanaka flatly rejected the task: 'God sees all, so it's an impossible task.'[15] God's omnipresence is also the theme of Psalm 139 in the Bible and of many passages in the Qur'an.[16]

The most famous story told about him recounts how, as a low-caste man, Kanaka was not free to go inside the Krishna temple at Udipi. He stood by a chink in the wall to look in, and so intense was his fervour, *bhakta*s say, that he provoked the image of Krishna to turn around on the pedestal. Originally facing east, the charming statue turned to face west, just to look towards this faithful servant. The temple priests left it as it was. The small window in the rear of the Udipi temple is called *Kanakana khindi* to this day. However, some disagree with this popular folk explanation of the unusual position of Krishna's statue and deny that Kanaka was responsible for it.[17]

Kanaka was said to have lived to the age of 98. It was a belief among *dasa*s that he was an incarnation of the brahman sage Vidura of the Mahabharata story, born to play a part in the present age of discord, the Kali Yuga. This view regarding a previous life would permit upper-caste people to accept a shudra studying sacred texts as an exception to the general rule which prohibited this.

Besides composing many songs, Kanakadasa is also known for his four poetic works: *Mohana Tarangini*, ('The River Waves of Enchanting Krishna'); *Ramadhyana Charitra*, ('The Story of the Ragi Blessed by Rama'); *Nala Charitra*, a Kannada recitative piece about Nala and Damayanti on the theme of suffering for a worthy cause – his most popular work in verse and the only version of this classic Sanskrit story known by most Kannada speakers; *Hari Bhakti Sara*, a series of 100 devotional verses to Krishna.

A Humble Grain Demands Respect: *Ragi's* Voice is Heard in the Land

The *Ramadhanya Caritre*, written by Kanakadasa in the Bhamini Shatpadi meter, a popular form for chanting and reciting, consists of 56 stanzas. In the poem Kanakadasa says that he would like the whole population to hear it: 'I'm telling you the Ramadhanya so the whole world will be taken by surprise and apprised of what I have to say.' The metaphors in the story reflect aspects of his age and society. It is a poignant story, dramatizing the sufferings and indignities of being categorized as lowly. While royalty, wealthy merchants and weavers could afford high-quality rice, poor people could afford to eat only the staple grain known as *ragi*. In the story deeper truths gradually emerge as a conversation among different types of grain ensues. Kanakadasa uses the voice of the character *ragi*, a sesame-seed-sized grain which is a staple food of common folk, to criticize the social structure, responding to prejudice of pandits and to the arrogance of some *haridasa*s.

Set in the context of the story of Lord Rama's life, like an episode from the old *Ramayana* epic, this account of conflict among different varieties of grain is lifted from the level of historic struggle to a timeless sacred level by occurring in Lord Rama's presence.

The story involves Rama, who is on his way to Sri Lanka, arriving at the ashram of the sage Muchukunda. Many saints and sages are gathered there, and they listen to a conversation between Rama and Muchukunda. At the mealtime, the resident holy man who is host serves food to Rama and his retinue. Rama, on behalf of his retinue and the people present, addresses Hanuman, asking him to speak. Hanuman, the extraordinary monkey-devotee, son of the sometimes tricky and trouble-stirring wind god of the Vedas, responds by praising the virtues of that reliable popular grain called *ragi*.[18]

At the behest of sage Gautama Maharshi, all kinds of grain have been brought for a feast, and various people extoll the properties of the different grains. *Ragi*, by coming into contact with the blessed touch of Rama, is delighted to become known as 'Ramadhanya'.

Rama then asks Gautama Maharshi: 'Which grain is best?'

Gautama Maharshi gives his opinion: 'The itsybitsy grain, *ragi*, is the most nutritious one you'll find in the entire land!'

On hearing this assertion, *bhatta* paddy, high-quality rice with the husk still on, is outraged. Considering himself to be a very major grain in this or any other assembly, very popular, well loved, a fancy luxury item often preferred and celebrated, probably the main world-class favourite of all time, *bhatta* paddy bitterly objects and feels that the pride of place should be given to him. So, paddy accuses Gautama of obvious bias. 'Outrage!' he complains. 'A sage like you! What is the meaning of this! Giving pride of place to *ragi*! With wheat, myself and other famous staple grains present, *ragi* is called the best? Not fair!' paddy fumes, scowling with resentment.

The conflict between *ragi* and paddy does not end there. *Ragi* keeps quiet, despite the grumbling and verbal attacks, feeling that it does not behove him on such a solemn occasion to bicker, banter, rebuke and bite back. But paddy, furiously provoked, challenges *ragi* insistently, accusing *ragi* of being 'one without a proper birth'. And he even mutters haughtily, 'Go burn your idiotic pride, you flaming dolt!'

Paddy humiliates *ragi* until the poor little grain can take it no longer. *Ragi*'s tiny eyes turn red-hot with anger, and the miniscule grain demands to know, 'What are these abusive terms you slur me with, these wretched, mean-spirited insults?'

'Do you expect a reply? Well, it isn't fitting to answer you. No need to talk to those of your position,' paddy says. Then he keeps quiet. *Ragi*'s response makes no impact on the offenders.

And innocent little *ragi*, there in the presence of Lord Rama himself, knows how futile it would be to argue with such thick-skinned arrogance. But a duel of words ensues, because *ragi* just can't help but observe out loud that rice is the customary Hindu offering given to the dead. Rice in this light is rather inauspicious and unappetizing – the corpse-white food of death. The listeners stir, losing their appetites, knowing *ragi*, the trickster in an innocent's clothing, has a point there.

When Rama sees the devastated paddy sitting there so upset, downcast and glum, with all these bad feelings stemming from the fact that *ragi* has been praised, he tells paddy: 'Come here, paddy. Why worry your head about it? Why accuse and attack, full of rage, just because we extol this tiny little fellow named *ragi*? We praise him because in famines he rescues and sustains humanity. That's a good trait to have, isn't it? You have to admit you're more aloof, almost heartless at times. When's the last time you gave yourself to poor and starving folks? But no one denigrated you, we only pointed out how *ragi* is full of compassion.'

Rama, being diplomatic, and loved by all, does not want to slight or abandon rice. He tries to smooth things over. Some writers have seen a resemblance between Rama in this tale and Vijayanagara ruler of Kanakadasa's time, Krishnadevaraya, after a triumph. Symbollically, Rama is on a platform above all the others, beyond caste bias. Metaphorically, God is the transcendent unity which allows all the varieties to exist, and cares for all. God is not entangled in the drama of their playing out their various parts, but is the omnipresent witness. Yet, he shows fondness and appreciation for the devoted and humble servant *ragi*.

Kanakadasa does not say, 'All grains are identical, you can mix them together and forget the different names.' He does not argue for the homogeneity of unicaste sameness, which would be an unrealistic demand in a world of variety, but pleads that each kind be given its due, be respected for what it is on its own merits and virtues, and not be given automatic spiritual rank according to a rigid system authorized by those who feel superiority is their birthright. (Modern Westerners may ask, 'Why reform and not revolution?' As Gary Snyder wrote, individual enlightenment has been the mercy of the East, while social revolution has been the mercy of the West.) *Ragi* should be given credit where it is due, for sustenance and generosity. This reasoning about social status uses grain metaphors to highlight the overlooked or underestimated value of the 'lowly' as life-sustaining and very worthy of respect. Thus Kanakadasa shifts focus, re-examines taken-for-granted logic based on ossified customs, myths, habitual routines and non-adaptive addictions to privileges of birth status and injustices. In the story, *ragi* is respectfully called 'Shudranna', 'elder brother *shudra*'. The symbolism seems obvious today, but it was original at the time.

The character *ragi* is like a brown-skinned trickster, pretending naively to speak his mind, innocently turning the tables and upsetting the white rice, and then, when ire is stirred, acting surprised. Language and storytelling are devices which the disadvantaged may use as a defence. As a character in a Jean Genet play says, 'By stretching language, we'll distort it sufficiently to wrap ourselves in it and hide, whereas the masters contract it'.[19]

Kanakadasa enjoyed the respect which high status brought him in his own community, and seems to have been deepened and exalted by significant crises in his life, such as the dramatic religious turning point on the battlefield which made him a *dasa*. Yet among the *dasa*s he was sometimes treated as lowly. The symbols of Vaishnavism gave him the means to try to persuade others to reconsider their rigid ways. Only in the face of confrontation and demands for justice does the half-conscious power of the status quo accede and show a little merciful flexibility, just as the guru Vyasaraya, not wanting to offend anyone, gave the Kuruba man a buffalo mantra, yet later was willing to speak for the rights of the good man of low birth. Kanakadasa reminds us that spiritual goodness is no automatic birthright of priests, and lowliness must not be blanketly associated with disadvantaged communities. This is a plea for spiritual recognition, dignity according to what one does and what one actually is. It is a demand for respect for the spiritual worth of a pious life, for virtuous deeds, a rejection of unearned stereotypical labels. It is a demand that *bhaktas* live up to supposed bhakti ideals, as if to say: 'In this realm where the beloved rules, let small-minded conventions never spoil the true feelings we experience, but instead ever expand to include true devotees wherever they might originate, in the meritocracy of bhakti.'[20] In his poems Kanakadasa was a philosopher and sometimes a protester; in songs he was also a questioner, considering strange contradictions, besides being a humorist and worshipper.

Criticisms of Caste by Kanakadasa and Other *Bhaktas*

The caste system has many complexities, and it is usual for modern scholars to concentrate on simplified aspects of it, which they condemn on moral grounds. A few scholars have tried to describe the actual relationships within the caste system, without letting modern assumptions blind them to the complex workings of this Hindu organization of society which evolved and hardened and sometimes relaxed over the centuries.[21] Between the 1100s and the 1300s new views emerged. Devotees of Vishnu were forming into new communities – those following Madhvacharya, and those following Ramanuja. Ramanuja told all who would listen that people were equal, regardless of their castes or genders. He freely associated with tribal disciples as well as brahmans. Among Shaivites, Basava also condemned archaic ritual distinctions and upheld the equality of sexes, castes and untouchables in spiritual worthiness.[22]

Thirteenth-century Virashaiva poets such as Palkuriki and Somanatha denounced social problems caused by caste rigidities. And Telugu folk-poet Vemana wrote verses in South India before the time of Kanakadasa, criticizing caste prejudices:

> Though there are many castes, and personalities vary,
> people are all of the self-same human race; cotton shares
> a basic sameness, though pillows have different shapes;
> divine consciousness is affirmed by all true faiths.[23]

In his series of Sanskrit verses, *Hari Bhakti Sara*, Kanakadasa questions the logic of the strict birth-based systems of ritual purity/pollution which divided life in India so stultifyingly:

> Once food has been tasted, people call it 'polluted'.[24]
> Well, don't frogs and fish taste the water of sacred rivers?

Yet we drink it reverently calling it 'holy *tirtha* water'.
All holy men revere and drink the milk of cows,
yet the calves have already been tasting and drinking it down.
And the sage Vyasa has already tasted all knowledge,
yet men of wisdom are glad to imbibe it again
– 'purity' or 'pollution' – it's all in your head;
Lord Kaginele Keshava, please protect us always.[25]

In songs, too, Kanakadasa uses a symbolic reasoning to raise serious questions about these issues:

What does it mean to be 'of high birth';
What does it mean to be 'of low birth'
When we consider a good man's true worth?

The lotus is born from pond-bed muck
but we offer it to God in worship;
milk is secreted inside a cow's udder
but the highest caste drinks it ... What does it mean to be 'high born' ... ?

Musk is effluvia oozing from deers' pores
but the high-born smear it on their pure bodies.
To what caste does Narayana belong, tell me?
To what caste does Lord Shiva belong? What does it mean to be 'high born' ... ?

To what caste does the soul belong?
To what caste do life and love belong?
To what caste do the five senses belong?
If a soul is united with Kaginele Keshava
What does it mean to be 'of high birth' ... or 'low birth' ... ?[26]

Kanakadasa, in yet another song, asserts that the only *holeya* or pariah is the miser who hoards his wealth, implying that highness or lowness is determined by generosity and ethical conduct, not birth.[27] This logic, pointing out prejudice regarding pure and impure categories, is used by the North Indian poet Ravidas[28] and other saints. It has a modern ring to it.[29]

Annamacharya sang: 'What if he's this, what if he's that – doesn't much matter about his caste – whoever he is, all alone he comes to know Lord Hari at last.'[30] Ravidas sang: 'Families with members who truly follow their Deity are beyond high or low caste, beyond nobility and poverty.' And Kabir noted: 'If caste was really what the Creator had in mind,/why hasn't anyone so far been born/marked with Shiva's three-lined sign? ... No one is really lowly born. The only lowly ones are those/who never talk about Lord Rama.'[31] God-consciousness determines rank in the spiritual world, according to these poets.

All of these arguments showing the non-ultimacy of high/lowbirth groupings are meant to loosen up a fixed idea and break an addiction. Kanakadasa is fighting against endlessly repeated habits and community practices, value systems and hierarchies claiming extra-human origins – orientations dichotomizing purity/pollution, auspicious/inauspicious, holiness/unworthiness, divided on oversimplifying categorization and judgement according to birth status. He attempts to melt the frozen infrastructures of people's conditioned presuppositions. He warns:

> Don't break your clan into warring factions
> – do you even know how your clan began?
>
> Everyone who was ever born came through the same passage–
> from the womb they pass out by way of the vagina.
> There is no earth that has not been stepped on by humans.
> Almost nothing exists that hasn't been cooked and eaten.
> There is no higher or lower. Remember the Lord; don't break your clan …
>
> Isn't water the mother of all the communities?
> Do you know the origin of the community of water?
> Like a water bubble the human body is ephemeral.
> Try to find the real abode, offer your praise,
> chant and meditate, o mortal – and don't split up your clan...
>
> Hari is the highest of all; Hari is everyone's Lord.
> Everything is full of Hari; the one who knows this
> and contemplates the lotus feet of Kaginele Adikeshava,
> he alone is born in an 'upper caste' – don't break your clan
> into warring factions – do you know how your clan began?[32]

This reasoning has a levelling effect in religiously attuned minds. It induces a humility in which the precarious illusion of height can yield to common ground, by the contemplation of origins, and waters, and the non-discriminatory Lord. As a North Indian contemporary of Kanakadasa, the poet Kabir, puts it, 'it's pointless to ask the caste of a saint; all are on the same search for the sacred'.

Kanakadasa also sings in humility: 'I bring grass to the house of my betters, who offer their flowers to our Lord … I'm the son of a *dasa* by birth, orphan of a born *dasa* … '[33] When the high-born in South India hear this today, sometimes they realize Kanaka's multidimesional depth, and, melting, they admit his greatness.

Dasa of *Dasa*s to *Deva* of *Deva*s, and the Rhetoric of Reversal

It is a truism that the central and basic metaphors in civilizations usually pass unnoticed; because they are assumed literally to depict reality, and not just serve as an interpretation, they are taken for granted as the way things are.[34] The Vijayanagara people had such metaphorical terms. Terms such as 'Nayaka' and 'Dasa' imply whole metaphorical systems. For the deeply spiritual, one alternative kind of 'hero' it was possible to become the paradoxical *haridasa*, the militant musician, the married renouncer, the fool of God and anti-hero.

Dasa is a seasoned traveller of a term, associated with a lot of historical baggage. It was not used positively in the Vedas, so far as I can tell. *Dasyu* was the 'other', or even 'enemy', a negative designation for people who were lowly, ignorant and superstitious – a class to be subjugated, in Vedic language.[35] '*Dasa* of the divine', servant of Lord Hari, is a term that comes later – for example, in the name of the great poet Kalidasa, meaning 'servant or slave of Kali' and Ramadasa, a name of Hanuman, the ideal servant of Lord Rama. To take the name *dasa* is to humble oneself.

In the classical Hindu law text, *Manava Dharma Shastra*, we find *dasyus* mentioned as people of tribes other than communities born from the mouth, arms, thighs and feet of the Cosmic Person at the origin of time, whether their language is that of Mlecchas or Aryans.[36] In the same text the *shudra* 'bought or unbought' is said to have been 'created by the Self-existent to serve as slave to the brahman.'[37] In the *Bhagavata Purana* the term *dasyam*, one of the nine aspects of devotion, means the practice of the devotee identifies with playing the role of servant to the Lord, and *padasevanam* is the practice of serving the feet of the Lord, not bound to serving the world, being concerned with the soul, not the body.

What was the original intention and tone of the term *haridasa*? It can be translated as 'servant of the Lord' or 'slave of God'. It has the sense of a subordinate: God is absolute; all else is different, lesser, needy. It acknowledges a bond of dependence, the servant creature waits upon the Lord and Master. Humans cannot presume to coordinate themselves independently; that would make them the same as God (the *advaitin* view, which is denied by Madhva and the *haridasas*) – they must subordinate themselves. At best, they are servants, levelling their egos and taking orders from the master. The religious humility suggested by the term *dasa* has Western counterparts, as in the New Testament teaching 'The last shall be first'.[38]

There are similar terms in medieval Western quest stories, such as the Celtic tale of Peredur. There, 'servant of God', somewhat like the term *haridasa*, signifies a hermit dedicated to a non-worldly life, one whose energies are set aside for spiritual contemplation. To use a self-effacing term like 'slaves of God' was a way of rubbing the noses of worldly people into what they were slaves of: wealth, pleasure, ego, status. The logic resembles that of Christ becoming a servant and teaching that whoever would be the head of all should serve all. The Qur'an[39] speaks of the Messiah and angels as 'slaves of Allah', implying that, if angels have such a relationship of servitude, how much more should mortal men be submitted to the divine master. And in sura 23 'a party of my slaves' is mentioned, designating the faithful.[40] The implication is that by sacrificing ordinary status, religious people can open their potential to realize the nature of life and find extraordinary experiences of self-transcendence.

One who has had the experience of being a master knows the state of servitude in a different manner from a born servant. Hence Kanaka's change from 'Nayaka' to 'Dasa' is a dramatic one. (It is a greater change to go from master to slave than from *nayika* to *dasi*, which means the lady in waiting, the longing lover, becoming the courtesan, dancer, erotic mate of the Lord.) Both Shrinivasa Nayak, the jewel-selling brahman who became the singer-saint Purandaradasa, and his contemporary, Kanaka Nayak, the Kuruba chief, converted, becoming *dasa*s. They lost worldly status to gain spirital prestige.

But the question remains, how revolutionary is bhakti? Is it really a dissolver of caste? Is it a relaxer of the rigidities at certain times, such as at *bhajana* singing, without actually destroying the structure? (The structure includes a guild-like system of professions, disciplines and responsibilities besides inherited injustices, and hence even Gandhi, striving for justice, did not seek its total destruction.) Is it a system of rhetorical ideals and the same old practices? A way out for individuals through spiritual realization, rather than political activism?

In India we expect not brittle breaks, but more gradual organic shifts – further evolving complexities. Even Buddha used taken-for-granted caste society symbols to explain his values, saying that the 'true brahman' (really pure seeker) is the one who meditates and so on.

According to some scholars, 'the *Bhagavad Gita* is a revolutionary work which challenges the sacerdotal tyranny over a caste-ridden society and introduces the idea of *bhakti*, a cult of the Bhagavata sect, into the old Upanishadic conception ... '[41] But the *Bhagavad Gita* also shows Krishna declaring to Arjuna that he is the source of the caste system, an order which channels energies.

The outcome of the pre-Vijayanagara Shaivite saint Basava's and the Lingayats' lives shows how difficult it was to escape caste. The old saying, '*Eadem, sed aliter*' means 'the same things but in different ways'. Unlike the *lingayats* or Tengalai Vaishnavas, many leaders of the bhakti movement of the North rejected the idea of caste. *Lingayats* claimed superiority to orthodox brahmans and buried their dead in sitting position, like sannyasins. The *lingayats*, it sometimes seems, became one more caste or separate community developing, in time, their own sense of superiority.

The great Vaishnava *acharya,* Ramanuja, is depicted in traditional tellings of his life as saying, 'Is it the wearing of a sacred thread that makes one a brahman? He who is devoted to God alone is a brahman.'[42] He developed *prapatti.* or surrender, as the means by which grace could flow to people of lower castes, because the *upasana*s, taught in Vedic literature, were closed to them. Given a mantra, he shouted it from the rooftops, for the benefit of the lower castes, expanding Vaishnava devotion to sectors previously left out of its promise. At least, that is the symbolism and drama in his life story. (In our age Gandhi renamed outcastes, *harijans*, meaning 'children of God'.)

Ramananda (the teacher of the iconoclastic poet Kabir, the Hindi-speaking Rama storyteller Tulsidas and the Hindi hagiographer Nabhaji, among others) wrote: 'Let no man ask a man's caste or with whom he eats. If he shows love to Hari, he is Hari's son.' Though Ramananda had a *smarta* brahman background, bhakti saints of this time often came from various classes: Kabir was a weaver, Dadu a cotton weaver, Namdev a calico painter, Raidas a barber, Nanak a grocer, Ravidas a cobbler.

The *Chaitanya Bhagavata*, a text celebrating the Bengali saint Chaitanya, says of the holy untouchable: 'A *chandala* attached to the name of Krishna is not to be despised as a *chandala*; a brahman who is dishonest is not to be respected as a brahman.'[43] And the North Indian saint Narasimha Mehta, though born a brahman, preached and practised freedom from caste habits, emphasizing that a man's actual life determines his greatness. In one song[44] he characterizes a saint as one who helps others egolessly, is humble with respect for all, considering *all as equal*; he has no greed or anger, is always happy, and those who associate with him are happy, too. Such a saint is a blessing to his family, the song declares.

The effects of such a spiritual–philosophical value system can change lives in ways that more confrontative modes may not. Paying attention to what actually *is* brings a grounded responsive attitude. There are many statements in bhakti literature about unearned privilege accorded to the unworthy being an affront to the spiritually worthy who have earned respect the hard way, but have been denied their rights. 'If a man is made into a brahman through an initiation rite or through recitation of Vedas, why can't a lower caste man become a brahman by doing the same?' This example shows the value of the actual over custom.

Even so, a story told about the North Indian Krishna devotee Namdev is instructive regarding the limits of abrogating strict custom in the name of true devotion. In this story[45] Lord Krishna eats leftovers from devotee Namdev's plate. Krishna expiates his infraction of the rules, circumambulating the brahmans to get back into their good graces.[46] The same story asserts: 'He who says his caste and family are pure, has no repentance in his heart; then how can he ever meet with the Holder of the Disk [Krishna]?'[47] Krishna is unrepentant about having taken food from Namdev's plate, saying that no devotee was the equal of Namdev. Nevertheless he submitted: 'I will accept whatever penance you may prescribe for me.' He circumambulates the brahmans and bathes and smears himself with cowdung and ashes as the scriptures prescribe.[48] And it is said that, like a mother loving her child Krishna cares for devotees – 'he pays no respect to their caste or family'.[49] Thus, whereas, in Kanakadasa's story the stone statue turns and the Lord responds, in this story the Lord reciprocates, honours the devotee and humbles himself by participating in the bhakti relationship. It is a vision that the spiritual boundary is crossed, but the social order is still respected. The tension is held, not disbanding the old, but not denigrating the new either.

How Tolerant Was the Vijayanagara Era?

Religious intolerance which had flared up in antagonisms among Hindus during the twelfth and thirteenth centuries was on the decline before the brothers and Vidyaranya founded the Vijayanagara empire, and it is said to have been quite negligible before the Tuluva dynasty came into power. Thus, by the sixteenth century the region was under a more open-minded variety-encouraging rule.

A European traveller named Barbosa who observed goings-on in Vijayanagara described the king as allowing great freedom, so that every man could come and go as he wished, living according to his own beliefs without suffering any persecution, and without having to be questioned as to whether he was a Christian, Jew or Moor. He said that the governors ruled with justice.[50] Krishnadevaraya, and then his brother Achyuta, made gifts to brahmans of all sects, and gave land for both Shaiva and Vaishnava enterprises. A Hindu named Rangai Nayakayya gave funds for a mosque to be constructed. Devaraya II built a mosque in the capital for his Muslim soldiers.[51] And Ramaraja, Krishnadevaraya's son-in-law, used very inclusive symbolism in the state ceremony in which Muslim soldiers offered their obeisance to him: a copy of the Qur'an was placed before the king so that the soldier would be honouring his faith when he bowed, showing not 'either/or' but 'both/and' symbolism. This inclusive symbolism was like the coin of Caesar, using not force but persuasion.[52]

In Vijayanagara there were Arabs, Jews, Portuguese and other Europeans, Malayans, Chinese and Parsis. While the bulk of society was Hindu and was organized into castes, it was not as rigid as many Westerners presuppose. There was a connection between caste and occupation, but the link was not unalterable. Despite protests from conservatives, new historical opportunities and changing situations were always factors reshaping people's lives and their means of livelihood.[53] Some brahmans, such as Shripadaraya's family, engaged in agricultural work.

Figure 9.3   Foreign male dancers, based on a sculpture in Vijayanagara

Encouragement of a variety of kinds of religion and sensitivity to issues of mutuality are traits of some of India's most celebrated rulers. Emperor Ashoka (273–232 BCE) is known for an inscription that reads: 'He who does reverence to his own sect while disparaging the sects of others, with intent to enhance the splendour of his own, in reality by such conduct inflicts severest injury on his own.'[54]

Though Vaishnavism 'found favour' with the sixteenth-century rulers of Vijayanagara, it was not exactly a state religion, although it did become more popular. The state valued, encouraged and promoted the various sects and communities, including Shaiva and Jaina. Krishnadevaraya, often called the greatest of the Vijayanagara rulers, tried to harmonize faiths, rebuilding the Virupaksha temple and other Shaiva shrines, giving land grants to pilgrim places such as Tirupati, Ahobalam, Tiruvanamalai, Amaravati, Chidambaram and Shrishailam. He employed both Vaishnava and *smarta* brahmans.

In the fourteenth century Bukka I, according to an inscription, was petitioned by the Jainas of Anegondi, Hosapattana, Penugonde and Kalyaha, complaining that Vaishnavas were unjustly killing them. So the king had representatives of the Shri Vaishnava faith from 18 *nada*s (regions) brought before him. These included the *acharya*s of Shrirangam, Tirupati, Kanchi, Melukote and, with them, Jaina leaders. He told them that he would not allow any unjust actions harmful to the Jains, nor would he let the Vaishnavas cover their deeds with religious excuses, and he also passed a decree that the Jainas would have the sole right to use certain musical instruments customary to them in their five temples (*basti*s) which he protected.[55] In another version of the edict the king proclaimed that there was no difference between the Vaishnava and Jaina *darshana*s (world-views), joined the hands of the two sects and issued the decree.[56]

The text *Amuktamalyada*, traditionally said to be written by Krishnadevaraya, advises kings: 'Be always intent upon protecting your subjects … . The people of a country wish the welfare of the king who seeks the progress and prosperity of the country.'[57] It is an old sentiment in India. Emperor Ashoka's 'Borderer's Edict' proclaims: 'All men are my children, and just as for my children I desire that they should all enjoy happiness and prosperity both in this world and in the next, so for all men I desire the like happiness and prosperity.'[58] To promote the many sects and world-views was to promote social uplift, noble values and harmony, according to this Indian tradition. Pleas for tolerance and signs of universalism are found in songs of Purandaradasa, Kanakadasa and Annamacharya. Annamacharya, who was Kanakadasa's contemporary, asserts in a song that it does not matter what caste one is born into – all alone one comes to know Lord Hari in the end.[59]

There are many signs that bhakti had a loosening effect on caste rigidities. Pleas for tolerance and signs of universalism are found in the songs of Purandaradasa, Kanakadasa and Annamacharya. Kanakadasa is still remembered today because he voiced hope and aspirations for the common people who have their own virtues, like *ragi*. As with most things in India, whatever one says must be qualified with exceptions and awareness of complex interrelated issues and counterforces, to prevent inadequate oversimplified conclusions, to avoid reducing and understanding something greater in terms of something lesser. We cannot say bhakti was a panacea, but we can say this much: because of voices such as Kanakadasa's, caste was not all-determining in the realm of spiritual values in South India in the Vijayanagara empire and in later times.

Some say the Madhva school influence declined rapidly after the reign of Krishnadevaraya, but on the level of songs kept in circulation among villagers, its popularity was alive and well to some extent, influential long after its peak of creativity. Vyasaraya did not succeed if the goal was officially to convert all to his *matha*. But his followers' songs popularized his teachings and gained wide currency in the region. So, culturally, there was a deep impression made in people's lives. Bhakti values sung by children, women and village men helped form the heartbeat of the ethos and became part of the regional cultural identity.[60] Kanakadasa made a lasting contribution to this process. His songs are still sung, centuries after the fall of Vijayanagara. His Kannada narrative, *Nala Charitre*, is the only version of that famous Sanskrit epic story which most Kannada people ever know. His full-bodied life transcended easy caste clichés, earning spiritual honours and dignity. The people of Karnataka today affirm that Hari had good reason to pursue the reluctant Kanaka who fled but was destined to serve as a *haridasa* and to compose such moving lyrics. Such a life, and the works which flowed from it, can function as an archetypal sacred attractor to the changing generations with their hopes and needs. As Duke Ellington said of music, 'Either it's agreeable to the ear or it isn't – you don't need to always categorize it', so R.D. Ranade said of mystical thought that humanity cares for its visionary glimpses in literature without worrying about distinctions of creed or caste or race.[61] Kanakadasa is one of those beloved sources of spiritual inspiration.

Notes

1   This chapter, in a shorter form, was originally presented as a paper, 'The Singer-Saint Kanakadasa's Response to Encounters with Caste Prejudice', at the Midwest Regional American Academy of Religion, Chicago, 21 March, 1998.

2   Francis Thompson, "The Hound of Heaven at http://poetry.elcore.net/TheHoundOfHeaven.html (accessed 1 July, 2003).

3   Birappa was a Polegar and military chief, a shepherd leader and revenue collector, and Bacchamma was his wife in stories of Kanakadasa's life.

4   According to D. Javare Gouda, former vice-chancellor of Karnataka University, who wrote of Kanakadasa characterizing him as 'Vishvamanava', universal man, Everyman, on the occasion of the 500th year celebration of Kanakadasa. See *Janapriya Kanaka Samputa: A Commemorative Volume to Mark the 500th Birthday Celebrations of Sri Kanakadasa* Bangalore: Directorate of Kannada and Culture, 1989 also *Isabeku Iddu Jaisabeku: An anthology of Kannada Kirthanas* by Various Dasas, ed. Shyamsunder Bidarakundi. Gadag: Alochana Prakashana, 1989. See further, Gouri Kuppuswamy and M. Harihan, *Compositions of the Haridasas*, Tirandrum: College Book House, 1979,; A.P. Karmarkar and N.B. Kalamdani, *Mystic Teachings of the Haridasas of Karnataka*, Dharwar: Karnatak Vidyavardhak Sangha, 1939; R.D. Renade, *Pathways to God in Kannada Literature*,

Bombay: Bharatiya Vidya Bhavan, 1989. Sadguru Sant Keshavadas also wrote with admiration of Kanakadasa's accomplishments in *Lord Panduranga and His Minstrels*, Bombay: Bharatiya Vidya Bhavan, 1977, pp. 87–95.

5   *Nayaka* is an honourific term meaning 'captain' or 'chieftain' and is used for the local leaders as well as for a regional governor. It is a title of prestige, also meaning 'hero', so many people wanted to be a *nayaka*, or be called a *nayaka*. In the *Mahabharata* it connotes a military leader. A man could be a hero in several ways: as a big landholder, as a respected community leader, delegated governor, viceroy, lover, wealthy merchant and so on. It is significant that desire for prestigious status often promoted self-similar symbolisms and behaviour at various levels of a system. That which is admired is imitated, and emulation percolates through a system. Brahman poets glorified *nayaka* heroes, the glamorous examples of the martial caste. Kings taking the throne were called '*Nayaka*s', mates coupling with the heroine who is the land. Wealthy merchants and leaders of various sorts, including upwardly pretentious status seekers, sometimes added '*Nayak*' meaning 'chief' to their names.
It is significant that a hero of the 1500s had a few truly new options, not a wide spectrum of freedom; he could not adventure into Europe which was the home of the new traders from Portugal, for example, or experiment with untried ways, taking risks. Perhaps it would have given Hindu culture more resilience and adaptability in the world that was coming into existence if there had been practical men and women who could confront 'the irreducible stubborn facts' not as bits of *maya* from just one more time in the process of degenerating cycles in the later Hindu time scheme, but as orderly accessible discoverable rational secrets of the universe. Although the Vedic concept of *rita* held out such an order, the Buddhist view, and Shankara's view which checkmated it, did not. Thus innovators, inventors and discoverers did not develop in Vijayanagara. Mystery and yogic experience of sacred consciousness formed the heart of reality for classical Hinduism, not rational order and cracking laws of the universe. This means that in the early modern world there was a weakness built into South Indian Hindu society, a missing hero capable of holding the new emerging complexity, respecting, looking seriously and responding to the other as other. The regionally divided subcontinent would have to wait to become 'Mother India', a land able to foster sons like Gandhi and Tagore, Nehru and Aurobindo. Perhaps this lack amounts to a failure to be alert to warnings and to envision the magnitude of the unavoidable upcoming challenges just as Aztec and Incan priests and shamans of North America and Siberia-Alaska were ineffectual in responding to the overwhelming new influx of unfamiliar European germs and technology. Exponential change brought a runaway condition that none could control. There was a capitulation, a giving in, a taking in, an introverted gaze of preoccupation, ancient-rooted but seemingly defenceless – easy prey to powerful outsiders. One radical spiritual response was to become a *haridasa*. Kanaka Nayaka was a great man, but was limited in his options as a bhakti hero.

6   As with many practices of Hinduism, the activities at this temple may not conform to simplistic expectations of outsiders; the *archaka*s, priests offering praise there are *lingayat*s, and have been for generations. Since this is a temple to a form of Vishnu, most would expect non-Shaivites to officiate there. History's complexities in India and elsewhere are more dynamic more than simply linear.

7   For songs which he composed in Belur, Kanakadasa used 'Velapuri Keshava' as a signature.

8   In the Western world St Augustine is known for his reluctance to change his life, and Francis Thompson's 'The Hound of Heaven' is also an archetypal account of such a situation in Western poetry.

9   The war is not named. Inscriptions offer examples of possible conflicts that it might have been. In 1504, for example, there is an inscription praising a Hindu with a Muslim title, Chittapa Khan, for retaking possession of Warangal fortress from the Muslims. See Robert Sewell, *The Historical Inscriptions of Southern India*, New Delhi: Asian Educational Services, 1983 (reprint).

10 Keshavadas, *Lord Panduranga and His Minstrels*, p. 89. the 'bursting sea' phrase is from 'Hound of Heaven'.

11 'Strange attractor' is a term from chaos science. See John Briggs and F. David Peat, *Turbulent Mirror*, New York: Harper & Row, 1990, pp. 45, 109, 168.

12   Perhaps a Western counterpart would be the charismatic African-American, Sojourner Truth, who said that, without any previous teachings, she encountered what she felt was the presence of Jesus.

13   The stories of Dhruva and Ekalavya are archetypes of this kind of solitary inward discipline.

14   Some say it was the 'buffalo' vehicle of Yamadharmaraja which came and moved the stone.

15   U.R. Anantha Murthy uses this legend to contrast a character to whom God has become 'a set of tables learned by rote' in his novel *Samskara*, Delhi: Oxford University Press, p. 92. The story is reminiscent of a tale purported to be a Jataka (lives of the Buddha-to-be), 'The Master's Test'. In that tale a teacher tells his disciples to go where no-one is watching and take a wayfarer's money without harming him. They go, but one remains, explaining that the master's plan seems impossible 'because there is no place where no one is watching ... even when I am quite alone, my self is watching ... '. The teacher is glad, saying that this disciple is the one who has grasped the lesson which the others has failed to catch. See Noor Inayat, *Twenty Jataka Tales*, Philadelphia: David McKay Co., 1939, pp. 79–80. Inayat drew from translations by Ayre Sura and J.S. Speyer.

16   In the King James version of the Bible, Psalm 139 asks: 'Whither shall I go from thy spirit? Or whither shall I flee from thy presence? If I ascend up into heaven, thou art there: If I make my bed in hell, behold, thou art there' and so on.

17   On the Krishna statue, M.A. Vasudeva Rao, in 'The Udupi Madhva Matha', *Seminar*, (456), August. 1997, writes: 'Although the miracle of Kanaka is still believed to be true by many devotees, the *sannyasis* and other pandits of Udupi base their reasoning on "historical" evidence. They argue that Krishna did not turn and the *matha* was constructed in this special way (in most other monasteries and in all temples, the deity faces East).' My thanks to Dvaita philosophy scholar Deepak Sarma for this information.

18   The Latin name of this cereal grass is *Eleusine coracana*. There were a number of grains raised in the Kannada region. Varieties of rice were classified as white or black (or red). The king and nobles ate *rajana*, the best white rice. Black rice was cheap and used by the poor. Muslims preferred wheat. *Reddis* and other agriculturalists lived on *ragi*. See N. Venkata Ramanayya, *Vijayanagara: Origin of the City and Empire*, Madras: University of Madras Press, 1933, pp. 388–89.

19   Jean Genet, *The Blacks: A Clown Show*, New York: Grove Press, 1960, p. 27. There is an Ethiopian proverb, 'When the great lord passes the wise peasant bows deeply and silently expels gas.' On the topic of the subversive use of language by the disadvantaged see James C. Scott, *Domination and the Arts of Resistance: Hidden Transcripts*, New Haven, CT: Yale University Press, 1990.

20   I have not yet seen the paper by K.S.S Shivanna, 'Kanakadasa's *Ramadhanya Charitre* – It's Socio-Economic Significance', presented at the 40th session of the Indian History Congress, Waltair, 1979, but it is said to discuss the point.

21   On caste as complex system see Louis Dumont's *Homo Hierarchicus: The Caste System and Its Implications*, Chicago: Chicago University Press, 1998, and Bernard Cohn, India: *The Social Anthropology of a Civilization*, chapters 10–11, in *The Bernard Cohn Omnibus*, New York: Oxford University Press, 2004. Kees Bolle has also probed the issue interestingly in his essay 'Views of Class, Caste and Mankind', *Studia Missionalia*, 19, 1970, pp. 165–75. McKim Marriot of the University of Chicago has also published extensively on this.

22   A number of the points in this paragraph are based on material in T.N. Mallappa, *Kriyasakti Vidyaranra*, Bangalore: Bangalore University, 1974, p. 68

23   Vemana, *Verses of Vemana*, ed. and tr. A.L.N. Munty, Kakinada: Sripathi Press, 1978, p. 21. This is my versification of the text.

24   Food which is tasted, for example, by way of a ladle touched to one's lips and tongue, is tainted by the inauspicious substance of saliva.

25   Kanakadasa, *Hari Bhakta Sara*, tr. Sant Bhadragiri Keshavadas, Bangalore: Vishwa Shanti Ashram, 1986, verse 101.

26   Versified from T.M.P. Mahadevan (ed.), *Seminar on Saints*, Madras: Ganesh and Co., 1960, p. 246.

27   *Sadhu sajjana*, in *Kanakadasara Kirtanegalu*, ed. B. Shivamurthy Shastry and K.M. Krishna Rao, Mysore, Government of Mysore, 1965, p. 62, #72.

28   John S. Hawley and Mark Jurgensmeyer, *Songs of the Saints of India*, New York: Oxford University Press, 1988, p.26.

29   Consider, for example, the line in the American movie *Fried Green Tomatoes* (1991): 'He won't sit next to colored, but he eats eggs that shoot out of a chicken's ass.'

30   *E kulajudemi* by Annamacharya; Telugu lyrics in *Annamacarya Kirtanalu*, Tirupati: TTD, 1977, no. 29, p. 29. Also in Adapa Ramakrishna Rao, *Annamacarya*, New Dehli: Sahitya Akademi, n.d., p. 78–79.

31   Hawley and Jurgensmeyer, *Songs of the Saints of India*, p. 54.

32   *Kula kula kulavendu* by Kanakadasa, *Janapriya Kanaka Samputa*, Bangalore, Directorate of Kannada and Culture, 1989, p. 26.

33   I.M. Vittala Murthy (ed.), *Janapriya Kanaka Samputa*, Bangalore: Directorate of Kannada and Culture, 1989, p. 19.

34   In other words, the master narrative metaphors are usually background presuppositions, taken-for-granted archetypes; ideology is usually indirect and peripheral, rather than blatant and obviously labelled.

35   Mirrea Eliade, I believe, somewhere noted that Goshala's father was a Manka, one who wandered and displayed pious images, a non-Aryan, and so, a *dasyu*. Eliade commented that this term meant something like 'native' used in European colonial times. Being in that category, Manka was forbidden in Aryan society from any occupation but a servile one. It would seem that Europeans later became like the Aryan elite earlier had been in India, in their arrogance and unawareness of non-European ways. The illusions involved in a sense of superiority are seen best from a distance.

36   *Manava Dharma Sastra*, II.45.

37   Ibid., IV[D] 413.

38   Matt. 18:30; 20:16; Mark 10:31; Luke 13:30

39   Qur'an, sura 4, verse 172.

40   Ibid., sura 23, verse 109.

41   K. Krishnamoorthy, *Essays in Sanskrit Criticism*, Dharwar: Karnatak University, 1974, p. 281.

42   Swami Tapasyananda, *Sri Ramanuja: His Life, Religion and Philosophy*, Madras: Sri Ramakrishna Math, 1990, p. 2.

43   *Caitanya Bhagavata*, Madhya, chapter 1. Cited by Bhaskar Chatterjee, 'Social Perspective of Caitanyaism', in N.N. Bhattacharyya (ed.), *Medieval Bhakti Movements in India*, New Delhi: Munshiram Manoharlal. 1989, p. 322. This sentiment, and others, such as Ramanuja's above, are similar to the statement in the *Bhagavata Purana*: 'I believe a pariah who has dedicated to God his mind, speech, actions, wealth and life is much more worthy than a brahman who has turned his face from Lord Vishnu's lotus feet, even if the brahman has the twelve signs of greatness: austerity, knowledge, subtlety of sense perception, beauty, good ancestry, wealth, splendor, wonderful glory, physical prowess, intelligence and yogic skills.' *Bhagavata Purana* VII.9.10.

44   Narasimha Mehta's song *Vaishnav-jan*. Thanks to Dr. Chandrahas Shah, Arlington, Massachusetts, for the text and translation of this song.

45   *Stories of the Indian Saints: Translation of Mahipati's Marathi Bhaktivijaya*, tr. Justin E. Abbott and Narhar R. Godbole, vol. I and II bound in one, Delhi: Motilal Banarsidass Publications, 1996 (reprint).

46   Circumambulation is a ritual of reverence – holy places, such as shrines and temples, are circumambulated by pilgrims. By circumambulating the offended brahmans, Krishna affirmed their holiness, and they forgot the offence.

47   Ibid. Vol. I, verse 108, p. 202.

48   Ibid., verse 128.

49   Ibid., verse 168.

50   M.H. Rama Sharma, *The History of the Vijayanagar Empire*, vol. I, Bombay: Popular Prakasshan, 1978, p. 153.

51   John Briggs, (tr.), *History of the Rise of the Mahomedan Power in India till the Year A.D. 1612*, *translated from the original Persian of Mahomed Kasim Ferishta*, Calcutta: Editions Indian 1966 (reprint of 1829 edn.), p. 431.

52   N. Venkata Ramanayya, *Studies in The Third Dynasty of Vijayanagara* Madras: Madras University, 1935, p. 318.
53   Nilakanta Sastri, *A History of South India*, Madras: Oxford University Press, 1976, pp. 313–14.
54   Ashoka's Rock Edict XII.
55   *Epigraphia Carnatica* IX. Intr. p. 24; cf. EC IX Ma 18.
56   Ibid., II SB, 344.
57   Krishnadevaraya, *Amuktamalyada*, Visakhapattanam: Varald Ticar Trust, 1978 Canto IV. v.205–6.
58   D.R. Sircar, *Inscriptions of Ashoka*, Delhi: Publications Division, Government of India, 1957, p.26.
59   *E kulajudemi* by Annamacharya. Cited in note 31 above.
60   The practice of congregating like one big family and singing songs together in a *bhajan* session, like singing in other religious gatherings, is the enactment of a model of a possible ideal world – an ideal of a way of life of hope for humanity's future. In 1998 I heard an interview with American folk-singers Peter, Paul and Mary, in which they described folksongs in this way.
61   R.D. Ranade, *Mysticism in India*, Albany, NY: SUNY Press, 1983, p. 21.

CHAPTER 10

Achyutaraya: The Coronation after the Coronation

"The king governs and protects the larger world
just as a peasant nourishes his little patch of land.
Kampan Ramayana[1]

The Ritual Beginnings of a Reign

When Krishnadevaraya died in 1529, his half-brother Achyuta, son of Narasanayaka and his third wife Ombamba, became king. Achyutaraya was born after Narasanayaka returned from a pilgrimage to Rameshwaram on the tip of the subcontinent.[2] Achyuta, who had been staying at Chandragiri fort, went to the mountaintop temple at Tirupati. There, with water from the conch shell sacred to the deity Venkatesha, he was consecrated in the presence of the Lord of that place. Then he proceeded to another holy centre to the south-east; he was consecrated at Kalahasti, as if to be blessed publicly with religious power and recognition before being consecrated a third time in the capital at the widespread empire's power centre, Vijayanagara.

Since the coronation ceremony expresses the integral religio-legal or sacral-political assumption of authority it is a highly complex ritual with symbols representing all the levels of existence – celestial and metaphysical, terrestrial and social – involved in the reordering under new leadership, the official taking charge, which it enacts.

This ritual action was the transforming rite by which existence could be shaped and sovereignty established. This was a momentous time. The initial thrust determines much. Things done wrong, or omitted, are seeds of future conflict and disorder.

To know the auspicious times the *mantrin* consulted the astrologer-priest who checked the patterns of stars to find the best correspondence for important activities – the beginnings of things. Traditionally, the astrologer-priest selected auspicious times for such events as marriages and consecrations of rulers. The right configuration of stars in the sky is linked to the right time for the best configuration of events in people's lives on earth. The king links the cosmos and society integrating their powers together into a workable whole. Moderns may ask for evidence of the 'whole''s unity. There are some aspects of life shared by all in a traditional society, offering a shared cultural destiny and unity of outlook. For example, in traditional India, most women wore the same form of dress – the *sari* – though some were cotton and others were silk. Similarly, concepts of dharma and karma provided a cohesive view for many in society. In the *Kampan Ramayana* it is said that the king governs and protects the larger world just as a peasant, on a much smaller scale, nourishes his own little patch of land. The peasant is the little man who gives to the king the fruits of his labours on that land-patch. The king is the 'big man' who pays his revenues to God, the cosmic person or supreme being, by distributing the fruits of his realm's 'patch' to brahmans, who worship and specialize in relating to the absolute, promoting culture and prosperity and enhancing royal honour. Both king and peasant are beholden to the giver of life, their common divine reference point beyond this world of limits and changes. And the divine giver on the vastest scale of all is seen as caring for the whole cosmos. The organizing principle here is a kind of fractal-pattern logic with self-similarities at different scales. It reflects a cosmic pattern of religious rationale, existence in a whole context of meaning: a continuum of consciousness which links peasant, king, and God in an ordered lifeway. In effect the priest says, 'Here is the highest vision of how it works, the continuum of man, cosmos and beyond; if we preserve and incarnate this vision all will be well.' Celebrating the unfolding vitality of existence requires the marking of cycles with festive occasions displaying the beauty of flowers, songs, waters of rivers, mango leaves over doorways, the offering of coconuts, aromatic incense smoke, the light of flames, the giving of one's word. Collecting and arranging representative elements of the whole macrocosm, making a social–religious mesocosm centred around the microcosm – the king; this is the Hindu way of re-establishing order, making it continuous with the order in existence from time immemorial, grounded in cosmic patterned images.[3]

The central focus of the ritual was the fixing of the cloth band around the ruler's forehead, and the placing of the crown on his head. Once this was done and the emblems of kingship were conferred, royal commands could be pronounced in the kingdom under authority of his name, in his power, legitimately. From that point on, his sovereignty was a fact of authority, accepted and enforceable.

Waters, Women, Music, Quickening: Phases of Achyutaraya's Coronation[4]

Rajanatha III wrote the Sanskrit text *Achyutarayabhyudaya*, which describes in verse the ascension of Achyutaraya to the throne, between 1536 and 1542.[5] The ministers prepared for Achyutaraya's coronation rite, to complete the transformation already begun, so that he would fully become a *nayaka* or hero, of the *nayika* or heroine who was none other than the earth. This is symbolic of the serious task of taking responsibility for protecting the whole land.

From a common-sense distance or a linear–literalist perspective, this marriage might seem a surreal, monstrously grotesque or arrogant mismatch – a small man wedding an immense mass of soil – but from within the poetic vision, the logic symbolic of sovereignty, it also has a deep and necessary logic. The king is representative of the divine transcendent mating with the natural world below – earth – and he stands for the holding force that can hold it all together in firm form – dharma. The religious imagination augments the proportions so that they seem symmetrical, not a total mismatch. The incommensurateness is toned down through connections of order that seem almost inevitable, dignified by the mysteries of sovereignty.[6] In this logic unruly but fertile nature needs the refining and organizing power the ruler represents.

The ritual mating of man and land involves archetypal symbolism. This ritual symbolism has worldwide variations, as Robert Moore and Douglas Gillette have pointed out:

> Always, the king's culminating ordering generative act was to marry the land in the form of his primary queen. It was only in creative partnership with her that he could assure every kind of bounty for his kingdom. It was the royal couple's duty to pass their creative energies on to the kingdom in the form of children. The kingdom would mirror the royal generativity, which, let us remember, was at the Center. As the Center was, so would be the rest of creation.[7]

This is the very specific logic in Hindu kingship.

The *Achyutarayabhudaya* describes the king's willingness to begin his work of 'shouldering' the burden of the earth by poetically associating the moment with such archetypal earth-bearing images as the primal world-holding tortoise, as well as Adisesha the cosmic serpent who bears Vishnu, and the elephants who hold up the directions of the compass. The king is thus linked to those visions of the original foundations of existence.

The *Achyutarayabhudaya*[8] describes how water was ritually drawn from sacred *tirtha*s, east and west, and from seas and rivers, to be used for the consecration rite in which the king is bathed, sprinkled and quickened. The ministers knowing Achyutaraya (who, like Rama, was depicted as tall with long arms) had great confidence in his inborn ability to govern.

The pious Achyutaraya, who, as we have seen, had already been consecrated at Tirupati with water from Vishnu's conch shell, arrived in Vijayanagara to see colourful banners hanging from homes, flapping festively, greeting him and giving shade, and streets decked with ornaments. The palace was decorated with paintings of beautiful women and the court was brilliant with colourful silks, pearl garlands and festoons of gems and yak tail whisks.

In the courtyards elegant women made elaborate *rangoli* (auspicious geometric designs) with the fine dust of crushed pearls, skilfully shaping the auspicious signs of order and beauty with powder released from their fingers.

Beautiful women from a variety of regions joined together to celebrate and demonstrate their provinces' allegiance. While the women of Aratta land played resonant vinas gracefully, the Konkani girls were beating out rhythms on *mridangam*s; while the Kalinga ladies pounded sweet-smelling musk, the Lata women mixed sandalwood ointment with camphor, and the wonderful fragrance

**Figure 10.1 Lord Venkateshvara, the deity at Tirupati, based on a sculpture in
Vijayanagara**

filled the air. As the women from the Virata and Saurashtra regions prepared the
betel, the Trigarta girls were arranging the wicks in the oil lamp to be waved before
the king. As the women from Avanti, Kunti and Andhra fashioned garlands of lovely
smelling flowers, the Vidarbha ladies made garlands with shiny mica pieces
embedded in them to be draped in the hair, and the Nepali girls prepared incense
from aloe. The activities of the girls echoes the *gopis'* deeds in the *Bhagavata
Purana* and in other lists of women's activities in Hindu literature.

The palace seemed like auspiciousness incarnate, and everything was vibrant
with joyful anticipation. In the far distance the rumblings of huge drums could be
heard, echoing as they were pounded loudly inside mountain caves. The very
mountains round about were quivering, almost bouncing and jumping with joy. They
were resounding with happiness that day because they knew that the king could

Figure 10.2   Male folk-dancer, based on a sculpture in Vijayanagara

lighten life by taking on the burden of the earth. As the chamberlains chanted the victory call, Achyutaraya along with close members of his family, proceeded with dignity to the elaborately ornamented hall where the consecration would take place. The recitation of praise of the divine opened the rite.

The rhythmic beats of *mridangam*s reverberated, vinas and flutes played solemn tones, kettle drums rumbled, cymbals clashed, horns sounded, accompanied by the loud pounding of the big military drums; the deep tumult rumbled, marking the time as momentous, imminent with deeply significant events. Altogether the vibrations of these instruments had an amazing sound, a deep resonance that was harmonious and impressive, commanding attention and focusing it. They created awe and reverence.

Achyutaraya, already recognized and consecrated by the grace of Hari, was further endowed with the emperorship by means of formal rites there in the central palace of the capital, celebrated with musical offerings and symbolic displays of life, beauty and joy.

The Quickening of the King

> " ... And I am still the breath you require
> My veil the vapor of your vast empire."

Paul Valery[9]

The women sprinkled fragrant water on the king from their golden vessels. Achyutaraya, the Tuluva king, was consecrated with water coloured with kumkum and auspicious minerals. Upon the consecration dais, water mingled with red sandalpaste was flowing for the king's ceremonial bath. After the symbolic bathing, the king put on new pure white silk. After the rest of the rite had been performed, he sat on his throne, and the servant women waved the *niranjana* lamps in front of him, to bless him and ward off any inauspicious influences.[10]

Achyutarayabhyudaya verses describe the consecration as the marrying of sovereign and the land. The high priest representing spiritual authority, and the king, representing temporal power, joined together in symbolic actions and prayers to enact ritually taking possession of the land. With the tying on of the headband, the king became the centre of authority and prosperity in the kingdom, and was recognized as such.

Beautiful women danced with joy in graceful celebration of the moment, dependent vassals from different provinces of the land fanned him with chowries on either side. The royal umbrella, emblem of rulership, beamed with pride as if trying to announce to the people that this king would be a just sovereign, a just ruler following the tradition of the original law-giver, Manu.

In the rite, kings who ruled various provinces held symbolic emblems. The Kalinga king held a golden vessel. The Magadha ruler held gem-studded sandals; the Shaka king held a chowrie with branches of whisks; the king of Lanka held a ceremonial sword. These kings first respectfully showered golden petals on the new king, to show their allegiance, then gave him the gifts they held and made the formal gestures of honouring him.

Thus symbolically anointed and crowned, recognized and celebrated and honoured as was right and fitting, in harmony with the various dimensions, entities and beings, the king was in place and on line, ready to run his programmes, rule his realm like a timeless archetypal ideal pattern of dharma. At the same time, his queen, Varadambika, was anointed and his son, Chinna Venkatadri, was consecrated as Yuvaraja, crown prince, even though he was young and had not been fully trained. He was a kind of 'back-up copy' to ensure the continuation of the line.

And so, sprinkled, blessed and hailed by representatives from the land, Achyutaraya took the reins of sovereignty. The enthronement represented a rebirth in the king's life; anointed, he was called the 'Child of the Waters of the best of Mothers'. Holding the wealth of rulership after the consecrations, he distributed gold to brahmans as part of the celebration, and they honoured him.[11]

The *Manava Dharma Shastra* states that the king is made up of eight cosmic deities, including Varuna and Indra: 'Hence the king surpasses all other beings in splendour ... He is a great god in human form.'[12] The king becomes more than an ordinary human; he becomes a semi-divine being, a fit mate for the land. By chanting the Vedic mantras, the priests performing the ritual bring the king's authority and power into being in that specific time and place, thereby centring anew the old empire's life.

Envisioning Mythical Images, Ritual Practices and Artistic Portrayals as Fractals of Hinduism

The ritual 'Quickening of the King' forms a microcosm containing many aspects of Hindu tradition. Exploring the enthronement more deeply would further reveal the way in which the parts are all enfolded in the whole: if you pull one strand, every fibre in the net quivers; if you begin one story, you end up echoing and implying them all:

> Just as its mythic descriptions and art indicate, Hinduism can begin or end at any one of its representations, as each paradoxically curls back on itself constantly foreshadowing the rest ... . Each layer is truly a representation of the whole with the cascading pattern of representation infinitely cycling in on itself like the colourful paisley pattern that India is so famous for and that a Westerner, Benoit B. Mandelbrot, recognized in the mathematics of the irregularly appearing forms of nature which he named fractals.[13]

All of Hinduism's principles can be found in not only the symbolic actions and relationships of the brahman priest, the warrior king, the bountiful earth and the pious and industrious people, but also in the mythic images of the holy: 'in Shiva/Brahman/Purusha who are represented as Nataraja, who is danced as Bharata Natyam, who shines as Surya and Chandra, who play as man and woman, who appears as the manifest awakening of its transcendental nature, who is Shiva/Brahman/Purusha ...'[14] The continuation of the polity is the continuation of the ancient brahman vision, and the continuation of the lore, systems and practices in one home is potentially the seed of the whole empire. The Hindu lifeway and symbol system bear in their depths hopeful seeds of regeneration, urges of vitality reaching towards physical health and the power of the psyche. With every end in Hinduism a long-lasting resilience adapts to make a new start. Raw nature must be carefully shaped and refined in time-tested manners. Gather the priests and auspicious women, gather the waters, the flowers, the clay. The old king is dead, the new king is in power; long live the king. Repeat the cycles within cycles within cycles.

I would like to highlight how we can see fractal-like patterns in both structures of Hindu society and images of the nature of the divine. Elsewhere I have mentioned how Indologist Madeleine Biardeau shows the atemporal structure of classical Hinduism's world: 'in each territorial "unit" – which can be as small as a village with its chief – one finds, theoretically at least, the totality of the Hindu socio-religious structure and its values.'[15] This is very much a fractal image: all in each. The whole is reflected in the parts. Also, previously I mentioned Burton Stein's observation, that in Vijayanagara the 'locality units of the political system ... [w]ere reduced images' of the imperial centre – that is, fractal-like smaller-scale replicas of it, just as the practices at great religious institutions, such as temples and *mathas* served as models for the actions of ordinary people of the Vijayanagara era, fractal-like smaller-version patterns echoing the originals.[16]

On the mythological–ideological level, the origins of different castes are associated with different parts of the cosmic Person who was sacrificed and divided in the beginning, becoming the different parts of the universe.[17] The Laws of Manu, referring to this, assert that if one acts contrary to, or oversteps, the boundaries of one's role in society, one disturbs the overall order. The logic (as in European feudalism) gives an order in which the members are participants in a chain of being.[18] Individual bodies (sharing the same *atman*, or spiritual self[19]) make up the body politic, and this is based on, and reflects, the body cosmic, the original Person. Thus, there are fractal-like patterns of part/whole correspondence and transcendence on the part of persons in the Hindu world-view. Without using the concept of fractals this is articulated by Madeleine Biardeau in this way: 'at the level of secular society, both theoretical and concrete, there was no place for the human individual as such; the individual is only a unit within his group, caste or lineage, which determines his place in the hierarchy ... from his group he receives a certain idea of his duty ...'[20] His role depends on his birth context in society. But such an isolated identity is a temporary experience in the long run, rather than the ultimate reality. 'The day he feels too strongly the relativity, or indeed the vanity, of what is expected of him he breaks away from the group and attends to what is most essential and permanent within himself – the *atman* ... [attaining] liberation, through knowledge or yoga, only by shedding all differentiation, by being absorbed into the Absolute where it finally loses all that remains of empirical individuality.' In this view, the ego is dissolved and there is a merging in a more encompassing state of being, as the person's spirit (atman) merges in Spirit (*paramatman*).[21]

There is also a fractal-like pattern of multiple forms of God in Hinduism, with the cosmic whole found in each form and in all of the forms together. As Biardeau explains, 'Each Hindu deity is part of a complex. If the Absolute is located anywhere, it is this complex and not one or another of its members. It is in this sense that "all the gods are merely forms of *Brahman*." Let us say that together they all constitute *Brahman*.'[22] This concept is a vision of cosmic totality, self-similar organically related parts of a larger composite on different scales: fractal-like. In the wholeness of Brahman the various aspects dissolve in the mystery of pure consciousness, sacred unity as described by the Upanishads and later philosopher saints such as Shankara. Fractal patterns thus help us not only to imagine a wholeness in which the infinite is found in finite beings, but also to mentally plot natural processes and principles of organization, natural–cultural structures and visions of the transcendent.

A great historian of the Vijayanagara empire, Burton Stein, seems to view the segments of the 'segmentary state' in South India as having a somewhat fractal quality; he describes the organization at different levels expressed in the following way: '[the] segments are structurally as well as morally coherent units in themselves.'[23] We can see how the segments, which 'are its territorial units, each of which, from the largest – the kingdom – to the smallest – the village – resembles the other in its organization. The most important segments of the Hindu state are neither the kingdoms to which they are attached nor the villages of which they are composed, but the 'localities' (*nadu*) and supra-localities (*periyanadu*s).'[24] And considered altogether, these 'segments comprise a state in their recognition of a sacred ruler whose overlordship is of a moral sort and is expressed in an essentially ritual idiom'.[25] The *nayakas* carried out all the different applications of the given policies governing the empire, and, together, this can be considered as a fractal.

Indologist Ron Inden sums up Louis Dumont's similar view as follows:

> [Dumont] argues that the dominant caste replicates at the village or local 'level' the royal function. This apparently makes it possible, at least in principle to understand the kingdom by looking at the village. It is also important in another respect, for it means that if one demonstrates the subordination of power to hierarchy at one 'level' in this segmented, holographic system, one has also shown it at the other levels.[26]

This structure, of microcosms in macrocosms, each part reflecting the whole, is consonant with the nature of cosmos and consciousness depicted in Hindu philosophy. For example, the *Yogavasishtha*, an eleventh or thirteenth century Sanskrit text attributed to Parthasarathi Misra, which integrates *advaita* and Vijnanavada Buddhist views, states that the universe is like a ripe fruit which appears from the activity of consciousness (*chit*). Furthermore, it states, there is a branch of a tree with innumerable fruits like it, a tree with thousands of such branches, a forest with thousands of such trees, a mountainous region with thousands of such forests, a territory with thousands of such regions, a solar system with thousands of such territories, a universe with thousands of such solar systems, and many such universes contained in what resembles an atom within an atom; and that consciousness is the subtle sun lighting existence.[27] This cosmic containment, the vastness of the whole replicated in the smaller parts, each of which is whole at its own level, is a vivid way of conceptualizing aspects of wholeness, unity and the mystery behind life. *Atma* and atom, all in all, all in each, each in all, each in each – in some ways, modern physics and cosmology have affinities with this view.[28] The symbolism of kingship and Hindu philosophy concerning the structure of cosmos and consciousness offers much food for thought.

Practical Problems at Ground Level

Ideology usually offers ideals for men to reach for, not actual attainments. What is the meaning of the symbolic acts of consecration, all the rites of taking on kingship?

If 'the meaning of a communication is the behavior that results',[29] then actual outcomes show a dissonance between intention and eventuality. After the celebrations Achyutaraya of the third dynasty Tuluva family spent his days coping with many difficulties. He was kept busy fending off problems arising from internal rebellions, defending the realm against foreign aggression, and trying to root out the bandits who harrassed pilgrims and traders, not to mention the intrigues and conflicts with his rival of the Aravidu family, Ramaraya, who sought to co-opt power from the time Achyutaraya was a child. The Aravidu family was to become the fourth dynasty of Vijayanagara. There is evidence that Achyutaraya strove to govern with dharma as his guide until he died in 1542.[30] His cultural activities included music (there is a specially designed vina associated with him), the construction of new suburbs, temples, pools and philanthropic causes.[31]

Whilst the complex and colourful symbol system and ritual enactment of assuming power focus attention on an important turning point and give credence to authority in the social system, the investment functions for believers. The ornate poem *Achyutarayabhudaya* celebrates the signs and metaphors of legitimate rulership with Achyutaraya at the very centre. But the Nayakas and the formally patterned routines of the system itself actually govern. (As Czar Alexander said on his deathbed: 'I never ruled Russia. Ten thousand clerks did.') Together, the captains or governors made up the system like a composite rudder, and the emperor was like a 'trim tab', the little rudder in the big rudder that steers the ship of state. Those who did not honour, acknowledge or abide by the rules of that emperor–*nayaka* symbol system paid little heed or homage to its public figurehead. Outsiders – Muslims, Portuguese, rebels, bandits and others not impressed by the rituals and religious display, and so not swayed to submission – destroyed the order as much as they were able. They sprang attacks or launched alternative agendas of exploitation or thievery in the consecrated territory, fighting the will of the system's protector.

The elaborate consecration with flowers and soils, throne and bath, ointments, music and dance, rites of brahman and *kshatriya* – the 'marriage' of protector and earth – consists of poetic images, attractors stimulating awe, and memorable reminders of interconnections. While the timeless ideal is beyond the grasp at any given moment, it offers meaning and a programme, signs of a way of properly exercising power and implementing orderly policies – a standard to reach towards, a goal for dedicated energy. The image of the cosmos-quickened king-husband represents the perfect idea of sacred power, but realistically much depends on the abilities of governors and clerks, commanders and soldiers. To enforce the order against the forces of decay takes discipline, efficiency, and loyalty. Territorial rivals to the north were to gather forces and 23 years later, in 1565, the centre would give way, mere anarchy would be set loose, and there would be a failure of the light of strategic imagination at the twilight of the last great old fashioned Hindu realm of Karnataka.

It is a truism in systems theory that 'the mode of failure of a complex system cannot ordinarily be determined from its structure'.[32] In other words, the overall system may appear to be in good working order to those close to it, and even those overseeing its operations. The system's routine processes seem to be proceeding in ways that look familiar and enduring. The crucial variables are discovered by accident; the unviable becomes known as the system fails to survive or faults are recognized after runaway change begins to take place.[33] Some have seen the *nayaka*s as part of the cause of the Vijayanagara empire's fall. These feudatory leaders and regional kings or viceroys for the emperor, instead of just protecting their own areas became kings betraying other kings, involved in other areas' business. They overextended their interests and activities. Divided among themselves, the *nayaka*s could not fend off the determined five sultans to the north who tirelessly harrassed them: 'When a fail-safe system fails, it fails by failing to fail safe.'[34] Just when the guards, the systems of alerts and alarms, were unconcerned and the spies saw no problem there came a great cataclysm. The catastrophe was the defeat of the City of Victory. Krishnadevaraya's reign had been the high point, but '[s]ystems tend to malfunction conspicuously just after their greatest triumph',[35] as Arnold Toynbee noted after studying over 20 civilizations. Typically a successful strategy that is repeated too long becomes a formula for failure. Typically, the army is made ready – but to face the dangers of the previous war. Unprepared for the new unfolding unanticipated conditions, not noticing the new threats, trained to react by rote, if one does not want to be bothered by small intrusions, one may have to respond to, or collapse under, major overwhelming invasions.

In some form and combination of distinctively South Indian stresses that is probably what happened to Vijayanagara. In the end, the royal survivors became rivals, burning each other's palaces.[36] Proverbs about wholes and parts sometimes capture important principles: 'A house divided against itself cannot stand', especially against a strong enemy who can 'divide and conquer'. We shall return to the theme of how the capital fell to invaders in 1565, in the final chapter of this book.

Notes

1   *Kampan Ramayana*, I.180. See David Shulman, *The King and the Clown in South Indian Myth and Poetry*, Princeton, NJ: Princeton University Press, 1985, p. 50. This suggests a fractal-like pattern with several levels of self-similarity: the peasant works his plot, the king rules the world as the peasant works his plot; and, of course, God rules the cosmos, within which smaller creatures have their domains.

2   Vasundhara Filliozat, *Vijayanagara*, Delhi: National Book Trust, 1999, p. 50. Filliozat sees Achyutaraya as more of a culture-lover than a sword-wielder. Vaishnava kings sometimes seemed more pleasure-loving than Shaivite kings.

3   To paraphrase Mircea Eliade and chaos theory, chaos is never conquered once and for all, it is only temporarily hypnotized. A simple order seems to hold it for a while, an illusion of order prevailing until the basic dynamic turbulence returns. The reign of human control is a repetitive myth and ritual on the face of the basic basin: chaotic process.

4   D. Sridhara Babu, '*Kingship: State and Religion in South India, according to South Indian Historical Biographies of Kings (Madhuravijaya, Acyutarayabhyudaya and Vemabhupalacarita*',

dissertation, University of Gottingen, 1975. esp. pp. 57–60. Thanks to Rajanikanta Rao for helping me locate this text. The word 'quicken', which I use several times in this chapter, means to make alive ritually, to stimulate and kindle, to enter a new phase – the king's consecration and coronation are a 'quickening', an enlivening of the royal power in him.

5   Ibid., p. 15.

6   For some patterns and symbols of 'sovereignty themes' in Western Grail literature see Chapter III of *Peredur: A Study of Welsh Traditions in the Grail Legends* by Glenys Geetinck, Cardiff: University of Wales Press, 1975. The symbolic logic, the ritual rationale, is quite clear. Lakshmi, the consort of Vishnu, the Preserver of the Universe, is conceived of as the prosperous sovereignty of the *raja*. A king without Lakshmi at his side finds his unfortunate realm in chaos and drought, illness and degeneration, poverty and infertility. A king needs to be whole, whether in the East or West, because wholeness is a sign that the goddess of Sovereignty is with him.

7   Robert Moore and Douglas Gillette, *King, Warrior, Magician, Lover: Rediscovering the Archetypes of the Mature Masculine*, San Francisco: Harper, 1990, p. 60.

8   *Achyutarayabhudaya* III 20–53.

9   Paul Valery, 'The Youngest of the Fates', *Selected Writings*, New York: New Directions, 1964, p. 27.

10   The king's enthronement rituals included a clay bath with pieces of clay from many sites, which had a symbolic correspondence with the king's bodily parts, to anoint him as a cosmic person. See Ronald Inden, 'Ritual, Authority, and Cyclic Time in Hindu Kingship', in J.F. Richard, (ed.) *Kingship and Authority in South Asia*, Madison: University of Wisconsin Press, 1981. The different kinds of clay selected from different places calls to mind a Midrashic legend. In this Jewish tradition, God took clay for making Adam (meaning 'man' in Hebrew) from every part of the world, using every colour of the earth to ensure universality and basic homogeneity of the human race. See also J.C. Heesterman, *The Ancient Indian Royal Consecration*, The Hague: E.J. Brill, 1957. All the potential parts of the human race are thus found in the wholeness of the first man.

11   For more on Hindu Kingship see Richards, *Kingship and Authority in South Asia*; also Ananda K. Coomaraswamy, *Spiritual Authority and Temporal Power in the Indian Theory of Government*, New Haven, CT: American Oriental Society, 1942 (reprinted New York: Kraus, 1967).

12   *Manava Dharma Shastra* VII 3-8. As I mentioned elsewhere, the king recapitulates Indra's victory over chaos, and becomes the archetypal *kshatriya* (warrior or knight) through a series of investitures. See John Weir Perry, *The Heart of History: Individuality in Evolution*, Albany, NY: SUNY, 1987 pp. 98–99 for a discussion of sacral kingship and psychological symbolism.

13   Sofia Diaz, 'Bharata Natyam: A Hindu Fractal', *Anthropology of Consciousness*, I# (3–4), 1990, pp. 19–20.

14   Ibid.

15   Madeleine Biardeau, *Hinduism: The Anthropology of a Civilization*, Delhi: Oxford University Press, 1994, p.120.

16   Burton Stein, *Peasant State and Society in Medieval South India*, Delhi: Oxford University Press, 1985, pp. 367–68.

17   *Rig Veda* X.90.

18   Louis Dumont, *Homo Hierarchicus: The Caste System and Its Implications*, tr. M. Sainsbury, Chicago: University of Chicago Press, 1974, pp. xvii, and pp. 1-20, etc.

19   The *atman's* nature is an unalterable wholeness, which is why 'when fullness is taken from fullness, fullness remains' (*Isha Upanishad*). Ordinary linear images do not help us picture this concept, but fractal imagery does. The *Upanishads*, tr. Swami Nikhilananda, New York: Harper and Row, 1963, p. 89.

20   Madeleine Biardeau, *Hinduism*, p.121.

21   Ibid.

22   Ibid.

23   Burton Stein writes of the 'segmentary state' in *Peasant State and Society in Medieval South India* Delhi: Oxford University Press, 1985, pp. 23 ff.

24   Ibid.

25   Ibid. See also Ron Inden, *Imagining India*, London: Blackwell, 1990, p. 206.

26   Ibid., pp. 206, 153.

27   For a translation, see *Yogavasishtha*, tr. Hari Prasad Shastri, London: Favil, 1937.

28   Cosmic holism is seen in quantum physics even the smallest changes of atomic particles change the whole, because of mysterious subtle interconnectedness; in ecology there are interdependent food chains and interactive organisms and environments; in molecular biology there is DNA, with the code of the whole organism inscribed in each cell and so on.

29   John Gall, *Systemantics: The Underground Text of Systems Lore*, Ann Arbor, MI: General Systemantics Press, 1990, p. 102.

30   K.A. Nilakanta Sastri, *A History of South India from Prehistoric Times to the Fall of Vijayanagara*, Madras: Oxford University Press, 1981, p. 287.

31   Filliozat, *Vijayanagara*, pp. 50-51.

32   Gall, *Systemantics*, p. 78.

33   An ancient Egyptian example is the precarious pyramid of Snofru, which collapsed when it was almost completed. Snofru had tried to outdo his grandfather Zoser, but he did not know that Zoser's structure was already at the maximum size into which such materials could safely be constructed. Snofru exceeded the scale of possible building and the structure collapsed. Cheops, wishing to learn from the mistake of Snofru, built his pyramid more cautiously, mindful of making a better distribution of the stresses. His pyramid was solid and stable, and his successors followed that method. Their pyramids worked, and this success inspired more and more to be built. At this point, on another scale, the whole Egyptian state, overburdened with excessive stresses of building monumental pyramids, broke down under the pressure into anarchy – the centre could not hold. See Ibid.

34   Ibid.

35   Ibid., p. 35.

36   Filliozat, *Vijayanagara*, p. 55.

CHAPTER 11

Conclusion: Bad Blood – Wounded Pride and Retaliations

> *... there is a moment which follows pride in the boundless extension of the territories we have conquered, and the melancholy and relief of knowing we shall soon give up any thought of knowing and understanding them. There is a sense of emptiness that comes over us at evening, with the odor of the elephants after the rain and the sandalwood ashes growing cold in the braziers .... It is the desperate moment when we discover that this empire, which had seemed to us the sum of all wonders, is an endless, formless ruin ... that the triumph over enemy sovereigns has made us the heirs of their long undoing*
>
> Italo Calvino[1]

It is a humbling experience to try to encompass a distant empire and its centuries of events in our reflections. There is always more to learn, and we can never know all. We can gather many samples, many overviews, and patches of knowledge; there are accounts and documents and artefacts to sort out in the attempt to draw conclusions. Eventually, time and necessity overtake us, and we must sum up findings or try to arrive at a formulation of views with regard to unresolved questions. Some points register and make strong impressions in the search despite the constantly shifting perspectives. To explore impressions from the literature, consider some useful emerging vocabulary terms of our day and to try out tentative conclusions seems a necessary risk. On discovering that there are many variables, we find ourselves revising, adjusting, relativizing or discarding most of our conclusions, eventually coming to accept that although a variety of approaches makes a simple consensus impossible, sometimes views can converge in a composite, if tentative, synthesis. It takes many views to seek a larger whole understanding, so we must be pragmatic and gather our viewpoints where we can. From Firishta and Nuniz, Nilakanta Sastri and Herman Kulke, Burton Stein, Mulk Raj Anand, Phillip Wagoner, Vasundhara Filliozat, Anna Libera Dallapiccola, George Michell and other people brought together in discussion and debate, we can access a rich profusion of voices and topics for reflection.

Sensitivity to Initial Conditions and End Results

In the stories of Vijayanagara's origins the hare-and-hounds legend describes an event which signalled the auspicious place of beginnings. It is a legend capable of multiple interpretations. Although some may dismiss it as meaningless, in my view, even if it is not an historical event, the anecdote uses images repeated in folklore and legend – images which have archetypal qualities and stand for hopes and dreams. Far from being random, myths use images of wonder to explain 'how it all began', like the momentous landslide that grows from a tiny grain of sand. The images depicting the situation belong to a worldwide vocabulary of dynamically expressive symbolism. For example, as previously mentioned if you know the *Rig Veda*, you can find a passage that has a similar pattern, in which a riddle describes backward-running rivers, a jackal driving a wild boar from the brushwood, a hare swallowing a razor, and the *rishi* singing the mantra mysteriously sundering a distant mountain with a clod.[2] In the Mahabharata epic, Bhishma asks 'Can a dog kill a lion?' and describes a group of lesser kings barking like dogs at a lionlike king.[3] Though used for different purposes and involving a shift to the next scale of size, the image is nevertheless that of a weaker power turning against a seemingly greater one.

In the Vijayanagara legend the image – although it has some variations – is specifically of unexpected resistance. T.M.P. Mahadevan writes of copperplate grants dated 1336, recording that Harihara hunting on the southern bank of the Tungabhadra saw a *hare and a hound together*, despite their natural enmity.[4] In a verse narrative described in *Sri Vidyaranya*, an official publication of the Vidyaranya Vidyapitha Trust, the episode is described a bit differently: Vidyaranya asked the princes to build a new city on the spot where *'hares chased the hunting dogs'*,[5] and they did so. Whatever the variations, this is an image that taps the archetype of a large-scale reversal. In other cultures, similar possibilities are condensed into kindred images. For example, in Zen there are sayings which serve as puzzles to solve, images to fathom. One is: 'A wide marsh swallows a mountain; a badger neatly beats up a leopard'.[6] This, too, speaks of a seemingly overwhelming adversity defeated by a bold assertion of autonomy. It is like the Zen saying 'A rabbit conceives and bears a tiger'.[7] Another Zen saying concerns the inherent creative power in human beings which, when called upon, can rise to life's challenges: 'When needed, it turns tiger; not used, it turns rat.'[8] The wisdom carried by sages or other authentic spiritual leaders helps people face challenges by getting in touch with the necessary archetypes: models of heroism and diligence, sacrifice and loyalty. Creative powers which stagnate and go to waste may be perverted into poison; repressed imagination may be diverted into demonization.

The African American blues singer Leadbelly's 'All Out and Down' blues song ends with the image of a woman who could 'make a preacher lay his Bible down .... make a rabbit hug a hound'.[9] There is also the story told by American singer-songwriter Arlo Guthrie about two rabbits who ran away from dogs into a hole. One says; 'What can we do now? If we leave, we're dead.' The other says, 'Yah, but if we stay here, eventually we'll outnumber them.' Arlo Guthrie thus voices the hope that a population with certain values (those held by his folksinger father) would grow. Similarly, by staying in the charmed circle by the Tungabhadra river, guided by the Merlin-like Vidyaranya, 'the brothers' grew in number, as it were, until they formed an empire; the underdogs overcame adversity and won autonomy.

There is a characteristically Hindu ideal – that detachment ennobles dedicated action. It holds that only someone as dedicated as a cave-dwelling hermit, beyond attachment to the physical world, is fit to guide the king to the throne at the centre. Each empire seeks to fulfil its own dynamic possibilities in its own unique period of time. And in the cycles of time's reversals that which was high becomes low: 'The fox steals up to the approaching lion: the jackal drives the wild-boar from the brushwood … . The great I will make subject to the little: the calf shall wax in strength and eat the bullock', as the Vedic seer sang long ago.[10] We could go on giving examples from verses and proverbs worldwide. The point is that the wise man has the depth and clarity to mirror the situation and to give puzzles to solve with life itself – enigmatic images to fathom. The wise notice the clues and read the signs of the times. They 'know the end from the beginning'. The story credits Vidyaranya with that power. The folk mind tends towards the archetypal. The story of the hare makes the success of the empire seem inevitable. Equally, the story of the false conch signal at the empire's ritual beginning makes its failure seem inevitable. The stories make the origins, developments and end of the empire seem foreordained in the way that destiny is written on an individual's forehead. Such stories all fall within the context of divine *lila*, or folk imagination, not secular history.

Because conditions were ripe, the resolve of two small groups of brothers made a great difference in South India in the fourteenth century – the changes, as the realm grew, exemplify the 'butterfly effect'. For three centuries the Vijayanagara empire represented a large-scale creative surge, made up of smaller but sustained creative surges in generations and smaller creative urges in individuals, embodying a new empire incarnating the generative order in the society.[11] Today, we have a new understanding of order and hierarchy – one in which:

> the general principle is immanent, that is, actively pervading and indwelling, not only in the less general, but ultimately in reality as a whole. Emerging in this fashion, hierarchies are no longer fixed and rigid structures, involving domination of lower levels by the higher. Rather, they develop out of an immanent generative principle, from the more general to the less general.[12]

The Sangama brothers, seeing the need to build upon tested patterns of the past, to structure society in a way that was known to have endured, called upon the spiritual knowers of the past to renew the system. Vidyaranya was experienced, he had 'drunk the water of 36 wells', studied with a guru, lived in Banaras, offered sacrifices, raised a son, grown in knowledge and acquired wisdom. He had become a master who knew the past and, in a sense, held it all together for the present founding of the future. Vidyaranya re-established the familiar attractors that had patterned great Hindu kingdoms of the past. (The structure of the system of government and society shaped by Vidyaranya was partly based on the record of past functioning – how Hindu kingdoms of the past had worked for centuries. The brahmans were the repositories of the groundplan, and so they and the other elements of society had no choice – democracy had not been introduced, and would not be for another 600 years. If a Hindu empire were to speak it would sound like the epics and folksongs of India, Vedanta and *Dharma Shastras*, and a potemtial empire-founder would have to know those and other expressions of Hindu lifeways as well as know the world, including rulers, traders and peasants of tropical regions, and yogic seekers in the Himalayas.) Like the Western archetypal Merlin, Vidyaranya is the guide who protects the ruler and the kingdom with his knowledge. The legendary Vidyaranya's power is mysterious, far-reaching and unknowable, like Merlin's; it is neither specific nor predictable; it is a non-linear element in the world of governance and dominion. He was a wild card the Muslims had not noticed in the deck. I have emphasized the systemic patterns involved not to condone any injustices, but to avoid a narrow oversimplification that focuses only on politics or economy (or worse, on blaming whole classes of people out of some anachronistically righteous rage.) The people remembered themselves when the Vijayanagara empire formed. As one more local example of a universal ordering process they organized themselves a state, the empire grew and flourished, and 'the rise of Vijayanagara as a champion of Hindu revival led to a spurt of musical activity all over the South',[13] a burgeoning of bhakti creativity in the fine arts. For Hindus in South India, Vidyaranya, an agent of Hindu self-organization, helped bring order out of the chaos of the times. He (or archetypal folk memories of him) spearheaded a movement that re-established the old attractors that could pattern folk energies.

The Importance of *Nayakas*: The Network of Domains and Governors

> *The most powerful metaphors in any society are not the purple ones which immediately spring to mind like 'progress,' 'growth and development' in Western societies today, but the ones least likely to occur to us, the ones we have hidden from our conscious selves by constant wear and tear.*
>
> Donald Miller[14]

Unconscious levels of the Vijayanagara lifeworld become more evident in terms and symbols used in taken-for-granted ways. Hidden 'metaphoreality' seems fully real, foundational, 'taken for granite' at any given time and place. The desire for life and joy is imaged by the *devadasi*, and the need to die to the world and be devoted to the ultimate is imaged in the renouncing *haridasas* and sannyasins. The rulers of the segments in various provinces of the state were called *nayakas*, and this name may also constitute a hidden metaphor of the period we are exploring.

Nayaka is a Sanskrit term (from the root *ni*, 'to lead') meaning 'leader'. In the Mahabharata epic it also means 'king', and over the centuries it has connoted a spectrum of meanings: 'chief, lord, principal, general, commander', and, in the *Bhagavata Purana* for example, 'husband'. In Sanskrit dramas it meant romantic 'hero' and passionate 'lover'.

By the early 1500s in South India, *nayaka* meant feudatory leaders and regional kings or viceroys for the emperor, and members of a new supralocal military class had that official title. Both Purandaradasa and Kanakadasa, though from very different backgrounds and echelons of society, were sometimes called *nayaka*s, showing, I suppose, that it also meant 'important man' or 'leader'.

The term *nayika* meant 'noble lady, mistress, courtesan, the heroine in dramas' and, in literary works, a class of female personifications representing illegitimate sexual love. The *nayaka–nayika bhava* is expressed in the *lovers*' relationship, the aesthetic and bhakti moods of longing and union. This archetypal attractor is a central metaphor for devotion – a distinctive strategy developed to its full by the Hindu religious imagination – for example, in songs such as the *ashtapadi*s of Jayadeva, the *pada*s of Kshetrayya and the *shringara kirtana*s of Annamacharya.

Whilst we should not think of the symmetry as perfectly simple – *nayaka* as beloved of *nayika* – I also want to insist that it is not non-existent. A new bureaucratic class, the *nayaka*s and Poligars or Palayakkars, representatives of the elite in cities and townships, had been growing as a segment of society situated between king and people.[15]

As Burton Stein has said, 'Temples and *matha*s were prime instruments for Vijayanagara political purposes; they enjoyed a moral standing which no kingdom could ignore or oppose. Every temple ... represented ... as a single entity the diverse peoples whose worship it attracted.'[16] There were shrines for village deities, shrines for tutelary deities of dominant landed people, as well as territorial deities and other centres of religious life and power. Vijayanagara kings had to win over the allegiances of a variety of these religious centres in order to enjoy the support of the various communities they represented. The leaders of sectarian *matha*s were quite powerful among the people – they controlled wealth, had prestige and exercised necessary powers of ceremony. They often sent agents to teach, train and receive support from their constituents. The kings supported some of them and, in return, some of them served as spiritual advisers (*rajaguru*s) to the kings. (For example, the head of the Tengalai *matha* at Tirupati was important during the reign of Saluva Narasimha. The head of Ahobilam *matha* was the leader of the Vadagalai branch of Vaishnavism. Shrishailam was an important Virashaiva *matha*. All received support).

Karyakarta was a title for agents of the king – regional assistants who were not autonomous authorities. In contrast, as the structure changed, during the second half of the Vijayanagara empire, the title *nayaka* came to signify a local lordship. Burton Stein contrasts the new organization with the absolute rights held by settlers who cleared the forests and cultivated the land. The new rights were rights of agency derived from a king who could parcel out areas in exchange for revenue and military support. Prebendel rights (granted by the state) were in potential conflict with traditional rights from the community already in existence. The development came during the reign of Devaraya II (1406–1422), who attached more importance to soldiers and their military service to the king. (He also introduced Turkic strategies and Muslim mercenaries in his military operations.) The title *amara raja nayaka* from that time comes from *samara*, war, and *nayaka*, leader, commander or captain. The *nayaka* lordship exercised authority given by the central powers of Vijayanagara rule, either *mahapradhani* or king, and it weakened locally derived rights.[17] Appadurai has described how money and land circulated to connect kings with their important commanders, the heads of major Hindu traditions, Vaishnava and Shaiva, and the sacred centres such as temples. The kings and leaders exchanged wealth and resources for honours at the temples through influential local leaders to gain the upper hand over groups of people who might otherwise be resistant.[18]

In the second half of the Vijayanagara empire, during the sixteenth century, many inscriptions attest to this vast territorial rule by the king's authority. Noboru Karashima's studies concentrate on Tamil inscriptions, but also reflect the situations in other regions. (By 1364, Madhurai, far to the south in Tamil Nadu, had been incorporated into the Vijayanagara empire, as we saw earlier.) The Tamil inscriptions studied by Karashima indicate that the *nayakas* often enjoyed a close relationship to the king, working for him as agents in distant segments of the empire. Some of them kept military contingents for the king's use and some had their own territorial division (*sirmai*).[19] Some *nayakas* sought the king's permission for tax remission and land grants. '*Nayakas*, depending on the king's authority to legitimize their rule in the locality, tended to seek the king's favour.'[20] One method was to make donations for the king's karmic merit (*punniyam* or *danman* in Tamil Nadu). *Nayakas* had their own subordinate officers, and there was some further infeudation. *Nayakas* also made donations for other purposes, including their own merit, and also gained social benefits from close association with temples. For example, Achyutappa Nayaka, because of his donations and compassionate acts in persuading Kondama Nayaka to give certain privileges to the Shrimusnam temple, was honoured with a 'watchmanship' over 38 villages of the temple, and guardianship of the temple treasury. These brought him not only income, but also *prasad* (worship offerings of food) and prestige.[21]

In the areas of North and South Arcot, the Vellar valley in the Kaveri delta studied by Noboru Karashima, inscriptions provide sociohistoric information helpful in reconstructing patterns of the past; they are like surviving melody fragments useful in reconstructing lost ragas of the lifeways there. Noboru Karashima's findings suggest that, until the middle Chola period (around 1000 CE), local homogenous organizations seemed to be the rule, with no importance given to members as individuals; the rise in status to important local leadership positions, with its attendant increase in political power and economic strength, came later.

In the fourteenth and fifteenth centuries Vijayanagara warriors were administrators and officials of the court. Yet even though they might govern a region, command a military campaign and serve as agents for revenue collection, they did not usually control their own territory. The growth of the *nayakas* system from 1450 to 1500 structurally promoted social stability.[22] In the sixteenth century the *nayakas* became like feudal lords; they comprised a pan-empire elite having feudal relationships with the king and other *nayakas*, and were positioned between the more high-status and powerful individuals and the subordinate, lower status groups. This feudal and hierarchical system embraced the big landholders in the villages in all the *nadu*s, as well as the peasants and artisans. Artisans and other local leaders settled in many Tamil temple precincts or temple villages during the fifteenth century, building and enhancing temple structures with their expertise and skills. Temples were major consumers of important goods. Sixteenth century inscriptions bear witness to the development of trade in many localities, which expanded greatly in comparison with Chola trade, and, as a result, the taxes from artisans, merchants, weavers, craftsmen and traders thronging the roads with wares, correspondingly increased.[23]

In the sixteenth century *nayaka*s responded to trade that had been developing since the thirteenth century by bringing artisans to their localities in Tamil Nadu, and by protecting and patronizing those craftsmen. These developments were closely linked to the growth of foreign trade in such commodities as sugar cane and pepper. Shipping and trade in the port towns along the Vellar river were booming in those days.[24]

After a period of little conflict among landholders and cultivators in Tamil Nadu, oppression led to revolt in the fifteenth century, followed by the reclamation and colonization of land by new cultivators. The early fifteenth century was marked by conflicts between the invading Vijayanagara administrators and big landholders on the one side, and the class of artisans and cultivators on the other. (As Burton Stein put it, some areas, such as the Kaveri delta, although rich, were not easy cows to milk.[25]) With firm rule by the *nayaka*s established during the second half of the fifteenth century, the inscriptions cease to reflect these social clashes.[26]

*Nayaka*s gained rights from the king to obtain revenue from specific plots of land, from particular villages, and the management of certain temples. Their relationships with landholders and cultivators, and with artisans and merchants, was not just as tax collectors or administrators for kings but as landlords controlling production in the locality through a lord–vassal hierarchy, like the feudal lords in Europe or Japan. *Nayaka* strength and independence increased towards the end of the sixteenth century. Thus the social formation of the sixteenth century was quite different from that of Chola times (850–1200), in which the state seized direct control over the people. Stein asserts that the *nayaka* system is a system only in the reports of Portuguese visitors. On the other hand, Noboru Karashima argues that it functioned as the state system in Tamil Nadu for 150 years, from 1475 onwards, in many ways not unlike European and Japanese lord–vassal relations in medieval times.[27]

Around a third of the taxes went to the king, though sometimes as much as a half did. The greatest number of revenue inscriptions date from 1501–1550, the heyday of the empire, during Krishnadevaraya's reign. The decline in the number of records from 1451–1500 probably reflects the troubled conditions of the Oriyan invasion period (1463–1464). The steep decline from 1551–1600 reflects the conditions of turmoil after the fateful battle of Tallikota, (or Rakshasi-Tangadi) in 1565, the loss of the ruler and capital of the empire.[28]

In terms of spatial division, 'most of the area of our study was parcelled out to *nayaka*s as *nayakkattanam*s during the 16th century and afterwards'. 'Bisnaga'

(Vijayanagara) was divided among 200 *nayaka*s under Achyutadevaraya, according to the Nuniz's account, with some much more important than others.[29]

According to Karashima, who studied the rationale of the system of authority, under *nayaka* rule 'a social formation generated in earlier centuries seems to have become dominant',[30] but the fall of the central power of the empire and political interference by European powers in the seventeenth century, plus the great expansion of foreign trade, made another change in South Indian society; destruction or drastic change of the formations established in the sixteenth century.[31] The *nayaka*s derived their authority from the king, and the power structure replicated in various scales and various degrees of self-similarity. Reflections on these authority patterns, besides being found in inscriptions, are found in proverbs and in verses of poets and singers during that period. With the king as the figurehead standing for the whole system, the *nayaka* network forms a fractal of social relationships. As is the case at other levels of existence there is a kind of default action. The dominant image of power is the king. Instead of invention there is repetition of the patterns associated with the king's rule on the smaller level of the king's subordinates. Since the king is so important we need to explore further royalty's symbolic rationale.

The King Contains the Realm: Fractal-like Microcosmic Imagery

What is the deepest logic of the structure, what is the ideology and natural form – the pattern – which should not to be depicted as overly smooth simplistic reduction to power politics, nor as so messy and chaotic with beliefs and human feelings and ravages of history, that it is incomprehensible and unrepresentable? Right-brain perceptions of Vijayanagara depict it as a whole, through artistic vision, metaphors; the left-brain process works out the details of the parts, the lines of the code, the breakdown. I would suggest that homologies depict a fractal-like ideology; the encompassing pattern is fractally structured. Like father like son; like big man, like little one – similar entities exist on different scales. Often we hear that the king shares attributes with the deity. According to the classical Sanskrit literature of statecraft, the king is a composite being 'made out of the permanent elements of Indra, Vayu, Yama, Sun, Fire, Varuna, Moon and Kuvera'.[32] And the king is Vishnu. Furthermore, '[t]he kingdom is an organism of seven limbs, viz., the Sovereign, the Minister, the Friend, the Treasure, the State, the Fort, and the Army'.[33] And '[t]he sovereign is always possessed of the attributes of seven persons, e.g., father, mother, preceptor, brother, friend, Visravana or Kuvera and Yama'.[34]

Proverbs and verses are condensations of situations expressed in metaphor; they are like brush strokes characteristic of a whole pattern in a painting. A few may suggest the South Indian sociopolitical landscape in miniature perspective and give an indication of scale and relative weight of the king's importance: 'As the king is, so will the people's virtue be'.[35] The wise king is equal to ten wise men learned in the Veda.[36] Another proverb says that a bad king devours demonically, and we are told to visualize the following equation: ten slaughterhouses are equivalent to an oil press; ten oil presses are as bad as one tavern; ten taverns equal a brothel; the evil of ten brothels is on a par with the negative impact of one bad king.[37]

The metaphor of fractal geometry is useful here in visualizing interrelations. Since fractals are non-Euclidean patterns in nature, and they seem to share some characteristics with consciousness in the Upanishadic view (the principal of the whole) they form a useful metaphor. Their space-filling quality reflects the pervasive space-filling quality of consciousness (Vishnu, *atma*, and Brahman have this meaning at root) which, although formless, is associated with order and vitality, *prana*. It is axiomatic that the energy flowing in a system serves to organize it, along the lines of least resistence.[38] Fractals help us conceptualize whole–part interrelationships.

As the *Hitopadesha* asks, 'What would a king be without his vassals, and his elephant drivers and his elephants, without the swaying tassels of gold and the waving of fans of silk, and without the symbolic royal umbrella, and with no horses and banners?':[39] all his trappings and appurtenances, and the kingdom, make a king.

Thus, traditionally in the Hindu theory of statecraft, the king is one element in a network of symbolic forces, a web of existence and status. The view emphasizes hierarchies and interdependence. The 'circle of kings' is made up of the king, the enemy, the power adjacent to both and also power from outside. Each of these has allies and allies' allies. In this complex 12-element system of interrelations each part has elements of minister, land and people, fort, treasury, military – making 72 elements. The powerful king must encompass and dominate from the central hub of all these elements by the wise use of resources, in classical statecraft. The wholeness–partness aspect of this hierarchy has fractal-like composite qualities.[40]

Literature typically idealizes the king's control or his influence over surroundings, including neighbouring kings. He is often pictured as having mirrorlike toenails which reflect the lesser kings who bow before him. And in a twelfth-century inscription narrating the story of Jayasimhadeva, the king is so powerful that when other rulers hear he has become king, they suffer dramatic decline: 'the Gurjara king was ruined, his arms' strength overcome by Muslims, and the lord of Karnataka abandoned lovemaking; other rulers ran away in fear, crossing the ocean.' Such hyperboles serve to dramatize the king's greatness.[41] There is a tendency to see the ruler as an archetype, the embodiment of the self of his realm, and ultimately as an integral part of the cosmos.

The king's first duty is to protect dharma, which means defining, deciding it. As we have seen, the *smarta* sage Vidyaranya was picked to synthesize Hinduism anew. The Sangama brothers had gained some real-politik governing know-how from their experience with the Muslims who employed them, and drew on the Hindu code of statecraft from Vidyaranya, the sage-preserver of the seeds of dharma. At first, they had no knowledge of the fine points of Hindu polity but knew nevertheless that traditional sanction was what they wanted. In Hindu kingdoms the laws of growth and organization derive from the interaction between brahman sage and warrior king. The sage embodies the way to *moksha*; the king embodies the three other goals of life, spending his days promoting dharma by caring for dependents, promoting *artha*, the growth of prosperity, attainments, abundant life, and, after his daily duties have been discharged, exemplifying the pursuit of *kama, joie de vivre*. He is a healthy specimen, a living standard of the full life, enacting the people's fulfilment. In the Vedic *rajasuya* rites the king is depicted as all the people together in one embryo – all in one, one for all. There are different scales of existence, varied roles and duties, but the same life is encompassed in a synechdochal figurehead, a representative man.

South India had traditional areas called *nadus*[42] of 20–100 square miles, and a number of these is called a zone. Several zones clustered together is a subdivision. Several subdivisions make up a macro-region, such as was held by a Vijayanagara ruler. The land is considered to be the wife of the king; the king is called the husband and *pati* (lord of the land, 'protector'), and the king and the land together are father and mother of the people who are the children. As Ron Inden points out, the 'Hindu family was defined by the sharing of a single body and code of conduct'.[43] The earth is subordinated to the king like a wife and there are regular royal celebrations of the earth's menstruation and ritual sowing in spring. (This is why in the Ramayana epic, King Janaka found Sita in a furrow while ritually ploughing the earth – the same story is played out in different ages and regions.) The kingdom is homologized to the human body and its capabilities and necessities.

The king is the focal point, the meaning and integrity of the kingdom, and in subtle form he contains the cosmos; his body is the symbol of his realm's well-being, order and cohesion. And his work is the reintegrating of the parts of the *purusha*, the primal cosmic being dismembered in the original sacrifice before time began. By coordinating the *nayaka*s reporting to him, and through their concerted efforts, he unifies the realm. As the *bhupala* or 'earth-lord' he is a microcosmic representative of the macrocosmic being of the *purusha*. In this world-view symbolism the inner and outer realms are inseparable. The king is supposed first to conquer his own senses. He rises before dawn, exercises, is rubbed with oil, rides his horse, master of himself; and when he can govern his senses, he can bring larger external parts of the whole under control – his people, allies, and rivals.[44] The placing of the throne (facing east like the cosmic person at the origin in *Rig Veda* X.90) in the centre of the capital replicates archetypal acts and continues old patterns.

In a ritual bath using different clays from various regions of the earth the king's body is symbolically anointed to correspond with parts of the world.[45] For example, his head is a mountain top, the highest point of earth; his heart-mind is the royal centre, the control centre of his body and realm; his arms are the earth, torn up and gauged by bulls and elephants – earth's body marked with aggressive male energy or virility; his loins are the courtesan's doorway, a place of concentrated sexual potency. In this ritual, representatives of various realms sprinkle river waters, giving powers of all the gods, beings and substances in the universe.[46] Unity of cosmic hierarchical levels within levels, wheels within wheels, networks within networks are symbolized in many ways. The annual reconsecration of the king brings wealth, fame and the death of foes. The annual rituals unify the realm and become festivals celebrating the body politic's selfhood. The different encompassing cycles of the royal day, year, reign and dynasty all give order to time with the unity of fractal-like hierarchy.[47]

In Hindu philosophical ideals the king becomes king by victory over others, but is truly a king by virtue of his own self-mastery,[48] shown by taking a brahman-sage as adviser. As Burton Stein writes:

> Caste was surely one of the principles of social organization in sixteenth century South India. But there were other kinds of affinities that were more important. Certainly, political and religious affiliations and their interrelationship during Vijayanagara times was of the first importance, if on no other basis than the evidence of that time speaks much more about chieftaincy and sect than about caste. But it is necessary to admit that not much is known about the religious component of local identities then, however more is known about that than the usual preferred explainer of most Indian social phenomena – caste.[49]

Worship is the way through which the parts which, in isolation, have no meaning or cohesion themselves, are brought together – the members joining in, individual and family and clan entities partaking of transcendent being, renewing their lives, unifying, integrating and radiating negentropy.[50] Vishnu has the cosmos as territory, with kings under him. The kings have their kingdoms as territory with *nayaka*s under them. The *nayaka*s have smaller fiefdoms as territory, and subordinate chieftains and loyal communities under them.

In Brahmanic ritual kingship, visionary correlations with roots in the Vedas symbolize power relations. The incorporation is enacted symbolically by the ruler – priests, kings, gods and castes are 'capable of being replicated in territorial segments of larger systems as an ideology of homologies'.[51] Different scales, similar patterns, same principle:

> Local chiefs, heads of local agricultural groups are homologized to great kings, as their tutelary gods are homologized to great vedic gods. The method of incorporation is the technical medium of ritual carried out by trained priests – increasingly within the special context of temples.[52]

This depends on the strength of an original vision, deep poetic correspondences with ongoing resonances, the power of religious experiences.

There is multiplicity within the three different types of kindred groupings given in the *Dharma shastra*: *kula* (kinsmen), *shreni* (guildsmen), *gana* (territorial assemblies of the people); each is fairly autonomous but looks to the king as ultimate earthly power, while the king, correspondingly, looks to cosmic power, all in the self-same system. Smaller-scale echoes of the overall shape from the three groupings are found in proverbs: 'When the king's wife climbed up to the top of the palace, the potter's daughter-in-law climbed on top of the hut';[53] 'When Akkanna and Madanna mounted their state palankin, Sarrappa got on the bund of the tank [pool] to make himself equal';[54] 'When crowbars are blown around by the wind, the leaf platter asks "What's my fate to be?"'[55] The greater is related to the lesser. Losses are seen as experientially proportionate: 'The loss of a wing is the same to a mosquito as the loss of a leg to an elephant.'[56] Repercussions from the level above are felt by those beneath: 'When the cows fight the calves get broken legs.'[57] 'If one of the royal family strikes a villager's child, Narayana will strike his child.'[58] 'When he went to Gudur to tell of his misfortune, the misfortune of seven villages met him.'[59] Nothing is discrete; everything is part of the net of consciousness. Each level has its resources and abilities: 'To keep an elephant you need a country; to keep a horse, a village, to keep a she-buffalo, a maidservant.'[60]

In the traditional configuration a strong kingdom has nine gates, following the pattern of the Vedic cosmic *purusha*, sacrificed at the origin of the universe, who has nine orifices. (All human beings have nine openings in their bodies: eyes, ears, nose, mouth, anus and urinary orifice.) The strong king, capable of self-control of the incoming and outgoing activities of his own body, is the necessary ruler of such a kingdom: *Bahu nayakam, stri nayakam, bala nayakam* 'Woe to the rule of many, the rule of woman, and the rule of child.'[61] In the body politic of the empire the *nayaka*s and other members of society are limbs or organs. One cannot do the work of another well: 'Can a woman who pounds rice for hire or digs up edible roots be brought to a temple to dance artfully before the Lord?'[62]

The king's dilemma, according to Indologist Jan Heesterman, is that he must be both part of the community and foreign to it. The settled agricultural community of villages (*grama*) and the wilderness (*aranya*) are complementary poles: 'In the *grama* one undertakes the [king's] consecration, in the *aranya* one sacrifices.'[63] The connecting of *grama* and *aranya* is enacted in the *rajasuya* ritual sequence of symbolizing unction; departure for war and conquest, return and enthronement is 'encompassed in a greater cycle of the *rajasuya* along the same lines' in an infinite series, much like a fractal pattern: ' … the virtual endlessness of the cyclical pattern does not only involve cycles encompassed by other cycles … . It equally repeats itself in an unending sequence and this means that the inthronization [*sic*] should again be followed by another *abhishekha*, another departure and so forth.' Nothing stands alone; different horizons and dimensions pulse with self-similar recursive cycles.[65]

In Hindu archetypes the cosmos is a cosmic person's body sacrificed; the kingdom is shaped like a human body; the temple is shaped like the Lord's body: Virashaiva poet and leader, Basava, and others speak of the human body as a temple: a society's limbs and parts are derived from the divine organism; the household is a body, the front door the auspicious face, the back the rear; the body is enlivened by little tutelary deities within. In the universe one thing is always being transformed into something else: the sun to energies, decaying life-forms to soil.[66]

Like father like son; like child like doll. Like God like king; like society like family. Like home like body; like body like organ. Like saint, like devotee; like ultimate like beloved. Like demon like enemy. World-views lie embedded in intricate representations, in recursive patterns and in mantras, rituals, life-cycle phases, in images such as Shiva's cosmic dance. Hidden patterns, like nets, lattices and tissues, knit the empire together, energies flowing in social transactions: eddies made of eddies, merchants dealing, farmers sustaining, leaders receiving and distributing tribute, religious culture flowing, services being rendered, nourishing blood circulating through society. The highways and byways, and networks of villages, make up a tissue that is like a fractal surface – vein-like creeks and artery-like streams, rivers and mountain passes, village roads criss-crossed by *haridasa*s and sannyasins. The roads and footpaths join lives in networks, connecting forest tribals and townspeople, the learned and the illiterate. Singers bring bhakti spirituality to the workers of the soil and the artisans, and housewives give food to wandering singers and mendicants. Circles of culture are unifying processes – poets weave bright strands from folk culture into their verses, and the people repeat and transform the poets' verses into their own way of speech. The richest women wear saris of finest silk and the poorest on the road wear the same shape of cloth, but made of worn-out plain muslin. Vemana said: 'The minds of kings are occupied with strategies of war; the sage contemplates ultimate reality; ordinary folk have their heads full of sex; thought processes depend on a person's individuality.'[67] Same human brain, same era, different drives. And, for the religious, all the differentials of complexity and relativity are dissolved finally in the same ultimate goal of *moksha*.

The parts of the empire are a unity because Hinduism as a whole is 'recursive ... self-referential, the behavior of one guided by the behavior of another hidden inside it',[68] like an intellectual *smarta brahman* within the Hindu body politic, raising anew patterns of cohesion to conceive of and practise, because they have learned the gist of the code, the vision of the whole, intricate and simple, while others are engrossed by everyday demands. *Smarta*s have often been involved in connecting the parts, seeing the connections. Historically they revealed the circuit of pilgrimage that united the subcontinent with seven sacred sites. They unified the regions with a calendar of annual festivals configuring time and thereby designating to Prajapati his proper 'clothes', clarifying the order. They orchestrated a worship of all the gods in one, *panchayatanapuja*, gathering various absract forms representing the divine on the same silver plate. They could shape an updated kingdom of coherence, a system generating information, via the traditional *varnashrama* dharma. It was that or become a Muslim province.

It was almost as if the five Sangama brothers were an antibody in an immune system. They had almost been incorporated into the foreign order, working for Muslims, being converted to Islam, denying their original heritage. Then, in time, they revived their original identity to turn decisively against the invaders like corpuscles in an immune system. They did not know the finer points of Hindu polity, but knew that that was what they wanted; the *kshatriya*'s attribute is will power and muscle – courage. They went to the head, the memory centre to get the vision and knowledge to reconstitute and synthesize Hinduism anew.[70] In this view, the emotion-powered *volte-face* in their hearts was the real seed of change both for their lives and their people's lives. The sage Vidyaranya was out in uncivilized wilderness full of potential; the king recognized what he lacked in the sage; their convergence created Vijayanagara. Vidyaranya was the expert on *smriti* and Vedanta, guardian of traditional memories; Harihara was the strongman leader needing plans.[71] Together they made the viable self-organizing pair at the core of an expanding Hindu kingdom held together by languages, symbols, caste, customs and geographic necessities.

'Both/And' Together Rather than 'Either/Or'

How valid is the criticism that Vijayanagara was an intellectually closed system, with no means of coping with upcoming challenges? Was it the Hindu religion that limited vision and caused failure? Was there too little self-criticism for the structure to endure in the complex modern era? Were the rulers' tools of analysis and interpretation inadequate to cope with incoming systems and forces? If '[t]hought itself is born of crisis and important crises',[72] aren't there signs of some intellectual energies at work?

Perhaps a certain amount of rigid thrall to the past did contribute to the empire's demise, but the Vijayanagara synthesis of Hinduism does nevertheless offer examples of fresh attempts to respond to the changing world. Krishnadevaraya succeeded because he was stirred by a *niti* proverb, like a man awakened sweating from a nightmare, frantic to check out the real number of troops he had to defend his kingdom. The *niti* literature (like *Tidings of the King*) teaches that his personal wariness and receptivity to wise advice were the factors that let him truly realize his power's potential. He made the City of Victory a fulfilment, a fruition of past hopes which Vidyaranya would have recognized. Hinduism has a sense of the past, the enduring, the auspicious, to help guide people in a dangerous world. As with all people, Krishnadevaraya's generation bequeathed an inheritance to the succeeding generations, in the form of their unfulfilled desires.

Phillip Wagoner's studies offer proof of the adaptiveness of Hindu polity – its ability to incorporate Muslim practices. Devaraya II changed the army, influenced by Turkic strategies, which included more archers, and employing Turkic mercenaries. Wagoner also contends that there is evidence that the *nayaka* system came into existence as 'an Indic adaptation of the Islamicate system of administration through *iqta* assignments'.[73] This structure, organized by the Suljuqs, involved 'an assignment of the right to collect land revenue, in return for which the *iqta*-holder was obliged to provide military service for the state'.[74] It was a formal and detailed arrangement which required careful record-keeping. Wagoner concludes that since Vijayanagara's *nayaka* system was so similar to the *iqta* system, it appears that it 'was developed as a direct adaptation from an Islamicate model'.[75] But is this necessarily an expression of a changing identity? Isn't it also true that one way of competing with enemies is to co-opt their successful methods?[76] Wagoner concludes that the historiographic representations he studied significantly 'proclaim Vijayanagara's rulers not as "saviors of the south"' ... but ... as "sultans among Hindu kings"'.[77] I feel that this view neglects the massive signs of Hindu identity and the concern to survive as a renewed form of Hinduism, not as Muslims. The Vijayanagara founders and sustainers were able to revise their lives and survive. I agree with Joan-Pau Rubies that:

> 'The fact that Vijayanagara was a Hindu political society which was essentially defined in opposition to the religious domination of Islam (even though in reality the Vijayanagara elites may have borrowed a number of practices from their Muslim neighbours) is of great importance, especially considering the analogous European tradition of confrontation with Islam.'[78]

Perhaps in emphasizing Muslim elements in Vijayanagara what Wagoner is noticing is the increasing complexity in that era in South India – we see evidence not of plain and simple Hindu resurgence, nor of total assimilation to Islam with indifference to Hinduism, but some resurgence and some assimilation. What joined them was the need to be who they were (Hindus), *and* to thrive in the world of their time, which was shaped by an ascendant Islamicate culture. The interrelations among the two cultures, the two kinds of order interacting, were probably more like a dynamical system than a linear one – chaotic processes, with simple patterns lurking under the complexity and complexity lurking under the simple patterns, rather than either/or. To pretend that either view alone suffices – 'They were only Hindu patriots' or 'They were only trying to be sultans with no thought of Hinduism' – is over simplistic and therefore inadequate. It is better to admit there was indeterminacy, dynamism and complex entanglements. Although the use of Muslim titles and styles of dressing and the Islamicization of Hindu culture at Vijayanagara are interesting and important, it is also significant that the Vijayanagara rulers did not convert to Islam and that the ideals sustained by brahmanic culture gave the empire its identity and legitimacy. As Joan-Pau Rubies says, 'Vijayanagara was simultaneously both a Hindu bulwark against Muslim conquests ... and a centre of adoption of a number of international Islamic cultural values.'[79] It was probably this syncretism, manifested in an ability to function with increasing complexity in new conditions, that allowed the empire to thrive as an adaptive complex system for over three centuries.

Systems of all sorts, whether man-made or generated by nature, arise, as Theodore Roszak says, 'from the most intricately creative of impulses'.[80] New civilizations arise from a creative surge: as David Bohm and F. David Peat remind us, 'all societies have ... started from a creative perception in the generative order',[81] and their decay is often caused by rigidly holding on to old knowledge and structures which no longer do enough justice to reality and an attendant vulnerability to corruption, decay, disorder, or attraction to forces that lead to disintegration. Decay often involves a sense of self out of touch with the vital reality of processes of which one is part. Adhering to the inadequate old ways makes illusions seem real, and demands denial and collusion among those holding desperately to the outmoded. Rigid clinging to the outmoded or indulging in debilitating addictions inevitably blocks creativity which comes with the free flow of new thought. Holding so rigid goes against the flow of time and change in the cosmos. According to Bohm and Peat, '[b]ecoming caught up in the false processes of a destructive generative order ... has been the ultimate fate of all known generations',[82] including Vijayanagara. To be too self-centred at the expense of relating to one's greater circumstances brings downfall.

Conditions in the Empire Before It Collapsed

> *Most people who miss, after almost winning, should*
> *have 'known the end from the beginning'.*

Tao Te Ching[83]

The Sangama dynasty of Vijayanagara ruled from 1336 to 1485. It was involved in repeated conflicts with the Bahmani sultanate to the north, and, towards the end of the dynasty suffered from internal instabilities as well. The second dynasty, the Saluva family, ruled from 1486 to 1505. It began with a successful general, Saluva, and signalled the rise of a class of generals with their own territorial backing as regents and founders of dynasties. This political organization set governing patterns for Vijayanagara during the first half of the sixteenth century. The instability that came in with Saluva's son, Immadi Narasimha, (1491–1505) was resolved by the ascendancy of the regent Narasa Nayaka, whose son Viranarasimha (1505–1509) founded the third, Tuluva, dynasty which ran from 1505 to 1542. Narasa Nayaka's brother, Krishnadevaraya (1509–1529) consolidated and centralized the empire, and through strong defence against strong men to the north and east and conquest, flourished at the peak of Vijayanagara glory. He was wealthy on a scale known to few other rulers in the world at that time. By the time his brother Achyutadevaraya took the throne (1529–1542), the Bahmanis had disintegrated into five sultanates, which formed a Deccani alliance. The fourth dynasty, the Aravidu family which ruled from 1542 to 1649, stemmed from Ramaraya (1542–1565) who was the regent for Achyutaraya's son, but took rule instead. Whereas Krishnadevaraya, after the battle of Raichur, was in a position to let one sultan stay in power rather than allowing Bahmani power to be split into four smaller strong kingdoms to contend with and wisely did so, later kings had to face the separate antagonisms and combined strength of the five kingdoms that succeeded the Bahmanis. After 1565, when the capital was lost to a coalition of those Muslim invaders from the north, rule was fragmentary, with *nayaka*s reigning independently in scattered provinces. Subsequently Vijayanagara was abandoned by Ramaraya's sole surviving brother, Tirumala.

Historians have hypothesized several reasons why the Vijayanagara empire ended when it did. Each of the reasons is suspect in isolation, but adding them together we can at least suggest a network of related possible reasons, thus pointing to discernible vulnerabilities and probable trajectories towards downfall.[84] After the reign of Krishnadevaraya – the high point of prosperity, administrative ability and cultural efflorescence – there was a decline. There were dissolute kings, if accounts such as those of Paes and Nuniz reflect the times accurately.[85] From bright light, dark shadows fall. Every flow has its ebb. In 1565, at the battle of Talikota,[86] the regent Ramaraya and his army of nearly a million were defeated by the combined Muslim forces.[87] The coalition forces captured the elderly Ramaraya (b. 1469) and killed him.[88] The invaders then took the capital, shattering the monumental beauty to rubble, and the authorities either died or fled. The sacred Vaishnava shrines were vandalized, though many Shaiva shrines were not harmed. (Vijayanagara commanders who were devotees of Virupaksha had made agreements to ensure that the Virupaksha temple with its exquisite sculptures would not be ruined, and so the fine details of those carvings can still be seen today.) Tirumala, next in line to rule, fled to Penukonda, and inscriptions dating from 1568 all describe Vijayanagara as a ruined city. The city, with its nine main gates open to vandals and plunderers' insults, was as defenceless as a body with unguarded openings. 'I laid out a beautiful city in the form of a man,' Vidyaranya is pictured saying in the *Vidyaranya-kirti*.[89] It was as if the man, the 'cosmic person' laid out by Vidyaranya at the inception of the kingdom had been beaten, robbed and left for dead in that fateful year of 1565 when the City Victory became the City of Ruinous Defeat. Several converging factors led to this dramatic downfall.

Why did the empire decline? Historian Nilakanta Sastri considers the Vijayanagara empire to have been as close to being a 'war-state' as a Hindu kingdom came, with military needs dominating the political organization. It employed a huge army, with military fiefs scattered throughout the realm, each headed by a *nayaka* entitled to collect revenues and govern as long as he kept the agreed number of troops, elephants and horses ready to fight at the emperor's command.[90] Other historians have also noted that:

> Vijayanagara at the zenith of its power displayed imperial grandeur. For over two centuries it was the bulwark against foreign intrusions into South India. But with the Hindu revival came rigidity. No dynamic new conceptions inspired the times, so that the far reaching changes in the political structure of the South were inevitable.[91]

A number of scholars have arrived at this conclusion: the great leaders enabled change, the weaker ones, too self-absorbed, lacked both the vision and the will to make the necessary changes effectively and were overwhelmed. Ideologically, according to some critics, the empire's leaders were insufficiently progressive, adaptive, eclectic and dynamic. Ramaraya, in some ways well suited to the niche he came to fill, was nevertheless precariously perched at the empire's head. Skilfully countering complex forces, playing off other rulers against each other, for some time he succeeded where lesser men would have failed. But, though very wealthy, he did not have the resources and advisers that would ensure the empire's unity beyond his time. A system that is too closed and rigid cannot find the necessary adaptive strategies; it lacks the flexibility to respond with intelligence and vigour to new challenges.[92]

In the view of many historians the Vijayanagara enterprise had put a temporary halt to a decline of Hindu cultural life, vigorously reordering life in a period of chaos:

> A history of the first millennium would have to give India enormous weight: the subcontinent housed a single civilization ... achievements it produced in art, literature and philosophy were exported with a moulding impact to China and Islam ... it was a civilization in expansion. With bewildering suddenness at about the turn of the millennium the inspiration seemed to dry up, the vision to turn inward and the coherence to dissolve ... [p]olitical dissolution accompanied the cultural decline.[93]

In this view the vision awoke again for a time, around 1336, flourished, and then in 1565 was put back to sleep. But no consensus exists. According to the Indian historian Romila Thapar, Vijayanagara was a 'static period' in South Indian history, not a time of conscious Hindu revival. Thapar sees the architecture and other arts as stagnantly repetitious, whereas others find it dynamic, innovative and eclectic.[94]

As I have mentioned in my retelling of the origin story of Vijayanagara, some versions, such as the Sanskrit text *Vidyaranya-kriti*, predict that the city would last for 360 years, then be destoyed because of a breach at a vulnerable point (*marma-bheda*). This story predicts in retrospect a precise-in-time but vague-in-cause, destiny of inevitable decline.[95] Perhaps this reflects the view that even noteworthy accomplishments are ultimately doomed in the *kali yuga*.[96]

The singer-saint Kanakadasa, who lived during and after the heyday of Krishnadevaraya, dramatically described social ills of the *kali yuga* in a song:

> Where did truth and duty go? The noble can't survive anymore,
> thieves and habitual adulterers strike it rich, the rest are poor.
> Relations among family members are mixed up and reversed–
> the wife plays the husband's part, it just keeps getting worse.
> Family members turn hostile, fools puffed up with pride
> forget God, guru, and elders. Decent holy people go unprotected;
> Vedic brahmans sit about idly; starving they beg for support.
> No one pays the soldiers, no helping rains shower the earth.
> Those with food and clothes are corrupted by being on the take.
> Immature dogs full of trickery multiply like cruel snakes,
> traitors to God win houses, gain cows, and wealth, and grain.
> Men leave wives for whores until their time is all drained out,
> kings do as mean dastards wish, involved in high intrigue.
> Earth groans under the weight, tottering, crying, 'Shri Ram, please!'
> The good wife seeking shelter with her husband has no clothes,
> loose women flaunt jewels and luxuries; so the Kali age goes–
> Good wives are rare, while many weak wives sleep around,
> they lose their place in heaven and bring their own ruin down.

> Worshippers of Shiva are clashing with the Vishnu devotees.
> Great offerings are made to the most horrific violent deities.
> Who could list the wrongs of the time? Lord Adikeshava; you know
> *Kali yuga's* power. Don't wait, help this world in the time of *Kali*, now![97]

Probably writing during the generations before the end of the Vijayanagara empire, Kanaka pictures a society showing symptoms of disintegration and disfunction. If he is describing daily life, it would seem to be in a state in disarray, not very viable when under attack. Or, it could reflect a decline occurring partly as a consequence of uncertainty after so many feuds and wars and depredations – *kali yuga* ills as hedonistic escape on the brink of life-threatening catastrophe. But tempering this reading, there is also a tradition of Vaishnava bhakti, of songs confessing sins and criticizing wrongs, forms encouraging the examination of conscience, and these are not necessarily to be taken literally. Kanakadasa's contemporary, Purandaradasa, likewise wrote some bleak lines about being protectorless, perhaps after Krishnadevaraya's reign was over.[98]

Vijayanagara is the story of four dynasties: the first, Sangama, was long-lived; the second, Saluva, was short-lived, the third and fourth, Tuluva and Aravidu, included high points of vigour but were entangled and, finally, the last one, which was really rule by regent, was disintegrative. The Vijayanagara state came into existence to fulfil certain needs, to satisfy certain desires. According to Ravi Palat, the logic of organization entailed an increasing centralization of political power and a concentration of resources in royal bureaucracy. The king's unrealistically high demand for surpluses of grain and revenue had led to a crisis in peasant agriculture by the time of Achyutaraya, and the momentum kept building when monetary payments were substituted for crop tributes owed by whole villages. The heavy demands led to tensions between villagers and the authorities who collected their dues. A further complicating factor was the fact that rights to a share of the yield were sometimes donated to temples or priests. In order to get enough revenue the state expanded the areas of cultivated land through irrigation projects. And a result of extensive state interference was that the economy became dependent on state protection. If you take an area over, you have to hold on to it. A precarious situation developed; if a political crisis were to develop, it would have a catastrophic effect on the economy. Dislocations of economic factors from both within and without, along with decades of civil wars among *nayaka*s built up into a distressing pressure until it reached the point of eruption with Talikota – the final straw breaking a tired camel's back.[99]

Also, European merchants, especially Portuguese, representing a totally different lifeway, and with political and moral codes different from those practised in South India, worked the coasts in such a way that the Vijayanagara emperor soon lost any firm control that he might have previously enjoyed. Arabs had monopolized trade for centuries. Arab merchants had begun settling on the west coast in the eighth century, gradually migrating inland. In the late 1400s Portuguese traders began to arrive and soon rivalled the Arabs in numbers. By all accounts the Portuguese were violently aggressive; in 1558 they destroyed Mangalore and other towns along the thriving Malabar seaboard. In 1560, at the time of the Spanish Inquisition, Goa was forced to embrace Christianity,

Figure 11.1   Arab standing before a seated royal figure, based on a sculpture in Vijayanagara

Indian ships were destroyed and 2000 Indian sailors were massacred. The people rebelled, and the Portuguese dealt harshly with them. At this time the Portuguese cut down 40 000 palm trees.[100] All the king's horses and all the king's men couldn't help those suffering these predations on the west coast. The entire trade had fallen into the hands of the Portuguese – and this is at least one of the reasons for collapse. The unifying force fell apart. Fishermen and others along the coast who did not want to live in misery or die began to convert to Christianity, pledging allegiance to the Portuguese ruler. And the Pandyan coast pearl fishery slipped through the emperor's fingers. Horses, those 'handfuls of wind made for flight and pursuit', no longer arrived by the shipload to re-energize the army's mobile strength – 13 000 per year during Achyutaraya's reign. (Marco Polo, who lived in the thirteenth–fourteenth century, wrote that horses being transported over such a distance often died from mishandling; kings had to buy thousands of new ones every year – an expensive prospect.) However, the fortunes of the Portuguese in India declined after the fall of Vijayanagara; they had no friendly power to trade with, and they feared that the Muslim sultans of the Deccan plains would take the ports which they had established. Furthermore, an era had ended elsewhere, too: After 1580 Philip II of Spain controlled Portuguese domains anyway. A flow had ebbed.

As Helen Keller wrote, history is basically 'but a mode of imagining, of making us see civilizations that no longer appear upon the earth'.[101] David Shulman has suggested that Annamacharya, living just before the height of the empire, was a lyricist reflecting the great changes of society in the time in which he lived. He sees 'a revolutionary shift in sensibility in South Indian *bhakti* poetry, a shift linked to the world of "mood" the irreducible moment of nuanced feeling and perception in the experience of an irreducible individual'. Shulman sees this mood as 'discursive and present-oriented in the context of a deepening subjectivity – both of the poet and the God he worships'. He believes that this change is probably related to the restructuring of political and social domains in fifteenth-century Andhra Pradesh and the reconstruction of the Tirupati ritual and Puranic worlds. He considers Annamacharya the voice of a new elite active in state building and in temple economy, articulating 'for the first time, the ethos of a newly integrated individualism at a moment of cultural and institutional expansion'.[102] The inward-turning cultivation of devotion in songs of longing and in rituals of adoring the sacred presence in the temple shrine has a long history and deep roots, so Shulman's contention must involve a new complexity and intensity, if it is true. Was individualism of this sort a cause for decline or a sign of strength? In any case, historian Nilakanta Sastri notes that the abiding differences between the society in the North and the South of India (and that great temples in the South still stand and are full of masterpieces) can be attributed in a large measure to the success of the Vijayanagara empire.[103] The difference made by the efforts of Vidyaranya and the five brothers, and by kings Kampana and Krishnaraya and others, and by *nayakas* great and small, in this sense is a victory that never ended, but continues on today.

As Octavio Paz noticed, 'The beginning of empires is similar: conquest and plunder. Their end as well is similar: disintegration, dismemberment. Each empire is unique, yet all empires are doomed to fall apart, just as orthodoxies and ideologies are doomed to split apart into schisms and sects'.[104] Systems (whether individual organisms or empires, the earth annually orbiting the sun or a galaxy turning) all self-organize, creatively improvise within their own given limits, and waver or gloriously thrive. And with the multitude of rhythmic changes which time inevitably provides, eventually they self-destruct. Each and all, every time, wane.

Bad Blood, Wounded Pride and Criticality: Falling When the Elephant Charges, Losing All

> *'They're [diverse physical, biological and human phenomena] all in something*
> *other that a state of equilibrium: the new word for this is criticality, which*
> *simply means that a system contains within it both sensitive dependence on*
> *initial conditions and self-similarity across scale. The possibility exists for an*
> *abrupt transition from one phase to another, and the likelihood of that happening*
> *is inversely proportional to the magnitude of the event when it occurs.'*
>
> John Lewis Gaddis[105]

Bad blood must be added to the reasons the empire suddenly failed. A series of insults exchanged between Hindu and Muslim rulers and their men, deliberate offences and affronts, stirred outrage and the desire for revenge. Rapacious insults and gestures of disrespect had significant consequences for both sides.

Offences and reprisals led to wars in early times – namely, the hereditary feud between the Hindu dynasty of the Sangamas and the Muslim dynasty of the Bahmanis. (The Bhahmani kingdom was founded in 1347 by Hasan Gangu, north of the Krishna River.[106]) In 1351 Ala-ud-din Bahmani waged the first Bahmani war, beginning the feud. The second Bahmani war came about in 1361 when Bukkaraya refused to pay tribute to Muhammad Shah and paraded Shah's money-collector on a donkey as a public humiliation, according to the Muslim historian Firishta. This led to the third war and the siege of Vijayanagara in 1366–1368.[107] The sixth Bahmani war, according to a Muslim historian, occurred when Devaraya I, son of Harihara II antagonized the Bahmanis by making a foray into their territory to satisfy his passion for a farmer's (or goldsmith's) beautiful daughter living in Mudgal. This occurred soon after Devaraya took power, in 1406. Another writer says the war began as the consequence of Firuz Shah Bahmani deciding to wage a jihad against the Hindu ruler.[108] The eleventh Bahmani war came in 1453, involving an assault on the forces of the weak king Viradevaraya III (1446–1465), who lost territory to Telugu Reddis, and to Orissan forces also. More examples could be given to show how old grudges often led to fresh attacks. Acts of cupidity and retaliation bloody the age like strange attractors which drew rulers into conflicts they could not escape. On reading of the 'fourteenth Bahmani war' one tends to think: 'How exhausting, three centuries of mutual antagonisms, a grudge match to the death! How much life spent fighting a permanent foe?' And the Bahmani conflicts were not the only ones. The Adil Shahi kingdom, established in Bijapur in 1490, also waged wars with Vijayanagara rulers, beginning in 1492.

In 1520 Krishnadevayara laid seige to Raichur to the north of the empire's border. He had a massive force, including 733 000 foot soldiers, 35 000 mounted horsemen, 586 war elephants with trunks armed with scythe-like blades, 12 000 water carriers and 20 000 courtesans. The king himself led near the front. The Bijapur shah's artillery decimated many advancing soldiers in the initial stages of the battle, but the tide turned and Krishnadevaraya was victorious. His men sacked the city and raped many women, a rankling offence which the Muslims would remember.[109] When Adil Shah's ambassador arrived at Vijayanagara and asked for the ruined city to be restored to its former state of wealth, Krishnadevaraya agreed to return all that had been taken – if Adil Shah would come and kiss his foot. This insult, too, the shah and his followers would not forgive or forget, even after Krishnadevaraya was dead and gone.

In 1565 Ramaraya, son-in-law of Krishnadevaraya, was regent, supposedly representing Sadashivaraya, a young descendant of Achyutaraya, but in fact functioning as the ruler. Ramaraya had great wealth at his disposal and he had generously been using it for a decade; he had also made some useful strategic alliances and had successfully kept the Deccani sultans divided for that time, but his soldiers, like Krishnadevaraya's before him, had sometimes gone too far. Ramaraya's interactions with powerful Muslim men were riddled with betrayals and indignities and careless of niceties. For example, Ramaraya rebuffed Sultan Ali, son and successor to Ibrahim Qutb Shah, to whom he had given power. When in 1557 Ali sought friendship, and Ramaraya's wife adopted him as a son, the old man showed him little respect, and this arrogance rankled him. When, in 1559, Ali asked for military help Ramaraya's soldiers cruelly wiped out a whole population of the dominions of Hussain Nizam Shah of Ahmadnagar 'from Porundeh to Khiber and from Ahmadnagar to Dawlatabad'.[110] Ramaraya's soldiers were said to have behaved with extreme cruelty, offending Muslim women's honour, destroying mosques and insulting the Qur'an. Ramaraya's contempt, voiced by his scornful tongue and evidenced in his arrogant actions, was no secret.[111] Ramaraya's soldiers committed offences that would come back to haunt him – the Muslims remembered how his men had raped Muslim women, razed whole towns to the ground and stabled their horses in mosques, a deliberate sacrilege that pierced the very heart of Muslim faith. In addition, Ramaraya snidely snubbed and belittled Muslim ambassadors and leaders, not letting them sit down in his presence and treating them with hostile contempt. When Hussain Nizam Shah asked for peace, Ramaraya told him, 'First restore Killian fortress to Bijapur, and then visit me and receive betel from me.' (Betel chewing is a South Indian sign of hospitality and friendship.) Hussain, in a precarious position, agreed, and gave back the fortress. When he went to Ramaraya's tent, Ramaraya did not get up to welcome him. Having forced himself to go through this humiliation of turning over the key to the fortress, Hussain could stomach only so much. After kissing Ramaraya's right hand in greeting he called for a basin and water to wash. This enraged Ramaraya, who remarked that if Hussain wasn't a guest he'd make him repent of this insult, and then he also asked for water to wash. The mutual self-disgust resulting from humbling themselves to meet each other and their subsequent mutual antagonism culminated in 1565 in Ramaraya losing everything he had – his head, his capital and his empire.

Already in 1564 the five Muslim sultans, all of whom had been insulted by Ramaraya, were allied against him, forming 'a general league of the faithful'. In January 1565, unforgetting and unforgiving, the five gathered their armies and moved south near Talikota, a fortress near the northern edge of the Vijayanagara border. Ramaraya, a spry 96 year old at this time, first attacked the Muslim forces with rockets, but soon lost many men. He tried to rally his troops. asking his treasurer to heap up gold, jewels and coins to show those who would fight well how they would be rewarded. He led the army against 2000 Muslim archers who stood in front of lines of cannons and smaller artillery and swivel guns. When all this firepower was unleashed it blasted his army severely, and 5000 more of his men died on the spot. Many of the dead had been hit by the large numbers of copper coins being shot from heavy cannons. Ramaraya himself fell to the ground when his elephant bolted and his carriers lost control of the litter he was in, and he was captured. This was the beginning of a cascade of losses. Ramaraya was decapitated by Hussain Nizam Shah and his head was displayed on a pike to frighten his soldiers.[112] The troops fled in panic and 100 000 of them were slaughtered. This was

Figure 11.2　Ramaraya, the last ruler of the empire which had Vijayanagara as its capital

the beginning which led to the loss of the great capital city, Vijayanagara, which was now defenceless.

This rout was the critical point; never before had such a wealthy and powerful old regent and commander been dislodged, and then beheaded, his fearful army routed, his capital taken and his whole empire broken. As a result, the illusion of control was shattered, and such superficial surface stability as there was destabilized under a cascade of irreversible change.[113] What illusions did Ramaraya, the uncrowned head of state, suffer from? Was he intoxicated by power, feeling that the only way to stay in control was to dominate as the visible head, making decisions on the battlefield? Did he have a deathwish? Where were his wise advisers – his Vidyaranya or Appaji? Hindus include under the concept *maya* the illusion that one is gaining control when one is in fact losing it. A beheaded head of state is a powerful image. The privileged head above others when removed in degradation mocks a man's life and power. The head of the foe historically has been coveted and used symbolically by the powerful, and still is today.[114]

The *nayakas*, instead of just protecting their own areas, had sometimes become power-players, monkeying around in others' areas. Divided among themselves, the *nayakas* could not fend off the determined five sultans to their north. They failed to draw on the potential energies of those who would have cooperated with them. This ignoring of the resources which might have helped them, and the fact that they looked towards supernatural forces for assistance rather than taking all the necessary practical precautions, went against evolutionary trends, according to Mulk Raj Anand.[115] Anand, who explored the psychological–religious motives and inspirations of the different dynasties, suggests that an enduring way of life needs a vision in tune with nature, sensitive to the way in which natural processes of evolution and survival work. A culture heedless of evolutionary concerns imperils itself and brings about its own downfall.[116]

The Vijayanagara *nayaka*s were challenged by the 'mean between a deficiency of severity and an excess of it'.[117] Thus, the old Vijayanagara empire, with its well-sung heroes, and worldly-wise sages, its lovers and musicians, poets, buffoons, craftsmen and tillers of the soil passed away and left its children to carry on anew in a different age, still bearing the Hindu way of life, prepared to consider necessary change. The past gives the present a legacy, a sword of wisdom for defence and a glimpse of the tough and wily sacred force behind existence, amphibious and uncontrollable as the Wild Boar which was the emblem of the Vijayanagara empire. Much of tradition involves working with appealing archetypes which help people fulfil the desires of the time.[118] Each generation must earn its awareness of deep dimensions of existence by sweat and angst and struggle, enduring unsettling experiences that challenge its talents in search of fulfilment.

In 1565 the emblem of the empire, the Boar,[119] *avatar* of Vishnu, and the sword, lost its strength. The crescent moon dimmed; the sun was eclipsed. The exhausted Boar, having lost the world it was holding up, while rescuing it from beneath the sea, said (just as the Boar emblem of the Guptas had said long before), 'It has slipped beyond me – but another rescue higher up on the spiral will succeed.' And the sword fell with a clatter in the stones, then stillness. Some consider this turning point to be the beginning of modern India. The crest of the wave curls and crashes then the undertow withdraws and there is a lull.

A poignant reflection from V.S. Naipaul's brooding on Vijayanagara focuses on its implications for today:

> ... every Indian should make the pilgrimage to the site of the capital of the Vijayanagara empire, just to see what the invasion of India led to. They will see a totally destroyed town. Religious wars are like that. People who see that might understand what the centuries of plunder and slaughter meant. War isn't a game. When you lost that kind of war, your towns were destroyed, the people who built the towns were destroyed, you are left with a headless population. That's where modern India starts from. The Vijayanagara capital was destroyed in 1565. It is only now that the surrounding region has begun to revive.[120]

Times change. There are endless regroupings and breakdowns, fractures and reunions.[121] Vijayanagara was a world of horses and lotus flowers, wandering *haridasa*s and temples, dancing girls and diamonds, ivory and pearls, gold and silver, buffaloes and parrots, rice and mangoes. It was a composite of ethnic regional ways of life, an Indian lifeway anchored in the ancient, not one designed to control nature drastically for short-term gain, comfort and convenience. At its best, Vijayanagara gloriously supported Muslims and Jains, as well as the Hindu majority.

Figure 11.3   Dancers and musicians performing before a royal figure

It appreciated diversity, encompassing many paths and voices, absorbing needed energies from many sources and trying out new combinations. It had a place for Vidyaranya and Ganga Devi, for Molla and Kanaka. At its worst, it was a compulsively repeated pattern of offences and acts of revenge.

As J.L. Mehta said,[122] it is difficult to discuss ideas with someone who appears on your doorstep with a sword, and proceeds to destroy your sacred images and maybe even your life. This holds true of the armed Hindu 'fundamentalists' of recent years, who have attacked innocent Muslims (and Christians) in a rage stemming from very old grievances. Terror is demonic injustice whoever perpetrates it. To disregard man's law and rashly take the power to end others' lives into one's own hands is always a mistake. It is impossible to give one's children a promising future by antagonizing foes. At its best, Vijayanagara was the centre of a tolerant eclectic realm of realms. That it was not based on a hatred of Muslims is good to know. (Many Muslim soldiers helped protect it.) The best qualities of Vijayanagara rule included broad-minded encouragement of all ennobling traditions, an entrepreneurial spirit, love of life and culture enriched by eclecticism, and a valuing of diverse voices.

A Concluding Consideration of Hindu-Muslim Relations

It is worth considering briefly the differences between Hinduism and Islam, the two world-views in the background of this discussion, from a couple of different perspectives. In his study, *The Long Recessional: The Imperial Life of Rudyard Kipling*, David Gilmour discussed how Kipling as a young man preferred Muslims to Hindus. He considered Muslims more straightforward than Hindus and found it easier to sympathize with their monotheism. His preference for Muslim dogma's simplicity over the phantasmagoria of Hindu deities, his belittling of the Hindu epics Ramayana ('trivialities') and Mahabharata ('drivel'), and his characterizations of Muslims as strong, bold men of action and of Hindus as sedentary and talkative, show that he saw Islam as a confident active faith of conquest, and Hinduism as fatalistic, apathetic, escapist, a breeding ground for social ills and injustice.[123]

Perhaps, as a colonialist, Kipling found it more convenient to see Islam as more reliably masculine, consistent and rigidly conformist, and Hinduism as more nebulous, tricky, changeable and childlike, more womanlike, fluid, playful and flexible in different situations. This kind of superficial assessment seems to involve a mistaken view of things, an oversimplification. This oversimplification – an attempt to find security, stability and dependable safety in a world of bewildering complications – comes with its own humiliations. Any kind of reductionism involves considerably suppressing the recognition of life's actual dynamics. It leads to convoluted ways of dealing with, or denying, the complexity of things, which is always fraught with contingencies and interrelations. Good intentions, or a firm belief in oversimplified views, cannot make things turn out as humans wish them to. Hinduism's non-linear complexity is in tune with deep structures. Even Islam uses the 99 most beautiful names of the one God to do more justice to life's complexities.

Many historians have portrayed the invasions of Muslims into the subcontinent as a clash of world-views: waves of Muslim invaders crashed into Hindu India. At the time, the impact was a great shock bringing massive change – like a continent drifting, crashing into a coast. But now, after so many years of Hindu and Muslim people living side-by-side, the 'coastlines' made by the original 'tectonic shifts' of invasion and political rule are no longer two separate shapes, but finely interlace, like fontanelle cracks in a skull. At this later date Muslims' and Hindus' lives are dovetailed, like the 'headwriting of Brahma', destined to go together, interlocked by fate. In such a fine jigsaw-puzzle interface of fates, none can claim to be all-important and exclusively privileged – all are mortals, all have their claim to greatness, as followers of the Vedas or the Qur'an, but none can expect to be the sole dominant power. And there is no need for such hegemony, as both Hindu and Muslim creative wisdom intuited long ago, heard in the voices of Kabir, Shirdi Sai Baba and Shahul Hamidi.[124] These and other saints and *sufi*s of India had followers from both traditions. These saints, like Vemana, suggest that much can be won by gentle intelligence: 'By gentleness we can pleasantly win everything. That is true victory. We keep our promises with gentleness. Bet everything on it. What troubles Dharmaraja overcame by means of gentleness!'[125]

Notes

1   Italo Calvino, *Invisible Cities*, tr. William Weaver, New York: Harcourt Brace Jovanovich, 1972, p. 5.
2   Ralph T.H. Griffith, *The Hymns of the Rgveda*, Delhi: Motilal Banarsidass, 1986 (reprint), X.28, p. 550.
3   *The Mahabharata*, tr. J.A.B. van Buitenen, Chicago: University of Chicago Press, 1975, vol. 2, p. 97.
4   T.M.P. Mahadevan, *The Philosophy of Advaita with Special Reference to Bharatatirtha-Vidyaranya*, Madras: Ganesh, 1969, p. 4.
5   *Sri Vidyaranya* (Publication No. 3), Hampi: The Vidyaranya Vidyapitha Trust, 1983, p. 34.

6   *A Zen Forest: Saying of the Masters*, ed. Soiku Shigematsu, New York: Weatherhill, 1981, no. 759, p.88.

7   Ibid., no. 841, p. 94, #841.

8   Ibid., no.1176, p. 118, #1176.

9   *The Blues Line: A Collection of Blues Lyrics from Leadbelly to Muddy Waters*, ed. Eric Sackheim, New York: Schirmer Books, 1975. p. 118. Compare the opening of Lightning Hopkin's song, 'She's Mine.': 'She's little and she's low, she's right down on the ground ... Well the way she acts make a rabbit hug a hound.'

10 *Rig Veda*, X.28.4,9 (*Mandala* X, hymn 28, verses 4, 9).

11 See David Bohm and F. David Peat, *Science, Order, and Creativity*, New York: Bantam, 1987, p. 164.

12 Ibid.

13 R. Rangaramanuja Ayyangar, *History of South Indian (Carnatic) Music*, Madras: Author, 1972, p. 34.

14 Donald Miller, *The Reason of Metaphor*, New Delhi: Sage Publications, 1992, p. 42.

15 The complex uncertainties regarding *nayaka*s are admitted by those who study history deeply: 'Warriors who used the title *nayaka* or *amaranayaka* ... cannot be defined easily in terms of particular office, ethnic identity, privileges and duties'. However, in Vijayanagara times a new level of supralocal chieftainship appeared. Warriors who had armed followings, joining kings in defensive and predatory warfare, rather independent, not so beholden to those above them, more autonomous in redistributing resources, constituted a kind of power that had not been found in South India previously. Burton Stein writes of *nayaka* enigmas in *Peasant State and Society in Medieval South India*. Delhi: Oxford University Press, 1985, pp. 369, 405–408.

16 Burton Stein, '*Vijayanagara*', *The New Cambridge History of India I.2*, Cambridge: Cambridge University Press, 1989, p. 103.

17 Ibid., p. 64. Some of these issues are discussed in Hiroshi Fukazawa, *The Medieval Deccan: Peasants, Social Systems and States*, Delhi: Oxford University Press, 1991; also in Noboru Karashima, *Towards a New Formation: South Indian Society Under Vijayanagar Rule*, Delhi: Oxford University Press, 1992, Chapters 1, 5, etc.

18 Arjun Appadurai has written of this in 'Kings, Sects and Temples in South India, 1350–1700 A.D.', *The Indian Economic and Social History Review*, XIV(1), 1977, and elsewhere.

19 Karashima, *Towards a New Formation*, p. 27.

20 Ibid., p. 29.

21 Ibid., p. 30.

22 Ibid., p. 17.

23 Ibid., pp. 30–33.

24 Ibid., pp. 43–63. Romila Thapar writes about *nayaka*s, tolls and taxes, loans from temples and merchants and artisans in the empire at large in *A History of India*, vol. 1, London: Penguin Books, 1990, pp. 328–31.

25 Stein, 'Vijayanagara', p. 51.

26 Karashima, *Towards a New Formation*, p. 178.

27 Ibid., p. 111.

28 Ibid., pp. 16–17, 197.

29 Ibid., pp. 83, 197.

30 Ibid., p. 178.

31 Ibid.

32 Shrimat Shukracharyyavirachitah, *Shukranitisarah, or the elements of polity* ed. and tr. Jivananda Vidyasagara Bhattacaryya, Calcutta: Sarasvati Yantra, 1890, I.141–143. An English translation is also available in *The Sukraniti*, tr. Benoy Kumar Sarkar, New Delhi: Oriental Books Reprint Corporation, 1975, p. 13.

33 *Sukraniti* I.121–122.

34 *Sukraniti* I. 121–122.

35 M.W. Carr, *A Selection of Telugu Proverbs*, New Delhi: Asian Educational Services, 1986, no. 1078, p. 109.

36 *Mahabharata*, I.42.27–31.

37 *Manu* 4.85–86. Cf. *Mahabharata*, 13.255.9.

38 Fractal patterns are self-similar at different levels of the infinite scale, from smaller than smallest to larger than largest, they are an iteration with organic cohesion, a sense of self, replicated with variations, nested within similar, equally complex patterns. Fractals are visual equivalents demonstrating cycles, although they are non-periodic, and demonstrating growth, like the progression of Fibanacci numbers. Fractals reflect a cosmic, holographic all-in-all order; they evoke a sense of coordinated organic wholeness through symbolic suggestions of essential patterns. Revealing order, fractals have a soothing, question-answering effect – there is a place for everything and everything in its place in the infinite scale of things, like a series of mountains and rivers around the globe, contextualized by infinity and hence at home in eternity.

39 Epiphanus Wilson (ed.), *The Literature of India*, New York: The Colonial Press, 1900, p. 32. My paraphrase.

40 *Kautilya Arthashastra* VI.2.22–39; *Manu*, VII.155–8; *The Arthashastra of Kautalya with the commentary Srimula of T. Ganapati Sastri*, Trivadrum: Government Press, 1921, 1925.

41 This is cited in Ronald Inden's excellent article about how ritual authority functions, 'Ritual, Authority, and Cyclic Time in Hindu Kingship', in J.F. Richards (ed.), *Kingship and Authority in South Asia*, Madison: University of Wisconsin South Asian Studies 2nd edn, 1981, p. 40.

42 A *nadu* or locality is a 'tract claimed, settled, and cultivated by a peasant people possessing a common ethnic identity, including a shared putative ancestry and, often, history of migration, a shared local loyalty, and a shared culture.' Stein, *Peasant State and Society in Medieval South India*, p. 416.

43 Inden, 'Ritual, Authority, and Cyclic Time in Hindu Kingship', p. 30.

44 *Visnudharmottara* II 65.47, cited in ibid.

45 It is interesting that in Jewish legends, God created Adam, the first man, from red, black, white and green dust gathered from the four corners of the world.

46 *Visnudharmottara* II.

47 See Inden, 'Ritual, Authority, and Cyclic Time in Hindu Kingship'. See also Burton Stein on the Mahanavami festival, in which the *nayaka*s paid rents to the Vijayanagara king, royal arms were anointed by priests and royal women, and rites of animal sacrifice and consecration of the ruler's kingship were performed. The city was a world microcosm. Stein, *Peasant State and Society in Medieval South India*, pp. 384–91.

48 Ananda K. Coomaraswamy, *Spiritual Authority and Temporal Power in the Indian Theory of Government*, New Haven, CT: American Oriental Society, 1942 (reprinted, New York: Kraus, 1967). The reduction of motive, ideology and so on, to 'nothing but' power relations betrays modern scholars' limited experience and vision, a disbelief that there is anything deeper to be known than Euclidean-simple materialist surface views. It is unreasonable to demand that we judge the depths as we would judge the superficial, implying that there is nothing momentous, only the trivial. For example, the French social scientist Pierre Bourdieu assumes that 'power relations are all that enter significantly into the construction of human societies ... a vision as totalizing as those he criticizes'. See Margaret Trawick, *Notes on Love in a Tamil Family*, Berkeley: University of California Press, p. 147. This amounts to a denial of complexity, closing down prematurely life's richness of motives and manifestations.

49 Stein, 'Vijayanagara', p. 102.

50 'Negentropy' is a term coined by the Austrian theoretical physicist Erwin Schrodinger's concept 'negative entropy' discussed in his book, *What is Life?*, Cambridge: Cambridge University Press, 1994. Negentropy refers to the observation that there is an organizing power at work in the universe – there is order at many levels of existence, rather than just entropy, disintegration and patternless, random disorder. Thus, negentropy means free energy, 'order for free', structural organization in systems at all levels of existence.

51   Burton Stein, 'All the King's Mana', in Richards, *Kingship and Authority in South Asia*, p. 146.
52   Ibid.
53   Herman Jensen, *Tamil Proverbs*, New Delhi: Asian Educational Services, 1997, no. 1076.
54   Carr, *A Selection of Telugu Proverbs*, no. 20, p. 3.
55   Ibid., no. 570, p. 57.
56   Ibid., no. 342, p. 34.
57   Ibid., no. 173, p. 17.
58   Ibid., no. 278, p. 28.
59   Ibid., no. 497, p. 50.
60   Ibid., no. 324, p. 33.
61   This Telugu proverb is found in A. Galletti di Cadilhac, Galletti's *Telugu Dictionary*, London: Oxford, 1935, p. 429.
62   A South Indian proverb.
63   Cited in W. Caland and V. Henry, *L'Agnistoma*, Paris, 1906 p. 26. See also Jan C. Heesterman, 'Brahmin, Ritual, and Renouncer', in *The Inner Conflict of Tradition: Essays in Indian Ritual, Kingship, and Society*, Chicago: University of Chicago Press, 1985.
64   Heesterman, 'Brahmin, Ritual, and Renouncer' p.12. *Abhishekha* means ritual bath or anointing.
65   Between order and turbulence, between monotone and white noise – the best of music is at the peak of complexity between the poles. 'Between totalitarian order and anarchy, lie reasonable social and political systems, and the best of them encompass a peak of ordered diversity.' John Briggs, *Fractals: The Patterns of Chaos: A New Aesthetic of Art, Science, and Nature*, New York: Schuster, 1992. p. 123. 'Simplicity and complexity are complementary', and a tension between them can enliven – 'I wouldn't attempt to grasp that complexity without having a conviction of the underlying simplicity.' Michael McGuire, *An Eye for Fractals*, Redwood City, CA: Addison Wesley, 1991, p. 124. Fractals imply a way out of modern nihilist-relativism, not over simplistic and not bewilderingly complex. Whorls made of whorls; the Sanskrit word for this is *vichitarangam* – the living planet earth, made up of lives, an organism of micro-organisms. See David Loy, 'Indra's Postmodern Net', *Philosophy East and East*. 43(3), July 1993, pp. 481–510. Nature, like some traditional Hindu organizing principles, is better represented by fractal, rather than linear, models.
66   Melinda A. Moore, 'The Kerala House as a Hindu Cosmos', in McKim Marriot, (ed.), *India through Hindu Categories*, New Delhi: Sage Publications, 1990. pp. 169–200.
67   Vemana, *Verses of Vemana*, ed. and tr. A.L.N. Murty, Kakinda: Sripathi Press, 1978, no. 26 p. 13.
68   James Gleick, *Chaos: The Making of a New Science*, New York: Penguin Books, p.179.
69   In the Hindu view, the unit of each year is Prajapati (Lord of Creatures, the divinity presiding over procreation, the protector of life, supreme god among Vedic deities, time personified, the sun – the name was later applied to Vishnu and Shiva). As time personified, the deity is all that exists. It is as if the *smartas*, by making the calendar and fixing the times of festivals, gave this form of the deity apparel – forms of an external appearance.
70   In culture there are recurrent processes, efforts of renewal, time-worn paths of repeated actions, circuitries of tradition and new growth. Vidyaranya revived the Hindu system with *smarta* traditional information, as an acorn's DNA preserves the oak's identity so it survives in a new tree. Vidyaranya was involved in the autopoiesis, or self-organization, of premodern Hinduism. This is a term used by Francisco Varela and others for a quality of living adaptive systems. 'Autopoiesis refers to the characteristic of living systems to continuously renew themselves and to regulate this process in such a way that the integrity of their structure is maintained', as Erich Jantsch writes in *The Self-organizing Universe*, New York: Pergamon Press, 1980, p. 7. Such a brahman, entrusted with organizing an empire, on the social level, is something like the Hox genes on the molecular level: ' … one Hox gene turns on and produces a transcription factor that kindles many other genes to create the uppermost segment of the body; then the next Hox gene down is aroused, and it helps build the next lower section of the embryo, and so forth … . Hox genes … encapsulate the entire human form: the chromosomes contain a physical and temporal representation of the body axis, of the child itself

– an idea with alluring artistic and philosophical undertones. It brings us back to the medieval notion of the homunculus, a tiny human being in every sperm cell that needed only the nourishment of the mother's womb to grow … .' Natalie Angier, *The Beauty of the Beastly*, Boston and New York: Houghton Mifflin Co., 1995, p. 86. Hox genes, like *rajagurus*, operate the master switches of system development, in a manner of speaking.

71 Rabindranath Tagore wrote an essay, 'A Vision of India's History' which explores the dynamic relationship of brahmans and *kshatriyas* over the centuries. See Amiya Chakravarty (ed.), *A Tagore Reader*, Boston, MA: Beacon Press, 1961, pp. 182 ff.

72 David L. Hall, 'Reason and Its Rhyme', *Journal of the Indian Council of Philosophical Research*, IX(2), January–April 1992, pp. 42–43. See also Hall's contribution to the book *Nature in Asian Traditions of Thought*, Albany, NY: State University of New York Press, 1989.

73 Phillip B. Wagoner, '"Sultan among Hindu Kings": Dress, Titles, and the Islamicization of Hindu Culture at Vijayanagara', *Journal of Asian Studies*, 55(4), November 1996, p. 318.

74 Ibid.

75 Ibid. See also Ravi A. Palat, 'The Vijayanagara Empire. Re-integration of the Agrarian Order of Medieval South India, 1336–1565', in Henri J.M. Claessen and Pieter van de Velde (eds), *Early State Dynamics*, Leiden and New York: E.J. Brill, 1987, pp. 174-77.

76 For more on the topic see Richard M. Eaton, Cynthia Talbot and Phillip B. Wagoner, *The 'Nayaka System' Reconsidered* (forthcoming).

77 Phillip B. Wagoner, 'Harihara, Bukka, and the Sultan,' in David Gilmartin and Bruce B Lawrence (eds), *Beyond Turk and Hindu,* Gainesville: University of Florida Press, 2000, p. 320

78 Joan-Pau Rubies, *Travel and Ethnology in the Renaissance: South India through European Eyes, 1250–1625*, Cambridge: Cambridge University Press, 2000. p. 18.

79 Ibid., p. 16.

80 Theodore Roszak, *The Voice of the Earth*, New York: Touchstone, 1992, p. 164.

81 David Bohm and F. David Peat, *Science, Order, and Creativity*, New York: Bantam, 1987, pp. 205–208. The 'generative order' referred to here is primarily concerned not with the outward side of development and evolution in a sequence of successive stages, but with a deeper and more inward order out of which the manifest form of things can emerge creatively, in Peat and Bohm's view. This order is fundamentally relevant both in nature and in consciousness; the 'implicate order' is a particular kind of generative order in physics, (p. 151).

82 Ibid., p. 209.

83 *The Way of Life According to Lao Tzu*, tr. Witter Bynner, New York: Capricorn Books, 1962, no.64, p. 66.

84 This summary is in part based on Joan-Pau Rubies' overview in *Travel and Ethnology in the Renaissance*, pp. 16–17.

85 Domingo Paes and Fernao Nuniz, *The Vijayanagar Empire*, as seen by Domingo Paes and Fernao Nuniz, ed. Vasundhara Filliozat, tr. Robert Sewell, New Delhi: National Book Trust, 1977, pp. 85, 145.

86 The actual battle site was probably over 25 miles south of Talikota, south of the Krishna river. See Robert Sewell, *A Forgotten Empire*, New Delhi: Asian Educational Services, 1982 (reprint of 1900 edn), p.199.

87 See K.K. Basu, 'Battle of Talikota from Muslim Sources', *Vijayanagara Sexcentenary Commemoration Volume*, Dharwar: Vijayanagara Empire Sexcentenary Association, 1936, pp. 245–54.

88 Ramaraya's officers had pleaded with him, but the stubborn old man was resolute, believing he would not need to retreat in battle. He underestimated his enemies, calling them 'children' who would soon run off. Arrogant to the end he told his men to capture two of the leaders alive so that he could keep them in iron cages, and told them to cut off the head of Hussain Nizam, who had insulted him, and to deliver it to him. Though 96 years old, Ramaraya was said to be as brave as a 30-year old. Ironically Hussain Nizam (also still stinging with remembered insults) personally cut off Ramaraya's head, reportedly saying, 'Now I am avenged of thee. Let God do what he will with me.' See Sewell, *A Forgotten Empire*, pp. 203–205.

89 Phillip B. Wagoner, *Tidings of the King: A Translation and Ethnohistorical Analysis of the Rayavacakamu*, Honolulu: University of Hawaii Press, 1993, citing the text *Vidyaranya-kirti*, pp. 165–69.

90 K.A. Nilakanta Sastri, *A History of South India from Prehistoric Times to the Fall of Vijayanagara*, Delhi: Oxford University Press, 1976, pp. 307–309. Sastri also notes that many differences in North and South India right up to this day are attributable to the success of the Vijayanagara empire, while it lasted.

91 G.S. Dikshit and Sumitra Srinivasan, in George Michell (ed.), *Splendours of the Vijayaganara Empire – Hampi*, Bombay: Marg, 1981.

92 This is suggested by Wagoner, in his discussion of the decline of Vijayanagara. See *Tidings of the King*, pp. 11–12, 68–69.

93 Felipe-Fernandez Armesto, *Millennium: A History of the Last Thousand years*, London: Black Swan, 1996, p. 105.

94 Romila Thapar, *A History of India*, vol.1, London: Penguin Books, 1990, pp. 334–36. See also, for example, Anna Libera Dallapicola, *Sculpture at Vijayanagara: Iconography and Style*, New Delhi: Manohar Publications, 1998.

95 Wagoner, *Tidings of the King*, p.169.

96 The *kali yuga* is a reference to the Hindu world-view which divides the cycles of time into a series of four ages. The *kali yuga* is the current age, in the Hindu view. The first age is seen as a golden age of order and well-being. The *kali yuga* is a period of discord, vice and disorder following a gradual decline.

97 *Kanakadasara Kirtanegalu*, ed. B. Shivamurthy Shastry and K.M. Krishna Rao, Mysore: Government of Mysore, 1965, song 172, p. 154. I base this English rendering on the translation from Kannada which H.L. Chandrashekara of Mysore made for me.

98 For example, in the song *Yakenani*, Purandaradasa describes being friendless, in a kingdom where there's no king to recognize him and he is penniless, etc. See William J. Jackson, *Songs of Three Great South Indian Saints*, New Delhi: Oxford University Press, 2002, p. 149. Vemana also describes the plight of someone born and raised on 'this land', but unable to pass land on to anyone, while a man from a foreign country rules. See Vemana, *Verses of Vemana*, no. 1118, p. 268.

99 Palat, 'The Vijayanagara Empire' pp. 182–83. See also Vijaya Ramaswamy, *Textiles and Weavers in Medieval South India*, New Delhi: Oxford University Press, 1985, pp. 167, ff.

100 Sewell, *A Forgotten Empire*, pp. 194–95.

101 Cited by Cynthia Ozyck in 'What Helen Keller Saw,' *The New Yorker*, 16 and 23 June, 2003, p. 195.

102 David Shulman, 'A Science of Mood: Telugu Poems from Tirupati and Kalahasti', paper delivered at University of Texas at Austin, 1998.
     Shulman sees mood as the 'defining feature' of Annamacharya's voice, and believes that it articulates a new sense of (and approach to) the divine presence in the temple at Tirupati. There is a confidence, a bold approach through a yoga of feelings and a daring exploration of meditative moods in the songs he sang. If this is a departure, it arises, in my view, from traditions already in existence. Shripadaraya sang colloquial *kirtana*s in Kannada which were popular before Annamacharya's Telugu ones. Envisioning the beloved as poignantly desirable and longing for the beloved's presence was celebrated in the *Gita Govinda* and *Bhagavata Purana* as well as in the songs of Tamil saints. But perhaps Annamacharya's deeper mood of individuality does mark a new beginning in South Indian history. Bhakti was a unifying rallying point for the Maratha kings who later faced the Europeans and tried to make a strong Hindu defence in post-Vijayanagara South India.

103 Sastri, *A History of South India*, p. 309.

104 Octavio Paz, *One Earth, Four or Five Worlds: Reflections on Contemporary History*, New York: Harcourt Brace Jovanovich, 1985, p. 205.

105 John Lewis Gaddis, *The Landscape of History: How Historians Map the Past*, New York: Oxford University Press, 2002, pp. 86–87.

106 T.V. Mahalingam, *Administration and Social Life Under Vijayanagar*, Madras: University of Madras, 1969, p. 2.

107 See chronology in George Michell, (ed.), *Splendours of the Vijayanagara Empire–Hampi*, Bombay: Marg Publications, 1981.

108 Sastri, *A History of South India*, p. 269.

109 Walter M. Spink, 'Vijayanagara – The City of Victory', *Journal of Indian History*, Trivandrum, Dept. of History, University of Kerala, No. 1, 1973, pp. 136–37.

110 Robert Sewell, *The Historical Inscriptions of Southern India*, New Delhi: Asian Educational Services, 1983 (reprint), p. 255. The Muslim historian Firishta is cited here.

111 Sewell, *A Forgotten Empire*, pp. 181–201.

112 Spink, 'Vijayanagara – The City of Victory', pp. 12–13. As late as 1829 the severed head of Ramaraya was annually slathered with oil and red pigment and exhibited in public celebrations by Muslims in Ahmadnagar on the anniversary of Talikot. And there was a stone replica of the head in Bijapur used as the opening of one of the sewers. These were displays of the memories of insults revenged. Readers who congratulate themselves on their own civility are cautioned to consider similar displays in their own societies' recent pasts. For example, Englishmen seem to have kept Oliver Cromwell's head in Cambridge for many years. See John Drummond, *Tainted by Experience: A Life in the Arts*, London: Faber and Faber, 2000, p. 51.

113 Some say that Shivaji, who later established Hindu rule where Muslims had taken over, had Ramaraya as a model or influence.

114 The unprecedented beheading of King Charles I in 1648, an execution sought by the Puritans led by Oliver Cromwell, brought a time of change. Oliver Cromwell's head was soon cut off and displayed in public for years, to restore order. See Claire Tomalin, *Samuel Pepys: The Unrivalled Self*, London: Penguin, 2002, pp. 10, 24, 133–37. Perhaps this beheading of the king was the point of criticality leading to the French and American Revolutions. More recently Cofer Black, CIA veteran and new State Department coordinator for counter-terrorism spoke of the world's need for proof of Osama bin Laden's death. 'You'd need some DNA. There's a good way to do it. Take a machete, and whack off his head, and you'll get a bucketful of DNA, so you can see it and test it. It beats lugging the whole body back.' Jane Mayer, 'The Search for Osama', *The New Yorker*, 4 August, 2003, p. 26.

115 Mulk Raj Anand suggests this in his reflections in Michell, *Splendours of the Vijayanagara Empire – Hampi*, p. 40.

116 Ibid., p. 7.

117 Pieter Geyl (with Arnold Toynbee and Peterim Sorokin), *The Pattern of the Past: Can we Determine It?*, Boston, MA: The Beacon Press, 1949, p. 22.

118 As Mulk Raj Anand puts it, 'tradition is mostly desired myth'. See Michell, (ed.), *Splendours of the Vijayanagara Empire – Hampi*, p. 8.

119 'The boar who saves the earth ... is originally Prajapati, who keeps her afloat by flattening and spreading her ... .' Wendy Doniger, *Hindu Myths*, New York: Viking Penguin, 1975, p. 184, citing *Taittiriya Samhita*. In the *Shatapatha Brahmana*, earth was the size of a hand-span, and Prajapati raised her up; she was his mate and also his dear abode.

120 V.S. Naipaul, 'A Million Mutinies', *India Today* (special 50th anniversary issue), 18 August 1997, p. 36. The Vijayanagara empire also comes in for some harsh words from Naipaul in his *India: A Wounded Civilization*, New York: Vintage, 1977..

121 And conclusions drawn depend on presuppositions and viewpoints. Note the depiction by B. Sheik Ali: 'With the breakup of the Vijayanagara empire in the 16th century, Karnataka fell into the hands of petty chieftains for nearly two hundred years until it was unified again under Haidar and Tipu.' *Encyclopedia of Asian History*, ed. Ainslie T. Embree, New York/London: Charles Scribners Sons/Collier Macmillan, 1988. Here 'unified' means put under a rule, a single tax system; the unification was rather brief, and one wonders how meaningful it was for many in the long run.

122 In a conversation at Harvard in 1979, before he retired.

123 David Gilmour, *The Long Recessional: The Imperial Life of Rudyard Kipling*, New York: Farrar, Straus and Giroux, 2002, p. 57.

124 Muslim holy man Shahul Hamid (1513–1579) settled on the Bay of Bengal. He and his followers were honoured by Hindu rulers. Today over half the pilgrims visiting his shrine are Hindu. See

Vasudha Narayanan, 'Religious Vows at the Shrine of Shahul Hamid', in William Harman and Selva Raj (eds.), *Dealing with Deities: Promising Gods in South Asia*, Albany, NY: SUNY Press, 2004.

125 Vemana, *Verses of Vemana*, ed. and tr. C.P. Brown, New Delhi: Asian Educational Services, 1986 (reprint of 1829 edn), no. 1092, p. 362.

Index